BLOOD AND POWER

BLOOD AND POWER

The Rise and Fall of Italian Fascism

JOHN FOOT

BLOOMSBURY PUBLISHING

LONDON • OXFORD • NEW YORK • NEW DELHI • SYDNEY

BLOOMSBURY PUBLISHING
Bloomsbury Publishing Plc
50 Bedford Square, London, WC1B 3DP, UK
29 Earlsfort Terrace, Dublin 2, Ireland

BLOOMSBURY, BLOOMSBURY PUBLISHING and the Diana logo are trademarks
of Bloomsbury Publishing Plc

First published in Great Britain 2022

A catalogue record for this book is available from the British Library

ISBN: HB: 978-1-4088-9794-2; EBOOK: 978-1-4088-9793-5; EPDF: 978-1-5266-5248-5

2 4 6 8 10 9 7 5 3 1

Typeset by Newgen KnowledgeWorks Pvt. Ltd., Chennai, India
Printed and bound in Great Britain by CPI Group (UK) Ltd, Croydon CR0 4YY

MIX
Paper from
responsible sources
FSC® C171272

To find out more about our authors and books visit www.bloomsbury.com
and sign up for our newsletters

To Paul Ginsborg

Contents

Preamble: A Family Story

My father used to tell a family story. Every summer, in the 1970s and 1980s, the entire Foot clan would gather at my grandparents' beautiful house in Cornwall. My grandmother Sylvia would preside over mealtimes – the great matriarch – delighted to have her three sons, her daughter, and assorted friends, grandchildren, uncles and aunts all there. Meals were served around a huge, long table. Discussions were often heated and usually political, but there were also silly jokes and games. This was a family steeped in politics. Four Feet had stood for parliament in the 1945 election, although only one had been elected. Three had been MPs at one time or another. My grandfather was a career diplomat, used to dealing with politicians and parties. There were photos of him in the house with Churchill, with the queen and with Yasser Arafat. My father was a militant, on the radical left. In his telling of the story, the debate has become intense, around the table. As often happened, someone accused somebody else of 'supporting fascism'.

Then, a small voice piped up. It was my great-grandmother, Aurelia Lanzoni, who was born in Kars in Turkey in 1867, but was of Italian heritage. She had lived in Bologna in the early twentieth century, and had witnessed at first hand the rise of the blackshirts and Mussolini. She was a tiny woman. There is a photo of her holding me as a baby, but she died soon after my birth, in 1965, and is buried outside Edinburgh. By then she had a shock of white hair. 'Ah, the fascism!' she'd say, in my dad's telling of the story. 'It was wonderful!!'

My great-uncle, George Tod, Aurelia's son, wrote a kind of autobiography which was never published but has remained within the family. In 1921, he remembered, he was at school in Bologna. 'My earliest memory of my grandmother is of her returning home in about 1920/1921, with her hair dishevelled, her hat squashed and in her hand, her dress torn and her nose bleeding. She had been attacked by a communist gang ... The town was in turmoil,' he wrote. 'Separate gangs of communists and Bolsheviks roamed uncontrolled.' George Tod saw fascism as positive. 'When Mussolini came, the gangs were routed, order was imposed, sometimes harshly and even unjustly but certainly a great improvement in security.' In short, he concluded: 'There was a rebirth in Italy.' Of course, he added: 'Fascist methods were not very gentle. Many carried the *manganello*, a sturdy walking stick. More of a staff than a stick. Very convincing. Security returned.'[1]

In this history of Italian fascism, the *manganello* will play a key role. For some, fascism was indeed 'wonderful'; for many others, it was a nightmare.

Prologue

Italy invented fascism. Out of the chaos of the First World War, in which nearly 600,000 Italian soldiers lost their lives, a new movement emerged which preached hatred for politicians and love for the fatherland. Fascists embraced violence, both in their language and on the streets. At first, they were overshadowed by a socialist uprising where revolution seemed inevitable during the 'two red years' – the *biennio rosso* – of 1919–20. But soon, groups of fascists, known as squads, dressed in black, were on the march in the countryside and cities of Italy, destroying a powerful union movement, crushing democracy and spreading fear throughout the country: 1921–22 were the 'two black years' – the *biennio nero*.

Many local fascist leaders emerged during this latter period, but by 1922 one man had taken charge. His name was Benito Mussolini and he had been a radical anti-war socialist until 1914. Mussolini was appointed prime minister at the age of thirty-nine after fascists carried out a semi-coup during the so-called 'March on Rome' in 1922. The liberal state thought it could contain and use fascism but it was making a very serious mistake. Mussolini would remain in power for nearly twenty-one years, setting up a regime which negated democracy itself, imprisoned or murdered anybody in opposition, and set out – no less – to create an entirely new nation, with a new set of heroes, myths and symbols. In many ways, Benito Mussolini seemed a very unlikely dictator. He had two real skills, honed in the first thirty years of his life: journalism and public speaking. His previous attempts at political organisation and militancy had usually ended in failure.

Having taken power through murderous violence, Italian fascism held onto it through further bloodshed and the occupation of the state. In power, fascism eliminated all vestiges of free speech. Violence was not just inflicted on its own people. A brutal military occupation of Ethiopia in the 1930s was backed by the use of poison gas and horrific massacres of men, women and children. Fascism eliminated its opponents with gusto, or reduced them to a state of fear. It also rewrote its own history, painting the fascist movement as a glorious defender of the fatherland, as a revolutionary and modernising force, but also as a return to order. Fascism was built on a mound of dead bodies, cracked heads, traumatised victims of violence, burnt books and smashed up cooperatives and union headquarters. Most of those who ended up governing Italy had committed crimes for which they were rarely investigated, let alone tried. None of this was inevitable. Yet somehow, over the years, this carnage has tended to be played down, or justified, even by anti-fascists.

In power, fascism was brutal. But it did not rule by force alone. It tried to win over Italians through cultural politics, welfare institutions, sporting triumph, colonial conquest and the invention or use of a series of enemies, old and new. Above all, in 1929 an historic pact was signed with the Catholic Church, in a masterpiece of diplomacy and alliance-building. Dissent was strangled at source. A secret police force controlled people's private lives, backed by an army of informers and spies.

In the end, Italian fascism overreached itself, buying into its own propaganda that portrayed a nation of warriors carrying '8 million bayonets'. In 1938, Italy introduced widespread discrimination against the Jewish population with a series of 'racial laws'. The 'Pact of Steel' was signed with Hitler in 1939. At the height of his power, in 1940, Mussolini launched into war against France and Britain. It began with easy triumph, but soon turned into disaster. After the Allies landed in Sicily in 1943 and bombed Rome, Mussolini was forced out of power. Fascism was over. A bitter civil war followed. In April 1945 Mussolini was shot trying to escape to Switzerland and hung by his feet from a petrol station in Milan.

There has been considerable historical debate about the meaning of Italian fascism. Was it a modern dictatorship, thrusting towards the future? Or did it hark back to the past? Was it essentially a nostalgic attempt to create what was called a 'new Roman empire'? How important was violence to its rise and permanence in power? Did the regime create a consensus in the 1930s? Did fascism transform Italy, or was it just a superficial dictatorship, whose influence faded quickly once democracy had returned?

Italian fascism looked forwards *and* backwards. It built extraordinary modernist structures, such as Florence railway station, but also neo-classical throwbacks. It encouraged and tolerated innovative forms of art and performance, as with the futurists, but it also covered Italy in dubious realist statues and images of its leader. It understood the power of the media and advertising, but it also glanced back longingly to a rural Italy which was fast disappearing. It was at times radical, but also radically reactionary, and often simply pragmatic. It claimed to be anti-system and anti-political, but most of its leading proponents were corrupt, and enriched themselves. These contradictions were also its strengths.

*

This is not a traditional history of Italian fascism. It tells the story of the 1920s and 1930s largely through the stories of real people – fascists, anti-fascists, socialists, communists, anarchists. Violence is a central theme. This book depicts victims, perpetrators and bystanders.[1] Without violence, before and during the regime, fascism would never have come close to power. It was fundamental, visceral, epochal and life-changing: both for those who experienced it, and those who practised it. Fascist violence brought something fundamentally new to the political scene: a militia party, whose use of murder, beatings, intimidation and destruction swept aside all opposition. Revolvers, nail-studded cudgels, fire and castor oil were all part of the weaponry of the blackshirts. In their wake they left thousands of terrified opponents, and hundreds of ransacked and charred buildings. This violence and its ramifications are ever-present in the stories this book recounts.

Like the Italians under the regime itself, historians have often become transfixed by the figure of Benito Mussolini, but Il Duce is not at the centre of this volume. We know much about Mussolini, but too little about ordinary Italians and how they lived through the dictatorship. How did Italians experience the regime? Who were the fascists and who resisted their rise? What happened to those who were beaten, widowed or orphaned by postwar violence?[2] How did it feel to be forced to drink a litre of castor oil, and then paraded through the streets, covered in your own excrement? During the rise of fascism, and under the regime, violence 'struck not only its victims but also its spectators', and 'every new act of violence evoked past acts and induced new terror'.[3]

Historians of fascism have also become fixated by the outputs and world view of fascism itself – studying the regime on its own terrain – its monuments, exhibitions, architecture, film and, of course, its leaders. This has led to a bias towards the 1930s and towards the so-called 'years of consent'. Violence has been underplayed and the victims of that violence, with a few exceptions, ignored. But violence ran right through the twenty years or so in which Mussolini held political power. It was everywhere, a constant presence. Without violence, which fascism excelled at, and used in a refined, radical and innovative way, Mussolini would never have come to power, or stayed there for so long. The framing of that violence, and the othering of socialist violence in the 1920s, was central to the way that fascism presented itself as a saviour, a heroic bulwark against Bolshevism and chaos. 'Good' violence was pitted against 'bad' violence. In this, the use of propaganda, 'fake news' and the judicial system were all central pillars of the story that Italian fascism told its people. Like my great-uncle George Tod, many Italians felt that fascism had brought order from chaos – and for this they were grateful. For many Italians, fascism was, as my great-grandmother said at that dinner table in Cornwall, 'wonderful'.

This book does not tell the whole story of Italian fascism. No work can do such a thing. There are thousands of books and articles and documentaries dedicated to Italian fascism and to Mussolini, covering every aspect of the regime from all angles – from jazz, to politics, to Mussolini's body, to his mistresses and lovers, to architecture, art and sport. This is a history told through episodes, fragments, massacres and trials, moments of violence and escape, defeats and victories, silences and noise, rhetoric and reality. It focuses on real people, on the emotional and personal tragedy, and triumphs, which fascism implied, for many people and their families. It reflects, as does all history, individual interests, foibles and quirks, and my own interest in micro-histories, stories and details. This book seeks to place the reader right in the middle of the events that brought Italian fascism into being and then into power.

In recent years Italian fascism has been at the forefront of political debate. The rise of right-wing populists in the 1990s, beginning with the extraordinary twenty-year era linked to the media magnate Silvio Berlusconi, has led to parallels being made with Mussolini's regime. Berlusconi was often compared to Mussolini, and his rehabilitation of neo-fascists, whom he brought into government, was seen as a warning signal for democracy itself. He defended the record of Mussolini, repeating the stereotypical depiction of Italian fascism as essentially benign and generally popular. Post-Berlusconi, global politics has also seen constant references back to the 1920s, and to Italy. Current right-wing Italian populist politician Matteo Salvini has used fascist slogans taken directly from the 1920s and 1930s. Donald Trump was dubbed the 'Mango Mussolini', and the attack on the US Capitol by armed rioters in January 2021 was frequently compared to the March on Rome itself, leading to an extensive debate around the question of whether Trumpism represented a return to fascism.[4] Mussolini himself had refused to accept the results of the 1919 elections in Italy, vowing to overturn them by whatever means necessary. A whole series of 'strong men' have dominated world politics, whose communication strategies and disdain for democracy have used models of masculinity mirroring Mussolini – from Putin's bare-chested horse-riding, to Muammar Gaddafi's use of rape and sexual assault.[5] Propaganda tactics and the spin put on events, as well as outright lying, are also features which were crucial to Italian fascism and its imposition of one (false) version of the past onto the present.

Italian fascism matters. It is still with us, as a warning, a prototype and a possible future. It was not a necessary evil. It did not treat its opponents lightly. It failed to bring order and stability. It was directly responsible for the 'premature deaths' of at least a million people, in Italy and across the world.[6] In short, it was a catastrophe, which also enabled and informed the rise of Nazism in Germany, and other fascisms and authoritarian regimes.

The people whose stories are told here were fascists, socialists – or sometimes socialists who became fascists – apoliticals, and others. Not everyone was coherent or predictable or linear in terms of their beliefs or actions. Some are relatively obscure figures. Many were victims; others were perpetrators of violence and oppression. Their testimonies date from before the days of fascism, through the Second World War, the postwar regime, and often into the post-1945 period, if they lived that long. Some of these tales are tragedies, some are odysseys, others are mysteries. All of them form a part of a larger history of fascism, and those who opposed the movement and the regime.

This history begins in 1911, in a barracks, in Bologna.

1911

A SHOT AT DAWN

'I am happy to have defended my comrades, give me those six
bullets that I have earned, so that my comrades will remember
me. I should not have been called to arms, the nine months
I served in the army were enough, and I always behaved well.
The King, General Spingardi [Minister of War during the Libyan
campaign] and the parliamentarians should go to war instead
of us, in order to conquer a land which the capitalists will then
exploit.'

Augusto Masetti[1]

Dawn, 30 October 1911. A courtyard of the Cialdini Barracks, in the
city of Bologna. Uniformed troops are being addressed by a Lieutenant
Colonel Giuseppe Stroppa, who is speaking from a stage. Stroppa tells
the soldiers that they no longer have any family beyond the fatherland,
and that the troops have been selected to go to war, the next day, in
Libya. It is time for Italy to become a great nation, and a great nation
needs an empire. None of the assembled soldiers had volunteered.

Suddenly, a soldier raises his rifle and fires a shot towards the officers.
The bullet hits Colonel Stroppa in the shoulder. It is reported that the
shooter then cries out: 'Long live anarchy, down with the war', as he pulls
the trigger. Stroppa is injured, the bullet passing through his body. As the
shooter is set upon and taken away he is said to shout: '*Fratelli, ribellatevi*'

(brothers, rise up!) and that he would rather die in Bologna than in Libya. That night in prison he tries to take his own life.

*

Augusto Masetti had been a bricklayer in the small central Italian town of San Giovanni in Persiceto, not far from Bologna. He had been conscripted (for the second time) and was twenty-three at the time of the Stroppa shooting. Masetti was soon vilified in the mainstream press. Some called him '*l'arabo di Bologna*', or the 'Arab of San Giovanni di Persiceto', a phrase intimating that he was a traitor, a friend of the enemy – the Libyan 'Arabs'.[2] But for anarchists, and many others, he was an instant hero, and soon became a potent symbol of anti-militarism and rebellion. A popular song told the story of Masetti locked up in 'Cell number 9'. He sometimes claimed to remember nothing of that morning – but he also seemed at other times to have a very clear memory of the shooting itself. His selective 'amnesia' remains a mystery.[3]

'Pro-Masetti' committees soon sprang up across the country, bringing together anarchists, republicans and socialists, as well as some Catholics. Campaigns proliferated in favour of Masetti, and other dissenting soldiers. His defence was taken up by the celebrated socialist lawyer Genuzio Bentini, who was admired and revered for his powerful oratory, and who also represented a socialist and fellow anti-militarist called Benito Mussolini.

According to the military code, Masetti should have been executed (shot in the back) but it was believed by the authorities that this would create a powerful martyr. An alternative solution was required. Two leading psychiatrists came to the rescue with a lengthy report, couched in obscure scientific language, which decided that Masetti's decision to shoot at the officers was not due to anarchism, or anti-militarism, but that Masetti was insane. He was, they argued, 'just a degenerate who reacted in a pathological way to the trauma of being called to arms and to the fact that his name was drawn by lot thus sending him to war'.[4] They also made reference to his appearance to justify their decision, measuring his head and body (his arms, for example, were described as 'monkey-like').[5] This diagnosis was useful for the state and the army, although it did little to silence the campaign in favour of Masetti, or the myths surrounding his act of rebellion. Pamphlets were published calling for his release: one was entitled 'Masetti has never been mad'.[6]

Masetti himself was silenced – shut away in a number of forbidding criminal asylums.

War and conscription divided Italians. Many were proud to fight for their country, whatever the cause, but huge numbers – possibly the majority – were not. Anti-militarism had been a constant feature of Italian society, as was militarism. But virulent debates on these themes took root and political form with the Libyan colonial war of 1911–12. Augusto Masetti's case was not forgotten, and his example was to re-emerge with force and passion in 1914, on the eve of a conflict which would lacerate the world and leave millions dead and injured. Masetti became an icon, for both sides. Fascism would first emerge around the fissures of these bitter and violent divisions – as both pro-war and radically anti-anti-war. Fascists judged Italians through their attitude to war.

1914

INSURRECTION: RED WEEK

'We don't yet know if we will win, but we can be certain that the revolution has begun.'

Errico Malatesta, 17 June 1914[1]

'People were killed for the sake of it … shots were fired at will – seventy of them – just to prevent people going to a city where the Statuto [Italy's original 1848 constitution] was being celebrated, which is a commemoration of constitutional liberty.'

Utopia, July 1914[2]

'It was not a blind uprising, but an insurrection with precise objectives. The context was not revolutionary, but there was a widespread feeling of revolution, a desire, the expectation of something new.'

Benito Mussolini, July 1914[3]

Every year, on 7 June, Italy marked the creation (or 'concession') of its first constitution – the 1848 *Statuto Albertino* – which had laid the basis for a united Italy. This was a national, non-religious holiday, when the fatherland celebrated – essentially – itself, and its monarchy. Usually, across the country, there would be a series of patriotic demonstrations, military marches, and the waving of the national flag. But on 7 June 1914, tensions were running high. Pro-Masetti campaigns aimed to use this occasion to contest the nation's right to fight wars.

Today, in the Central Archives in Rome, which are housed in a huge, fascist-built building on the edge of the city, there are vast numbers of files dedicated to individual 'subversives'. The so-called Casellario Politico Centrale is a key site for documents of this kind, organised by name and containing hundreds of thousands of individual files which run from the Italian liberal period, through fascism, and beyond. Usually, the more dangerous the person was considered by the Italian state, the bigger the file. Documents of all kinds are kept within folders and then stored in larger hard-edged box files. Some people's papers, exceptionally, take up more than one box file. Errico Malatesta's records stretch across *thirteen*.[4] As the historian Maurizio Antonioli has written: 'For the Italian government, Malatesta was the most feared of all.'[5]

Malatesta was an anarchist and a revolutionary – and by 1914 he was a legendary figure. For years, going back as far as the 1870s, he had tried to spark revolts in different places across Italy. Born in 1853, he was a diminutive, bearded figure, who dressed like the worker he was; age had not mellowed him and he remained a powerful speaker and writer. At the end of July 1913 Malatesta returned to Italy after a fourteen-year period of exile, which had followed an extraordinary maritime escape from internal exile on the remote island of Lampedusa in 1899.[6] Now he was back, and at the centre of events, once again.

It was almost as if Malatesta's mere presence was enough to cause a revolution. He had been imprisoned numerous times – and had taken on a mythical quality among the Italian left and the Italian working class – and, in an opposite way, within the state and the establishment. His appeal (and the fear of his supposed powers) went way beyond that of anarchism itself.

Malatesta chose to base himself in Ancona, on the eastern coast of Italy. For much of the twentieth century, this port city was a centre of radicalism and subversive thought and agitation. According to the authorities, there were 45,000 'subversives' in Ancona, out of a population of around 70,000 – including 780 anarchists, 20,000 or so Republicans, 7,000 socialists, 350 young socialists, 10 trade unionists and revolutionary syndicalism, and 7,000 'clericals' (who were strangely lumped together with the others).[7] Malatesta was soon immersed in anti-militarist activity, calling protest meetings to coincide with the 'Festa dello Statuto', in favour of Masetti and other soldiers who were suffering repression and torture due to their anti-militarist views and actions. 'This holy day,' wrote Malatesta, 'when the monarchy celebrates its splendours, should be transformed by the will of the people into a day of protests against the only and single institution which supports the monarchy: militarism.'[8] Banned by the authorities, the meetings went ahead in defiance of these orders.

*

On 7 June 1914, in Ancona, it was pouring with rain, so much so that most of the military parades in the city were called off. That afternoon, a Sunday, an anti-militarist meeting and illegal demonstration were planned. One of the speakers was the young republican Pietro Nenni, who attracted 'lively and unanimous applause' from the 500 or so people in attendance. He was followed by Malatesta and others. After the meeting, at around 6.35 p.m., the relatively small crowd began to file away. A group begin to sing '*l'Inno dei lavoratori*' – the workers' hymn – and started to march. Their route down a narrow street was blocked by *carabinieri*. The marchers felt trapped, with no obvious way out. There was pushing and shoving; stones were thrown. Then, amidst great confusion, a policeman discharged a shot in the air, presumably to try to disperse the demonstrators. In the panic that ensued, twelve *carabinieri* fired on the crowd itself. They thought, they later claimed, that they were under attack. Two demonstrators were killed on the street, one was fatally injured, and four others were hurt. The three dead were Attilio Giambrignoni, a twenty-two-year-old anarchist; and republicans Antonio Casaccia, aged twenty-four, and Nello Budini, who was just seventeen years old. Two dozen shots had been fired in total. Seventeen *carabinieri* were injured. News spread fast. It was another 'proletarian massacre' – to add to the long list of those killed by the state under 'liberal Italy' since the unification of the country in the 1860s.[9]

Revolt!

> 'This … revolution had no idea what its demands were, or what it desired.'
>
> Gaetano Salvemini[10]

How would the trade union and socialist movement respond to the deaths in Ancona? Would a general strike be called? Without waiting for the answers to such questions, spontaneous protests broke out.

Shops pulled down their shutters, and put up signs which read: '*Chiuso in segno di protesta per la strage proletaria*' ('Closed in protest at the proletarian massacre'). 'The city,' one journalist reported, 'is like a corpse.' He continued: 'The working masses have occupied the centre of the city, tumultuously.'[11]

On 8 June, the day after the deaths, an unsigned editorial appeared in the Socialist Party newspaper, *Avanti!* Its content was incendiary:

> Premeditated murder … murder without extenuating circumstances
> … there was a desire to punish Ancona, a hiding place for rebels.
> There was a desire to give a lesson, in blood, on behalf of the state
> and the men of order … Malatesta, the unions, the site for the
> Socialist Congress, the Republican groups … too much subversive
> news has been produced recently by this city … tomorrow, when
> the news has spread across Italy, in the cities and the countryside,
> the response to the provocation will be spontaneous … and we have
> a duty to support it and back it … the news from Ancona affects us,
> we are exasperated … the proletarian soul will be shaken.[12]

According to the journalist who wrote the article, *enough was enough.* The author of the piece was the editor of the paper – who was already well known for his vivid prose style, militancy and oratory. His name was Benito Mussolini.[13]

In the city of Ravenna, close to the east coast of Italy in the Romagna region, there had been tension in the air even before news filtered through about the deaths in Ancona. Thousands of rural workers entered the city on 10 June, some by boat. It seems that at a certain point a cry went up from the crowd to 'go to the prefecture', the seat of national power in most cities, as exercised through a centrally appointed prefect. Rumours abounded of revolutionary acts elsewhere, and of further casualties in Ancona. In front of the prefect's palace, in Piazza del Popolo, an angry crowd gathered. Bottles flew through the air and one hit a policeman called Giuseppe Miniagio, who later died in hospital of his injuries.[14]

Phone lines were cut, and the post office was invaded by the protestors. Others entered a church and religious furniture was used for barricades, with damage done to the altar. On 11 June the Prefect of Ravenna formally handed over his powers to the army in order, he claimed, to re-establish public order. In the disturbances that followed, some soldiers were taken prisoner. Most notoriously, a certain General Agliardi was stopped and disarmed at a roadblock set up by strikers in Cervia in the province of Ravenna. He was later released unharmed, after five hours. This was to become the most famous (for the revolutionaries) and most outrageous (for the state) moment of what became known as 'Red Week'. Meanwhile, outlandish stories circulated including one that the king himself – Victor Emmanuel III – had fled Rome.[15]

In the town of Alfonsine in the province of Ravenna there was, without any doubt, a revolution. 'People were called to the square by the sound of horns;'[16] a church and its priests were attacked and religious furniture piled on a vast bonfire. The priest, Don Tellarini, later described what he saw. 'Playing loudly with all their might the crowd occupied the square with their barbaric music, those dirges that the poor savages of Africa chant during their cannibal-like parties.'[17] Goods, food and wine were seized. A local monarchist club was attacked by agitators, portraits of the king and queen were thrown out of the window, as well as the billiard table. Church bells rang all night. The town hall was set on fire, its walls daubed with the slogan: 'Long live Masetti, down with the army'. On 21 June, 200 soldiers on horseback arrived to restore order.

During Red Week, one witness described how women in the factory town of Terni in Umbria 'filled their aprons with ashes; the mounted police came and they threw ashes into the horses' eyes'.[18] Another recalled: 'We were Terni's street urchins … we broke into the station, we tore up the rails, overturned the freight wagons, so no trains could come through with ammunition or soldiers.'[19] The rail route from Rome to Ancona, which passed through Terni, was blocked by demonstrators. There was a three-day general strike.[20] Shops closed and put up signs saying: *Lutto operaio* ('Working class mourning'). Protests continued after the strikes were called off. 'A clear type of revolution' was taking place across a wide area: 'churches were burned, stations invaded by the mob, barricades [were built] in the streets and "Freedom Trees" [trees or poles carrying flags and radical slogans, following a tradition going back to the French Revolution] were raised in the centre of squares.'[21]

Workers also went on strike in Milan. 'Shopkeepers were forced by strikers to shut their businesses, [but] not without resistance,' recalled one observer. A cart carrying bricks was seized. The 'bricks were collected and thrown at a train that was coming from Venice ... Soon after, a cavalry squadron charged the demonstrators. The police chief arrested seven people including the anarchist Aida Latini, who followed the agents to the police headquarters in Via Settembrini, waving a slipper in the air.'[22]

In Naples, a general strike was called as news from Ancona filtered through. A socialist and trade unionist called Francesco Misiano handed out leaflets to railway workers which called on them to support the action: 'Comrade Railway Workers ... those who fail to take part in this struggle and sell their souls for a few coins, are trampling on human dignity. Long live the strike.'[23] In clashes in the city, four demonstrators died, at least three thanks to gunshots, including a sixteen-year-old worker called Pietro Raimondo on the evening of 11 June. His mother had no photo of her only son and requested one of his corpse to remember him by. Barricades went up in various parts of the city and there were mass arrests. Misiano was sacked from his job with the railways.[24]

Under pressure, the national union leadership had reluctantly agreed to call a general strike on 9 June.[25] But strikes were also organised and called locally by many of the 'Chambers of Labour'– territorial labour organisations – with the occasional support of railway workers. There was much debate over how long the strikes should last but as they spread, they would turn out to be the biggest series of such action ever seen in Italy. The newspaper *La Stampa* reported that in Ancona: 'The general strike is complete, absolute, and is extended to all public activities.'[26] Railways ground to a halt, preventing troops being moved towards the rebellion.

Soon large parts of the centre of the country were paralysed by the strikes, accompanied by a chaotic form of revolt which appeared, to some, like a revolution. In Ancona, one journalist wrote: 'The population is gripped by panic, there is widespread fear that things will get worse, many people have barricaded themselves in their own homes.' Errico Malatesta appeared to be in command, for a short while; as the report stated: 'The tired, but harsh figure of ... Malatesta roared in many meetings, and the anarchist agitator is in charge of the crowd at this moment with his characteristic eloquence which inspires emotions, pain, pity, rebellion.'[27] Even Malatesta himself was taken by surprise by the force and breadth of the insurrectionary wave.[28] Malatesta wrote that 'the Romagna [region] is in flames'.[29] Later he claimed that: 'For a week we were in total charge.'[30]

It was said that at some point during Red Week, Ubaldo Comandini, a distinguished republican member of parliament, had stood up in a square, or a cafe, or perhaps even on the balcony of the town hall, in Cesena in central Italy, and proclaimed the Republic to the cheering crowds below.[31] He was said to have worn a suit and pince-nez, and sported a perfect moustache. The reality was rather more prosaic. Comandini had simply stated that, for a time, central government had lost control of parts of the Romagna region, including Cesena, where the communication lines had been cut. Nobody appeared to be in charge. It was a de facto Republic, but it was also very short-lived. Comandini actually spent most of his time during Red Week trying to calm protestors. He was quick to play down the extent of the movement in the days that followed, noting 'the absence of any action by the revolutionaries'. It felt more like a rebellion than a revolution. Churches were attacked in Cesena itself, and a customs post was burnt.[32] In other places priest's vestments were stolen, and the strikers wore them as a sign of both victory and humiliation. A clergyman in one town brandished a pistol to protect his church. In another, the water supply was cut off by demonstrators.

When the dust had settled, Comandini stated that 'it makes me smile when I hear talk of the proclamation of a Republic … the Republic was a fact. There was no sign of the government and the city was in the hands of the people. If this is a republic, it existed for a few days.' In short, Comandini's 'proclamation of the Republic' was no more than a tale, a myth.[33] As Comandini himself said, without any sign of the state or government, a series of 'incredible stories' spread quickly. It felt as if we were heading, he said, for somewhere 'unknown'.

There were numerous examples of spontaneous organisation, with citizens' committees being set up. Order was often maintained by the Chambers of Labour, which became, for a time, and in some places, a kind of de facto state, 'the only authority that was recognised as such'.[34] Excessive force was not used to put down the rebellion, in part because the authorities weren't entirely sure they could rely on the army. But this was also perhaps a wise choice strategically, avoiding escalating the bloodshed and creating more martyrs. The cannons were not sent in, although it should not be forgotten that sixteen demonstrators were killed, and more than 600 injured.

During the uprising, the anarchists tried – paradoxically perhaps – to maintain some sort of order. On the one hand they were clear that: 'This is no longer a strike, but a REVOLUTION'. But they also claimed: 'We do not plan, for now, to abolish individual property … there is no need to worry now if a hairdresser, for example, has served a client, or not, or if a shopkeeper has opened his shop.'[35] However, on 11 June the general strike was called off by the national union leadership by telegram. The trade union proclamation of 12/13 June read:

> The aim for which we acted has been achieved, but the ideals for which we fight have still not been realised. A unitary committee has now been formed which will bring together the forces of subversion and prepare our future actions. Now let us all return to work, to our homes, satisfied with what we have achieved, proud of the threat which burns in our hearts. From midnight … the strike is suspended!

Although there was local opposition to this order in many areas, almost as quickly as it began, the revolution fizzled out. Many later blamed the union leaders for their 'sabotage' of the revolution. Ludovico D'Aragona of the union federation later said: 'we could not go out onto the streets of Milan without being booed and whistled at … we were called traitors, sell-outs'.[36]

Red Week cemented the idea on the revolutionary left that a general strike was an appropriate response to attacks on the movement, and to violence from the state. This weapon would be used time and time again in the postwar period (with little success). Others criticised the uprising as a 'revolution without a programme' which, in the words of the (at that time) socialist Gaetano Salvemini, 'didn't know what it wanted or what to ask for'. But Salvemini also warned: 'The riots … are a sign of a crisis.'[37] Future Socialist Party leader Giacinto Menotti Serrati said that: 'Stones thrown against the troops are not enough … I do not think that the situation in Italy allows us to seriously contemplate a revolution.'[38] Serrati had been one of the first leaders to call off the strike action, in Venice, where he was secretary of the Chamber of Labour. Reformist socialist Claudio Treves called the protestors 'hooligans' and argued that they had nothing to do with the change socialists desired.[39] But Mussolini disagreed, writing that: 'It was not a blind uprising, but an insurrection with fairly precise aims. There wasn't a revolutionary situation, but there was widespread sympathy for a revolution – a desire, the expectation of something new.'[40]

Escape

Red Week was over and as the state forcefully reasserted its power, mass arrests took place all over the country. But where was Malatesta? The most spied upon and followed person in Italy, with all those files and police reports in Rome, had disappeared, much to the embarrassment of the police. Rubbing salt into the wounds of the state authorities, Malatesta soon gave an interview. He was in London, where he taunted the Italian state for failing to arrest him. He claimed that he had managed to slip past his guards, had stayed with a monarchist (to throw them off the scent) and had then taken a train to Switzerland.[41] He also analysed what had just happened in Italy. It wasn't, he declared, 'a movement that was prepared or desired … but … the revolution was about to happen'.[42] The decision to call off the strike, he said, had caused confusion. He stated he had not been 'the leader' of the revolt, which had, in fact, not produced any leadership at all.

Red week was a rebellion without a programme. It was inspired by anti-militarism and republicanism, by the acts of individuals such as Augusto Masetti, and was imbued with strong aspects of anti-clericalism. But what ideas was it promoting? Who was in charge? It had united (briefly) anarchists, trade unionists, socialists and republicans – but why? For the historian Marco Severini, 'a good part of central Italy was paralysed and isolated for a number of days, increasing a sense of utopia but also fears, exaggerating the role of agitators and militants who would soon be forgotten, and leaving a tragic trail of bloodshed which would prove to be a preview of the destruction of the world war'.[43] No one at the time was able to pinpoint its purpose with any coherence. It was a violent spasm, in anticipation and yet also protesting at the violence that was to come, and the sacrifices that would be made. Some two weeks later, Archduke Franz Ferdinand was shot dead in Sarajevo, sparking a series of events which would lead rapidly to a global conflict. The protagonists of Red Week quickly split in the face of war – some backed the conflict; others were radically opposed.

1915–18

THE GREAT WAR

'Everybody recognises that the war represents an historical break, in the sense that a whole series of questions which piled up individually before 1914 have precisely formed a "mound" modifying the general structure of the previous process.'

Antonio Gramsci[1]

'Four years of pain, suffering, of violent conditioning, of contempt for your own life and that of the others, of enforced subservience, of compulsory discipline, have created an environment full of anger, hatred, passion and fury.'

Enrico Dugoni[2]

Allied to Germany and Austria-Hungary through the Triple Alliance of 1882, Italy initially remained neutral in the First World War, on the grounds that the alliance was a defensive arrangement. Then, on 24 May 1915, it declared war on Austria-Hungary. The decision was taken by the king and a minority of the cabinet, without the approval of parliament, after secret meetings in London at which the Entente powers promised that, in the event of victory, Italy would be able to annex the regions of Austria-Hungary largely populated by Italians.

Most Italians were opposed to joining the war, although an organised and violent minority had campaigned vigorously in favour. Over five million Italians were called up, and the conflict caused serious strain in a country which had only recently been unified and whose population identified far more with their local village or region than with the nation. Most of the fighting took place around the Isonzo river in the north-east, but the front stretched west through Trentino and Alto Adige. The infamous and seemingly endless 'battles of the Isonzo' claimed 200,000 lives for an advance of twenty-five miles. In the trenches 'the clear distinction between life and death' collapsed.[3] It was also a 'white war', sometimes fought in the mountains at heights of over 3,000 metres, where more soldiers died from the cold than from Austrian gunfire.[4] Even today, more than a hundred years later, bodies are still pulled out of the melting glaciers every year; all are given military funerals. In August 1916, under pressure from France and Britain, Italy also declared war on Germany.

War divided Italians in violent and radical ways. That conflict, with its myths, 'many histories' and deep economic, social and political transformations, changed the face of Italian life.[5] Less than fifty years after its unification, Italy went through a brutal form of modernisation compressed into four years. Italy was an agrarian country when it entered the war in 1915. Its army was mainly drawn from rural areas (two-thirds of war orphans would come from rural backgrounds). Millions were uprooted from their land and forced to fight – underfed, badly supplied and ineptly led. The family, the 'bedrock' of Italian civil society, was ripped apart as men were conscripted and sent to the front, women entered the factories and peasants moved to the towns. The human cost was horrific.

Over three and a half years, nearly 600,000 soldiers in the Italian army were killed, and many thousands terribly injured. As a proportion of the population, these casualties were higher than Britain's. Many Italian towns and villages were destroyed and thousands of people made homeless. Italian military justice was especially harsh. Since there was no great enthusiasm for the war (and a fair amount of open opposition), the tactic adopted by the generals was to terrify their troops into fighting. It isn't known how many soldiers were executed in total; some were killed through the practice of decimation – the random shooting of one in ten troops – as an example to the others. By the end of the war, something like a million military trials had taken place – a figure that makes clear the failure of the harsh regime adopted by General Cadorna, commander-in-chief of the army until 1917. Mutinies were common and suppressed by force. More than a hundred summary executions took place at the front in a desperate attempt to keep the troops in order and there were 150,000 desertions. Meanwhile, on the home front, things were beginning to disintegrate.

Rice and bread: Milan and Turin in revolt, 1917

Industrial transformation had brought women into factories and out of their homes in huge numbers. Female workers in wartime industries increased from 14,000 in 1914 to 198,000 in 1918.[6] In industrial Milan the role of women was profoundly altered by the war. Women entered the (mainly munitions) factories or took jobs on trams and buses, as the men left for the front. Industrial work was stressful and dangerous. There were over 30,000 industrial accidents in Milan in 1917 alone. Women, at the bottom of the scale, exhausted, underpaid and unskilled, were often the victims, and subjected to ridicule and harassment. When tensions in Milan reached fever pitch in May 1917, after two tough years of conflict and mobilisation, it was the women who moved first.

In May 1917 the temporary scarcity of the staple Milanese food – rice – was the spark. Protests swept across the province of Milan. The uprising began in textile factories, but these quickly developed more widely into riots against price rises.[7] One commentator described the demonstrators as being 'masters of Milan for 24 hours'.[8] Soon the demonstrations took on an open anti-war stance and on 5 May thousands of women marched from the countryside to the north and into the city, forcibly closing factories producing war materials and arms. Despite mass arrests and repression with some women being prevented from entering the city, demonstrations continued. Strikes extended across the countryside and to industrial towns on the outskirts of Milan. There were public order disturbances, and factories were vandalised to cries of 'Down with the war!'[9] Milan's protests fizzled out, but the authorities had been warned. Three months later, in Turin across to the west of Italy, it was the breakdown of bread production and deliveries that caused a collapse of order. Italy's other key industrial centre exploded into violent protests that threatened the entire home front sustaining the war.

On 22 August 1917, the bread failed to turn up in Turin. The authorities had known for some time that supply lines were under great pressure. Prices were rising and by the middle of the month the grain held in the port areas closest to Turin had run out.[10] Turin was central to the national war effort – producing munitions and equipment in its numerous factories and workshops. The city's workers and their families needed to be fed, so they could produce arms. Many protestors, as in Milan, were women. When they discovered that there was no bread, all hell broke loose. As Teresa Noce, future communist leader and resident in Turin at the time, later wrote: 'It was the women who started everything.'[11] It was said that a large car had driven by, and someone from inside had shouted 'Let them eat biscuits'.[12] It was claimed that this was the catalyst for the revolt. 'So, let's eat the biscuits,' someone responded on 22 August, and another echoed that 'this time, the biscuits aren't just for the rich, we will eat them as well'.[13]

Groups of women and children began to attack bakeries and other stores. Soon the army was called in. Now Italy's troops were fighting on two fronts, internal and external. Noce remembered the outbreak of violence. 'We heard the first gunfire. Nobody slept that night. Everything had stopped, from the factories to the workshops to shops to transport … barricades went up everywhere.'[14] There were reports of fraternisation between troops and demonstrators, but Antonio Gramsci, the Turin-based socialist and journalist, wrote after the war that 'we waited in vain for the soldiers to help us, but the soldiers were hoodwinked into thinking that the revolt had been provoked by the Germans'.[15]

Barricades went up and factories ground to a halt as the workers walked out. It felt very much like a revolution, but who were the leaders? There were none. Nobody was in charge. As Noce concluded: 'Without arms and without leadership, there was no way the uprising could win.'[16] A general strike was called for 23 August – 'All the factories were closed.'[17] Later, the then editor of *Avanti!*, Giacinto Menotti Serrati, was clear that 'this was not *our* movement'.[18] Lenin heard news of the revolt, and he wrote somewhat optimistically that 'there is no doubt that a world revolution is developing … in Italy there has been an explosion of the masses in Turin'.[19]

As the revolt developed, and word got out as to what was happening, Serrati himself set off from Milan, where he was based, in an attempt to reach Turin. The two cities are less than a hundred and fifty kilometres apart, but it was wartime, and he was closely watched, with the authorities anxious to try and prevent him travelling. Serrati somehow made it to Chivasso, on the edge of Turin, on the morning of 24 August. He then walked towards the city to a place called Gassino (ten kilometres away) and, after avoiding the clutches of the *carabinieri*, finally arrived in Turin that evening. By the next day, he was back in Milan.

Serrati had not come to lead a revolution. In fact, he attempted to calm things down and end the strike.[20] At no point did the socialist leadership see the possibility of the events of August 1917 in Turin leading to a wider revolution – just as they hadn't during Red Week in 1914. In retrospect, however, this was probably the most insurrectionary moment of the entire war on the domestic front. Gramsci later wrote: 'Those women workers and male workers who rose up in August in Turin, who armed themselves, fought and died like heroes, but they wanted the war to end with the defeat of the bourgeois Italian army and the victory of the proletarian class.'[21] Leaflets appeared which stated: 'Proletarian blood has been spilt, but not pointlessly' and which referred to the war with the words used by the pope on 1 August 1917 – as a *'strage inutile'* – a 'useless slaughter'.[22]

On the streets, in Turin, the revolt was crushed in blood. Largely unarmed crowds were fired upon by troops, again and again. Many of the dead had been shot in the head. Ambulances found it is too dangerous to pick up bodies and the injured. Food supplies were hampered still further by the spontaneous barricades and the chaos. The revolt reached its peak on 24 August. Machine guns were brought in by the army and as one eyewitness wrote, 'lead was spread everywhere'.[23] Official figures of the dead varied wildly, and to this day many believe that the number of casualties was far higher than the forty-one admitted at the time, although different figures are alluded to at various times. Gramsci vastly exaggerated the numbers in his postwar writing.[24] However, in the early 1970s the journalist Giancarlo Carcano went through the documents and death certificates and found that the official numbers were broadly correct.[25] Who were the forty-one dead? Most were, not surprisingly, striking workers. At least five women were killed, as well as three soldiers who died repressing the revolt. Some of the demonstrators had been armed. A state of war was declared in Turin – martial law, effectively. On Sunday 26 August, the revolt came to an end and the barricades were taken down.

Repression and trials

Once the shooting was over, further repression was swift, with mass arrests in the working-class areas of the city. 'Those arrested were beaten ferociously and packed onto lorries.'[26] Ordinary people were picked up, seemingly at random. Many were prosecuted through the so-called 'quick trial' (*direttissimo*) process, which could be completed in a matter of days, a procedure reserved for 'exceptional' events. At least 822 people were arrested in the first wave and 326 were charged, with 264 found guilty after 'quick trials'. Some of those arrested were found to be deserters in hiding, and people faced a mix of civil and the harshest military justice.

Italy's authorities painted the revolt, or *moti* ('uprisings'), as a conspiracy whipped up by anti-war agitators and planned – or at the very least inspired – by socialists, anarchists and 'enemy powers'. To this end a series of socialist leaders were arrested and charged, often via military tribunals, with extremely serious crimes. Serrati was picked up in Rome on 29 May 1918, accused of 'indirect betrayal', and locked up for the rest of the war.

Thirteen people were finally called to trial in June 1918. An impressive group of left-wing lawyers was mobilised to defend Serrati and others, including the legendary socialist member of parliament, the bearded, tall, Giuseppe Emanuele Modigliani, brother of the famous painter. Serrati decided to stage a political defence. After a few delays, the trial finally began on 10 July. Prosecutors used speeches Serrati had made well before the revolt as 'evidence'. He had spoken in Turin on May Day in both 1916 and 1917, when his words were described as 'inflammatory'. But the key moment for the authorities was a meeting with representatives from revolutionary Russia who visited Italy in August, which it was claimed, improbably, was the trigger for the revolt itself (which broke out some days later). It was said that Serrati had called at that meeting for the people of Turin to: 'Rise up ... at the right moment' and had said that 'a spark is all that is needed'.[27]

At that infamous demonstration with Russian representatives on 13 August (the Bolshevik revolution, of course, had not yet happened), which was much picked over in the trial, Serrati had live-translated a speech by the Russian, Josif Petrovič Goldenberg. This was a big meeting, which some claim attracted around 40,000 people.[28] It is not clear if Serrati spoke good Russian, and he was charged with wilful mis-translation – of making a more incendiary speech than that actually given by the representative from revolutionary Russia. Reports of Serrati's 'free translation' stated that: 'He embellished Goldenberg's words whilst translating them.'[29] According to the journalist Giancarlo

Carcano: 'He [Serrati] said that the Russians were in agreement with the Italian socialists in wanting the immediate end of the war, and that the Russian delegate was convinced of the imperialist aims of the Italian war, and concluded his speech with the cry "Long live the Italian Revolution" while inviting the Italian workers to copy the actions of their Russian comrades.'[30]

Serrati denied any connection between these meetings and the subsequent revolt, pouring scorn on the whole idea. In 1918, as the tide was turning their way, the socialists transformed the trial into a political opportunity. Serrati stated at the outset: 'I am no expert in law, the law in my opinion is an expression of power. Today, you are in power and you are the law.'[31] He argued he had always been a socialist ('I have expressed these ideas for 25 years') and that being a socialist was not a crime in itself.[32] 'I am accused of having translated the words of Goldenberg, badly.'[33] Serrati was also accused of 'insurrection against the powers of the state'. He openly admitted his failure to lead. This had been a revolt which had broken out without any kind of socialist leadership – a bread riot: 'it was a movement which had nothing to do with us'.[34]

'I have had everything in my life,' concluded Serrati, 'as much as a modest militant could hope for. I have only one quality: my faith.'[35] A verdict was handed down on 2 August. Serrati was found guilty. Despite the fact that the judges described him as 'a willing traitor' he was given a relatively light sentence of three years and six months. Modigliani was 'unable to halt the bile of the judges … who once again showed themselves to be backward and conservative'.[36] Serrati only spent a little more time in prison before an amnesty saw his release in February 1918 from Turin's Le Nuove prison.

Serrati went back to editing *Avanti!*, the socialist daily whose print run rose massively in post-Great War Italy. While in prison he had continued to write for the paper, using the byline 'N.48', his cell number. His respect among the masses rose hugely due to his trenchant opposition to the war and the lively nature of his journalism, and the fact that he declined to become a parliamentary deputy. He later wrote that the trial of 1918 had been 'the most beautiful moment of my life as a rebel'.[37]

August 1917 in Turin soon entered the pantheon of 'what if' moments in the history of the Italian left.[38] *If only* there had been leadership, *if only* the proletariat had been armed, *if only* the troops had been willing not to shoot on the demonstrators, as in previous moments of insurrection and rebellion in Italian history. As with Red Week in 1914, Turin 1917 was seen by some as yet another missed opportunity, another betrayal.

CAPORETTO AND VITTORIO VENETO: FROM DEFEAT TO VICTORY, 1917–18

'Italy is moving towards a situation with two great parties: those who were there [in the war] and those who weren't ... the millions of workers who will return to the furrows of the fields after having been in the furrow of the trenches will create a synthesis between class and nation from an antithesis.'
Benito Mussolini, 'Trincerocrazia', 15 December 1917[39]

When Austrian troops broke through Italian lines in October 1917 at a place called Caporetto, on the border with what is now Slovenia, it felt like a catastrophe. Having done so, they advanced towards Venice. A chaotic retreat saw large parts of Italian territory invaded. Hundreds of thousands of Italian prisoners were taken, and arms and supplies abandoned. Refugees flooded out of the occupied zones and fled from the cities close to the new front line. Many more abandoned their arms. The apocalyptic aftermath of defeat was described vividly by Ernest Hemingway in *A Farewell to Arms*.[40] The writer Carlo Emilio Gadda, who took part in the chaotic retreat and was imprisoned for months by the Austrians, said at the time: 'My moral life is over,' and later: 'The shame of the defeat became increasingly strong. I think about history: I will be placed among the dishonourable.'[41]

General Cadorna blamed his own soldiers, accusing them of a 'military strike'. In a letter he wrote that 'the men are not fighting'.[42] One of the generals held to account for the devastation at Caporetto was Luigi Capello, who had become known as 'the butcher' for his activities in the Libyan war.[43] Capello was also 'active as a Freemason'.[44] He has been described as 'dynamic' and 'alarming' ... 'bulking larger than life ... a plain-speaking warrior, learned in the arts of war, implacable in attack'.[45] Capello essentially saw his troops as cannon fodder. As the historian Mark Thompson writes, the 'main effect' of Capello's tactics on his troops was 'exhaustion and resentment, mounting into hatred'.[46] Capello, as we shall see, would go on to play an unexpected role in post-Great War Italy. In Rome, the government fell. Caporetto, and the reaction to it, had deepened the violent fractures which the war had already opened up in Italian society.

General Graziani

To 'keep order' behind the lines, in the wake of Caporetto, another general, Andrea Graziani – well known for his brutality – was provided with his own firing squad. He took to his task with some gusto. As Thompson writes: 'He had 19 men shot in the back for sundry offences on the morning of the 16 November alone, another man, Alessandro Ruffini, was shot for saluting without taking his pipe out of his mouth.'[47] After the war, *Avanti!* ran a vigorous campaign against Graziani, citing these and other incidents.[48] Graziani later said that his decision to have Ruffini shot was 'a necessary if harsh act which helped to persuade the other 200,000 stragglers that in that moment there was a stronger power than their anarchy'.[49] General Graziani became, for many, a 'symbol of repression'.[50] But for others, such as the future *squadrista* and fascist, Ferruccio Vecchi, he was 'an unalloyed hero'.[51]

Two trials were held relating to these events after the war, but Graziani was cleared in both and he became a powerful figure under fascism. He died in February 1931, aged sixty-seven. His body was found at dawn, near a railway line close to a new station under construction in Prato, Tuscany, by railway workers; he was dressed in black and his feet were close to the rails. A train ticket was found in his jacket pocket. He also had 6,000 lire on him, in cash. It was a mysterious death, not least because the body was found on the other side of the tracks from where his train had been travelling. His coat, bag, hat and umbrella were left on the train. What had happened? Had he opened a wrong door by mistake? The liberal daily *Corriere della Sera* wrote that after Caporetto, Graziani was a 'hero' who had managed to 'give demoralised troops a sense of strength and faith, and the ability to resist the enemy gain'.[52] Judicial enquiries concluded that Graziani's death had been 'accidental', although doubts remained. He had been the only passenger in the three first-class carriages on the train.[53] The press claimed that 50,000 people attended his funeral in Verona.[54]

In 2005 the name of Alessandro Ruffini (the man shot on Graziani's orders for saluting while smoking a pipe) was added to those of forty-nine other victims inscribed on the war monument in his city, Castelfidardo in central Italy. This rehabilitation was organised by the local council, after a book appeared which detailed the tragic events of 1917. It had taken nearly ninety years for the pointless death of Ruffini to become part of the official memory of the war.

*

After Caporetto, much of the blame for territorial losses were laid at the door of the so-called 'defeatists'. Italy's army regrouped and dug in on the banks of the Piave river. Meanwhile, a new military hierarchy was put in place. General Cadorna's leadership ended with the debacle of Caporetto and he was replaced by General Armando Diaz. A vast patriotic effort on the home front began with the aim of preventing further encroachments into Italy, invaded for the first time since unification. Some of the harsh conditions and absurd disciplinary methods used earlier in the war were toned down. Big promises were made to the troops, including land, bread and – eventually – peace.

The fact that the Italian army was able to reorganise and win a victory at the battle of the Piave river in June 1918 (thanks in part to the internal collapse of the Austro-Hungarian armies) could not wipe away the shame of Caporetto. *Fare caporetto* came to mean 'to run away quickly' and Caporetto became a synonym for 'disaster'.[55] Despite the eventual victory, the retreat in 1917 had crystallised divisions over the war, and gave birth to stereotypes about Italian soldiers that have not faded away even today.

The battle of Vittorio Veneto, close to the Piave river, brought a final Italian triumph. An armistice was signed on 3 November 1918, but celebrations were muted: Italy had lost hundreds of thousands of men for very little extra territory, and the idea that it had been a 'mutilated victory', in the words of the nationalist writer and poet Gabriele D'Annunzio, soon took hold. This was a victory which came at momentous human cost. Soon the conflict would move back to the home front, as the soldiers returned from the trenches.

Divided Italians

At the time of the armistice, over two and a quarter million men were still under arms. Half a million Italians would die of 'Spanish flu' in the postwar pandemic. Deep fissures ran right through the nation. Italy was both made and broken by the war, which left behind deep physical traces – trenches, barbed wire, unexploded bombs, bullet holes, rubble, and of course corpses. War had created a violent generation, and not just among the soldiers themselves. Pacifism and revolt on the home front saw the rise of Italian Bolsheviks, who wanted to 'do as in Russia'.

Defeatists

On the one side of the divide were those implacably opposed to the war. These individuals were often referred to disparagingly as *disfattisti* – defeatists. Ercole Bucco, Pietro Farini, Francesco Misiano, Giuseppe Modigliani and Giacomo Matteotti were all hostile to the war. All spoke out against the conflict. All became hate figures for their anti-war radicalism, and targets of violence and judicial repression, but also immensely popular for the same reasons. All became symbols of the deep tensions opened up by the conflict, and would go on the be key figures after 1918. They will play a central role in this book.

Born in 1884 in the deep south of Italy – in Ardore in Calabria – Francesco Misiano joined the Socialist Party in 1908 after moving to Naples. During Red Week in 1914 he was involved in the general strike in the city, and was sacked from the railways, where he worked, as a result. Misiano was in Turin in 1915 during the first mass protests against the war and he later continued his struggle within the army itself, as a conscript, carrying out open, anti-militarist agitation among the troops in his barracks. For this, he suffered harassment and torture, was threatened with being sent to the front line and to the most dangerous zones of the conflict, and was even locked up in a psychiatric hospital for a while.

After escaping from his barracks in Cuneo in the north of Italy, he was accused of desertion. As a consequence, Misiano fled to Switzerland and Germany (he faced execution in Italy) and only returned home in 1919. In Switzerland he met Lenin and the two men became friends. Lenin returned to Russia in 1917 to lead the revolution. In Germany, Misiano took part in an armed revolutionary uprising which led to his imprisonment there. He became a prominent political figure, a go-between with personal and political connections to the Bolsheviks and Lenin himself. At one crucial point he was even entrusted with a letter by Lenin to bring back to Italy.[56]

Misiano's anti-war militancy was public and radical, and he personified radical anti-militarism in wartime and postwar Italy. 'When the intervention in the war was close, in 1915,' he later stated, 'I was one of many thousands who fought against that intervention by Italy. I spoke in numerous meetings in Piedmont, Liguria, Tuscany, Lombardy and you were aware of this, the police knew about it, the government, everyone knew what was my attitude to the war … in the face of the war I fought against the war.'[57]

He made no secret of his hatred of a conflict that had caused such deep rifts among Italy's citizens. Standing as a candidate in the 1919 elections (while still behind bars in Germany) he was elected with a large number of votes in both Naples and Turin, despite the fact that he had been unable to campaign. Soon afterwards, Misiano's election was validated. He became famous and infamous at the same time: popular among the revolutionary base and among workers; hated by many others.

Giuseppe Emanuele Modigliani came from a distinguished family. He was often known simply as Mené. It was impossible not to recognise him. His beard ('a prophet's beard') was long, and by 1919, mainly white.[58] He was Jewish, from the port town of Livorno – and he worked, like so many socialist intellectuals of that time – as a lawyer. A socialist reformist, he was a legendary orator; it was said that he had 'a tenor's voice'. Arrested many times, he was idolised by the working-class base, although often marginalised by the ideological battles within the party before and after the First World War.

A pacifist, Modigliani opposed Italy's intervention in wars in both 1911 and 1915, which made him into a hate figure for many – a marked man. Anti-Semitic propaganda was already circulating in his home town of Livorno around the time of the Libyan war, which depicted him as mixture of a Turk and a stereotypical Jew. Along with other defeatists, he was blamed by many for the near defeat of the Italian army at Caporetto in October 1917, and was referred to disparagingly as 'The Marquis of Caporetto' (a title that was also used for his fellow socialist, Claudio Treves, who was also Jewish).[59] He duly became a target for violence. In November 1917 posters were put up naming him and containing threats: 'We will avenge the shame we have suffered with their blood.'[60]

A month later, in Rome, Modigliani was recognised in a restaurant by two men who shouted that he should be 'chucked out of the place, he is not worthy to be here'. A scuffle ensued, 'during which the parliamentarian claimed he was grabbed by his beard'.[61] Subsequently, he was attacked or threatened on numerous occasions. For his supporters, Modigliani's beard was very important: it made him seem like 'a priest from [the opera] *Aida*'.[62] To others it was seen as symbolic of his power and masculinity – a much sought-after trophy for fascist squads, who pledged to use it 'to clean Mussolini's boots'. Fascists and nationalists tended to be clean-shaven or sport small goatees or just moustaches.

*

Ercole Bucco was a potent speaker and an incendiary agitator who first emerged as a radical in the small agricultural centre of Cento, south-west of Ferrara, and then in the city of Bologna. Thin, with small, rimmed glasses ('he always wears gold-rimmed glasses')[63] and a moustache, there was something of the dandy about him. Born in 1886, he grew up in Cento and joined the Socialist Party at a young age. Like many socialists, and Italians in general, he experienced emigration and was constantly on the move. In 1912 he became secretary of Cento's Camera del Lavoro and was soon making a name for himself with his radical organising powers, energy and oratory. His potted biography in his police file referred to him as 'lively and impulsive' but also educated and intelligent, and a 'tireless' organiser as well as 'violently anticlerical and anti-militarist'.[64] In a 1914 pamphlet he wrote that 'The cause of the war is a barbarian cause; the cause of peace is a cause of civilisation.'[65] From 1915–19 he served as a corporal and driver in the army.[66]

Entire cities, at times, seemed to oppose the war. Pietro Farini, who ran a chemist store, was a leading socialist in Terni. In 1915, he had been attacked by pro-war demonstrators. But during the war, on May Day 1917, he called on the peasants to light fires 'to salute their sons who are in the war, and call for an end to the massacre'.[67] In his unpublished autobiography, Farini remembered that: 'At the end of a beautiful day ... at dusk, in the valley, on the hills, on the mountainsides, we saw the fires rise, dozens, hundreds, thousands, ... toward Rome ... toward the Abruzzi, on the mountains ... on the road to the north where machine guns were sowing death among Italy's sons ... Terni seemed enfolded in a huge fire ... a sea of lights out of which [the people] voice their sharp call for peace.'[68]

*

The Polesine is an agricultural area to the east of Italy, which was marked in the early twentieth century by poverty and violent rural class struggle. Giacomo Matteotti came from the region and his radical pacifism in the run-up to and during the war made him a hate figure for many, and a hero to others. His home town was close to the front; so, to minimise his influence, he was called up to the army and moved around to keep him away from the troops. In the end, he was posted as far away as was physically possible, to a barracks in a tiny village in the province of Messina in Sicily.[69] In Palermo, it was said that when 'the restaurateurs had feared fascist reprisals if they served him, Matteotti had shrugged and gone hungry'.[70] The authorities described him at the time as: 'A stubborn and violent agitator, capable of attacking Italy's national interests on every occasion.'[71] Benito Mussolini later wrote of him that 'he hated war'.[72]

Interventionists

> 'Blessed be the youths who hunger and thirst for glory, for they will be sated.'
>
> Gabriele D'Annunzio, speech at Quarto, 5 May 1915

In 1914 Benito Mussolini, the talented socialist journalist and orator who had originally made his name as a fiery speaker and agitator, especially in opposition to war, changed his mind. He had been willing to go to prison for the anti-militarist cause and had been a strong and fervent supporter of Red Week. In 1910 he wrote that the Italian flag 'is a rag to be planted on a dunghill. There are only two fatherlands in the world: that of the exploited and that of the exploiters.'[73] But now, suddenly, and shockingly for the socialist movement, he became a powerful advocate in favour of Italian military intervention. This 'great betrayal' led to his expulsion from the party and sacking as editor of *Avanti!* He quickly created a new daily newspaper in Milan called *Il Popolo d'Italia*, and volunteered to fight, despite having already done military service. In August 1915 he was called up and experienced the trenches, before receiving a shrapnel wound. There are doubts about the details of Mussolini's participation in the conflict, but a powerful myth was soon created. He wrote a 'war diary' from the front which was published in segments.[74]

Others soon followed Mussolini's lead. Roberto Farinacci stood six feet tall with 'broad shoulders and an equally ample waistline, ruddy complexion, and jet-black handlebar moustaches'. He often wore a black hat and carried a 'a knobby walking stick'.[75] Born in 1892 in Isernia near Naples, his background was modest (his father was a policeman). In 1906 he and his father moved to the northern provincial city of Cremona, where he later worked as an assistant telegraph operator on the railways (his father had also started working in the same sector). He became part of the union movement and joined the Freemasons. After 1915 he became aggressively pro-war. His long political and local rivalry with Guido Miglioli, a Cremona-based radical Catholic and pacifist, began during the conflict itself. Farinacci began to experiment with what would become familiar fascist tactics – including the violent disruption of meetings. His talents were above all in one area – that of brutality, both physical and verbal. His language soon took on extreme tones. In 1918 he threatened Miglioli, who, he said, 'deserved to be forever put out of circulation', and insulted him as a 'German, sell-out, traitor, coward, sodomite'.[76] Farinacci soon began to carry a gun.

1919

FASCISM IS BORN

Few people noticed them at the time, but two smallish meetings held in Milan on 21 and 23 March 1919 later took on a mythical quality. The venue was the rather grand Palazzo Castani and more specifically the Sala riunioni del Circolo dell'Alleanza Industriale – in the centre of the city, in Piazza San Sepolcro. A somewhat ragbag collection of people turned up, and in far fewer numbers than was hoped. Those present on the 23rd were later given a striking collective title: *San Sepolcristi*, or sometimes 'the first fascists'. They included leading futurists (an artistic and cultural movement which exalted war) such as Filippo Tommaso Marinetti, and key figures in the later history of the movement such as Farinacci, Leandro Arpinati, Italo Balbo, Michele Bianchi, and Mussolini's brother, Arnaldo.

There were artists, poets, writers and a fair number of journalists. Most had fought in the war, often as crack troops in special units. All had supported intervention. Many came from the left – including ex-anarchists, ex-syndicalists and ex-socialists. The formation of the 'Fasci Italiani di Combattimento' wasn't front-page news, even locally in Milan. The meeting was reported on page 3 of the *Corriere della Sera* in a perfunctory twenty-three-line piece.[1] That was it. Yet, this was without doubt an historic moment, which would globally shape the rest of the century and beyond. It was the day that fascism was officially born. A programme was issued which was pro-war, hyper-nationalist, republican, anti-political and anti-socialist. Yet the real baptism of fascism would be on the streets of Milan, in April 1919, less than a month after that movement's official birth.

THE FIRST *SQUADRISTA*

Ferruccio Vecchi was born in the province of Ravenna in 1894, the youngest of five children. His father's occupation was recorded as 'milker'. In 1915 he volunteered for the war and fought with the crack *arditi* troops, who, it was said, attacked the enemy trenches with gusto and were adept in hand-to-hand combat, often using daggers and grenades. Vecchi was one of the key figures in the formation of the first fascist groups in March 1919 in Milan. He nursed a sense of bitter resentment about the war years, writing in 1919 in *L'Ardito*, a proto-fascist newspaper: 'We would like to thank the army and apologise for the fact that we did not all die as was our hope and our duty.'[2] A new civil war was beginning to take shape and Vecchi was well aware of this, as he argued: 'The enemy is not only German … it is also Italian.'[3]

Vecchi was a key figure in the founding moment of *squadrismo*, which was born in blood. In April 1919 he took part in the first act of *squadristi* mayhem, an event which was also to define fascism itself. Milan's city centre saw armed clashes between fascists and nationalists, on the one side, and socialist and anarchist demonstrators, on the other. Marinetti, the futurist, described the events of that day in his diaries as a chaotic battle, an episode of urban guerrilla warfare. He was both a witness and a protagonist of those clashes. The 'enemy', he noted, were singing 'Bandiera Rossa ['The Red Flag']' as they marched and included 'anarchists, red flowers pinned to their chests, three women in red shirts [and] two youths holding up a portrait of Lenin'. There was then a gunfight and unknown fascist gunmen shot dead three young workers, including a young woman, Teresa Galli, who lived and worked in the working-class neighbourhood of Bovisa. Marinetti and his followers had won. 'The battle,' he concluded 'lasted an hour.'[4]

An armed attack followed on the offices of *Avanti!*, the Socialist Party daily newspaper. This type of *squadrista* 'action' – an assault on a building, followed by looting, violence, burning and destruction – was to be repeated thousands of times over the next few years. The *Avanti!* raid in 1919 was a prototype, a model for the future, an example of 'positive' devastation. It would often be retold, narrated and represented over subsequent months and years. Similar actions were subsequently carried out against private homes, trade union offices, political party headquarters, newspaper presses – alongside beatings of individuals. The *Avanti!* fire was a model for how the blackshirts would act; an example of organised violence as a new and devastatingly effective political tactic.

Vecchi's account of that day was heroic and he depicted the attackers as a small intrepid minority. Once inside they laid waste to the building, setting it on fire: 'books, pictures, tables, collections of newspapers and all kinds of editorial equipment – all this was thrown out of the windows up high onto the streets below, and from here into the canal which stood nearby ... an immense plume of smoke, tongues of fire and star-like sparks rose into the April sky'.[5] A further key feature of that day – which would also be seen many times in the years to come – was the way in which police and *carabinieri* allowed the fascists to act with impunity. Fascist violence was tolerated – even encouraged – by the representatives of the state, right from the outset. Many sympathised with the aims of fascism itself and approved of its actions. The state was not neutral.[6]

The famous journalist Paolo Valera was an eyewitness: 'There were more than a hundred soldiers and *carabinieri* stationed around *Avanti!* that day, in two lines, one in front of the other,' he wrote:

> In an instant the attackers were on the ground floor, and then they moved up the stairs to the editorial offices, those of the administrators, the storerooms, the printing press on the first floor. The few people working at the newspaper escaped via the roof. But why did the soldiers and *carabinieri* do nothing, outside, indifferent, spectators of the crime which was taking place above them in a tumultuous way? Those responsible for this act of piracy were never apprehended.[7]

After the attackers left, Valera entered the building:

> I saw the damage a few hours later. It seemed the work of a gang of crazy people who were working with fire, hammers ... pickaxes to break through, knock down, destroy ... The office of the Editor [Serrati] was a disaster. The floor was ruined. There were large marks on the wall, smoke stains, signs of demolition ... the rooms of the library appeared to have been attacked by demons ... Bonfires of books had been lit – books by Marx, Engels, Lenin, Trotsky and

others … The typeface letters had become … a confusion of letters all mixed together … destructive flames took hold of registers, chairs, old newspapers and those waiting to be sent out … that which survived the fire had been thrown out of the window and into the canal … *it appears that the war has taught people to kill.*[8]

Through the actions of men like Vecchi, fascists had discovered a new way of doing politics. Organised military-style violence, directed against people and things, was their tactic of choice and became a way of life. It would be carried out by groups of (almost always) men, armed with guns, cudgels, clubs and batons – who would be called *squadristi*, and their movement was dubbed *squadrismo*. They usually wore military uniforms or black shirts, and travelled in trucks, moving swiftly and caring little or nothing for the law, human life, property or accepted norms of political interaction. The blackshirts, as they were also known, were a tiny minority in 1919, but their time would come. For the moment, despite the *Avanti!* attack, they were forced to take a back seat. The reds were in the ascendency.

RED YEAR

'Every village, every town had its own Marat and its own Lenin.'

Pietro Nenni[9]

'It was easy in those days to raise the blood pressure of the crowd with dazzling oratory or with low level demagogy and be carried in triumph choreographically … people became famous in fifteen days only to be seen as a disgrace in the next fifteen days.'

Antonio Gramsci[10]

'In 1919 the Italian working class had neither programme nor leaders … All Italy was out in the streets.'

Angelo Tasca[11]

My grandmother, Silvia, daughter of my great-grandmother, Aurelia – who had thought of fascism as 'wonderful' – left an unpublished and unfinished autobiography. Silvia was born in Bologna in 1910 and was in the city during and after the First World War. 'In that tired, hungry, cold, ancient Italian city there was no rejoicing. People wept,' she remembered:

Why did they weep? It seemed right. People wept for the waste of
life, for the futility of war, for the farce of victory, from self-pity,
from past senseless suffering, people wept out of weakness surveying
the scene of disaster of cities without young men, of hospitals full
of the maimed, of Northern fields abandoned to the wreckage of a
war fought without means, without military knowledge, without
the will to fight. Where to find the strength and courage to clear the
mess? Where to begin? Mother of God give us strength.[12]

Italy's 'two red years' following that conflict were a heady mix of revolt,
democracy and chaos. Strikes hit every sector of the economy, from
railways to factories. Even priests and football referees went on strike.
Millions of peasants rose up, occupying land and demanding basic
rights. In June and July 1919 shops were looted across the country in
insurrectionary 'cost-of-living riots'. In Milan the uprising erupted
on the morning of 6 July. Tension in the city had been rising after
first reports of disorder elsewhere had come flooding in. Two hundred
and ten shops were sacked that day in Milan and many goods were
transferred to trade union offices for 'protection'. 'Shutters have been
pulled down, or smashed,' wrote *Avanti!*, 'glass windows are broken.'[13]
    Some shopkeepers slashed their prices in desperation, while others
simply closed. It felt and looked like a revolution. It was a joyous
atmosphere, with chants dedicated to Lenin and the Russian Revolution.
A lorry carrying twenty-four tons of potatoes was held up and the
vegetables distributed to the crowd. Just outside the city, a factory
was looted and twenty-five tons of salami taken. Order was restored
only with the help of the factory's workers. Consumers revelled in
the overturning of the power relationship between themselves and
shopkeepers. In central bars, drinkers demanded that the price of a
Campari be halved. July 1919 also saw millions of workers down tools in
solidarity with Bolshevik Russia during a so-called 'International General
Strike'.

THE 1919 ELECTIONS

On 16 November 1919, 5.8 million Italian men went to the polls in the
first national election since the end of the war, although turnout was a
relatively low 56 per cent (women would not vote in Italy until 1946).

For the liberal incumbents, while they just held on to power, it was a shocking result. One hundred and fifty-six socialists were elected, many of them self-professed revolutionaries; 1,834,000 Italians voted socialist and the Socialist Party (*Partito Socialista Italiano* – PSI) vote went up by almost 1 million – more than double than that of 1913, the last time an election had been held. The PSI gained more than a hundred seats and became the largest single party in parliament. A hundred Catholic deputies also entered parliament, after the Vatican had sanctioned the formation of Italy's first Catholic electoral organisation – the Italian Popular Party (*Partito Popolare Italiano* – PPI). No fascists were elected.

The first days of the new parliament were not auspicious. On 1 December the king came to the parliamentary chamber to make his traditional speech opening the new parliamentary session. But many socialist deputies abandoned the chamber as the monarch entered, singing 'The Red Flag', calling for a socialist republic, hailing Lenin and waving red carnations. The signal for the protest was given by Lucio Serrati, brother of the editor of *Avanti!*, who stood up and shouted out: '*Viva il socialismo*'. The socialists had taken their seats more than two hours before the king had been due to arrive, in order to prevent other parties blocking their protest by occupying all the spaces. Even the clothing they wore was different: 'Dinner jackets ... shiny clothing, swords ... have all disappeared from Italian public life,' reported *Avanti!*, 'the heavy proletarian boot has crushed everything.'[14] The socialists didn't have a completely free rein, however. As they were leaving the building, a number of socialist deputies were attacked by nationalists and soldiers.

The next day, the socialist deputies protested over the oath they were obliged to swear before taking up their posts.[15] Over the next few years, *every single one* of those 156 socialist deputies (and many Catholics and liberals) would suffer violence at the hands of nationalists, fascists or the police. One would be murdered by fascists. Many were beaten on numerous occasions; a number would suffer serious injury, be forced out of their homes and escape into exile.

In 1919–20 across the country, from north to south, there were frequent – almost daily – clashes between demonstrators and police, *carabinieri* and a newly formed body called the Royal Guards. Entire cities or even regions rose up in revolt. Mantua's 'red days' in early December 1919, sparked by the attacks on parliamentarians in Rome, saw riots, looting, strikes and street battles. The local prison was invaded by demonstrators and the railway station attacked. Soldiers were disarmed by the crowd and tramlines destroyed. Gun shops were emptied. After three days, however, the revolt fizzled out. Seven people had been killed in various clashes; 296 people were eventually sent to trial in eleven trials and 173 were found guilty, but mostly of minor crimes. The maximum sentence was six years.[16]

A public enquiry into the events surrounding the Caporetto 'defeat' in 1917, which dragged on throughout 1919, opened wounds still further and hardened positions around reciprocal accusations of 'defeatism' and the brutal and incompetent management of the war by the government and army leadership. The radical artist Giuseppe Scalarini's forceful cartoons in *Avanti!* depicted mountains of dead and injured and laid the blame firmly at the government's door (and that of the Church). On the other side of the divide, wounds were paraded as political weapons. Uniforms were seen as a sign of pride (for the nationalists) or a provocation (for many on the left).[17] Competing monuments were erected (and destroyed) in a brutal memory war.

RED BARONS

In parts of Italy, around this time, trade unions and socialists, working together, took effective economic control. Networks of cooperatives linked to local government institutions threatened private commerce. Compact, combative and well-organised rural strikes left the landowners with no way out. It seemed that years of struggle and organisation were finally coming to an end. The final victory of the rural proletariat and their organisations appeared close.

Socialist leader Giuseppe Massarenti had been organising rural day-labourers in the small Emilian town of Molinella, on the plains between Bologna and Ferrara, for over thirty years.[18] In 1897 a forty-day strike in the town led to the first written contract for the local agricultural workers, and union recognition. The union in that area became extremely powerful, winning concessions over labour supply and forging unexpected alliances between sharecroppers and day-labourers. In 1903 Massarenti was forced to flee to Switzerland after a prison sentence was imposed on him for defamation. He returned in 1905 and became mayor of the town in 1906, a post he would hold until 1914. Massarenti utilised taxation, roadblocks and cooperatives to help strikes to succeed. He also organised electoral registration of the previously disenfranchised. This 'model' of administration attracted bitter attacks from the landowners, politicians and journalists, who dubbed Molinella the 'Republic of the Beggars'. Massarenti was accused of being a 'red tsar' who had created a 'state within a state'. He became a hate figure for landowners, liberal opinion and soon, for the fascists.

In 1914 the Socialist Party managed to elect all members of the council in Molinella by standing two lists. But, in the same year, on 5 October 1914, five people, among a group brought in to try to break a day-labourer strike from the Veneto, were killed in clashes with striking peasants just outside Molinella. Despite the attempts to link Massarenti with intimidation and threats, he himself preached non-violence. 'He used to say, it is better to be beaten twice than to beat somebody else once.'[19] Yet he was immediately blamed for the 1914 'massacre'.

Mass persecution followed the clashes.[20] Three thousand troops were sent to Molinella, which was effectively placed under military occupation. Massarenti was charged with murder, suspended as mayor and had to flee to San Marino, a tiny mountain republic located entirely within Italy which had a history of taking in refugees or those on the run. The local council in Molinella was dissolved within a week. Militant sharecroppers were evicted, and dozens of workers remained in prison or were interned (in Sardinia) for years – serving 'a thousand years of pre-trial prison time'.[21]

After an unexpected legal victory in June 1919, Massarenti returned to Molinella in triumph. He had been in exile for nearly five years. Thousands greeted him, and Molinella became a focus for some of the most bitter struggles seen during the tumultuous postwar 'red years'. Fines were imposed on landowners for the damage caused by the 1914 repression, evicted sharecroppers were given back their farms and one contract now covered all kinds of rural labourers and rentiers.[22] In the 1919 elections, the Socialist Party won another landslide with 93.6 per cent of the votes in Molinella. His enemies – the landowners – called Massarenti 'the Devil'. Leading journalist Mario Missiroli wrote numerous critical pieces and books about Massarenti.[23] Missiroli described Massarenti as 'the baron of Molinella. He is the law. He guarantees all freedom, all tolerance, everything that happens.'[24] The combination of reformist power and institutions and revolutionary rhetoric terrified the landowners and middle classes. Many soon turned to the blackshirts as a bulwark against social revolution. Massarenti's triumph would be extremely short-lived.

The leader of the national landworkers' union after the war was Argentina Altobelli. Very few women made it to the top of the Italian trade union and socialist movement. Altobelli, an extraordinary figure, was an exception to this rule – a woman in a man's world – and as a result, she was often criticised, caricatured or marginalised. Born in Imola in 1866, Altobelli organised rural and rice workers, many of whom were women. An avid reader, she was highly educated and popular among her base, and was said to be a rousing speaker, inspiring a song which included the line: 'Argentina Altobelli was the one who woke us up.'[25] Very few women spoke at public meetings in that period, but Altobelli was holding forth to crowds from the 1880s onwards.

In 1909 Argentina's husband died, leaving her alone with two children. She started up a newspaper aimed at women workers and was elected to the central committee of the Italian Socialist Party. She became leader of a rural workers trade union (the Federterra) and fought long battles for workers' rights. After the war, landworkers flocked to the Federterra. The union rapidly recruited over a million members. Many would be mobilised in vast social struggles, land occupations and strikes during the red years. Rural workers would often sustain terrible injuries, which meant that they were unable to work – and thus forced to live in near starvation, along with their families. Altobelli led the struggle for insurance and safety at work. The police became interested in Altobelli well before the rise of fascism, keeping detailed records on her life and activities, which were diligently deposited in Rome and in other police archives across the country. In one early report it was said that Altobelli 'is very active in the organisation of the local agrarian proletariat ... she is always on the move and she inspires the crowds who welcome her ... especially the women. A good-looking youth, she is a fluent speaker, and exercises a great deal of authority over the ignorant masses who always follow her orders and advice.'[26]

1919ISM: MAXIMALISTS

In the wake of these struggles, revolutionaries took over the leadership of the Socialist Party. There was a feeling in the air of rebellion and change. Some called this combination of words and action '1919ism'. In

1919 a short pamphlet was published in Bologna titled: *'Chi non lavora, non mangi'* ('who does not work, shall not eat').[27] The pamphlet argued for the replacement of the middle classes. 'Our adversaries in the class struggle,' the pamphlet argued, 'are not just the big capitalists, but all those who, due to the structure of the bourgeois economy, play the part of intermediaries.'[28] In a socialist society, this class of 'intermediaries' was no longer required. The author of the pamphlet was one of the most high-profile revolutionaries during Italy's red years – Ercole Bucco.

Bucco was a leading exponent of the maximalist – or revolutionary – wing of the Italian Socialist Party which took over the party in the wake of the Russian Revolution in 1917. One of their slogans was *Fare come in Russia* - 'Let us do as in Russia'. Confusingly, they became known as maximalists because they backed a (shorter) revolutionary programme, as opposed to the reformists, who supported a longer and more moderate 'minimalist' agenda. During the red years, the maximalists gained control over the party, and part of the union movement, usurping the traditional reformist leadership. As with many of the maximalists after the war, Bucco's rise to fame was rapid.

Elected to parliament for the first time with the 'red wave' in November 1919, Bucco became secretary of the Socialist Parliamentary Group, and he also took over the potent Confederation of Labour in the radical city of Bologna in central Italy. Bucco quickly wrote to the Prefect of Bologna with a stark statement: 'I do not recognise your authority. I am here to replace you.'[29] A charismatic speaker, he called for revolution on many occasions, and for the setting up of soviets. 'It is not enough,' he said, 'to cry "long live Russia", or "long live Lenin". We must imitate the Republic of Soviets in the work of reconstruction and in the daily battle to create a communist society.'[30] Bucco openly supported revolutionary violence, arguing: 'I reject violence as a method because it destroys the soul and crushes the personality, but I exalt violence which is exercised as a form of liberation in order to create, generate, produce.'[31]

MALATESTA IS BACK!

'If we let this favourable moment pass, we will have to pay a
heavy price for the tears of blood and fear we have inspired in the
bourgeoisie.'

Errico Malatesta, 1920[32]

On Christmas Eve, 1919, Errico Malatesta, the veteran anarchist firebrand who had fled to London after his dramatic escape following Red Week in 1914, finally made it back to Italy. In Britain, he had worked as a mechanic and electrician. He travelled in secret on a cargo boat via Cardiff to Taranto in the deep south of Italy, and then by overnight train up to Genoa. Newspapers had been full of rumours about Malatesta's homecoming for months. He was eagerly awaited, or feared, depending on which side you were on.

On arrival Malatesta was greeted by wildly cheering crowds and forests of red and black flags. It was a kind of *Malatestamania*. He embarked on a madcap series of meetings and demonstrations. It was a time when 'those poor devils who [had] a similar goatee to Malatesta were hoisted on shoulders with shouts of "Long Live Lenin!", "Long Live Malatesta!"'[33] As he remembered: 'My arrival back in Italy was crazy. Wherever I went thousands of people greeted me with applause and cried out "Long live the revolution".'[34] Unlikely plots were hatched. Everything seemed possible. The charismatic leader of the maritime workers' trade union, who had facilitated the veteran anarchist's return, also attempted to broker negotiations between Gabriele D'Annunzio and Malatesta, for a highly unlikely and fanciful 'march on Rome', or an insurrection of some kind. But these plans came to nothing.

When Malatesta came to speak in the industrial town of Terni there was a huge turnout. As one witness remembered, the crowd was so thick that, 'had you thrown a fistful of rice in the air, not one grain would have touched the ground'.[35] He held the crowd in the palm of his hand: 'Malatesta was a spellbinder ... those people, they could speak for hours without an outline, a piece of paper, anything; back then they spoke without any support, and their arguments were sound, were new.'[36]

Malatesta had been unsuccessfully trying to foment a revolution for over forty years. By now sixty-seven years old, his very presence had an incendiary effect. Most people could not hear a word he said among the vast crowds, but his charisma and reputation were enough.[37] The authorities were terrified of this frail, bearded figure, and even Mussolini – who admired Malatesta – welcomed him back. 'Today,' he wrote in April 1920, 'Malatesta is the star that obscures all the leaders of the Socialist Party. His influence on the Italian working masses is extremely powerful.'[38] On 27 December 1919, Malatesta spoke at the

Piazza di Carignano in Genoa, his first public meeting since his return. There was a massive turnout. According to Paolo Finzi: 'The Genovese workers left their workplaces at midday' to hear him speak.[39]

As Malatesta crisscrossed Italy addressing crowds in halls, factories and public squares, there were constant calls in the press and from politicians for his arrest, although he appeared to have committed no actual crime. 'Evidence' against him consisted almost entirely of his own speeches and articles – and these were often framed as 'incitement to civil war' or 'conspiracy against the state' which were both designated as crimes under the criminal code. State bodies were, however, wary of creating further unrest through the martyrdom of an old and physically frail man.

A Second Red Year
1920

Italy's second red year saw social and political tensions rise still further. Strikes paralysed industry in its heartlands in Turin, Milan and Genoa. Bitter struggles swept across Italy's 'breadbasket', the Po Valley, with its vast and landless rural proletariat, who had been organised into powerful 'leagues'. Harvests were threatened. In Turin, a lengthy strike in April 1920 brought out hundreds of thousands of industrial workers in protest against the loss of just an hour's pay, due to the clocks going forwards. Factory councils, similar to soviets, were formed. In one factory the workers moved the clock hands back themselves.

Ancona had been the capital of Red Week in 1914, and now, in June 1920, the people of the city rose up again, after a mutiny among troops against a possible war in Albania. A further revolt quickly spread across central Italy, with strikes, barricades and over twenty deaths. The leader of the rebellion among the military was called Monaldo Casagrande, but he was soon given a nickname – 'Malatesta' – in honour of the more famous anarchist. General Sanna, from Sardinia, was sent to quash the insurrection, which he did successfully, using cannons and warships stationed off the coast of Ancona.

Huge victories were won by the working class and the peasantry during the red years – the eight-hour day, employment rights, pay increases, controls over who was hired and fired in the countryside. But there can be little doubt that the constant strikes, riots and violence at that time also created a 'great fear'. There was an atmosphere of civil war.

In 1920, Giuseppe Massarenti from Molinella was one of the key leaders of an epic ten-month rural strike in Emilia. This was class conflict at its most stark, and brutal: employer directly against peasant, without mediation. Massarenti became mayor of Molinella again in November 1920, as the Socialist Party took every seat on the council. Molinella was symbolic for fascists, landowners, parts of the middle class and the liberal state as a town synonymous with hated 'red' power.

Ercole Bucco, the maximalist, was also involved in those dramatic struggles in the Emilian countryside. He was accused of controlling the strikes, and it was said that he personally issued (unofficial) permits to allow people to move from one area to another. The fascist historian Giorgio Alberto Chiurco later described Bucco as one of the 'bosses of the Province' in 1920. Chiurco claimed that Bucco imposed an illegal tax on grapes in order to finance union activities.[1] The employers were forced to give in almost everywhere.

In June 1920 five people were shot dead (and 150 wounded) by the *carabinieri* in Terni. Socialist leader Pietro Farini was indignant, and it was said that 'he picked up two and a half kilos of shell cases and took them to Rome, to parliament'.[2] According to one testimony, he then asked the chamber: 'Who fired these? Is it the people who are armed with this kind of weapons? Of course not!'[3]

Italy's red years culminated in the occupation of the factories in August–September 1920. Over 500,000 workers took control of their places of work, kicking out the bosses. Some continued to produce goods. Red and black flags flew over industrial buildings in Milan, Turin, Genoa – including the famous factories of Fiat, Pirelli, Campari, Alfa Romeo – and right across the rest of the country. Some of the workers gathered arms and stood guard. A ship was launched by the occupiers and named *Lenin*. Workers answered the phone at Fiat describing themselves as the 'Fiat Soviet'.[4]

In September 1920, with factories across Italy occupied by their own workers, a crucial meeting was held by the socialist hierarchy in Milan. The movement debated two motions. It was an extraordinary (and unprecedented) moment. A *vote* was held as to whether there should be a *revolution*, or not. Bucco was one of the signatories of the revolutionary motion, which lost (by around 591,000 proxy votes to 409,000). By this point he was a national figure of some importance. Like many other maximalists, Bucco often expressed contempt for parliamentary democracy, stating: 'We have always felt disgust for democracy, and seen it as a horrible thing ... when a house is about to collapse it is better to leave it to collapse … and we can then reconstruct the building from its ruins otherwise we will always have a structure full of patched up areas and plaster with rotten foundations.' Bucco worked as an architect outside of politics – hence, perhaps, the choice of metaphor.[5]

Following the failed 'vote on the revolution', the factory occupations were called off and a deal was signed. Bosses and supervisors assumed control, again. Wily liberal prime minister Giovanni Giolitti had decided not to intervene, and his circumspection paid off, as the movement dwindled on its own. Italy's red years were over. The workers involved in the occupation 'knew they were doomed to defeat', Antonio Gramsci wrote later, 'yet they held out for a month'.[6] It would be another movement that moved into the space the left vacated and would take control of the streets. This was a movement made up mainly of young men, many of them veterans from the recent war. They would soon take Italy by storm. The 'Black Years' were about to begin.

Black Years
1920–21

A FASCIST SQUAD

Thirty to forty men, all standing. Most are looking straight at the camera. They all seem young, and there is one small boy in the front. All are in uniform, but not all the uniforms are the same. Most are wearing black shirts. One is on a bicycle. Some have hats. One has a bugle. Many have guns. Others are carrying cudgels, long sticks, metal truncheons. Some have helmets. Most are clean shaven, although some have moustaches. None have beards.

This is a fascist squad, ready to go out on a raid. Groups like this formed all over Italy from 1920 onwards, and they often took these kind of team photographs before and after their attacks: transmitting a sense of collectivity, pride, masculinity and joy. The squads also documented the damage they caused, inspired by the early fascist 'actions', especially the assault on the offices of the *Avanti!* newspaper led by Ferruccio Vecchi in Milan in April 1919, and beatings of individual socialists.

In April 1920, Vecchi was part of the attack on socialist leader (and *Avanti!* editor) Giacinto Serrati in Milan's central Galleria. Serrati's beard was partly cut off and he was punched in the face and kicked. This incident was also captured in a celebrated photograph, and hailed by fascists in years to come as a combination of violence and prank. Vecchi was himself set upon by socialists two days later as revenge. *Squadristi* language was always violent. Vecchi, for example, shouted down the Neapolitan socialist deputy, Arnaldo Lucci, from the parliamentary gallery during a debate on the war, calling him 'the vomit of the nation'.[1]

Squadristi took pride and pleasure in burning, looting, and beating their enemies. Raids were carried out in a festive atmosphere, accompanied by alcohol, laughter and song. None of this was done in secret. There are hundreds of images from that time of books on fire, smashed up offices and printing presses, and even of individuals as they are attacked or humiliated. The *squadristi* also kept images of their own dead and injured – their 'martyrs'.[2] Between 1919 and 1922 hundreds of *squadristi* began to operate across the country. Local leaders emerged in every region, city and village. Fascists were most brutal, visible and effective in areas of heightened political and social struggle.

Soon, local *squadristi* leaders emerged. They became known as *ras*, after the name given to a provincial viceroy in Ethiopia's Amharic language (although some claim it was derived from an Abyssinian word, meaning 'chieftain').[3] Almost all had fought in the war. Some were aristocrats, some were landowners, while others came from the left. Many rose to fame and power with great rapidity, becoming celebrities and household names almost overnight. Local connections were so strong that it was often difficult to separate their names from the cities or regions were they operated. All used violence to accrete power and influence, orchestrating beatings, murder and the destruction of property on a grand scale.

RAS: GIUSEPPE CARADONNA AND ITALO BALBO

> *Ohe per la madonna*
> *noi siamo gli squadristi*
> *di Peppino Caradonna*
>
>> Squadrista song: 'Oh for the Madonna/
>> We are the *squadristi*/of Peppino Caradonna'

> *Manganello, manganello, tu rischiari ogni cervello*
>> Squadrista song: 'Cudgel, Cudgel, you will
>> straighten out every brain'

Giuseppe Caradonna was a *ras* whose base was in the deep south, in Apulia – the heel of Italy's foot. He was qualified as a lawyer, and had attended university in Naples, but his income came from his work as a farmer and landowner around the small town of Cerignola on the

Puglian plains. Caradonna adopted radical ideas as soon as he returned home from the war. He had been hailed as a war hero, and on his homecoming was soon making a reputation as an ardent speaker.[4] In May 1919 Foggia's prefect reported that: '[Caradonna] declared that it was time that the old Italy was swept away, that of the tax collector, the plainclothes police officer and the Italy which dishonoured the army by forcing it to rush from city to city and intervene in the struggle between capital and labour.'[5]

There was a long tradition of voter intimidation in this area of the south. Local landowners also used violent gangs to impose order and attack opponents.[6] These ferocious proto-*squadristi* were known as *mazzieri*, because of the weapons (*la mazza* – a cudgel or club) they carried to perform their dirty work. They were the middle-men enforcers of the Puglian great estates. Social conflict here was ferocious: 'Violence was the essence of the relationship between landlords and farm workers in Apulia.'[7] Caradonna was sometimes referred to as the *re dei mazzieri* (the king of the *mazzieri*).

Caradonna was soon involved in bitter local struggles. After 1918, the peasant movement had gained the upper hand under the charismatic leadership of a trade unionist called Giuseppe Di Vittorio, who was also from Cerignola. As a public official reported, the landworkers' union here 'achieved a membership of 18,000 numbering virtually every adult day-labourer in its ranks ... The organisation of the working class ... is perfect.'[8] In many ways, fascism in Apulia was little more than an extreme version of class violence. It made no attempt to convert the working masses to any cause and instead used beatings, intimidation and destruction to force workers into line. As the historian Frank Snowden has argued: 'In Apulia, fascism was squadrism and nothing else.'[9] Caradonna was the strategist and leader of this violent movement which drew on veterans and students, but also utilised criminals and the *mazzieri*.

This movement was a mixture of organised crime and paramilitary vigilantism, overlaid with elements of class struggle. Caradonna had experienced the class struggle in Cerignola at first hand, his own grain stores and wine cellars having been 'destroyed in union reprisals for his intransigence'.[10] There was nothing sophisticated about the fascist message. Join us, it said, *or else*. This message was translated through deeds, not words. Caradonna soon became known as the 'Duce of Cerignola'. Like many of the *ras*, he had no particular qualities, apart from his sense of ruthlessness and bravery. He produced no writings of note, had no real political skills, and was insignificant as a politician in terms of innovation, although he was skilled at obtaining resources and power. His success was entirely thanks to his unwavering commitment to the use of violence, and his key role in directing that violence to the crushing of socialism and trade unionism.

In this bitter struggle, however, the use of violence was not one-sided. In February 1921, 'the strikers in Barletta … burnt down the house of a landowner and destroyed agricultural machinery … while in Cerignola, Caradonna's farm and hay were set on fire'.[11] Fascist counter-violence was swift, extreme and seemed to have the full support of the local state and the forces of law and order. Within weeks democratic and labour organisations were destroyed – physically and politically. These institutions had been built up over decades, through the hard work and dedication of workers and intellectuals. They often had libraries, theatres, meeting places, bars, conference halls, and all of this was targeted and destroyed. It was not just the crushing of a movement, but also of their memory, their past and their future. The thought of rebuilding from scratch was, for many, simply too much. This destruction left a deep sense of trauma and loss. In 1921 Caradonna was elected to parliament with an incredible 133,414 votes – just behind powerful liberals such as Antonio Salandra and way ahead of the socialists.[12] That 'perfect' trade union organisation disappeared almost as quickly as it had risen.

Caradonna built up a strong bond with an eccentric Italian friar called Padre Pio from San Giovanni Rotondo in Apulia, who was said to have stigmata, and was himself gathering a large following. In San Giovanni Rotondo in October 1920, thirteen socialists and bystanders and a carabiniere died in clashes between fascists, socialists and the police during the celebration of a left-wing victory in the local elections in that small town. Fascism had allies in the Catholic Church right from the beginning, especially in the struggle against the rise of the left.

*

Since its golden age in the fifteenth and sixteenth centuries, the stunningly beautiful city of Ferrara had been living off past glories. Before and after the First World War, the city and its surrounding countryside saw intense and extremely violent social conflict. It could be argued that squadrism first took root in Ferrara, under the powerful and charismatic leadership of a former soldier and bank clerk with a small goatee beard called Italo Balbo. There, and in the surrounding countryside, he developed and perfected particularly violent tactics.[13] It is said that Balbo pioneered the use of castor oil as a punishment for fascism's victims. Ferrara's fascists crushed the socialist and union movement in the wake of violent street battles. Socialists were effectively banned and the city became a centre for *squadristi* 'expeditions' to other cities, where similarly brutal attacks on other socialist groups were carried out. Balbo quickly took total control, and his local power base would remain in place for nearly twenty years.

THE DESERTER

The most high-profile individual targets for the fascists were the prominent 'defeatists'. Many were horrified by the election of leading anti-war campaigners to parliament in 1919. The leading defeatists were unrepentant about their open opposition to the conflict, and their attempts to undermine the war effort. Mussolini was outraged and much of his ire was directed at one man – *the deserter*: Francesco Misiano. In 1920 Misiano finally returned to parliament, following a series of court cases. He was not cowed, and during a debate in February cried out: 'Down with the war!'[14] In July of that year, parliament was finally called on to debate what had become known as the 'Misiano case'. Deputies were asked to authorise his trial by a vote, thanks to laws protecting parliamentarians from the political use of judicial processes. In this instance, the specific case being referred to was an accusation of desertion. Misiano was to be tried in Palermo (the closest military tribunal to his birthplace in Calabria).[15]

Misiano made an impassioned defence of his actions in front of parliament.[16] His opening words – 'Honourable colleagues … I believe that this time you will allow me to speak' – hinted at the difficulties he had experienced making his voice heard in the past. His entire speech was later published as a pamphlet entitled 'The Deserter'.[17] Misiano's defence was political, not legal. 'I would like to declare immediately,' he continued, 'that I am guilty, I acted according to my conscience, in perfect coherence with my principles. I am an internationalist.' He made no attempt to hide his hatred of the war and his political work again it. 'In the face of the war, I fought against the war, I spoke out, wrote articles against the war, and carried out propaganda activities among the workers in which I demonstrated my aversion to the European war.' Misiano confessed that he had 'made a pledge in those demonstrations with the working class ... that my hand would never pick up a rifle in order to follow the politics of the ruling class, and that I would never fight for the ruling class, and that I would never go to the trenches ... and I would never use arms to obey the bourgeoisie.'[18]

In a potted history of his recent life, Misiano outlined his opposition to the war. He appropriated the word 'desertion' to argue that he had not *deserted* the working class at any point:

> I would have been a deserter if I had gone to the front and obeyed
> your orders and gone against my conscience ... when on the 17 May
> 1915 in Turin a general strike was declared to protest against the war,
> I did not desert from my place, I did not desert the battle in favour
> of the socialist movement. I was among those who spoke out and
> assumed the responsibility for my ideas, I was among those who,
> when the demonstration reached Piazza Castello, were shot at by
> the bullets of the cavalry. Some fell there. And then, when they had
> arrested me and taken me to prison, and the magistrates interrogated
> me, I affirmed my internationalist principles and I laughed in the
> face of their threats, which I took as a compliment.[19]

It was a magnificent and yet perhaps foolhardy speech: a revolutionary expression of anti-militarism, in the heart of parliament.[20]

In the debate that followed, Misiano found support among leading moderate socialists. The legendary socialist lawyer, deputy and orator Genuzio Bentini (who had represented both Augusto Masetti *and* a younger, anti-war Mussolini) spoke eloquently in Misiano's defence. Bentini was said to be one of only three orators that Mussolini was in awe of (the others were Filippo Corridoni, a trade unionist who died in the First World War, and Giuseppe Giulietti, eccentric and charismatic leader of the maritime workers' trade union). Bentini argued that Misiano's best defence was that he had decided not to defend himself at all, and predicted that Misiano would use any future trial for propaganda purposes: 'He will speak for all those who cannot speak, for those in the background, for the forgotten people, for the socialists who suffered during the war and thanks to the war.'[21]

This case, Bentini argued, was one of 'political persecution'. Misiano had been elected by the voters and this legal process was political, not personal. He was no coward, and had fought bravely during the uprising in Germany: 'the honourable Misiano possesses two forms of courage – that muscular courage that you glorify and exult ... and the spiritual courage of socialism ... honourable colleagues ... do what you will ... Deserter? But we need more of these kinds of deserters.'[22] Gaetano Salvemini, however, spoke in favour of allowing the trial to go ahead. The law, he said, should be equal for all. The parliamentary vote saw a clear majority *against* Misiano, as Bentini had predicted. Misiano's trial would now go ahead. A long delay followed with a game of legal cat and mouse between Misiano and the judicial authorities.

Misiano was never able to live a normal life again in Italy, even inside parliament. Newspapers accused him openly of treachery and he became one of the key targets for fascist violence. For his biographer, 'He was forced to avoid endless attacks [and] aggressions from the nationalists and the fascists.'[23] He was given the official protection of Royal Guards, which earned him much criticism from inside and outside the movement – as he was accused of cowardice, or of being a 'friend' of the authorities he had criticised on so many occasions.

'Condemned to Death': Fiume, escape and near-death, August 1920

'Hunt him [Misiano] down, punish him immediately, with cold iron. This is an order.'

Gabriele D'Annunzio, 1920

'For his enemies, Misiano was also, and above all, a symbol.'

Franca Pieroni Bortolotti[24]

In August 1920 word spread that Francesco Misiano had travelled to Fiume, a port in Yugoslavia (today it is known as Rijeka and is in Croatia) which had a large Italian population and had not been assigned to Italy after the First World War. In September 1919 the city had been occupied by irregular troops and others led by the nationalist poet and soldier Gabriele D'Annunzio. D'Annunzio set up a puppet state in Fiume, with himself as leader, in protest at what he called the 'mutilated victory' and the Paris Peace Agreement drawn up at the end of the war.

People of all kinds flocked to Fiume – nationalists, fascists and future *squadristi*, but also artists, anarchists, free-thinkers, trade unionists and rebels. It was in Fiume that many of the key features of the fascist movement were created: the chants and language, the uniforms, the balcony speeches, the rhetoric, the cult of personality. 'Veterans' from Fiume (known as 'Legionnaires') would turn up in numerous *squadristi* groups across Italy. This occupation was illegal, but the Italian state and government prevaricated for months until D'Annunzio was finally kicked out of the city by the Italian army in late 1920.

When D'Annunzio heard that Misiano was coming to Fiume, he issued an order in the name of the (illegitimate) *Esercito Italiano in Fiume d'Italia* (the 'Italian Army in Italian Fiume'). Posters went up naming Misiano as a 'miserable deserter' who was to be 'hunted down', and sentencing him to death by 'cold iron'.[25] Yet, although Misiano did appear to be in the Fiume area for a time, it appears that he was on holiday, rather than intending to carry out political activity.

Nationalists found him on a beach, and he was forced to escape by jumping into the sea and then via, it seems, a train and a car. Misiano later remembered this escape as like something out of a film. He eventually made it to nearby Trieste, where he came down with severe pneumonia. Socialist guards protected him in hospital. He could not even trust the doctors and nurses. It was an anxious time: it appeared as if Misiano was going to die. There were bleak reports in the socialist and liberal press. Once he had recovered enough strength, Misiano left the hospital by a back door via the bathroom and was driven away from Trieste. Yet, when he arrived in Bologna he needed to be hospitalised again.

D'Annunzio was the first nationalist during this period to call openly for an elected deputy to be murdered. Fascists took this as a legitimate order. From that moment on, 'Misiano's life itself was in danger'.[26] It was a death sentence, pronounced by someone claiming to have government authority, but who was in reality in charge of an illegal militia. Fascists in general were open about their endgame. They wanted, in Mussolini's own words, which echoed those of D'Annunzio, 'the cancellation of those extremely sad elections which carried Misiano the traitor to parliament … we will do all we can in Italy to make sure the purge is total'.[27]

After Fiume in 1920, and Misiano's famous 'death sentence', he was never able to live a normal life again. One observer wrote that 'when he went out … nobody knew if he would return'.[28] Misiano was kidnapped on more than one occasion. In Rome he was seized and frog-marched through the city surrounded by dozens of armed blackshirts, soldiers and ordinary citizens; his hair was shaved off and he was forced to wear a sign around his neck saying: '*La patria va servita e io sono un disertore*' ('You must serve the fatherland and I am a deserter').[29] In the photos many of the kidnappers are smiling. There is a phrase in Italian which describes what happened to Misiano that day: he was being '*messo alla Berlina*' – publicly humiliated, derided, pilloried.[30] In all of the images from that day, Misiano appears dignified – and in one he is staring straight at the camera, in an apparent gesture of defiance. Misiano had become the lightning rod for the violence and humiliation directed at socialists and anti-war campaigners. But he was not alone, and it was not just revolutionaries who were targeted.

Dino Grandi, a fascist from Bologna who went on to become a key figure in the regime, later wrote up his version of the events in postwar Italy. His account was published posthumously. He claimed that the main target of fascist violence had been the revolutionary socialists, and that 'the old reformist and classical socialists were never harmed'.[31] He was either lying, or had a very poor memory. Moderates were often targeted, in the same way, and with even more violence, than those on the far left.

In July 1920 the bearded reformist socialist Giuseppe Emanuele Modigliani, who had campaigned against the war, was beaten up in Rome by fascists (he required four stitches in his head). His fellow socialist, Nullo Baldini, told parliament what he had witnessed: 'I saw a young man dressed in black move away from the group [of demonstrators] and with a stick he hit our comrade Modigliani in the face. I was 10 or 12 paces away, but I heard a clear cracking sound and it felt like the blow could have been fatal.'[32]

Political violence: the case of Francesco Misiano, July 1920[33]

For Mussolini and the fascists, the 'very sad' elections of 1919 had been 'anti-national'. *They*, the black-shirted *squadristi*, and not the electorate, had the right to decide who could serve, and who not. They cared nothing for the niceties of the liberal democracy or the rule of law. They would save Italy from the red menace and the 'traitors'. This analysis was soon extended to the many local and provincial councils elected with socialist majorities in October 1920. The fact that socialists were elected was not enough of an argument to allow them to take power – instead the fascists sought to expel them from office using violence. The first and most important testing ground for this *squadrista* strategy was the 'red' city of Bologna, where the revolutionaries were about to take office with a clear majority. The maximalists were in control and the first sitting of the new administration was scheduled for 21 November. In the run-up to that inauguration, the fascists attempted to impose their power on the streets. It would prove to be a central moment in the rise of fascism.

ERCOLE BUCCO'S LAST NIGHT IN POWER
BOLOGNA, NOVEMBER 1920

Ercole Bucco was one of a series of anti-war maximalist leaders who had risen quickly within the Socialist Party and union movement. In a short time he had been elected as a deputy, become secretary of the socialist parliamentary group, and taken control of the most powerful workers' organisation in Bologna – the Camera del Lavoro. He had been a key figure in the bitter and violent rural strikes which had swept across the Emilian countryside in 1920 – his ascent seemed unstoppable. Yet, his life changed forever on the night of 4 November 1920. It was the second anniversary of Italy's victory in the war, and local fascists had threatened to attack the building which housed the Camera del Lavoro – symbol of union authority. Armed 'red guards' had been brought in from a nearby town to protect the premises and Bucco was in charge. A first skirmish took place when the fascists attacked and were shot at from inside the building, injuring one blackshirt.

Bucco then appeared to lose his nerve. He disarmed his own 'red guards' and hid their weapons. It was then claimed that he called the police, who forced their way into the building, and seized numerous bombs, revolvers, ammunition and, they said, a machine gun. Ninety-six red guards were arrested, along with Bucco and another socialist deputy, Francesco Quarantini. The discovery of the cache of weapons was front-page news across Italy.[34] Later that night the fascists smashed up the Camera del Lavoro anyway, destroying property and stealing a banner.

Police statements made by Bucco were selectively released to the press. He refused to implicate the red guards, who were all released, but was accused of blaming his wife for some aspects of the fiasco. This double 'surrender' by Bucco (on the night, and in the police station) exposed him to ridicule and he was disowned by many of his comrades. His surname (it sounds a bit like the Italian word for 'hole') didn't help, and was used to insult him, calling into question his 'masculinity' as well as his loyalty. A song was sung about him:

Il fortunato è Bucco / Che mangia e non lavora
E quando è nei pasticci / Ci mette la signora.

(Bucco is lucky/ He eats and he doesn't work
And when he is in trouble/ He puts his wife in the middle of things.)[35]

Bucco's actions that night also seemed to confirm the overall historical judgement on maximalism. They talked the talk, but were incapable of organising a real revolution. Local fascists, on the other hand, were emboldened. It was their first major victory. For Bucco, it was not just a political defeat; it was seen as a personal humiliation. According to one historian: 'The entire city laughed behind Bucco's back.'[36] Bucco and Quarantini were released the next day and still had support in the city. A three-day strike followed in solidarity with those arrested, but petered out after the red guards were released without charge. Bucco's rise had been meteoric, and his fall was brutal. He resigned from the Camera del Lavoro on 9 November.

The Bucco fiasco laid bare the question of what was to be done in the face of fascist violence. Some socialists believed that it was now time to get organised, and to procure more arms and weapons. This armed organisation was largely seen in defensive terms. Five days before the inauguration of a new socialist local administration in November 1920, the Unione Socialista Bolognese (the city's socialist body) elected a new directorate – whose key figures included militants Vittorio Martelli, Armando Cocchi and Corrado Pini.[37] Remember these names – they would be in charge of organising the opening day of the new administration on 21 November – which was designed to be a day of triumph for Bolognese socialism and its maximalist wing.

ENNIO GNUDI, 'MAYOR FOR AN HOUR'
PALAZZO D'ACCURSIO, 21 NOVEMBER 1920

Palazzo d'Accursio has been the symbol of Bologna's municipal power since the mid-fourteenth century, and was also the site of papal power until Italian unification. It stands to one side of the huge Piazza Maggiore, right in the heart of the city. Inside, the beautiful, rectangular council chamber has a roof covered in baroque frescoes, and which, in 1920, was flanked by two sets of wooden chairs on either side, complete with desks. The main entrance leads to an internal courtyard. The layout of this building, with its various ceremonial rooms and access points, was at the centre of the events which shook Italy in November 1920.

On 21 November 1920 maximalist socialist Ennio Gnudi was appointed Mayor of Bologna. Forty-four out of fifty-seven councillors had backed him, thanks to his role and symbolic identity as a railway worker and trade unionist.[38] Gnudi himself later said that he had tried to turn down this appointment. A diminutive figure, he was sometimes referred to as 'the little maximalist Samson' and was admired in his local neighbourhood.[39]

After the vote, Gnudi stood up to make his first speech as mayor in the council chamber. He called the Socialist Party 'the sincere and genuine expression of the proletarian class ... [that] derives its power from trade union discipline. By electing as mayor a humble and simple worker the party has shown ... that the rights of the working class, the proletarian class, will be defended by the Council.'[40] No mention was made by Gnudi of the previous, reformist, moderate administration of the city, which had governed from 1914–20, or of Francesco Zanardi, its popular socialist mayor. Zanardi had not been reconfirmed as mayor, although he was elected as a councillor (he had first been elected to the council in 1895). The divisions between the two wings of the Socialist Party, which would soon split into two distinct parties, would also play a role in the events which followed.

In his speech, Gnudi also praised the Russian Revolution and asked those present to pay homage to an elected councillor – Erminio Zucchini who had died just weeks earlier – between the election and the inauguration, following a violent clash involving demonstrators and Royal Guards.[41] Gnudi's party had come to power with a manifesto which promised to 'take away weapons from the bourgeoisie and hasten the dissolution of its class power'.[42]

Turning to the councillors of the opposition, Gnudi made reference to the conflicts which had been seen in the city in recent weeks. 'If the opposition decides to use oppression against us,' he warned, 'we will defend ourselves, because we will fight for the interests of the workers.' Gnudi was confident that violence would not succeed against ideals which were to be found 'in millions of hearts, millions of minds across the world, and cannot be defeated with attacks and lies'.[43] These words were to take on new meaning in the light of what was just about to happen (and would also be used against Gnudi and the socialist movement). Within minutes, Gnudi would be proved completely wrong.

Following Gnudi's speech, the leader of the opposition, Giuseppe Albini, began to address councillors in the chamber inside. As Albini was speaking, Gnudi stepped out onto the balcony of the Red Room, above the majestic central square in Bologna. It was around 3 p.m. White doves with red ribbons tied to them were released into the sky.[44] A crowd of 2,000 or so socialist supporters cheered and clapped. 'Those doves were not carrying messages of peace,' the police claimed later, arguing that they had been a signal for violence.[45] A red flag had flown proudly from the nearby Torre degli Asinelli, but was removed almost immediately.[46]

Inside the chamber, Albini's speech was interrupted, mid-sentence, by 'noises from the piazza' (according to the minutes compiled much later). Albini continued speaking, but he managed just a few more sentences before 'outcry and violent explosions' from outside led to the 'chaotic exit from the council room of the president, many councillors and functionaries'.[47] The sitting was interrupted – but what was going on outside?

SHOOTINGS, MURDERS, BOMBS

While we will never know the precise details about the facts of that day,[48] quickly, very quickly, things started to go wrong with the socialist celebrations. As Gnudi stood on the balcony, a small number of fascist *squadristi* broke through the cordons set up by the authorities and joined some other fascists who were already in the square. Shots were fired, it seems, towards the palazzo. Further gunshots, it appears, came from within the palazzo itself. Gnudi later said that he saw 'a number of people fall to the ground' in the piazza. Inside the council chamber, there was panic. According to the investigating judges, one of the socialists looked out of the window and said: 'Our army has scarpered.' Genuzio Bentini remembered 'the speeches, the shots outside which pattered against the walls, like hail ... word spread that there were dozens of dead in the square ... I bent down amongst the shots, but I could not lie down as other people had already done so and there was no space.'[49] Ex-mayor Zanardi also took cover.[50]

So controversial was the initial reporting on what went on in Bologna's most important daily newspaper, *Il Resto del Carlino*, that the editor of that paper (the famous journalist Mario Missiroli) was eventually forced out of his job, and had to leave the city for a time. For many years a rumour took hold in the city that all the copies of that newspaper for 23 November – the first that reported on the events in Palazzo d'Accursio – had been completely destroyed. This rumour later turned out to be false.[51]

What is certain is that tensions in the city had been high all year, and the fascists were determined to disrupt the inauguration of a new, more radical socialist administration. Bologna's prefect, in charge of public order, was far from being an anti-fascist.[52] We know that the leader of the local fascist squads, Leandro Arpinati, had issued a stark warning via a poster which was seized by the authorities. The poster was a threat: it 'ordered' people to clear the streets and leave the 'final clash' to the socialists and the fascists. We also know that many people on all sides were carrying firearms and that there were some with other weapons, both in the square and within Palazzo D'Accursio, with its wide, elegant stairways and huge ceremonial rooms, and that there were hundreds of armed police, Royal Guards and *carabinieri* in the vicinity.

The Royal Guards and *carabinieri* themselves started firing at some point (they later said in response to shots from within the Palazzo). Some reports claimed that up to a thousand shots were fired. As well as the eleven people who died, sixty were injured including fifteen policemen or *carabinieri*. A leading fascist, Giorgio Pini (editor of the fascist newspaper *L'Assalto*) who was in the square that day, was later interviewed by the TV journalist Sergio Zavoli for a documentary about the rise of fascism. He remembered it thus: 'It seemed like it [the piazza] was covered in bodies which were lying everywhere... it

was absurd, hard to believe … apocalyptic ….'[53] Finally, the shooting
stopped: 'There were cries and shouts from all sides.'[54]

Victims and memory: the piazza and the council chamber

The names of ten of the victims of that day are almost unknown and
largely unremembered. For the record, they were: Antonio Amadesi,
a twenty-nine-year-old mattress worker; Attilio or Flavio Bonetti[ini],
who was twenty-eight years old; Gilberto Cantieri, a twenty-five-year-
old pasta maker (*pastaio*); Enrico Comastri, a pensioner and former
railway worker; Vittorio Fava, a sixty-year-old rural day-labourer; Libio
Fazzini, a twenty-eight-year-old carpenter; Marino Lenzi, a twenty-
four-year-old railway worker, who died in January 1921 in hospital;
Leonilda Orlandi, a thirty-six-year-old railway worker who also died
in hospital, the next day; and Carolina Zacchi, an eighteen-year-old
worker. Ettore Masetti, from Casalecchio del Reno, aged fifteen, was
shot in the stomach. He passed away three months later.[55]

For more than twenty years, under the fascist regime, these ten
dead were seen as 'second-class deaths', or simply ignored. Only
one death really counted, and received numerous public and private
commemorations and memorials – the eleventh victim, who did not
die outside in the square.[56]

The most important death of all – politically speaking, and because
of the way the tragedy occurred – took place *inside* the council chamber
itself that day. During the commotion caused by the uproar outside,
at some point a number of shots were fired towards the ranks of the
opposition councillors from within the palazzo. Witnesses saw a man
enter the chamber from outside and shoot in that direction. According
to one of the councillors, he was 'youngish … short, dressed in brown,
with a grey–green coat'.[57] But there were, at the time and since, a host
of different descriptions and versions of the event, including many who
claimed that there was more than one shooter. This individual shooter
(or shooters) was never identified, although there have been numerous
suggestions over the years. Two were injured by gunfire – one seriously –
and one was killed.

Councillor Giulio Giordani was struck by four or five bullets and
died on the way to hospital. He was a forty-two-year-old war hero and
a nationalist who worked as a lawyer. He was also a '*mutilato*', whose

leg had been amputated following a war injury. As a result he wore a prosthetic leg, which soon became a kind of 'relic'. Some compared Giordani to Jesus Christ himself.[58] His death was national news, and had a lasting impact. There were also stories of bravery among the opposition that day. In one version of events, another councillor, Aldo Oviglio, a lawyer and nationalist (who had once, like Mussolini, been opposed to the Libyan war), 'placed his gun on the table in front of him and pronounced these courageous words: "Kill me if you like, cowards, but I am not fighting a civil war." '[59]

Giordani's funeral on 23 November was a grand affair, organised and orchestrated by the city's fascists. Flowers were laid at the place where he was shot. On that day, the blackshirts, armed with batons and sticks, were in charge. Giordani had not been part of the nascent fascist movement, but his dramatic death made him into the first and in many ways most important 'fascist martyr' of all.[60] When fascism celebrated itself in grand style in 1932, Giordani was given his own sacred space in the prestigious 'Exhibition of the Fascist Revolution' in Rome – complete with his clothing, medals and the entire row of seats from the council chamber in Bologna in 1920.[61] For the socialist historian Angelo Tasca, 'the dead body of Giordani was exploited to the point of hysteria ... Nothing was remembered but the ex-soldier with a heroic war record, "killed in a trap" by the anti-nationalists.'[62] Leading fascist Emilio De Bono stated at the time that 'the death of Giordani ... was the spark which created the patriotic flame which led to the fascist revolution'.[63] Dino Grandi himself claimed that more than 900 people had joined the fascists in Bologna in the wake of Giordani's murder. He included himself in this number.[64]

A plaque to Giordani was later unveiled on his house, describing him as 'il martire' ('the martyr') who 'left here before his ultimate sacrifice'.[65] Giordani's death was a gift for fascist propagandists. They could claim that the 'Bolsheviks' had plotted to eliminate the democratic opposition by assassinating them, inside the council chamber, in cold blood. Giordani's widow and two young children were often utilised as part of the memory wars that erupted around this time.

By contrast, those involved that day on the fascist and nationalist side – both in the streets and inside the council chamber – found that it did their future career no harm at all. After local democracy was crushed by violence, Italy's cities were all run by unelected, centrally appointed officials known as *podestà*.[66] Leandro Arpinati (who led the fascist assault on the streets) became the *podestà* (unelected mayor) of Bologna from 1926 to 1929, and then a minister under Mussolini; Aldo Oviglio (a minority councillor) rose to become Justice Minister in Mussolini's first government; Angelo Manaresi (who was also among the minority councillors that day) was appointed *podestà* of Bologna in 1933–35; and Cesare Colliva, who was shot in the face, would also go on to be *podestà* from 1936–39. Effectively, the losers of the 1920 election ended up governing the city for the next twenty years.

Cancelling democracy: Who was in charge?

Ennio Gnudi's hopes of a day of triumph had ended in complete disaster.[67] He would never officially assume office. On 22 November Gnudi was back in the town hall, but it was the previous administration that met and discussed what steps to take next. It was as if the recent elections had never taken place. Officials in the council offices did not treat him as a mayor, and it seems that they wouldn't allow him to use the mayor's car.

Gnudi did not have his own executive (*giunta*), as it had not been officially appointed, thanks to the interrupted session on the 21st: he had no real power and had been abandoned by the reformist wing of his party, who were anxious to distance themselves from the events of that day. Many of his comrades were arrested. Some went on the run. It was an exceptional and strange situation. Such was the confusion among the socialists that despite the fact that ten of their supporters had been killed, no general strike was called in the aftermath of the events – something that would have been surprising in the context of Bologna, and Italy, at the time.

Acting as if he were mayor, Gnudi issued a conciliatory statement, calling on all citizens to help with a process of 'pacification'. He also expressed great sorrow for the violence inside the council chamber, and paid tribute to Giordani as 'a loyal adversary, who paid a heavy personal price for his faith in the war'.[68] But, confusingly, a statement was also put out by the previous administration, which claimed that 'a crazy person was responsible for [Giordani's] death'. Councillors from the reformist wing seemed to blame the maximalists, attacking those who 'desire liberty and deny it to others' and paid tribute to the values of Giordani.[69] 'In six long years,' they said, referring to the previous, reformist administration, 'we never preached violence.' Collapse was swift. By 3 December, five councillors had resigned, three had been arrested and one was on the run. The council majority was disintegrating without ever taking power.[70]

As the historian Luciano Casali has written: 'On 21 November [1920] onwards ... democratic life in Bologna came to an end.'[71] In February 1921 most of the rest of the socialist representatives from the new council – who had never taken up their seats – resigned, while Gnudi and a few of his comrades remained (theoretically) in post (but without the means to exercise any of their functions). In March all the opposition councillors stepped down and on 4 April 1921 the council was dissolved by central government.[72]

This was a catastrophe for the left, and a triumph for the *squadristi*. Fascism was able to present itself as a defender of democracy and free speech while, at precisely the same time, effectively abolishing both. Fascist tactics had worked perfectly. The disintegration of local democracy in Bologna would be a model which was exported across Italy from that moment on. Fascist violence had won the day and the playbook would be repeated in every corner of the country, until every single elected local council was disbanded.[73]

The events in Bologna in 1920 were to provide the fascist movement, and then the regime, with one of their most powerful propaganda weapons, the equivalent of Hitler's use of the Reichstag fire. Bologna, they could state, had been in the hands of murderous 'reds'. The trade unions and labour offices were, to quote the Bolognese fascist Dino Grandi (and Mussolini): 'a state within a state'. Bologna thus *justified* fascist violence (even though in many ways the events of that day would not have taken place *without* fascist violence). Democracy could not be entrusted to 'the reds' and Bologna became the blueprint not just for the destruction of local democracy, but for the overturning of democracy in general, and of the socialist and trade union movement.

PUBLIC ENEMIES

After 21 November 1920, Ennio Gnudi's life changed irrevocably, but not in the way he had hoped. He was now a marked man, blamed by many for the 'events of Palazzo d'Accursio' – a symbol, for some, of extremist, violent, municipal 'Bolshevism'.

Ercole Bucco was also a physical target from the end of 1920 onwards. Mussolini picked out Bucco by name, calling him 'human rubbish'.[74] Bucco was threatened continually by fascist squads and hassled by the authorities. When he returned to Bologna only a heavy police presence could save him from a beating. He could not even go to a bar for a coffee.[75] According to some accounts Bucco was kidnapped and beaten in Leandro Arpinati's cellar, which was said to be used for torturing political opponents, and forced to apologise for having called the police that fateful night in November 1920.[76] Strange and often untrue stories circulated about Bucco in the press, which he tried to counter with letters. It was said that his lover had killed herself, and that he had passed off another girlfriend as a Hungarian revolutionary.

Attacks on 'the deserter', Francesco Misiano, also intensified. In Bologna, in December 1920, he was besieged by fascists in a bar, and forced to flee. He accused the fascists of 'cowardice', saying that they had confronted him 'forty against just one'.[77] The passivity of the authorities in the face of these attacks emboldened the fascists to continue their violence. There was also open collusion between the army, the police, the state and *squadristi*. An anti-socialist alliance was taking shape.

Manhunt

On 18 December 1920, two socialist parliamentary deputies were attacked in the centre of Bologna, as they left the law courts (both were lawyers). Adelmo Nicolai was beaten by a group of fifty fascists and hospitalised with head injuries, and his father was also caught up in the violence. Nicolai was meant to have been Gnudi's deputy mayor. Soon afterward, Genuzio Bentini met the same fate, as his aggressors shouted 'Giordani! Giordani! Murderers! Murderers!' Bentini had been in the room when Giordani had been shot, acting as a scrutineer (he was also an elected councillor). 'A violent conflict' broke out in parliament when this news was brought into the chamber and the sitting was suspended.

Fascists also warned ex-mayor Francesco Zanardi – to his face – that they were no longer willing to 'tolerate' his 'presence in Bologna', and accused him of organising 'the murder of Giordani'.[78] On 21 December 1920, Zanardi was attacked and effectively kidnapped by fascists in

Bologna. He was forced to make 'patriotic statements' and ordered to leave town.[79] Zanardi refused to abandon the cooperative building where he was working, and which was part of an economic welfare system he had constructed during the war years when his administration was in charge, but he was eventually made to depart with a police guard in a lorry.

The dramatic events in Bologna in late 1920 heralded the rise of fascism across Italy. *Squadristi* membership rose precipitously. The scene was set for the 'black years' of violence and civil war.

1921

'For more than two years [he] had been unable to sleep at home for fear of endangering his family. Each evening the blackshirts had come to search for him. "For two years," he said, "I lived with my hand on my revolver. I can scarcely straighten my fingers now".'
Angelica Balabanoff, describing the fate of an unnamed Italian worker who had resisted fascism[1]

Personal attacks on socialists intensified in January and February 1921. Fascists demonstrated at the home of Francesco Zanardi, and he was again forced to leave the city in fear of his life. Money was thrown at him (to symbolise his supposed corruption) and he was subjected to constant insults. Dino Grandi, one of the other leading *squadristi* in Bologna, threatened and insulted Zanardi in the fascist press in March 1921, writing that 'Zanardi, in his cowardly hiding place, has a faint hope of returning ... but he can feel his bones fresh from a beating and he remembers nostalgically the stairs of Palazzo d'Accursio which he can no longer use.'[2]

Eventually Zanardi moved to Rome. But the violence continued. From the beginning, fascist violence made no distinction between revolutionaries and reformists (despite subsequent claims by leading fascists, including Grandi himself).[3] Zanardi was often dubbed the 'moral force' behind the murder of Giordani, despite his opposition to the maximalist wing of his party and his (historic and well-known) aversion to violence. Ennio Gnudi was similarly harassed. In May 1921 he was effectively kidnapped for a time by fascists, and he then decided to carry a gun. His house in the working-class Bolognina neighbourhood was the target of intimidatory tactics. Fascists stood outside at night, threatening and singing hostile songs.[4]

THE SPLIT
LIVORNO, JANUARY 1921

In January 1921, trade unionist Argentina Altobelli was given the almost impossible job of presiding over the Socialist Party congress in Livorno. It was a tumultuous meeting, with violent accusations, insults, and even weapons drawn. Outside, on the streets, the fascists were waiting to attack. Altobelli struggled to control the emotions and anger on all sides, which ended with one minority group walking out and forming an entirely separate party – the Italian Communist Party (PCI). The two wings of the party had been acting as different entities for some time – but now the split was official. At a time of mass fascist violence directed against socialists, the main political organisation on the left had divided into two, weakening any sense of opposition or even defence. It was a gift to Mussolini and his followers. Ercole Bucco joined the PCI in 1921, along with Ennio Gnudi and Francesco Misiano. Giuseppe Modigliani, Zanardi, Altobelli and Matteotti remained in the Socialist Party.[5] Gnudi stood as a communist candidate in the 1921 national elections and was later voted onto the central committee of the party.[6]

Divisions on Italy's left coincided with the run-up to the bitterly contested May 1921 elections, which were marked by a peak of fascist violence, across the country, from north to south. The *Corriere della Sera* estimated that between 1 March and 31 May 1921, 195 socialists and communists were killed and 774 injured; for the fascists the comparable figures were 64 and 226.

In March 1921, socialist deputy and anti-war campaigner Giacomo Matteotti, now thirty-six years old, stood up in the Italian parliament chamber to make a speech. He was described as 'thin' and 'agile' and was known as a commanding orator: sharp, fearless, clever and well prepared, and an expert in budgetary and economic matters. He dressed elegantly, often with a bow tie, and his pockets were usually stuffed with paper on which he took notes. On this occasion he was also very angry. Since the days when he was radically opposed to the war and his subsequent internal exile in Sicily, Matteotti's focus had become the fascist violence which had become widespread in his local area, the rural Polesine, in the north-east of Italy. He provided an almost literary description for his fellow parliamentarians:

> In the dead of night, while most gentlemen are in bed at home, the lorries of the fascists turn up in small villages, in the countryside, where not many people live. Naturally, they are accompanied by the leaders of the local landowners, guided by them, because otherwise it would be impossible to recognise, in the dark, in the middle of the countryside, the small house of the trade union leader, or the tiny local employment office. They gather in front of a small house and the order is given ... surround the building. They are twenty, and sometimes a hundred of them armed with rifles and revolvers ... they call the name of the union leader and ask him to come outside. If he doesn't respond, they say, we will burn your house, your wife, your children ... the union leader comes downstairs, he opens the door, they grab him, they tie him up, they put him on a lorry, they torture him in a horrible way and pretend to murder him, to drown him, then he is abandoned in the middle of the countryside, naked, tied to a tree! If the union leader is a brave man, and does not open the door, and uses weapons in his defence, then he is immediately killed in the dead of night. One hundred against one. This is the system in the Polesine.[7]

Like so many of his socialist colleagues at the time, Matteotti represented a rural constituency marked by poverty, exploitation and bitter class and political conflict. Matteotti had been described – disparagingly – by the moderate newspaper *Il Corriere della Sera* as '*Il Marat del Polesine*' ('The Marat of the Polesine') for what they saw as his revolutionary rhetoric among the peasants of his home area.[8] On 12 March 1921, two days after his intervention in parliament, Matteotti was due to give a speech in a little place called Casteluglielmo, near Rovigo, in the heart of that same zone. But he was kidnapped by local fascists, taken away on a lorry, and tortured. His own experience confirmed the truth of what he had described in the chamber. There were also rumours that he had been sexually assaulted, something which Matteotti denied, but which was used to humiliate him further in parliament and elsewhere. It was seen as a sign of his weakness – not an example of the brutality of his kidnappers. He was then dumped in open countryside. Yet, Matteotti's kidnap and his denunciation of fascist violence fell on deaf ears. There was no sign of a let-up in the fascist violence, which intensified in the run-up to new elections, which had been called for May 1921.

FRANCESCO MISIANO

NAPLES, MARCH 1921

Throughout 1921, fascists targeted individuals mercilessly across Italy. In March, Francesco Misiano's private home in Naples was singled out. According to the *Corriere della Sera*, the fascists used a person disguised as a tramp to spy on Misiano. Around 150 Neapolitan fascists besieged his house and refused to let him leave. The plan that day, they said, was to capture Misiano, put him in a sack full of 'shit and rubbish', and dump him in the central Piazza del Plebiscito. Misiano, according to the article, managed to hide in another house, where he was protected by 'a hundred' Royal Guards. 'The fascists [then] tried to reach his house across the roof.'

In the end, Misiano was able to slip away dressed 'with a cloak of the Royal Guards and a beret from the same troops', a detail almost certainly invented. The whole tone of this article, and its headline, seemed to suggest that Misiano was by now fair game, even for liberal opinion. The *Corriere della Sera* treated attacks on him as 'humorous', and the whole story was told in a light vein, as if it was a comedy, or a farce. In reality, Misiano had been subjected to another life-threatening and terrifying experience. His home had been targeted, and he had only avoided a beating, or perhaps worse, by fleeing.[9]

MASSACRE: EMPOLI, MARCH 1921

Violence was escalating on the streets. In and around Florence during February 1921 there were unprecedented clashes between workers, fascists and police, with uprisings and barricades. On the 27th, in the city's Via Taddea, Spartaco Lavagnini, a local communist leader, was murdered in cold blood by blackshirts as he sat at his desk writing an article. On the left, there was an atmosphere of fear and terror, as well as calls for resistance. In March 1921, Empoli, a small town just twenty-five kilometres from Florence, prepared for the *squadristi*.[10] While there were no fascist organisations to speak of in the town at the time, rumours began to spread that *squadristi* were coming. As news filtered through of killings and clashes in other parts of Tuscany, a general strike was called.

On 1 March 1921 suspicious-looking vehicles were spotted on the outskirts of Empoli. Abdon Maltagliati, president of the glassworkers' union and secretary of the town's Camera del Lavoro, had been travelling back on his motorbike from the dramatic Socialist Party congress in Livorno, when he came across two Fiat 18BL trucks parked by the side of the road. One of the vehicles had broken down. Maltagliati later said that it was thought the lorries were carrying *squadristi* on their way to Empoli. Fiat 18BL trucks were used by the Italian army and favoured by the blackshirts. They could carry a number of personnel, sitting along both sides in the back, and had roll-down canvas roofs. The fascists would often scrawl slogans on the side of their trucks and travel in them open-topped, singing songs as they went.

But these vehicles were not carrying fascists at all. On board were young sailors, sent to support strike-breaking efforts in Florence. They had left the port town of La Spezia for Livorno before moving on to Empoli.[11] Most of the sailors were conscripts from the south. From the photos that survive, they all appear extremely young; they are not in uniform, and are accompanied by a number of *carabinieri*.

Maltagliati sent word ahead to Empoli that the '*squadristi*' lorries were on their way. As the vehicles entered Empoli, they came under fire. According to historian Paolo Pezzino: 'Suddenly an empty tin container was thrown in front of the first lorry, and two revolver shots were fired at it.'[12] The attack on the sailors arose from a combination of genuine fear and also anger, and a sense of revenge. It was a 'them or us' moment. There was also an uncontrolled, almost mob aspect, to the violence.[13] The young men were shot at, pulled from trucks, and some were beaten to death. Various items were hurled at the lorries, from plates to boiling water. For Pezzino it was, 'a real battle', although no locals were killed or, it seems, even injured.[14] Socialist and historian of fascism Angelo Tasca put the Empoli killings into the context of a mix of terror, fury and paranoia. In some places, he wrote, the workers 'developed a persecution complex which ... drove them like hunted beasts into acts of unprecedented violence'. In Empoli, 'the whole neighbourhood rose in arms'.[15]

Three *carabinieri* and six sailors were killed that day, and another ten men injured. Some of the sailors who escaped the first assault were later attacked again. One drowned in the Arno as he fled. Of the dead, one was from Venice, one from Palermo, one from Avellino, two from Sassari (both were *carabinieri*), one from Cagliari (the other carabiniere), one from Naples, one from Olevano Romano near Rome and one from Trapani. Many were very young (Alberto Tulli was twenty-one, Enrico Rottin twenty-two). One corpse, that of Vincenzo Incarbone, was found with part of his right ear missing.[16]

At the subsequent trial it was claimed that Maltagliati and other socialist and union leaders had known full well that the men in the lorries were not fascists, but had still organised a violent response due to a kind of widespread 'hatred' of soldiers in general. But the evidence here is thin. Everything points to a case of collective rage and mistaken identity.

'Empoli's massacre', as it was dubbed, made front-page news. It was the greatest loss of life in an 'anti-fascist' attack (although the victims were not fascists) from the postwar period.[17] In parliament the right-wing deputy Dino Philipson was incandescent: 'Florence, with its centuries-old traditions of kindness and civility, has been disturbed for days by barbaric and vulgar violence,' he railed. 'The revolutionary aggressors of ... Empoli are the same people who deserted from the army, who fled in the face of the enemy. Now they hide behind barricades, because they are filled with hatred for the fatherland, which is greater than their hatred against the enemies of the fatherland.'[18]

The attackers were described in the press as being both 'beasts' and cowardly. It had been an 'ambush', by those who had been 'hiding' (a reference to those who had avoided military service during the war). In particular, there was a focus on the role of a small number of supposedly 'ferocious women'.[19] One story that did the rounds, and became the detail everyone remembered from Empoli, was that it was a woman who had not only bitten (or cut off, or ordered someone else to cut off) Vincenzo Incarbone's ear, but had also cooked and eaten it (or served it to their daughter for dinner, with eggs).[20] Another was that some women made soup from the bodies of *carabinieri* – '*carabinieri* soup'.[21] A further oft-repeated story was of local man, Lindoro Cantini, who had allegedly used his crutch to beat and finish off a dying sailor. This story worked well in contrast with that of Italian war hero Enrico Toti, who had supposedly – but almost certainly didn't – thrown his crutch at the Austrian enemy as he died during the First World War in 1916 and had become a major national and fascist war hero and martyr.[22]

Tales from Empoli portrayed 'anti-fascists' as animals, 'cannibals' even, who were less than human and consumed by a wild hatred. 'Fascist' violence, on the other hand, was depicted as patriotic, brave, honourable; it was *clean*, rational, surgical. Socialists were non-Italian – the enemy within. The form of violence (supposedly) used was connected to their exclusion from the body politic of the nation state.

Ten thousand people, it was reported, turned out for the funerals of eight of the victims (one had not yet been recovered, the man who drowned in the Arno river) on 5 March. One of the orators spoke of a crime committed by '100 human beasts' which had 'brought great shame to Empoli'.[23] Citing Dante, he said that not even seven generations would be enough to cancel the shame of these events.[24]

Once the barricades had been cleared, the fascists really did turn up, and in numbers – burning, looting and beating, as they rampaged through Empoli, undisturbed by police or *carabinieri*. Revenge was brutal. The city was 'crushed, ransacked, burnt'.[25] As police and *carabinieri* descended on the town, people were arrested en masse. The entire local council was picked up, apart from the mayor who went on the run.[26] An incredible estimated 500 people were eventually taken into custody, including all the leaders of trade union organisations and socialist bodies who could be found. One account even claims that five thousand people were arrested, though this seems unlikely. Those in prison were routinely tortured – with reports of the extraction of nails and the burning of skin with cigarettes. Empoli's left was decapitated at a stroke – most of its most influential figures were put behind bars, or went into hiding, from where they could no longer take part in active political agitation (this had also happened in Bologna after Palazzo d'Accursio). Some were picked up years later. A number escaped to San Marino from where they were either extradited or tried *in loco*. One absconded and spent some time on the run, before being seized. Five men evaded capture altogether.

Empoli's nine victims, like Giulio Giordani in Bologna, were quickly appropriated as 'fascist martyrs' (although none were fascists). In fact, the events in Empoli were a particularly powerful propaganda tool because the sailors were not *squadristi*, or politicians, but politically innocent, just following orders and driving to a town. They had played no role in the fascist violence which had created the context for their deaths. But fascist disinformation cleverly utilised them in both ways – as honorary 'fascists' *and* as young, patriotic, non-fascists – simple boys in uniform – national heroes. Thus the circle was complete: fascists were the saviours, *and* the martyrs. Empoli was a powerful moment. It was easy, after that event, to depict the socialists as out of control and fascism as the protector of the nation and the army, and even of democracy.

PROPAGANDA OF THE DEED: ANARCHISTS, REVOLUTIONARIES AND BOMBS

'A meeting place for the opulent bourgeoisie.'
                Description of the Cova 1817 bar, Milan, 1920[27]

In the heady atmosphere of postwar Italy, some were attracted to what was known as the 'propaganda of the deed'.[28] Small groups and individuals saw assassinations and violent attacks as having the potential to spark revolt, or revolution. Many of these proto-terrorists were anarchists, and the circumstances of the time made it relatively easy for them to carry out their actions. Bombs and weapons were plentiful and easy to come by. There was a long tradition of political assassination in Italy – including the murder of the king himself, Umberto I, in Monza, by an anarchist, Gaetano Bresci, in 1900.[29] The victims were often symbolic, but also included specific targets – police chiefs, industrialists, so-called 'war-mongers', *carabinieri* or simply members of the 'bourgeoisie'.

In the centre of Milan, close to the city's imposing gothic cathedral, stands the entrance to the Galleria Vittorio Emanuele. Opened in 1817, elegant shops and restaurants have always lined the side of this magnificent glass-topped arcade. It was (and is) a place to walk, and talk, and be seen. At one end of its cross-shaped structure, with its huge glass dome and mosaic-lined walls, is La Scala, the greatest opera house in the world. And on the corner of Via Manzoni, metres from La Scala, was one of the city's most renowned restaurants, cake shops and cafes: Cova 1817. Stendhal, Giuseppe Verdi, Giuseppe Mazzini and Ernest Hemingway had been among the clientele over the years. With its famous garden this cafe was a visible and central meeting place for

Milan's bourgeois intellectuals, journalists, artists and high society, and also during the nineteenth century for leading figures from Italy's nationalist movement. Inside, there were imposing pillars and tables with white tablecloths, mirrors and chandeliers. It was the epitome of belle époque elegance. In 1920, the anarchist daily *Umanità Nova* called it a 'a place where the opulent bourgeoise hang out, cocky and fat on their millions … parasitic and spoilt … profiteers … lazy thieves'.[30]

During the turbulent postwar period, the Cova was often targeted and its windows were smashed by demonstrators. In the summer of 1920 two bomb attacks had been directed at the restaurant. On 25 June a device thrown from a taxi killed a passer-by – army captain Federico Sacchi – and damaged the building.[31] Weeks later, on 7 August 1920, another bomb was hurled at the Cova, causing part of the ceiling to fall down and leaving shattered glass everywhere. The cafe was virtually empty at the time (just three Swiss guests were inside, who were then promptly arrested as suspects). Eyewitnesses reported seeing two young men running away from the scene.

Umanità Nova complained about outrage in the 'bourgeois press' concerning damage to 'the chalices which fizz with champagne'.[32] A number of anarchists were arrested in connection with the bombings. But the actual culprits were not picked up – two young anarchist men who had been radicalised during the war: Giuseppe Mariani, twenty-two at the time of the second bomb attack on the Cova restaurant, and Ettore Aguggini, who was just eighteen. Mariani had been accused of desertion in 1917, and, it is said, had serious mental health problems, and spent time in an asylum.

Malatesta in prison

In October 1920, after the occupation of the factories, the veteran anarchist Errico Malatesta was arrested in Milan.[33] He was held in the model star-shaped panopticon prison of San Vittore in the heart of the city, where he joined fellow anarchists Armando Borghi and Corrado Quaglino. Serious charges were levelled at these men, including 'conspiracy against the state' and 'criminal association'.

There Malatesta and the others languished, awaiting trial, for months. Again and again they demanded to be tried, or released, but to no avail. Finally, on 18 March 1921, the three decided to go on hunger strike.

A campaign for Malatesta's trial date to be set intensified. Mussolini also called for Malatesta's liberation. 'If Malatesta is innocent, release him; if he is guilty, after five months there is a moral and juridical obligation to put him on trial.'[34] There were real fears that he would die in prison. On 23 March 1923, *Umanità Nova* carried an appeal which claimed that he was indeed 'dying' (*'Compagni! Malatesta muore!'*).[35]

Workers came out on strike in his support, and not just in Milan, and many socialists called for action. Anarchists were convinced that the intention was to kill Malatesta, or let him die.[36] It was in this context that a small group of young anarchists decided to carry out a series of coordinated bomb attacks to protest at the continued imprisonment of Malatesta. Their main and most prestigious target was the police chief of Milan, Giovanni Gasti, whom they blamed for the veteran anarchist's detention. Malatesta himself had never supported the idea of 'propaganda of the deed' or bomb attacks. He had, instead, always preached social revolution.

The Diana massacre: March 1921

'What happened on 23 March 1921 at the Diana Theatre represents a watershed in Italian history.'

Fausto Butta[37]

A makeshift group of anarchists had been carrying out bombings for some time in and around Milan. In September 1919 a young man called Bruno Filippi had blown himself to pieces in a botched attempt, close to the exclusive Milanese city centre restaurant, Biffi;[38] and the following year saw the double strikes on Cova 1817.

Now, the anarchists decided on a major attack. On 23 March 1921, a group including Cova 1817 attackers Mariani and Aguggini, gathered explosives in Milan and packed between 160 and 200 cartridges of gelignite into a suitcase. After taking a horse-drawn taxi to their target, Aguggini placed this powerful bomb on the pavement, outside the prestigious Diana Theatre, and Mariani lit the fuse with his cigar. The two had pretended to ring the doorbell after paying for the taxi. It is likely that a third man, Giuseppe Boldrini, was also present.

Mariani later said that he had wanted to bomb the police station itself (in what would effectively have been a suicide attack) in a different part of town, but had been outvoted in the meeting of the group. Many versions emerged about the intended target over the years, and the men changed their story on a number of occasions. At the trial both Mariani and Aguggini claimed that the Diana Theatre was a generic objective; they did not mention their supposedly intended target of the police chief Gasti in their testimonies. Mariani said: 'We chose the Diana Theatre because our other plan was too difficult and because we knew that the theatre was frequented by functionaries and the bourgeoisie: we did not know that workers were also there.'[39]

Inside the theatre that night a packed house was watching *The Blue Waltz*, an opera by Franz Lehar, which had started at 8.30 p.m. Due to discussions between the chorus and the director of the orchestra (a union dispute was ongoing, typical in those times of strikes and militancy) the third act started late. Between 10.45 and 11.15 p.m. (there is some dispute over the actual time the bomb went off) a huge explosion ripped through the walls and a shop front. Tiny pieces of glass shrapnel penetrated the bodies of members of the audience above the orchestra pit, the orchestra itself and those in the front four rows. Journalists who reached the incident a few minutes after the explosion reported screaming and horrific scenes, with body parts, gloves and fragments of clothing lying on the floor.[40]

Twenty-one people were killed; 172 people were injured, many of whom suffered horrendous injuries. Two sisters in their early twenties, Lina and Ida Crippa, were caught up in the blast. Both the men who had accompanied them to the show were killed. Lina, a seamstress, lost both her legs and Ida also suffered lower limb damage. The Crippa sisters became potent symbols of the bombing, along with a little girl, the daughter of a shopkeeper, Leontina Rossi, who was killed outright. Later, the two Crippa sisters were visited in hospital by Mussolini and invited to official commemorations. They referred to the fascists as: 'True pioneers of the civilisation of today.'[41]

Individual stories from the massacre were heartbreaking. A man who had gone out to smoke in the interval lost his wife in the explosion. The victims were generally not from the 'bourgeoisie'. One was a butcher, many were musicians, and one female victim was a violin teacher. Politically, the Diana massacre transformed Mussolini's public view on the anarchists. He saw a political opportunity and took it, giving the *squadristi* full liberty in their actions in Milan and elsewhere and calling publicly for payback. Another bomb that same evening exploded at an electricity power station, causing damage but no injuries. A further assault was planned against the socialist newspaper *Avanti!*, but was never carried out.

In the wake of the bombing, the fascists took their revenge. That same day they attacked the newspaper offices of *Umanità Nova*, dumping books and furniture into a fire outside, and the new *Avanti!* offices in Via Settala in Milan, which were not yet ready for opening (after the infamous *squadrista* attack on the previous offices and printers in April 1919). Fascists turned up in Via Settala at two in the morning and threw bombs at the palazzo. A blaze spread along some wooden scaffolding and the fascists shot at the firefighters when they tried to put it out. *Avanti!* accused the police not only of failing to stop the fire and the attack, but also alleged that they had provided the fascists with bullets.

When news came through to their prison cells about the Diana bomb massacre, the anarchists were shocked. Borghi later recounted what happened next. 'Errico [Malatesta] told us that in the face of such an event and that massacre, our cause was reduced to nothing … we had to call off the hunger strike.'[42] The other two agreed, and the hunger strike was immediately abandoned. *Il Popolo d'Italia*, Mussolini's daily paper, used this decision to indulge in black humour: 'Those who were on a diet now have their bellies full … 17 dead and 100 injured: this is an unusual *aperitivo*, which the anarchist leaders can stuff themselves with in the canteen.'[43]

The liberal press blamed Malatesta for the Diana Theatre attack and an immediate connection was made between the veteran anarchist and the bombing. He was accused of having deliberately raised tensions, of violent language and of inciting social hatred. In an editorial, the *Corriere della Sera* wrote: 'Those sinister priests have offered up a horrible human sacrifice to their god Malatesta, who was refusing to eat in prison …' But, the paper continued, should we blame 'only the murderers? Why not the teachers, the poisoners? Their words have killed people, more than the shrapnel from the bomb. Their rhetoric acted in that dark alley, close to the unguarded door, sniffing out that imminent massacre.'[44]

Funerals and aftermath

> 'Milanesi! It is useless to shed tears and commemorate. It is above
> all pointless to make distinctions. There are not only criminals,
> there are also those who are responsible. Too much hatred has
> been sown – from the Socialist and Communist Parties to the
> Anarchists … to allow us to place the terrible burden of blame on
> the shoulders of the humble foot soldiers. We must take revenge
> … we will have our revenge!'
>
> Fascist poster, 1921[45]

After the attack, open coffins were laid out in Milan's magnificent
Monumental Cemetery. Journalists reported (or invented) a macabre
set of details: 'a foot blown off with a shoe on has ended up at the
feet of another body … close to the body of the lady there is a third
hand … nobody knows who it belongs to … the face of a man cut off
as if it was a mask'.[46]

Then, on 28 March 1921, Mussolini and the fascists transformed
the funerals into an exhibition of fascist power. Fascists travelled from
across Italy to be at the ceremony. Tellingly, no general strike had been
called by the unions in the wake of the bombing. Despite being a target
of one of the anarchist bombs that night, the Socialist Party itself was
presented in the press and by the fascists as creating the climate for
the Diana massacre to take place. Fascist representatives were allowed
to negotiate with state authorities on a par with the elected mayor of
the city, and were referred to as a 'patriotic association'. The fascists
demanded that the council – at that time led by the socialists – be
excluded from the funeral procession and ceremony. Their wish was
granted: Milan's legitimate elected authority was sidelined.

After tense discussions with all kinds of groups, an agreement was
reached. The state, not the council, paid for and sponsored the whole
ceremony. Angelo Filippetti, the socialist mayor, was only allowed to
appear alongside the bodies at the cemetery. There was to be no Milan
city flag, no socialist or union symbols, and no speeches. Some confusion
followed over the presence of *all* flags, but the prefect confirmed that
the national flag would indeed lead the ceremony. The threat of further
violence was always in the air, and a repeat of another Palazzo d'Accursio
massacre was feared. All this was a clear sign of how rapidly power was

ebbing away from legal local institutions and towards the *squadristi* and Mussolini.[47]

On the day of the funerals shops were closed and much of the city was draped in black. Bosses allowed their workers to take time off work to go to the funerals; factories ground to a halt. Around 150 orchestra directors attended as part of a delegation. A message of condolence came from the king, who was represented by the Count of Turin. The procession was elaborate, comprising *carabinieri* on horseback; soldiers; Royal Guard; a national flag with a guard of honour; groups of injured war veterans; twenty-two vehicles with wreaths; other soldiers and *carabinieri* on foot; and the clergy (in that order). Then came the carriages with seventeen coffins followed by relatives.

Mussolini was there, and an estimated two thousand 'crack troops, nationalists and fascists', who arrived at around 10 a.m., marching in formation.[48] They came from ten different cities as well as Milan, and all had their own regional banners. Flowers were thrown from windows throughout the procession, which lasted three hours, as crowds thronged the route. People climbed up into trees for a better view. A plane flew low and dropped flowers. At one point there was panic after what sounded like a gunshot led to a crush and a man broke his leg.[49] In the days that followed the funerals, other victims of the bombing died, leading to further funerals and mourning.

A pattern was taking shape. Violence was blamed on the left as a whole. Martyrs and victims were appropriated by the fascists. The state stood by and watched, or actively enabled fascist attacks and reprisals. In the wake of Palazzo d'Accursio, Empoli and Diana, *squadristi* were able to create an image of themselves as the saviours of Italy, the defenders of the soldiers who had fought in the Great War, and the only force that could prevent the Bolsheviks taking control. Middle-class and moderate public opinion started to move towards fascism. Meanwhile, the socialists and the unions were in retreat and disarray. Divided, scared and torn between a desire to fight back and calls to respond with non-violence, their tactics were unclear and often counterproductive. When they did respond with their own violence, as in Empoli, the outcomes were disastrous: fascist revenge, mass arrests and repression, and collapse of the institutions controlled by the left. The rise of the blackshirts appeared to be unstoppable. Further violence in the run-up to the 1921 general election reinforced the increasing power of the *squadristi.*

RENZINO, TUSCANY, APRIL 1921

'While the fascists fight openly, the communists use the cowardly tactic of the ambush.'

Benito Mussolini, 1921[50]

'That which took place on 17 April [1921] was not, and could not have been, the work of human beings who had, or have had, a mother, but of animals.'

La Nazione[51]

Across Italy, in the run-up to new general election in May 1921, *squadristi* 'punishment raids' became commonplace. There were even special sections of newspapers to report on them. With general elections imminent, fascist activity was frenetic and the target for the blackshirts this time was Foiano – a small agricultural 'red town', and a key fascist objective – to the south of Arezzo in Tuscany. The first attack was planned, somewhat unusually for the fascist playbook, for a Tuesday: *spedizioni* – raids – were usually held at weekends, when their activities were more visible and their targets were more likely to be at home.[52] All over Italy, 'every Sunday [brought] gloom, a death rattle, tears, and, at the same time, hatred and damnation'.[53]

As usual, the fascists announced their intentions publicly. This was not hidden violence; it was played out in the open, accompanied by intimidation: elected officials would be kicked out if they were socialists; intimidatory letters were sent in advance promising violence to city mayors, giving them the chance to resign or face the consequences. Any 'insults' against fascists, they warned, would be met with further, rapid counter-violence. These pledges were usually kept. They were not empty threats.

A first 'expedition' to Foiano on 12 April was relatively mild, with beatings of socialists and a show of force. This time, said the blackshirts, the socialists had got away lightly, but they would, they promised, be back soon. If the officials insisted on staying in power, they would be removed by force. Socialists and other anti-fascists were faced with a stark choice. They could give in and resign from their democratically elected positions (as many did, across Italy) or they could fight back. Any appeal to the police usually fell on deaf ears.

As promised, a second *spedizione* took place on Sunday morning: 17 April 1921. Twenty-two fascists left Arezzo at dawn on trucks heading for Foiano. They were armed with weapons taken from a local barracks, and led by a serving army officer. Some were in official uniforms. The line between the state and the fascists had become blurred. One participant had been in Fiume with Gabriele D'Annunzio. Violence and death threats followed in the town – as in the classic script for a 'punitive expedition'. The work of the group seemed to be done – and needed to be as one of their members was due to play in a football match later that afternoon. Lunch was the next item on the agenda as this was also a day out. While the fascists ate and drank, happy with their morning of beatings and intimidation, local leftists were preparing a surprise for them, just outside town, on the way back to Arezzo, in a small hamlet called Renzino. A number of men and women hid themselves in the bushes and trees on the side of the road. Phone lines had been cut, and a roadblock set up.

At 3.30 that afternoon, one of the *squadristi* lorries began to head back to Arezzo, when it was hit by the ambush. The vehicle was overturned. One fascist was shot dead, and two others killed by a combination of the lorry crash, gunfire, 'an axe' and a pitchfork. Another lost two fingers and there were other injuries. The rest escaped.[54] For the fascists the event became known as 'the massacre of Renzino'. The attackers were vilified, and fascist revenge was swift and brutal. Squads soon returned to Foiano, this time from all over Tuscany, and then as far afield as Rome, burning down buildings and murdering as they went. The killings were indiscriminate. One worker in Foiano was tortured and then executed. No fascist was arrested in the aftermath; but 107 non- or anti-fascists were taken into custody.

Fires were started in a farm close to where the ambush had taken place and in the town itself. The fascist violence continued unabated. *La Stampa* reported on one such example: 'The fascists moved the residents away and set fire to the house. The flames raged furiously for about an hour.' By morning, 'the smoke was still rising from what was left of the buildings, and all around fire was rising from the sheds and haystacks which had been set alight during the night'.[55]

Meanwhile, a propaganda operation was in full swing. The victims of the fascist attacks were largely forgotten: they disappeared from history, as in the aftermath of Palazzo d'Accursio. Some victims were more important than others. Three fascists had died and around eight or ten non-fascists, (the real figure for the latter group was probably greater than this).[56] Some victims of the fascists were taken to Arezzo before being killed. One was shot twenty-seven times. Revenge also hit socialists in Arezzo itself, where some were kidnapped, including the director of the city's psychiatric hospital. The whole sequence of events would soon become known as 'Bloody Sunday'.[57]

Many newspapers led the next day with the events of Foiano. *La Stampa's* headline was 'Ambush by communists against fascists'.[58] For Mussolini's *Il Popolo d'Italia* it was a 'ferocious ambush' and the attackers were 'cowards'.[59] The use of the word *imboscata* ('ambush') carried two meanings. On the one hand it attempted to show that the socialists and the left were spineless and unable to face the fascists in an open, face-to-face 'fight'. But it also carried another meaning: *imboscati* was a collective name applied to those who had supposedly 'avoided' the war – deserters, pacifists and also workers who had not been called up because of the industrial requirements of the conflict. Thus, *imboscati* were not just those who hid behind bushes (literally meaning those who *hide in the woods*) and shot at fascists; they were also people who had not participated in the conflict, or had actively worked against the army (and thus the nation) during the war – in the minds of the fascists and others. The contradictory depiction of socialist violence – as cowardly *and* brutal – was always placed in contrast to the fascists who claimed they always fought their battles 'in the open'.

La Nazione, a Tuscan daily, sent a journalist called Bruno Bacci to report on Renzino. His articles set the tone, and laid down the fascist version of the events of that day. By 1921 middle-of-the-road newspapers were all beginning to fall into line.[60] Bacci wrote, in reference only to the ambush, of an 'explosion of the most brutal form of hatred'. *La Stampa* claimed that: 'Everyone participated in a sort of competition to see who could act in the cruellest way … it was frightening … with axes raised, the peasants hit out in a crazy way.'[61]

VOTES AND BLOOD: MAY 1921

In Cerignola, the town in Apulia in the south of Italy which had seen constant clashes between the *ras* Giuseppe Caradonna and trade unionist Giuseppe Di Vittorio and their followers, the 1921 election took place in a climate of extreme violence. Di Vittorio – the most charismatic of the local left-wing leaders – was in prison. Murderous conflict marked the run-up to the election. For three days Cerignola was in the midst of an armed struggle, with barricades, shootings and chaos. Both sides used guns, but the *carabinieri* appeared to arrest only socialists and trade unionists.

Election day saw 'a pitched battle'.[62] Potential voters were beaten – or simply shot dead – on their way to the polls. While socialists fired at fascists and landowners, fascists forced people back into their homes and shot at their doors to make sure they did not go out. A family of four were fired on by fascists – and a mother and one of her sons were killed, while another son was injured. At the subsequent trial these deaths were blamed on the victims themselves.

Nine people were killed in Cerignola on the day of the ballot, all of them from 'proletarian organisations'.[63] Out of 10,119 people who had a right to cast their vote, only 3,309 actually voted (and a mere 133 of these opted for the Socialist Party). Many of the leaders of the union and cooperative movement had already been forced out of town, along with elected officials.

In the agro-town of Minervino Murge, thirty kilometres or so from Cerignola, similar tactics were utilised in the run-up to the election and on the day of the ballot. Individuals were targeted. Meetings were effectively banned for the socialists. Posters were torn down. *Elettori dubbi* – 'doubtful electors' – were searched by fascists close to the polling booths and 'socialist electors' were 'beaten and forced out'.[64] Socialist deputy Arturo Vella was 'brutally attacked and beaten' in the town of Barletta. Caradonna visited him while he was recovering in a hotel, informed him he would have preferred that he had been shot dead, and ordered him out of town immediately.[65] Through violence, the fascists systematically removed all vestiges of elected local government from the entire region – town by town, city by city, town hall by town hall. As historian Simona Colarizi once wrote, Caradonna's fascism was 'a real terrorist dictatorship'.[66]

*

Attacks on socialists intensified in the run-up to the election. Giuseppe Emanuele Modigliani was targeted again in May 1921.[67] A young fascist had been shot dead after a train was fired on from a field in Tuscany. The fascists then discovered, by chance, that Modigliani (who had no connection to the shooting) was travelling on a different train between Pisa and Viareggio. He was struck with clubs and fists, and spat on: he fainted. According to his biographer Aldo Santini, 'he suffered a knee injury and lost some hair [in the attack] … the train was stopped for a long time … the fascists said that they would only allow it to leave if the deputy shouted out "Long live Italy" from a window. Functionaries and the police tried to persuade him to do so, but he refused. Calmly, he replied that "I would not even shout out 'Long live Socialism' if I was threatened." '[68]

Molinella, the small town in Emilia dominated by the unions and the socialists, would be the final 'red' area in that region to fall to the *squadristi*. After the red unions had been crushed, the fascists attempted to force locals to join fascist unions. Fascists tried to force their flag to be flown at the town hall and the socialist vice-mayor Giuseppe Bentivogli was 'tied to a seat, beaten, insulted, but would not give way'.[69] He would suffer numerous attacks in both Molinella and Bologna in the 1920s. Massarenti was chased out of town with the arrival of a thousand *squadristi* – including Italo Balbo – in June 1921, just after the national elections. He later wrote: 'We were beaten, starved, banned, massacred.'[70] Some estimated there were over seventy episodes of violence in the town of Molinella in this period. Many resisted, despite the unemployment and poverty which resulted. 'If we can't kill them, at least we will make them starve to death,' wrote the local police commissioner. Massarenti preached non-violent resistance, but this strategy had no success against the fascist attacks.

The May 1921 Elections

Despite the violence, intimidation, threats, and the split in the Socialist Party, the left vote held up relatively well in the May 1921 election. One hundred and twenty-three socialist deputies were elected, and fifteen communists. The Catholic vote increased slightly, and the Catholic Popular Party sent 108 deputies to Rome. But the key political fact from that election was the entry of thirty-five fascist deputies to parliament, including many of the *squadristi ras* – such as Leandro Arpinati, who had orchestrated the events in Bologna in November 1920; Giuseppe Caradonna, whose activities had led to voter suppression in Cerignola and elsewhere in Apulia; and the violent *squadrista* leader from Cremona in the north of Italy, Roberto Farinacci. Mussolini himself finally made it to parliament, with 172,491 votes in the Ravenna constituency. The fascists were elected as part of national 'bloc' lists, which also included numerous liberals. The socialists were still the biggest party. The elections of 1921 were by no means free, nor fair, yet in comparison with what was to come they were relatively democratic.

THE EXPULSION FROM PARLIAMENT
13 JUNE 1921

'It is interesting to look at the way that the "deserter" Misiano was attacked by the fascists, and the inertia with which so many people, including the socialists, did not understand that in attacking Misiano, his persecutors aimed to target "all the adversaries of fascism". This is a lesson whose relevance has not been appreciated enough.'

Enzo Collotti[71]

In 1921, Italy's first fascist deputies brought *squadristi* violence into the parliamentary chamber itself in Rome. Tactics seen on the streets and in the countryside were now used in the plush corridors and the magnificent setting of the parliament building. Francesco Misiano was attacked there, an event which marked a milestone for Italy.

In May 1921, Misiano was elected to parliament again, this time via the Communist Party list. He was one of just fifteen communist deputies and one of two elected PCI representatives from Turin, where he finished ahead of Antonio Gramsci and was the first communist elected in that city.[72] Misiano was still extremely popular among the socialist and communist base. On the other side of the divide, however, he also inspired many to become fascists in the first place. Piero Zama, a leading fascist in Faenza, wrote: 'I became a fascist because I did not want to accept the spitting mob led by the charlatan Bombacci and the coward Misiano. A volunteer in the war had no choice.'[73]

On 13 June 1921, the opening day of that parliament session, the new fascist parliamentary group met in the early afternoon. These were the first explicitly fascist deputies to serve in the Italian parliament, and this was their inaugural day in the building. Misiano, a deputy since 1919, was sitting in the so-called 'transatlantic' corridor in parliament outside the chamber, when the fascist deputy Silvio Gai came up to him. 'Are you Misiano?' he asked. Misiano replied in the affirmative. 'Then get out,' said Gai. Misiano refused to leave, saying that he had been voted in to serve as a deputy. Gai stated that *his* voters had elected *him* to kick Misiano out. Gai then attacked Misiano. After the familiar battlecry, '*Fascisti! A Noi!*' ('Fascists! It is down to us!'), a number of armed fascists, including Giuseppe Bottai, surrounded Misiano and began to push him towards the exit. The *Corriere* reported that Misiano was whistled at and booed, but that the piazza was cleared by the police. The fascists claimed that Misiano had brandished a gun, and that Roberto Farinacci had taken it away.

In the debate that followed, the socialist Modigliani protested about the treatment of Misiano, while the fascists cried out: 'Deserter!' Modigliani proposed that the sitting should be suspended until Misiano was allowed back. Elected deputies, he said, could not be simply ejected from the chamber with violence. This unprecedented attack on democratic rights caused protests from others not close to Misiano politically, including the reformist Filippo Turati, who declared that 'there was a much greater desertion in terms of the laws of civility and humanity and it was called war'. It was a crucial moment for democracy in Italy. Farinacci displayed Misiano's pistol in the debating chamber as a trophy and placed it in full view of the government benches, close to Giovanni Giolitti, the distinguished liberal politician. Famously, Giolitti looked at it and then, supposedly, said laconically: 'I don't have a gun permit.'[74]

Italy's democracy and its parliament, which had been under threat before, truly began to die that day. Fascist deputy Aldo Finzi called Misiano 'an individual who has supported desertion' and claimed that he 'could not be allowed to enter parliament'.[75] Cesare De Vecchi, another fascist deputy who had just been elected, claimed that he had 'spat fourteen times in the face' of Misiano, and he was 'ready to do it again if that dirty deserter continues to defile Italy's parliament'. Antonio Gramsci wrote of these shocking events that 'the first action of the fascists in parliament is an act of pure and simple criminality, not one which can be assigned any political significance, not even with the most mind-bending thought processes'.[76] *Squadristi* across Italy, however, were delighted. Young *squadrista* Mario Piazzesi wrote in his diary: 'Yesterday, Misiano was kicked out of parliament. The kicks were obviously given to him by the fascists, because all the others, the right-thinking patriots, were not disgusted by sharing a bench alongside that scum.'[77]

Nonetheless Misiano was soon back in parliament. Eight days later, on 21 June 1921, he entered the chamber flanked by his communist colleagues. The fascist deputy Giunta said that Misiano 'could stay until 4.30'; if he stayed any longer 'he would be expelled'. Misiano remained in parliament where he made speeches and interventions in the chamber. His parliamentary life, however, became increasingly difficult as time wore on, as did life for him outside the chamber.

Mussolini was cautious after the 13 June attack, praising what had happened but arguing that this type of action should not become 'systemic': 'The Fascist Parliamentary Group ... maintained the moral pledge it had made with the electorate ... the commitment to stop the notorious deserter Misiano from entering parliament.' He could not avoid the classic criticism of Misiano's lack of courage: 'The deserter deserted and disappeared.'[78]

Fascist deputy Valentino Coda recognised the break in legality provoked by the fascist attack, but argued that the 'honour of parliament' had been saved. In this way Coda placed the concept of 'honour' in the face of a 'deserter' above the law itself. There was a higher 'law' to which the fascists adhered. Laws meant nothing to them. They had no time for the formalities of liberal democracy.

MURDER: GIUSEPPE DI VAGNO, 1921

Despite the climate of violence during the 1921 campaign, some socialist deputies were still elected in Apulia, including a lawyer called Giuseppe Di Vagno. On 25 September 1921 Di Vagno had gone for an early evening walk with comrades and friends in his home region, in the small town of Mola di Bari, in Puglia. He had just attended a meeting to open a party 'section'. In 1914, at the age of twenty-five, he had been elected as a councillor and then as a provincial councillor. He had opposed Italy's participation in the First World War and been interned in Sardinia as a result. In the 1921 general elections he was the second most popular candidate on the left in the Bari constituency. Some called him the 'Good Giant', thanks to his character and physical size.

Suddenly, while out on the walk, Di Vagno saw a number of 'decently dressed' young men emerge in 'single file' 'from the darkness'. Then, someone 'gave a command'. One of the men had his 'collar up, his left hand in his pocket, a brimmed hat, down on the eyes'. Shots were fired from close behind Di Vagno, two of which hit him in the back. He fell to the ground 'in a pool of blood', and, as the group of young men ran away, they threw a bomb and fired again. Another man – a railway worker – was injured. In some versions, a female passer-by who witnessed the assault lost her unborn baby because of the shock. Di Vagno was taken to a small local clinic in Mola. His situation was critical – he had serious internal bleeding, but he was still alive and could talk. Asked about those who had tried to kill him, he said: 'I can only say that my aggressor is a young man, tall, thin, dressed in grey, I think he is from Conversano [Di Vagno's home town]. If I saw him I would recognise him.' No more questions were asked because of his 'serious condition', and he couldn't sign this declaration. He underwent an operation but died the next day. Giuseppe Di Vittorio, the celebrated trade unionist, was with Di Vagno when he passed away.

Di Vagno had already been shot at in the past, at least once, and threatened on many occasions. Ten thousand people, it was reported, went to pay their respects to Di Vagno's body in Bari in the Camera Ardente, and his funeral attracted large crowds. His coffin passed 'under a sea of flowers, between two packed lines of people' in the pouring rain. His body was taken to a room in the station, and then transported by special train to Conversano for burial. Di Vagno was the first Italian parliamentarian to be killed by fascists – but he would not be the last. A general strike was called, as after other cases of fascist violence. All shops were closed in Bari, and the electricity in the city was cut off. No newspapers came out and the trains stopped running.

The police picked up a number of young fascists from Conversano, some of whom had gone on the run. It was said in Conversano that Di Vagno had been 'condemned to death'. The fascists had travelled to Mola in two cars, which they parked in the countryside before walking into town. There was little doubt that the right men had been arrested, but it was unclear who had ordered the killing.

In parliament Arturo Vella, who represented the same area, paid tribute to Di Vagno and blamed the local judiciary for having created the conditions for the murder of his colleague. Vella compared Di Vagno's death to that of other socialist 'martyrs' who had been killed in the postwar period, as well as international figures such as Jean Jaurès and Karl Liebknecht. Another local socialist deputy, Adelchi Baratono, pointed out in parliament that Di Vagno had been a marked man since 1914. Both men made reference to Di Vagno's unborn child (his wife was pregnant when he was killed). It was an emotional moment: the murder of such a popular parliamentarian could have been another decisive moment for Italy, but it failed to be. Fascist violence continued, unabated.

ANTI-FASCIST JEWS, ANTI-SEMITIC VIOLENCE AND THE RISE OF FASCISM

Jews were often beaten savagely during the rise and consolidation of the fascist regime; some were attacked and had their beards or hair cut off. Jews were often also socialists or oppositionists – and this latter attribute is often cited as being the main reason behind these beatings. Yet references to the fact that socialists were Jews were common in the fascist press, and anti-Semitic tropes were often used to criticise Jewish socialists. Claudio Treves, for example, was described in a paper titled *Il Fascio* in August 1919 as: 'A repugnant figure in terms of his appearance: he has a deformed face, piggy eyes, lopsided shoulders, brooding voice, a mocking smile ... Jewish, he is a classic type who provokes diffidence and antipathy against his race.'[79] This connection between anti-Semitism and anti-socialism was clearest in the case of Pio Donati.

Jewish socialists, fascists and policeman: Modena, 1921

> 'If we carry on like this a socialist deputy will no longer be able to leave their own home.'
>
> Anna Kuliscioff[80]

Born in 1881 in Modena in central Italy, Pio Donati came from one of the most well-known Jewish families in the city. The family had their own private synagogue. Donati joined the Socialist Party in 1909 at the age of twenty-eight. He worked as a lawyer and was put on trial, and cleared, for having organised a strike against the Libyan war.[81] He fought in the First World War. Donati sported a moustache and beard in 'an American style', according to his police file, and dressed elegantly and was said to be of 'of rare intelligence'. Police reports claimed that he was 'hated' because it was said that he was not a socialist out of conviction but because of the possibility it offered of personal gain and political power, although there was no evidence to support this claim.[82] Donati was elected to parliament in 1919 and again in 1921.

During this period he was forced off trains and physically beaten, his office was ransacked numerous times and his books were burnt. As Enzo Levi later wrote, 'Pio Donati's office was invaded three times, with files and furniture destroyed ... he was twice beaten by fascists ... his house was surrounded ... he only saved his life thanks to the help of his friends and some he didn't know.'[83] In short, his life was made impossible. According to the historian and journalist Giorgio Fabre, there was a clear link between the fascist violence directed against Donati and anti-Semitism.[84] Donati was given a semi-permanent police guard (of six officers) which he required for over a year. The stress relating to the constant threat of violence gave him severe ulcers, which were 'diagnosed as being of emotional origin'. Fascists were often to be seen outside his house and lawyer's studio, calling for 'death to Donati'. In 1921 events in Modena would take a further violent twist, and Donati would be right at the centre of it all.

On 26 September 1921, at about 10 p.m. in Modena, Royal Guards, instead of shooting on striking workers or left-wing demonstrators, turned their guns on fascists, something that was a rare occurrence at the time. It wasn't clear who had shot first. Six fascists were killed immediately, two died later. It was a huge national story. The fascists had been trying (again) to attack Pio Donati's office. It was said that the clash originated when a commissioner of the Royal Guards, Guido Cammeo, failed to act with sufficient 'respect' towards a group of fascists carrying a fascist banner and had not removed his hat. Cammeo was then attacked by fascists which appears to have been the signal for the Royal Guards to fire. Local fascists held Cammeo and Pio Donati 'morally responsible' for the deaths of the fascists in Modena.[85]

Once again, as on many other occasions, the fascists organised the funerals of their victims in grand style. Mussolini was present, and it was said that he kissed all of the victims' bodies. One of the fascists who died was Duilio Sinigaglia.[86] He was Jewish, and just twenty-four years old. Sinigaglia had participated in the war, and had been a fascist since 1919. He had also fought with D'Annunzio at Fiume.[87]

Fascist fury continued to target Donati in the wake of the deaths in September, but their anger was also directed at Cammeo, who was also Jewish and whose father was a rabbi in Modena.[88] A conspiracy theory spread around the town and in the fascist press which had anti-Semitic overtones.[89] Cammeo was said to be 'Donati's cousin' (he wasn't) and was accused of being 'a socialist'. He was described as 'anti-Italian' in the fascist press, which also underlined that fact that he was a Jew, like Donati. There were references to the fact that one of his real cousins, Carlo Cammeo, a socialist teacher, had been killed by the fascists in cold blood in Pisa in April 1921.[90] 'In the centre of Modena a large hand-drawn coloured image appeared, which depicted Donati passing a revolver to Commissioner Cammeo.'[91] Of course, the presence of Sinigaglia among the victims that day made the idea of a Jewish conspiracy even more absurd.

In January 1923, in another extremely rare moment in postwar Italy, Cammeo and other Royal Guards stood trial in Rome in relation to the events in Modena. In the vast majority of cases, fascists accused of violence had their cases dismissed, even when they were arrested. Hundreds of people had been shot dead or injured by the police, *carabinieri* and Royal Guards in Italy since the war, and in fact on numerous occasions in the nineteenth and early twentieth centuries, yet very few of these killings or assaults had ever been investigated. But the victims here were fascists, so the tables were turned. Police and military forces connected with the values of fascism, and the violence it used on the streets. Modena in 1921 was a rare exception to this general rule.

It took two trials for Cammeo to be cleared, in July 1923. Meanwhile, Duilio Sinigaglia became a key fascist martyr, more prominent than many others, especially in Modena itself. His supposed last words – 'We need to make the revolution' – allegedly whispered to Bolognese *squadrista* leader Dino Grandi, who was also (supposedly) there, became a battle cry for the movement.[92]

ON TRIAL FOR DESERTION: MISIANO, PALERMO, NOVEMBER 1921

Even after he was thrown out of parliament with violence, and attacked in Naples, Misiano continued to fight on, but the legal and political net was closing in. After parliament had voted to authorise the process, his trial for desertion before a military tribunal in Palermo, the closest geographically to his home town in Calabria, was finally held in November 1921, three years after the end of the war. In the run-up to the trial, fascists called for calm in Palermo, 'because every punishment inflicted upon him would only play into his hands providing him with the aura of a martyr and an excuse to avoid the trial'.[93]

It wasn't easy for Misiano to even reach Palermo. He had to travel in disguise and it was recorded that he got off at the wrong station. Large crowds gathered on the day of the trial at the military court in the city's Piazza Bologna. Misiano arrived early, at 8.30 in the morning. 'Thunderous applause' followed the words of the prosecutor. In his defence, Misiano complained about being called a coward. He also said that his state 'bodyguards' both failed to protect him from attacks *and* spied on him. Misiano blamed a previous lawyer for having failed to send a letter in time. The judges deliberated for an hour, and then it was all over. The whole process had lasted less than a day. Misiano was found guilty by the military court, and cries of 'Long live Italy, long live the army' rang out. In the aftermath, 'groups of nationalists and fascists marched through the central streets of Palermo singing their songs and parading the national flag'.[94]

Misiano was given a ten-year sentence for desertion. A 1920 amnesty had reduced the penalty for desertion from death to ten years in a military prison, but this sentence was suspended following the rules of another amnesty. Misiano would not have to serve jail time, but he could not be fully cleared, the court argued, because his lawyer had not acted in time to take advantage of a yet another amnesty. In many other cases these limits were not applied so strictly and it was clear that this was a decision heavily influenced by the political climate.

No appeal was lodged against the sentence, and it was only a matter of time before Misiano was officially thrown out of parliament because of his conviction. In early December, fascist deputies tried again to attack

Misiano inside parliament, and he needed protection from his communist comrades. Whenever he appeared in public there were cries of 'Deserter!' and 'Kick the shameful one out!' The fascists also called on the other deputies to abandon the chamber in protest at Misiano's presence, and many did, including some from the Catholic party – the Popular Party – as well as the former prime minister and liberal grandee, Giolitti.

In the public gallery, the *Corriere* reported, the *ufficiali* ('officers') present stood up and applauded the deputies who were leaving in protest at the presence of the 'deserter'. Misiano walked out 'pale' and of boasting a 'contemptuous smile' in the face of cries of 'traitor'. Threatened at every moment, and forced to flee, once outside parliament he was helped into a car by *carabinieri* and driven away. A further story was told by the newspaper, although its truth must be in doubt. Misiano, it was said, had forgotten his coat in his hurry to escape; when it was found it had 'a pendant with the effigy of San Gennaro [the patron saint of Naples and subject of a cult in the city] on it'. The news of this discovery, 'which immediately did the rounds, led to gales of laughter'.[95]

In an editorial, the *Corriere* supported the protests against the 'anti-national' Misiano, and called for him to be removed (according to the rules): 'So that the normal development of parliamentary procedures is no longer disturbed by his presence.'[96] The paper argued that this was a *moral* protest and 'nobody wanted to stop Misiano the deputy in carrying out his duties, and nobody wanted to chuck him out from his seat using violence'.[97]

Fascist deputies tried repeatedly to block the work of parliament when Misiano was present, leaving the chamber, calling for a head count, and shouting abuse, in addition to the physical violence which they threatened or carried out on numerous occasions. This behaviour was tolerated by the authorities, and there were no arrests or suspensions of fascist deputies. Fellow communist deputy Nicola Bombacci defended Misiano (both verbally and physically) and said that 'all means' would be used to stand up for him by the communist movement. Modigliani also continued to support Misiano's 'right … to sit in parliament'. He called the fascist attacks on Misiano a form of 'sabotage of the institution of parliament' and pointed out that the sentence passed against Misiano was not yet legally binding. By now, however, Misiano's options had run out. Despite being elected twice, he was formally removed. Many of the socialists abstained in the vote. Misiano's short and dramatic parliamentary career was over.

Meanwhile, Italy was beginning to bring to justice the protagonists of the dramatic events in Bologna, Empoli, Milan and Tuscany in 1920–21. These show trials framed the violence of the red and black years as almost entirely the work of socialists, communists and anarchists, who were depicted as brutal and cold-blooded killers. This framing was central to the creation of a narrative which saw the fascists as having saved Italy from 'red chaos'. The first trial was linked to the bombing of the Diana Theatre, and was held in Milan.

THE MALATESTA AND DIANA TRIALS
MILAN, 1921–22

'Who did not believe in the revolution?'

Errico Malatesta at his trial, 1921[98]

'The hour of justice has come and justice will be done.'

Omedei Zorini, prosecutor, Diana bomb trial, 1922[99]

In July 1921 anarchists Errico Malatesta, Corrado Quaglino and Armando Borghi were finally brought to trial, charged with 'conspiracy against the state' and 'criminal association', after their hunger strike had ended with the horrors of the Diana bomb. The allegations against them had nothing to do with that attack, but the context of the trial was marked by the aftermath of the massacre. On the second day of his trial, Malatesta made a powerful statement concerning the theatre bombing, claiming that it was the work of a 'madman' which had only served the interests of the enemies of anarchism and socialism.[100] In just three days, all the accusations against these three prominent anarchists fell away. Even the public prosecutor seemed to give up the case. The three were cleared by the jury of all charges.[101] Malatesta was released but was never allowed to leave Italy again. His years of exile were over.[102]

In some ways, the Diana massacre had achieved one of its aims. It had, perhaps, saved Malatesta's life; but at a further, and devastating, political and human cost. The plotters who had tried to free their hero and halt his hunger strike felt the full force of the legal and penitentiary system. The Diana investigation closed at the end of November 1921 and the trial finally began in 1922, lasting from 9–31 May. By then, two of the Diana bombers, Aguggini and Mariani, had already been convicted of the Cova cafe bomb attack in 1920, to which they had confessed and been given long sentences: twenty-four years for Mariani and twenty for Aguggini.[103] Whatever happened in the Diana trial, the two men knew that they would probably never leave prison alive. As the *Corriere della Sera* later commented: 'For Mariani any eventual freedom will not come under a bourgeois society … he is hoping, with the tranquillity of a fanatic, for a revolution.'[104]

At the start of the trial it was said that Mariani observed the packed court and said: 'So many people just to give me a life sentence.' Anarchist protestors later compared the courtroom to a 'slaughterhouse'.[105] Mariani and Aguggini were defended by the celebrated (and former anarchist) lawyer, Francesco Saverio Merlino and an extensive team. Merlino had been at school with Malatesta and had represented him in a famous trial way back in the 1870s.

On day one, journalists described the accused as 'smoking' and chatting. Mariani was wearing sandals, and said to be chuckling with 'his dry and metallic laugh'. The third bomber, Giuseppe Boldrini, had shaved off his beard and was wearing 'a round artisan's hat'. His hands were described as 'defaced by scars from the burns produced by an earlier imprudent bomb attack before the tragic attempt at Diana'.[106] Boldrini had not been convicted of any previous crime. The seventeen anarchists accused of various misdeeds were brought to the courtroom early in the morning, to avoid trouble in the streets.

There was little chance of a fair trial. Mariani and Aguggini's long sentences for the Cova restaurant bomb were noted at the start of the proceedings, and were well known to the jury. One of the survivors of the theatre bombing spat at the prisoners in their cage. There were frequent angry arguments and the president of the court had to suspend the session on a number of occasions. At one point a jury member expressed a desire to walk out in disgust at the statements of one of the defendants.[107]

When the survivors and relatives of the victims gave evidence, the accused decided to leave the courtroom. A father who lost his only son in the attack recounted that he had fought for three years in the war. His son was in a good mood that evening, and was 'singing' as he left the house. He next saw his son, literally, 'in pieces'. Another father told the story of how his seven-year-old daughter lost an eye in the tragedy. A harp player recounted how she had sustained an injury to her hand and been rendered deaf by the explosion. The Crippa sisters also gave evidence. They were carried into the courtroom and Ida shouted 'cowards' towards the accused (who were not present). There were reports of many people crying, and the whole court stood to pay tribute to the victims and the injured.[108]

Three of the anarchists accused of less serious but connected crimes were represented by Leonida Répaci and Franco Clerici.[109] Both lawyers were communists, and Répaci had been alongside Antonio Gramsci in Turin during the occupation of the factories in 1920. He was twenty-four years old and had only recently graduated in law. He would go on to be a celebrated writer, painter, journalist, poet, translator and founder of Italy's famous Viareggio literary prize.[110]

Répaci represented a minor defendant, Giordano Ustori. After the *Umanità Nova* printing press was destroyed by fascists in the wake of the bomb, Ustori, who worked as a printer there, found himself unemployed. He was eventually arrested and extradited from Switzerland to stand trial. Répaci was impressed by the character of some of the others on trial. Of Giuseppe Boldrini (who never confessed to the attack, but was implicated by Mariani and Aguggini, although they changed their stories at the trial itself) he said that he was 'unemotional and decisive, a man of action. If there had been a few hundred of men like him, in Italy, maybe history would have gone in a different direction.'[111] The press depicted Boldrini as a cold-hearted killer, but journalists struggled with the 'normality' of the other defendants. 'They all have a youthful appearance ... they are calm, almost serene. It is pointless to try and find physical signs of criminality, abnormal craniums, facial deformations, sinister eyes.'[112]

Mariani was the first in the dock, and his defence was political. He referred to the 'millions' of victims during the war. 'There have been many dead,' he said, 'and the bourgeoisie were to blame. These dead [from the Diana bomb] are a form of punishment. You wanted these deaths. You are responsible.' This statement provoked a furious response from Gino Rossi, a relative of one of the victims, in the courtroom: 'What bourgeoisie are you talking about,' he shouted, '... coward ... You killed my five-year-old daughter.'[113] Aguggini also referred to the victims of the war in his defence: 'We consider ourselves at war against bourgeois society.'[114]

In his lengthy and dramatic summing up, and in an extremely hostile atmosphere, Répaci used all the tools of rhetoric at his disposal. He cited Nietzsche and Catone, William Tell and the anarchist poet, activist and songwriter Pietro Gori. At one point some in the public gallery joined in with an anarchist song. Répaci compared the judiciary to directors of psychiatric hospitals. His summing up closed with an emotional and highly rhetorical and almost literary appeal, which discussed 'the beauty of that drama which is part of all our lives, a drama which requires the roar of stupidity and the smile of the martyr ... [and] which leads to a sublime synthesis of that for which we all yearn: freedom'.[115]

On 1 June 1922 the trial came to an end.[116] It had been relatively brief.[117] Both Mariani and Aguggini claimed in court that Boldrini was innocent, contradicting previous statements and confessions. The suspicion was that they were trying to protect him, given the lack of other evidence. Jury members were asked to decide and vote on 264 charges. They took six hours to complete their task. The accused chatted while they awaited the verdicts. One of them, according to journalists, even took a nap. Throughout the trial journalists attempted to depict the accused as cold-blooded, nonchalant and uncaring.

It took twenty-five minutes to read out the sentences. Mariani was given life with nine years in solitary confinement, and added forced labour. Boldrini was also given life with eight years of solitary and Aguggini thirty years with two of 'special vigilance'.[118] These were among the harshest sentences possible under Italian law at the time (the death penalty had been abolished in liberal Italy in 1889). All the accused listened to the verdicts in silence. The Crippa sisters were in court to hear the sentences read out. There were cries from the audience of 'murderers' and Boldrini was said to have shouted at the jury that they should 'all die'. Mariani was sent to the forbidding prison complex on the island of Santo Stefano off the coast of Lazio and Campania. The incredible semi-circular panopticon prison building there was known as 'L'Ergastolo' ('The Life Sentence'). Finished in 1797, it was in the shape of a huge horseshoe with ninety-nine cells, over three floors. The cells were just 4.5 metres by 4.2 metres. It was known as one of the harshest prison institutions in Italy, and a place from which it was impossible to escape.[119]

Ustori was cleared, but all the others were given custodial sentences. Mussolini was very critical of the court process, and the publicity surrounding it, claiming that the accused had been given too much space to state their case in court. 'Milan's fascists,' he wrote, 'will not allow ... that a trial against a gang of criminals is transformed into a political platform ... if this horrible spectacle does not come to an end, Milan's fascists – even if at the cost of being shot – will perform summary justice.'[120] Répaci paid dearly for his outspoken defence of his client. As he was walking through the city's La Galleria arcade he was attacked by fascists and 'horribly and bloodily beaten'.[121]

Italian anarchism had been dealt a severe blow, first by the bombing itself and then by the prosecutions. Malatesta was very clear at his 1921 trial: 'The revolution did not happen,' but what happened afterwards, as he predicted, were 'terrible reactions'.[122]

Year Zero
1922

Nineteen twenty-two was fascism's Year Zero. Across the country, *squadristi* continued their campaign of violence. Local democratic institutions fell, one by one, to fascist pressure. Forty councillors had been elected to the provincial administration of Cremona, in northern Italy, in May 1922. But this formal, democratic procedure was completely ignored by the local fascists. They did not recognise elections. In that same month, local fascist leader and *ras*, Roberto Farinacci, insisted that he be allowed to speak as the 'forty-first councillor'. Farinacci had not even been a candidate in the elections. For Farinacci, the institution in which he was attempting to speak no longer represented those who had voted for it, an electorate who were now, he claimed, all fascists. When asked who had elected him, he replied: 'I elected myself'. It was the last meeting of that provincial council. Farinacci later mythologised and rewrote these events in his diaries, published in 1933.[1]

Cremona's squads were among the most violent of all and their brutality had led directly to this situation of dual power. Democratic institutions were helpless in the face of the blackshirts with their clubs, cudgels and guns, which were used for constant threats, beatings and murders. Councillor Attilio Boldori was beaten to death in December 1921, and the only comment from Farinacci was that 'it is not our fault if his [Boldori's] skull was weak'.[2] In 1922, 281 councils were effectively overthrown. Most were replaced with central state control. When elections were next held, as in Bologna in 1923, the left usually did not even put up a list. Election results and democracy had come up against fascist violence, and the latter had won.

During 1922 sporadic raids and individual beatings were increasingly accompanied by high-level military occupations by *squadristi* of cities and entire regions. The blackshirts had created an alternative military force which was prepared and willing to march through Italy, burning and looting buildings and attacking individuals and symbols of power as they went. A novel and highly effective form of political activity was being experimented with for the first time – a *militia party*. Although the objectives for the blackshirts in the summer of 1922 were the provinces and 'red' cities, these were dress rehearsals. The final objective was central political power.

THE MARCH ON RAVENNA, JULY 1922

'The state has abandoned all its powers to the avengers. A state has formed within the state. A private army has formed alongside the national army. ... The old local powers who were kicked out thanks to the vote of the people rose up and organised – as in medieval times – gangs from outside to reimpose their control ... In Ravenna there was a Federation with over a hundred consumer cooperatives, it was a miracle of faith and work, an institution of which the proletariat was proud and which was admired and studied from abroad ...
A man presided over the cooperatives who, if he had dedicated himself to business instead of the proletariat, would have been among the richest men in Italy: Nullo Baldini. One night the enemy arrived. The state was, as usual, passive and complicit. The organisation is destroyed ... is this not a dagger to the heart of the nation?'

Claudio Treves, address to parliament,
August 1922[3]

'We must ... strike terror into the hearts of our enemies ... The entire Romagna plain right up to the hills saw angry revenge attacks by the fascists, who had decided to put an end to the reds ... once and for all.'

Italo Balbo[4]

By the summer of 1922 in Cremona, Ferrara, Bologna and elsewhere, the *squadristi* were in control. The state, police, prefects, army and *carabinieri* were all reduced to the role of onlookers, and often took sides, providing logistical assistance to the violent gangs.

In late July, thousands of armed blackshirts descended on the city of Ravenna. The 'March on Ravenna' was carried out like a military invasion. It took place out in the open, during the day, and was accompanied by a selective purge – the victims being socialists, republicans and trade unionists.[5] As Tasca later wrote: 'the fascists ... left a trail of smoking ruins, tortured bodies, and broken minds from Rimini to Novara and Ravenna'.[6] At least nine people were killed in Ravenna alone – which was the main target – but the attacks ranged across a vast area which included Forlì and Cesena (targeted on the way *back* from Ravenna, on 29–30 July).

Usually, the story of this major raid is told via the diaries of its most celebrated leader, Italo Balbo, who recounted his version of the events in 1932, ten years after they had happened. The March on Ravenna was preceded by a practice run (in September 1921, in the same city)[7] and was itself a form of practice for a future March on Rome. The authorities stood back and watched the carnage unfold. Socialist and trade union attempts to fight back, as with a 'legalitarian' general strike called in protest at the violence, or with clashes on the streets, were a disaster.[8]

Ravenna 1922 was an *anti*-Red Week, or perhaps a 'Black Week'. Fascist violence struck back in many of the places which had witnessed the anti-militarist uprising in 1914. Ravenna had been one of the key cities during the revolt of Red Week in 1914. It was as if the fascists wanted to destroy all memory, all trace, of the left in those same areas.

From 26–29 July 1922, thousands of *squadristi* rampaged through Ravenna. The police and *carabinieri* made no attempt to stop them. No arrests were made of fascists (although many socialists were picked up) and no charges were brought subsequently. Victims were too scared to go to the police to describe what had happened, or even talk to medical staff openly. 'People were cared for secretly and the doctors did not produce the documents which were legally required.'[9] The Casa del Popolo ('People's House', a sort of left-wing social centre or club) in the city was ransacked, and bombs thrown. 'After entering the offices, the fascists chucked out our registers and paper and everything was burnt.' Symbols were substituted. 'On the balcony, where there was usually a huge red flag, the Italian flag was raised.' By 30 July, the suburbs appeared 'deserted with windows closed and doors locked'.[10]

It was a massacre and an occupation, directed at socialists, republicans and the cooperative movement – and both politically and economically inspired. Fascists took control of the city, camping out as if they were a real army. They saw no need to ask for permission. 'The arrival of so many fascists this morning seems to have transformed Ravenna into a vast encampment,' observed *La Stampa*.[11] The devastation was not limited to Ravenna. There were, in the words of the fascists, 'spectacular raids in Forlì, Cesena and Cesenatico'.[12]

Bonfire: the destruction of the cooperative building in Ravenna

'The fire in that large building projected sinister flashes into the night, the whole city was lit up … There are no half-measures in civil warfare, unfortunately … When I saw the socialist organiser leave the building with his head in his hands and signs of desperation on his face, I understood the tragedy of the situation. His dreams and life's work had been reduced to ashes, along with the Palazzo delle Cooperative in Ravenna.'

Italo Balbo[13]

It was one of the most beautiful buildings in the city, but all that was left were 'walls and ruins', and the overpowering smell of smoke.[14] In his diaries, Italo Balbo often attempted to provide a noble version of the violent events he had organised and led in the early 1920s. In his famous and oft-quoted account of the 1922 attack on Ravenna and its surroundings, he dedicates space to the burning down of the central cooperative building in the city, housed in a famous and historic edifice known as the ex-Palazzo Byron. Balbo admitted that the cooperative movement in the area was a 'gigantic organisation … run in a largely honest way'.[15] The federation brought together ninety-two cooperative organisations, owned 6,000 hectares of land and rented out a similar amount.[16] It was a place of national importance: 'one of the cornerstones of socialism, representing twenty years of work'.[17] Cooperatives had consistently undercut the landowners and shopkeepers and provided support for the lower classes. But early in the morning of 28 July 1922, fire ripped through the building after *squadristi* had smashed the interior to pieces.[18]

Ravenna's extraordinary cooperative movement had been built and fought for by workers and peasants under the guide of a local leader called Nullo Baldini, who had spent much of his life creating institutions of reformist counter-power. The cooperatives in the city and surrounding area represented, according to historian Luciano Casali: 'The site of maximum economic power for Italy's socialists.'[19] When the fascists turned up at two in the morning, Baldini was there with another official from the cooperative movement, Giacomo Bindo, as well as the building's porter and his wife. As those inside were forced out, *La Stampa*, in contrast with Balbo's version of events, reported that Baldini was, in fact, beaten. His office was reduced to 'rubble' and 'a pile of ruins and furnishings'.[20] The paper went on to describe the burning of the cooperative building as 'a very painful day'. What is left, it asked, of 'the Ravennate cooperativism of Nullo Baldini? ... the political and military authorities' had left 'the fascists free to do as they wished'.[21]

Baldini's defeat sent shockwaves through the left. Liberal opinion was also shaken. *La Stampa* praised the 'thirty or so years work' of Baldini to build the cooperative movement, which had helped in relieving unemployment, prevented peasants leaving the land and had modernised systems of production and distribution.[22]

Balbo wrote in 1932 that this orgy of destruction was inevitable. The socialists were the *enemy*, they had to be *annihilated* – every trace of them had to be wiped out. Balbo tried to claim that he had acted with respect for his rivals: 'I gave orders that Baldini should be moved along without being harmed or even insulted.'[23] Balbo underlined that the fascists needed an enemy that had to be forced into submission – 'we need to terrify our adversaries'. Balbo's squads were in control. *They* were giving the orders. Balbo threatened the police – he claimed – in order to obtain transport and other support:

> I announced to [the chief of police] that I would burn down and
> destroy the houses of all socialists in Ravenna if he did not give me
> within half an hour the means required for transporting the Fascists
> elsewhere. It was a dramatic moment. I demanded a whole fleet
> of trucks. The police officers completely lost their heads; but after
> half an hour they told me where I could find trucks already filled
> with gasoline. Some of them actually belonged to the office of the
> chief of police. My ostensible reason was that I wanted to get the

exasperated Fascists out of the town; in reality, I was organising
a 'column of fire' ... to extend our reprisals throughout the
province...[24]

Italy's state was providing the means for illegal criminal gangs to carry
out their activities with greater efficiency. The dividing line between
legality and illegality was increasingly blurred.

Balbo draws heavily from the *squadristi* playbook here in his use
of the term 'reprisals' to justify violence. Eventually, the lorries full
of *squadristi* left for their next target city – Cesena.[25] 'We went,' he
wrote, through 'all the towns and centres in the provinces of Forlì and
Ravenna and destroyed and burned all the Red buildings ... It was a
horrific night. Our passage was marked by huge columns of fire and
smoke.'[26] Five other cooperatives were burnt down. *Avanti!* referred to
the events in Ravenna as a 'proletarian massacre'.[27] People were reduced,
the newspaper wrote, to defending 'their houses, their women'.[28] Nearby
Alfonsine – the same small town which had attempted a revolution
in June 1914 during Red Week, burning down a monarchist club and
exalting the anti-militarist anarchist Augusto Masettti – also succumbed
to the fascist violence.[29]

What happened in the wake of this widespread and so destructive
'punitive expedition'? Some historians have written of wholesale disgust
across Italy.[30] There is no doubt that the activities and the obvious
immunity from prosecution of the fascists caused 'terror' among the
local population. Lists of names were published of those who, according
to the fascists, deserved 'punishment'.[31] *Squadristi* orders stated openly
that all the leaders of the three radical parties in Ravenna – socialist,
communist and republican – had just twenty-four hours to leave town.[32]
Obviously, none of this was legal, but many socialists didn't wait around
to see what would happen – 'all the leaders made themselves scarce'.[33]
There were reports of 'communists' being chased across the countryside
by armed fascists. In short: 'The fascists were able to stay in Ravenna as
the new bosses. They had conquered the city.'[34]

PALAZZO MARINO, MILAN, 3 AUGUST 1922

One by one, the last bastions of socialist power, and democracy, were
picked off by the *squadristi*. In August 1922, blackshirts occupied Palazzo

Marino, the vast building in Milan, opposite La Scala, which serves as Milan's town hall, and which had been governed by the socialists since 1914. Gabriele D'Annunzio, who was, coincidentally, staying in a Milan hotel, was persuaded by fascists to make a speech from the balcony. It was around 11.30 p.m. on 3 August, and a large crowd had gathered in the square. D'Annunzio arrived by car, saluting his audience and waving his hat. According to the *Corriere della Sera* the crowd suddenly fell silent, '*come per incanto*' – 'as if they were under a spell'.[35]

It was the first time D'Annunzio had addressed a crowd from a balcony since Fiume. It was not an explicitly fascist speech, but its setting, the sentiments he expressed, and the very fact that he made it, were powerful endorsements of fascism and its violent methods. 'It is not we who breathe but the nation which breathes in us,' he told them; 'it is not we who live but the *patria* [fatherland] which lives in us.' He also made a clear anti-socialist statement which would have been understood by the crowd in front of him: 'For too long, the language of the Italian flag has been silent here.' This was an explicit reference to constant debates in Milan over the war, the socialist administration and the flying of the national flag. D'Annunzio concluded that: '*L'Italia ... la Nazione che ha ripreso possesso della sua città.*' ('Italy ... has retaken possession of its city.') *Squadristi*, in short, were the real patriots, the *real* Italians, while the elected council were the anti-nation.

The speech was published in full in the *Corriere* the next day, and then in book form, although it was later said that few in the square could hear a word he was saying, given the number of people there and the background noise.[36] On 4 August, *Avanti!*'s offices in Milan were attacked by fascists yet again. In the wake of the armed occupation of the town hall, Milan's prefect soon removed the elected mayor, who was replaced with a government commissioner. Another democratic building block had fallen to violence.[37]

BARI VECCHIA AND ANCONA, AUGUST 1922

Bari Vecchia (Old Bari) is a tight-knit group of tiny streets, squares and courtyards within a kind of urban peninsula which reaches out into the sea. Then, as now, it is almost a separate place from the rest of the city of Bari, surrounded by walls and the sea. It has its own distinct dialect and has been compared to a kind of 'ants' nest'. In August 1922 there were dramatic clashes in Bari Vecchia during a general strike. Both sides were armed. The anti-fascists attacked a *carabinieri* barracks and a police station, but their victories were extremely short-lived. Caradonna, the local fascist leader, threatened to bring more than 2,000 *squadristi* to Bari, and the entire neighbourhood was surrounded. Numerous arrests followed. Machine guns and armoured vehicles were used by the state, as was a *torpedineria* (torpedo boat) stationed in the bay. Alongside Bari Vecchia, Italy's last red bastions were crushed – Bari, Ravenna, Andria, Milan, Molinella, Trento, Bolzano. Fascists across Italy in 1922 'marched' on these cities and towns en masse, brushing resistance aside.

Ancona had been the city where Red Week began in 1914. In early August 1922 the *squadristi* arrived in force. The taking of Ancona was surprisingly straightforward, although there were clashes, injuries and deaths. Ancona's anarchists were the main focus of resistance, and the principal victims in the aftermath of defeat. Buildings linked to the socialists, anarchists and Republican Party were all attacked and ransacked. Seven died (one of them a fascist) during the occupation, but opposition was only 'sporadic'.[38] It was a clear sign that the fascists were now in charge.

Mussolini was delighted. 'There is something prodigious about the fascistisation of Ancona,' he noted. 'This beautiful and powerful city … did not live up to the reputation that had been created there by a few professional socialists.'[39] Red Week, which Mussolini himself had supported, was not just a distant memory, it seemed light years away. A hyper-militarist and nationalist organisation was now in control. It took four days to capture and pacify Ancona, under the leadership of Silvio Gai, one of the fascist deputies who had attacked Misiano in parliament in June 1921.[40] For historian Ercole Sori, 'the taking of Ancona by the fascist squads appeared to be the necessary premise – logistically – for an attack on the capital itself'.[41] It was now time to attempt to take national power – in Rome.

The March on Rome
October–November 1922

By the autumn of 1922, the fascist movement meant to snatch political power, to take control of the state, to seize *Rome*. But how would this be done? The only way the fascists knew how to act was through violence, and the threat of further violence. This was the movement's greatest asset, the novelty it had introduced to modern politics – the armed party, the combination of political and military action.

In October 1922, an irregular 'army' of thousands of armed private citizens rose up at various locations in Italy, occupying government buildings, train stations and post offices. All were volunteers. The threat of an armed attack on Rome was then utilised to try to leverage political power. A disorganised march of sorts, towards the capital, then began. None of this was without victims, as has sometimes been claimed. Much blood was spilt. Many people died before, during and after the March on Rome (nobody seems to know exactly how many, but some have claimed that this figure could be as high as fifty dead, with between seventeen and twenty-two killed in the capital city alone).[1] Hundreds more were injured. Damage to property was extensive. The prelude to the march took place in Naples.

SAN CARLO THEATRE AND PIAZZA SAN CARLO
NAPLES, 24 OCTOBER 1922

'We want to become the state.'

Benito Mussolini, Naples, 24 October 1922

On 24 October 1922, Giuseppe Caradonna – landowner, war hero, *squadrista*, fascist – rode into Naples on horseback. It was a highly symbolic moment which carried echoes, for the participants, of national hero Giuseppe Garibaldi's march up Italy in 1860, which led to unification. That same day, some 40,000 blackshirts descended on Naples from across Italy. Benito Mussolini addressed his supporters inside the sumptuous San Carlo opera house, which was 'packed' with 'fascists … spectators' and dignitaries, including the mayor, the intellectual Benedetto Croce and parliamentarians.[2] Mussolini was announced by trumpets and greeted with 'wild applause, which lasted for a good few minutes', followed by the 'fascist hymn'.[3] He was dressed in a black shirt. It was a speech which was full of menace. 'Fascism,' he said, 'must become the state.'[4]

The audience appeared to be very much in agreement. There were chants of *Ro-Ma, Ro-Ma*. Mussolini added a more specific threat: 'Either they give us the government or we will take it by descending on Rome.'[5] Naples resident and celebrated thinker Benedetto Croce was also seen applauding 'fervently' as the fascists filed past.[6] Mussolini then left, and a fascist congress took place, but in the middle of a debate the leading *squadrista*, Michele Bianchi, expressed his frustration: 'Fascists, what are we doing in Naples? … I want to be in Rome by midday.'[7]

There was a plan for a national insurrection. The March on Rome had four official leaders, three *squadristi ras* (Michele Bianchi himself, Italo Balbo and Cesare De Vecchi) and a former general (Emilio De Bono). The first step was to occupy public buildings across Italy, then thousands of armed blackshirts would congregate at five sites around Rome. This would be as far as the march would go while negotiations took place with the political leaders in the capital. If the central government did not give way, then there would be a push on Rome itself. The first cities to move were in the centre and the north of Italy.

THE MARCH BEGINS
CREMONA, 27 OCTOBER 1922

'Those of you who accuse our revolution of being a comic opera, you should be reminded that in Cremona and Bologna we lost twenty dead for our revolution.'

Roberto Farinacci[8]

In Cremona, on 27 October 1922, the lights went out at around 6 p.m. Soon afterwards, without meeting much resistance, Roberto Farinacci's fascists took full control of the city's police station and occupied the prefect's office. Blackshirts also seized the city's post office and telephone exchange. After being forced out of the prefect's office, a further attempt on the prefect's palace took place later that same evening. Vehicles were driven at the building at speed in a bid to smash its 'massive doors'.[9] Four fascists were left dead in the shoot-out that followed. Cremona's prefect asked for reinforcements.[10] By the next day, Farinacci had marshalled greater numbers and the troops were ordered not to fight back. The local state had effectively conceded power. Farinacci then 'sat at the prefect's desk [and] began to issue proclamations'.[11] He had taken over some of the powers of the state, and seemed able to order arrests, and free others from prison.[12] The prefect, army and police had been at the sharp end of extreme fascist violence for some time. Their opposition to the takeover soon faded away. Elsewhere, even this semblance of resistance would not be forthcoming. Soon, Cremona's blackshirts were on their way to the capital.

The occupation of Foggia in the south of Italy was dramatic and efficient. On 27 October, after riding into Naples, Caradonna and 1,500 *squadristi* returned to Apulia, and proceeded to take control of key public buildings in Foggia with the use of force. Like Cremona, the southern city was plunged into darkness as the electricity was cut off. Blackshirts went on to take control of 'the prefect's palace, the post office, the telegraph and telephone offices as well as the air force barracks where they seized arms'.[13] There was some token resistance from the authorities, but no fascists were killed. Across Italy, the response of the army and the state was extremely patchy.

FASCIST HEADQUARTERS: THE HOTEL BRUFANI

'At the Brufani people come and go, there are a number of onlookers, who also have brought along their cameras. It looks like the drama will have a happy ending.'

Antonino Répaci[14]

At one end of Perugia's sumptuous central Corso Vannucci, perched on top of a ridge overlooking the sweeping plains below, with Assisi in the distance, stands the Hotel Brufani. For many years, this hotel was managed by British owners.[15] It was here, strategically, that the fascists decided to set up their general headquarters for the March on Rome and it was here that the four 'leaders' stayed (presumably, for free) while the march took place across Italy. In Perugia it was reported that 3,000 fascists were ready and awaiting orders. By midday on 27 October these men were all at the edge of that city. They proceeded later that night to occupy the prefect's palace, the station, the telegraph office, the post office and other 'public places'.

In Milan, at around the same time as the Cremona clashes, Mussolini had gone to the theatre to see the Hungarian Ferenc Molnár's play *The Swan*. One of his staff tried to attract his attention but was waved away until the end of the act. Then, he was informed of the beginning of the 'march' in Cremona.[16]

AN UNSIGNING: THE KING AND POLITICIANS IN ROME

'Your Majesty, the army will do its duty; however, it would be
well not to put it to the test.'
                              Marshal Armando Diaz to King Victor Emmanuel III,
                                                                October 1922[17]

In October 1922, the prime minister Luigi Facta found himself in charge of a fragile liberal administration. As Facta slept, his *chef de cabinet*, Efrem Ferraris, became alarmed by reports of fascist occupations and disturbances coming in from across the country. There were also stories of fraternisation between blackshirts and regular troops. He later wrote: 'In the night I witnessed, in the silence of the great rooms of the Viminale, the disintegration of the authority and power of the state.'[18]

Ferraris woke Facta at 3 a.m. on 28 October, and the ineffectual prime minister finally decided to act. In the face of fascist uprisings across Italy, and attacks on government and public buildings, martial law was announced to prefects at 7.50 a.m. This measure allowed for the use of the army on the streets, and special military laws to be put into place. A national state of siege (with martial law) was an extreme action, a last resort which had often, if not exclusively, been used against the left in the past. It had also usually been applied to specific parts of Italy, not the whole country.

As the orders went out, fascists were disarmed in some areas. But there was a problem. All decrees needed to be signed by the monarch, the head of state, under Italy's constitutional system. At 8 a.m. on 28 October, which was a Saturday, a call was made from the prime minister's office to that of the prefect in Perugia. But it was not the prefect who picked up the phone. Instead, it was the leading fascist, Michele Bianchi – one of the designated leaders of the March on Rome – who answered. Bianchi, it seems, called on the government to avoid bloodshed between the army and fascists. There could be little doubt that the Italian state was losing control.

The king was faced with a stark choice. At 9 a.m. Facta, a weak politician who had shared electoral lists with some of the fascists who were now moving ominously towards Rome, presented the monarch with the order for a state of siege (martial law). He expected the monarch to sign. Earlier discussions had suggested that the king's assent would not be an issue. To Facta's astonishment, the king refused to do so. Antonino Répaci, in his classic and influential account of the March on Rome, was in little doubt that that the army could have repressed the march in a matter of days, if not hours. As he wrote, in a classic piece of counterfactual history: 'with the use of martial law, and the deployment of regular armed forces, it would have taken forty-eight hours, or even less, to round up the fascists'.[19] Denis Mack Smith, the eminent British historian of Italy, agreed that the fascists would have been easily crushed if the state and the army had been used against them.[20]

Within hours, Facta had resigned. A new telegram to prefects was issued at midday, containing no mention of martial law. It had been, in the historian Richard Bosworth's words (quoting Répaci): 'a political poker game'.[21] Ever since, there has been wild speculation as to why the king took this dramatic and fateful step. Was he unconvinced about the loyalty of the army? Did he think that the Duca d'Aosta, his cousin, was preparing a kind of coup? Did he lack the courage for the fight? Was it true that 'he shrank from bloodshed'?[22] Or did he simply think it was time to let the fascists take over?

NIGHT TRAIN

At this time, Benito Mussolini was in Milan, a long way from the action. He took and made constant phone calls. (For Mussolini's base in Milan, see Figure 6.) As armed blackshirts gathered across

Italy, taking control of government offices, hotels and other buildings, often in his name, he waited to see how events would pan out. Mussolini acted with caution. He took no direct part in the march. But, as Répaci has written, 'Mussolini, in Milan, was behaving as if he was already in charge.'[23] He became more powerful by the minute and he negotiated, accepting nothing less than the top job for himself.

By refusing to sign the state of siege decree to install martial law, the king rejected the option of resisting the *squadristi* by force. In the face of blackshirt violence and the threat of further attacks in his own capital city, he then appointed the *head of the fascist movement* (who had, let us not forget, a mere thirty-five deputies in parliament) as prime minister.

Once his accession to power had been guaranteed, Mussolini caught the 8.30 p.m. night train from Milan, the DD17, which pulled into Rome at around 10.55 a.m. on 30 October. According to Martin Gilbert: 'At one point he [Mussolini] thought of stopping his train outside Rome and entering the city on horseback. In the event, he made the whole journey by sleeping car, and arrived at Rome station as his blackshirts pillaged the houses of political opponents and forced the editor of one liberal paper to drink the "fascist medicine", castor oil.'[24] The 'March' on Rome thus also took place on train tracks. Many of the marchers took trains, both to Rome and above all on their way back home. Mussolini's train was late, due, it appears to hordes of cheering blackshirts at every station it passed on its way through Italy.[25] Hundreds of people went to the station to greet Mussolini.

Mussolini's arrival by train allowed for theatrical and mythical aspects to be constructed around this march. Already, events were being carefully framed by Mussolini the journalist, in his own newspaper. Newspaper editor and senator Luigi Albertini was quoted as saying that Mussolini had 'published a supplement to his newspaper where he announced his own triumph, and let word spread that he would leave for Rome in the evening and he would like crowds to accompany him. This is why he did not travel via a special train.'[26] By taking the train Mussolini was able to separate himself from the blackshirts, to appear as a statesman, a man of order, but also an ordinary man.

MARCHING TO ROME

Meanwhile, thousands of *squadristi* were making their way to Rome, on foot, by road or by train. Many marched in their black shirts, with sleeping bags hung over their shoulders, sporting a variety of hats, facial hair and weapons – guns, batons, metal bars, daggers. Some displayed their medals; others instead wore their army uniforms. Men made up the vast majority of the marchers, but there were also some groups of fascist women. By the time they got to Rome they were cold, wet, hungry and often very tired.[27] The king and the head of the army, Armando Diaz, paid homage to the massed blackshirts with a military salute, and many replied with outstretched stiff arms. At least three generals marched alongside the *squadristi*.

Mussolini checked into the Hotel Savoia in Rome, and his next appointment was with the king, in the Palazzo del Quirinale. Already, this supposed revolution was being carefully choreographed. On 30 October 1922, Benito Mussolini, dressed in a black shirt (clumsily combined with a bowler hat and spats)[28] shook the hand of the king. Legend has it that he also said: 'I bring you the Italy of Vittorio Veneto.' Other versions include him saying: 'I come from the battlefield' (a phrase used symbolically, of course – in reality he came from his office and a train station).[29] Mussolini was eager to establish continuity between the fascist march and the war itself. A month before the march he had told a crowd in Cremona that: 'It was on the banks of the Piave that we began a march which cannot be halted until we reach our ultimate goal: Rome.'[30]

Crowds gathered outside Mussolini's hotel in Via Ludovisi, near the Via Veneto. Fascists stood guard. At around 12.15 Mussolini arrived from the Quirinale preceded by a motorbike. He was greeted with 'long applause' and then made the first of many 'balcony speeches' to the crowd below, flanked by leading fascists and blue-shirted nationalists. Standing on a chair, with 'strong and clear voice' he addressed the crowd: 'Fascists! Citizens! The fascist movement has won everywhere. I have come to Rome to provide the Nation with a Government. In a few hours, the Nation will not just have a Ministry, it will have a Government. Long live the King! Long live Italy!'[31]

It was an extraordinary, and fateful moment. The revolutionary socialist of Red Week, the man imprisoned for opposing the Libyan war just ten years earlier, had become Italy's prime minister, with the backing of thousands of members of illegal, criminal and violent paramilitary associations. Very soon, the event would be recast as a *revolution* by the regime. Was this, as Gramsci later put it, 'the moment in which an ethical and political system collapses and another is formed with fire and iron'?[32]

BLACK DAYS

Beyond the parades and military salutes, during the time of the 'March', Rome was terrorised for days by thousands of *squadristi*. Socialist buildings were besieged and ransacked all over the city. Most of the violence targeted socialists although some were murdered or beaten up because they were simply in the wrong place at the wrong time. People were killed caught in crossfire, standing at their windows or in doorways, while others were shot dead in the street for reasons which were unclear. One, a thirty-year-old war-wounded veteran, Attilio Battaglini, was shot in the head by Tuscan fascists close to Rome's station at about 2 a.m. He died in hospital soon afterwards.

Despite Mussolini's words to parliament, it simply wasn't true that the fascists had 'held back' during and (in particular) after the March on Rome. Beatings were being carried out by fascists all over the country, as well as in the capital, and the greatest outbreaks of violence took place after Mussolini was appointed prime minister. A new wave of blackshirt raids on trade union and socialist premises and property swept across the peninsula.

In Rome there were attacks on dozens of private dwellings, including those of the communist deputy Nicola Bombacci and the liberal politician Francesco Saverio Nitti.[33] Nitti was a hated figure for fascists, in part because of his 1919 amnesty which allowed many accused of desertion to walk free, but above all thanks to his opposition to the Fiume occupation by D'Annunzio, who dubbed him *cagoia* (an invented word approximating to 'scared shitless' or 'shitty').[34]

A hundred or so armed fascists surrounded Nitti's villa in Via Paolo Farnese in the Prati neighbourhood. Some climbed the walls surrounding the house. Nitti was not there at the time but his house was ransacked. Bombacci's house was also looted, his furniture and books thrown onto the street and burned, and a sign was left on his door saying: 'Flat To

Let'.[35] Bombacci's secretary, Dandolo Lemmi, was also the victim of fascist violence. Recognising him in the street, the fascists cut off his 'long beard' and his hair and forced him to drink half a litre of castor oil. His face was painted white, red and green, and he was paraded around town on a lorry with a card around his neck saying, 'Long live fascism', a cry he was also forced to repeat.[36] It is said that the fascist leader De Bono put an end to this 'spectacle'. Meanwhile the house of Elia Musatti, a Jewish socialist deputy, was ransacked.[37] In total, there were at least nineteen deaths in Rome, in various clashes across the city. Private tragedies accompanied public violence. A woman called Adele Montorzi tried to poison her fiancé because, it was reported, he wouldn't take her to the fascist parade.[38]

Violence and deaths relating to the march were not confined to Rome. In Rivarolo near Genoa on the night of 31 October the home of socialist deputy Clodoaldo Binotti was attacked by fascists, who 'turned it upside down, smashing everything'.[39] In Turin the Camera del Lavoro was invaded by fascists and the *Corriere* reported that 'today the fascists played the Royal March from the central balcony of the Camera del Lavoro, the national anthem and '*Giovinezza*' (a fascist song). Lieutenant Bagnasco spoke to the crowd in the name of the fascists.'[40] It was said that in Turin the future Communist Party leader Palmiro Togliatti narrowly escaped being shot by *squadristi*. In Bologna fascists laid siege to the prison, taking possession of two machine guns and freeing thirty-four inmates. In another raid, an aeroplane was seized and in a further attack on a barracks two fascists were killed. The blackshirts also took control of the train station. A train for Rome was commandeered by 600 blackshirts and a fascist killed himself by mistake with his own gun. In Ravenna during the period of the March on Rome, fascists occupied the prefect's palace and flew fascist symbols from the building. They also attacked the prison, releasing some fascists. Local papers generally supported these activities, showing, once again, what the historian Alessandro Luparini has called 'the conscious, blind abdication of so-called conservative Italy in front of the shameless illegality of the fascists'.[41]

For some, the March on Rome was the final blow to their capacity to resist and continue to live a normal life. Pietro Farini was a socialist deputy (elected by over 70,000 people in November 1919) from the Umbrian industrial town of Terni. He suffered numerous attacks from fascists on his person and on his property in the postwar period. In June 1920 he stood up in parliament and said that: 'If the *carabinieri* and the police come against us bearing arms, we will defend ourselves.'[42] But there was little he, or his supporters, could do in the face of continual assaults from the fascists. Resistance to fascism in Terni was strong, but the fascists eventually crushed even the strongest pockets of anti-fascism. Farini's pharmacy was razed to the ground in an arson attack by *squadristi* – the fire 'lasted from 11 a.m. to 7 p.m., with mad chanting and dancing'.[43] His house was then burnt down after the March on Rome.[44] Soon, the fascist squads would take charge in Terni, driving Farini out of town altogether, despite the force and power of the workers' movement in that factory town. Farini was eventually forced into exile in the USSR.

For the third time in the postwar period, at the time of the March on Rome, the *Avanti!* offices in Milan were attacked, putting the most influential left-wing daily paper out of circulation for over two weeks. Fascists occupied the newspaper building.[45] The bookshop was ransacked. Furniture and typewriters were simply stolen, with the police looking on, and loaded onto lorries. Then the building was set on fire. A small theatre was also destroyed. Those who openly criticised the actions of the fascists in the crowd were taken away to be questioned. Mussolini, it is said, ordered the attack in order to prevent reporting on the events of the march, from the most important socialist newspaper (which he had once edited).[46] He also wanted to hamper the coordination of the Socialist Party and prevent a general strike being called. The paper later gave its own account of the attack in Milan. *Avanti!* was put out of action until 14 November, when it came out in a shortened edition. 'Our factory,' the paper wrote, 'is in ruins.'[47]

REVENGE

Specific flashpoints during the political violence in Rome in late October 1922 were linked to previous clashes. On two occasions in 1921 and 1922 the fascists had come off worse after gun battles with socialists, communists and anarchists near the San Lorenzo neighbourhood in the city, which stood close to the main railway station. The area was laid out on a grid network, and was bristling with socialist institutions and 'subversive' traditions.

On 9 November 1921 fascists fired at railway workers from a train. Many of the residents in San Lorenzo were employed on the railways and an engine driver called Guglielmo Fannetti was killed in those first clashes. Strikes were called, followed by further violence when a group of fascists tried to march through the neighbourhood. When the blackshirts got to Piazza Tiburtina, they 'were greeted by numerous pistol shots, and the fascist Franco Baldini was killed'.[48] Violent street-fighting spread across the city, before the blackshirts decided to leave the capital. *Avanti!* wrote of the 'complete debacle of the "raid" on Rome'.[49] The defence of the neighbourhood had been partly organised by the Arditi del Popolo – a loose grouping of armed, active anti-fascists.

In May 1922, on the anniversary of Italy's entry into the First World War, San Lorenzo was again the focus of fascist activity. The occasion was the second funeral of a controversial war hero, Enrico Toti, a one-legged patriotic cyclist who had attempted to join up with Italian troops during the war. After his death in 1916, he had become a national figure, with statues dedicated to him across the country.[50] It was decided to rebury him in Rome's Verano cemetery.

Toti's second funeral was organised in grand style, and the fascists were ready to take full political advantage. The hero's body passed through various cities (Trieste, Venice, Bologna and Florence) on a slow train heading for Rome. In order to get to the Verano cemetery, the funeral procession needed to pass right by San Lorenzo. For the Arditi del Popolo, the procession, packed with blackshirts, was a perfect target. A ferocious gun battle ensued, causing panic.

After the funeral, crowds who had followed the coffin were attacked again.[51] According to one description: 'From the street and houses of San Lorenzo, there was continuous firing. From many windows there were ceaseless revolver shots … shutters opened and from each one of the windows revolvers were emptied…'[52] One person was killed and ninety injured.[53] According to historians Majanlahti and Osti Guerrazzi: 'The "battle of San Lorenzo" was a bitter defeat for the fascists, and increased the hostility of its leaders towards the capital city.'[54]

Fascist propagandists also claimed that Toti's coffin itself had been shot at. Mussolini, addressing his fascist base, wrote that the blackshirts should 'consider yourselves materially and morally mobilised from this moment on'.[55] Mass arrests (of socialists, anarchists and communists) followed. Over 180 people were picked up, and the socialists accused the police of ransacking their library, ruining over a thousand books.[56] A general strike was called in protest. For many *squadristi*, the March on Rome provided an opportunity for payback for those defeats in the streets. San Lorenzo was a key target. That neighbourhood needed to be taught a lesson.

GIUSEPPE BOTTAI AND THE BATTLE OF SAN LORENZO

General Piola Caselli: 'Do you intend to enter Rome?'

Bottai: 'Exactly.'

General Piola Caselli: 'My advice is that you do not go through San Lorenzo. This could become an order if you do not take this advice.'

Bottai: 'I'm sorry, my route will go through San Lorenzo and I will not change it.'[57]

In 1922, Giuseppe Bottai was a blackshirt leader, operating mainly in the Abruzzo region and in some areas around Lazio. As a fascist deputy he had proudly spat in Francesco Misiano's face during 'the expulsion' in June 1921. During the March on Rome he was at the head of *squadristi* columns which descended on the city and which clashed with anti-fascists around San Lorenzo on 30 October.

In the original plans for the march, Bottai's fascists were to surround San Lorenzo, neutralising any possible resistance there.[58] But after arriving in the station of Tor Sapienza, Bottai declared that he wanted to take his blackshirts *through* San Lorenzo. This was a risky strategy, given past tensions in the area. There were (failed) negotiations via intermediaries, including figures in the Arditi del Popolo (who later denied that these discussions had happened). No cheering crowds were seen here, unlike in other parts of Rome. A journalist reported that: 'The neighbourhood is deserted; windows are closed almost as a sign of hostility.'[59] Almost inevitably, a shoot-out ensued. Newspapers reported a 'battle between fascists and inhabitants'.[60]

A smaller group of fascists entered the grid-like neighbourhood, firing as they went. Missiles – bricks and tiles – were thrown from some of the working-class blocks. General Sanna, whom we have already met as the officer who suppressed the Ancona revolt in

June 1920, arrived on the scene. Machine guns were then used by the Royal Guards and the army, not against the insurgent fascists, but towards residential blocks. A body was found in a doorway, a young man in a pool of blood, still holding an umbrella. Among the fascists there were only a few slight injuries. Further shooting took place around six that evening between soldiers in armoured cars and people inside houses. In response, the Royal Guards fired through the windows of the buildings. *La Stampa* initially claimed there were five dead in the neighbourhood, including one woman; other reports claimed that eight people died that night, while yet others put the figure at thirteen (the number which has most often been settled on subsequently).

Fascist *squadristi* also used the clashes and the context of the March on Rome to settle scores with the Arditi del Popolo (the armed organisation set up by parts of the left to counter fascist violence on the streets). Argo Secondari was an anarchist and war veteran (he volunteered to fight in the war and was awarded three medals for military valour). In 1921 he was one of the Arditi del Popolo's founders. We have two photos of Secondari in uniform. In the first he is in his official army kit – fresh-faced, dignified, perfectly turned out, with a slight moustache. In his second he is just as elegant, but clean-shaven; he wears a polo neck and has a dagger in his belt – the unofficial uniform of the Arditi del Popolo.[61]

Like those of other anti-fascists, Secondari's house in Rome was targeted – in his case on 31 October 1922. Secondari himself was then viciously set upon by ten or so fascists.[62] In July the previous year, he had escaped from a similar attack after his comrades intervened. This time, however, the fascists found him alone. Secondari suffered 'a serious injury to the right part of his brain and concussion', and 'was struck so violently on the head that he remained an invalid for the rest of his life'.[63]

Another house to be attacked that day was of another Arditi del Popolo leader, Giuseppe Mingrino, who had left town to avoid the fate that befell Secondari. Fascists ransacked Mingrino's house and burnt his possessions. They also claimed they had found 'fifty' 'used' bombs.[64] The defeat in San Lorenzo in October 1922 marked the end of the short and turbulent history of the Arditi del Popolo, which was officially disbanded in December 1922. Popular anti-fascist armed resistance would not emerge again on a mass scale in Italy for more than twenty years. Fascism had gained complete control of the streets.

*

Three days after the lights went out in Cremona and Foggia, Mussolini was installed as prime minister. Most of the blackshirts soon began to return home, usually by train, but it was not until 7 November that all the insurgent *squadristi* finally left Rome and the march was over. Less than three years had passed since his electoral humiliation in November 1919, when socialists had printed fake Mussolini death notices, and there were sly rumours that he had thrown himself into one of Milan's canals in despair. Mussolini the anarchist, the socialist, the soldier, the republican, the fascist, the journalist had been replaced (or had merged) with Mussolini the prime minister, statesman and politician. Few people expected him to remain in power for long. Nobody had really believed it would happen at all, until it did.

MUSSOLINI IN POWER

On 16 November 1922, Benito Mussolini stood up in parliament and made his first speech as prime minister. After the debate, deputies would be asked to vote for, or against, his government. It was a speech laced with menace and threat. 'I refused to win too convincingly, and I could have done so. I said to myself that it is wise to act cautiously after a victory ... With 300,000 young people, armed to the teeth, all of them ready in an almost mystical way to follow my orders, I could have punished all those who defamed and incited fascism.'[65]

'I could have,' Mussolini continued, 'made this drab silent hall into a camp [*bivacco*] for my squads.' At this point he was interrupted by applause from his supporters and by a solitary cry, from the bearded, Jewish socialist, Giuseppe Emanuele Modigliani: '*Long Live Parliament, Long Live Parliament.*' Mussolini's reply to Modigliani was brutal. It was also prophetic. He was telling everyone what he was going to do, to them, and to democracy. 'I could have barred the doors of parliament and created a government which was only made up of fascists: but I didn't want to, *at least for now.*'[66] For the historian Salvatore Lupo, Modigliani's words 'fell into a void amidst bewildered servility'.[67]

At this point, 'an icy silence took over the chamber'.[68] Mussolini's threats continued. He had not ordered more beatings and killings, but he *could do so*, at any time. 'Our adversaries stayed in their safe spaces: they went out whenever they wished, they could circulate freely.' For now, he was saying, you can 'freely circulate' (this wasn't true); but this 'freedom' was *entirely in his power*. Giacomo Matteotti, socialist, parliamentarian, lawyer and victim of constant *squadrista* attacks in 1920–22, understood very clearly how threats and actual violence had led to this point. 'There was a strong sense of potential violence,' he said; 'a threat "against all those who were generously spared by fascism during the March of Rome" because only in this way could fascism maintain a majority and keep power against all those who didn't support it.'[69]

Mussolini then asked for 'full powers ... because I want to take full responsibility'. He was being crystal clear that simply managing the old liberal state was not enough. *We* are in power, he was saying, but the violence isn't over; I can turn it on and turn it off when I want to; I could have 'beaten up parliament' but – 'for the moment' – I don't want to.[70]

Giovanni Giolitti, the arch liberal, a hate figure for fascism for years, also fell in behind the new government. After Mussolini's so-called *Discorso del bivacco* ('Speech of the camp') Giolitti was surrounded in parliament by a number of socialists and liberals, calling on him to support parliamentary democracy against the fascists, but he refused to do so. Emilio Lussu, who was in parliament that day, wrote that Giolitti's 'face appeared covered in an impenetrable mask. He looked up and with his long and bony fingers, tapped lightly on the desk.'[71] Pietro Nenni, the republican protagonist of Red Week in Ancona in 1914, who had followed Mussolini briefly into fascism before turning to socialism, wrote in *Avanti!* after Mussolini's speech, that 'bourgeois democracy is dead'. He also harked back, ironically, to Mussolini's republican past, referring to him as 'my old prison comrade'.[72]

Most of the other liberals moved quickly into line, convinced, it seems, that they could control or profit from fascism – or that this was a phenomenon that would not last. They did not take Mussolini at his word: an historic error. Giovanni Amendola was reported as saying 'there is nothing to be frightened of. Mussolini too will get caught in the constitutional toils, and finally we shall have a government.' In the following months and years, Amendola would be attacked by fascists on numerous occasions, ultimately dying from his wounds in 1926 after a vicious beating in Tuscany the previous summer from fifteen or so *squadristi* armed with nail-studded cudgels.[73]

On 17 November 1922, a vote of confidence was held. All, or nearly all, of the big names in parliament backed Mussolini. Giolitti voted in favour, as did Facta, who had tried to stop the March on Rome with the use of the army just weeks earlier. Former prime minister Nitti (another hate figure for fascism) took a stand and abandoned parliament in protest forever.[74] Only a few liberal deputies abstained, including the eighty-year-old Sardinian liberal deputy, Francesco Cocco-Ortu, who had failed to win over the majority of his colleagues to his position.[75] For the anti-fascist Emilio Lussu it felt like the end of a civil war.[76] One side had won and now taken power.[77]

Some liberals understood what was happening, however, outside of parliament. Piero Gobetti, the brilliant Turin-based journalist, intellectual and activist, wrote in November 1922 that: 'The fascist revolution is not a revolution but a coup carried out by an oligarchy.'[78] Gobetti himself would soon fall victim to fascist violence. He was twice beaten by *squadristi* and died in exile, at the age of just twenty-five, in 1926.

A future president of democratic Italy, Giovanni Gronchi, voted in favour of Mussolini in the Lower House, as did one of the most important political figures of post-1945 Italy, Alcide De Gasperi. Both would soon also have reason to regret their actions, like so many others. De Gasperi was forced to undergo an official 'trial' by *squadristi* in 1926 and went into hiding, before being sent to prison the following year. He spent most of the period of the regime working in the Vatican Library. Gronchi, meanwhile, 'withdrew from politics' in the 1920s and 1930s.

*

Mussolini was the youngest prime minister in Italy's history. He claimed to not draw a salary, the beginning of the widely held myth that he did not 'personally' profit from his time in charge of Italy. Soon, on 16 November, he was given the 'full powers' he had requested in specific areas, and took personal control of the Ministry of Foreign Affairs and the Ministry of the Interior. Power was concentrated almost as never before in the hands of one man.

Fascism could do what it wanted, when it wanted, almost without consequences. It now had political power *and* military control. It was pretty clear where the army's sympathies lay. In Mussolini's first government, the minister of war was the military hero Marshall Diaz, and the head of the navy was also in the cabinet. These two powerful military men flanked Mussolini as he sat in parliament, waiting for Italian democrats to effectively seal their own fate by voting in favour of his first government.[79] In short, the army and the navy, which two and half weeks earlier had been asked by the previous prime minister to shoot on the fascists led by Mussolini, were now seemingly his loyal allies.

FREEING AND EMPLOYING THE BLACKSHIRTS: AMNESTY, IMMUNITY AND A NEW MILITIA

Throughout this period Benito Mussolini presented himself as a leader of a violent revolution, as well as the only person who could control the *squadristi*. His message depended on his audience. He had clear ideas about how to consolidate his power and he moved with great speed. A sweeping amnesty was issued on 22 December 1922, less than two months after the March on Rome.[80] It was a long text, but the first part was the most crucial: 'An amnesty is granted for all crimes to be found in the Penal Code, the Military Penal Code and the Naval Penal Code and other laws (including financial measures) committed either by political movements or for political reasons, when they have been carried out *for nationalist reasons*, either indirectly or directly.'[81]

It was clear in the lengthy preamble to the amnesty that this would be applied to one side only, from the recent civil war. For example, the preamble claimed that 'recent events ... have allowed internal divisions to be resolved and have put the nation back in a stable and safe situation'. Crimes had only been committed 'in the heat of the moment'. In a key passage, the text excluded acts which took place in order 'to try to crush the existing order, state organisations and the norms which lie at the base of social interaction'. This was a reference to socialist or trade union agitation and violence. These acts would not fall under the amnesty, but would be met with the full force of the law.

But there was an obvious contradiction here. During the March on Rome fascists had attacked the state itself, and its institutions – prefect palaces, army and police barracks, post offices, telegraph stations, railway stations and airports had all been targeted. How was this to be explained in terms of the amnesty? But those who drew up the decree had an answer. That violence had 'only *appeared*' [emphasis mine] to have been 'hostile to the state, but in reality [it] was inspired by ends which coincided with those of the state, and should be included with those which fall under the amnesty in article 1 of the decree'.[82] It was linguistic gymnastics.

As if things weren't clear enough, the preamble spelled out that 'this formula corresponds to those which, in parliamentary debates, are used to distinguish between the actions of national parties and those of the parties on the other side of the divide'. The circle was closed. The socialists were defined, *by law*, as anti-national, and the fascists as *pro-nation*. Ergo, all violent acts by the former were, simply, crimes. Violent acts by the latter would fall under an amnesty – including murders, rape, beatings, kidnappings, attacks on property. Fascists who had killed others would be released. Illegality was legalised. Legally, therefore, union member Luigi Masin had been taken from his bed in April 1921 and shot by fascists in the middle of the night, in the Polesine countryside, in front of his family, 'in the national interest'.[83]

The amnesty was also to be applied to the police and the army for supposed 'crimes' which were linked to 'keeping public order'. Further amnesties were extended to crimes involving the illegal possession of firearms, something which had often been seen among fascists after the war. It was an ambitious decree: in its own words, it wished to enable 'the liquidation of the past' with the aim of a 'pacification of the country'.[84] The decree was also applied retrospectively. It was signed by the king on 22 December 1922 and countersigned by Mussolini.

Mussolini's amnesty was soon to have an impact on ongoing trials and investigations, including that of the murderers of elected socialist deputy Giuseppe Di Vagno. Politics and the new amnesty quickly intervened in the case connected to this homicide. In December 1922, just over a week after the amnesty was issued, the appeal court decided that the killing of Di Vagno had been 'carried out by young men who were members of the Fascio di Combattimento and determined by a political motive for nationalist reasons'.[85] Shooting a socialist deputy in the back was officially a patriotic act, thanks to the fact that it was carried out by fascists. Di Vagno's killers walked free. Murder had become legal. Local *squadristi* continued to harass his widow (including singing fascist songs under her window) and anybody who visited her in Conversano.

Meanwhile, what was to be done with the *squadristi* themselves – the semi-criminal associations and their thousands of activists which were still very much at large and active across Italy? The fascist squads were officially 'dissolved' on 12 January 1923, although a number continued to operate.[86] Many of these men were then brought into the state machine itself, in a militia called the MSVN. At a stroke, this achieved two objectives. First, the blackshirts were rewarded for their part in the 'Fascist Revolution'. Second, their methods were legitimised, made official, sanctioned. *Squadrista* violence had not been abolished, but became part of the system of law and order in Italy. Previously, democrats and others had appealed – often desperately – to the state for protection *from* squadristi violence. This had sometimes been provided (very grudgingly) either through police guards or by the arrest of *squadristi* themselves. Now, the *squadristi were* the state. Their violence was no longer even technically above the law, it *was* the law.

A parallel or alternative state began to be constructed, with new institutions – a state militia, the Fascist Party itself (Partito Nazionale Fascista – PNF), semi-secret groups of thugs and killers under Mussolini's direct or indirect control, hit squads, a vast political police network to add to that already in place, and a new governing executive-like institution outside of Italy's constitution, known as the Gran Consiglio (which met for the first time on 15–16 December 1922). Fascist violence did not end in October 1922: it changed. Fascism and violence were intertwined and inseparable.

THE MASSACRE OF TURIN
DECEMBER 1922

After the March on Rome, the *squadristi* were off the leash. Even Turin, the bastion of the factory occupations in 1920, and the heart of the workers' movement, a place where many anti-fascists had taken refuge from the blackshirts, was no longer a relatively safe haven.

The seventeenth of December 1922 was a cold, dank, foggy night in Turin. In the working-class neighbourhood of Barriera di Nizza, twenty-two-year-old Francesco Prato, a communist who worked on the trams selling tickets, shot three fascists sometime between 10 p.m.

and midnight. All three fascists were taken to hospital. Two of them, eighteen-year-old engineering student Lucio Bazzani and twenty-seven-year-old railway worker Giuseppe Dresda, were seriously injured. Prato himself was also hit in the leg. Dresda died the following morning, while Bazzani would pass away on the morning of the 19th.

There are at least three versions of the shootings which sparked off the subsequent massacre. A dominant version on the left was that this had nothing to do with politics, but was linked to a dispute over Prato's affair with the daughter of an ex-anarchist-turned-fascist baker.[87] A final version contradicts the official account, claiming instead that it was Prato who was the victim of a fascist ambush. Nobody will ever be able to ascertain exactly what happened. There is no way of telling which of these versions of the facts, if any, are true. Historians are also divided.[88]

Prato was good-looking and an 'elegant dresser'. Some described him as a 'ladies' man', but he was also seen as a 'man of action', who disliked mere political discussion. It was said that he had planted explosives on behalf of the socialists.[89] He was known as part of the armed guard who defended Antonio Gramsci's left-wing newspaper, *L'Ordine Nuovo*. According to one account, Prato was already 'hated by the fascists'.[90]

Prato fled the scene and after initially staying out of sight in a cellar for two days, he was moved to a number of different sympathisers' apartments. He was forced to stay in bed, clutching a pistol the whole time, while his leg wound healed. It was later said that his hiding place was close to a police station. A 'comrade' doctor extracted the bullet from his leg, and fitted him with a cast (the bullet had struck the bone). In February 1923 he was taken secretly to Milan in a taxi (one newspaper claimed he was disguised as a woman) and from there to Switzerland and eventually the USSR. In 1938 he was sent to a gulag after being accused of being a spy. He died there in 1943, and was rehabilitated in 1956.[91] His full story was only revealed in the 1990s, when the Soviet archives were (briefly) opened up.

Massacre

'We wanted to set an example, so that the communists would understand that they cannot attack fascists without consequences'

Piero Brandimarte[92]

As news of the 'clash' between Prato and the fascists broke, numerous fascists began to arrive in Turin from across Italy as soon as 18 December 1922. Many were fresh from the March on Rome and armed with guns and daggers. Socialist Teresa Noce later spoke of 'an explosion of ferocity'.[93] Gramsci described the following days as the final attack on the Turinese working class. It is said that a poster was put up in the city during this time reading: 'We do not cry for our dead, we avenge them. I order the *squadristi* to assemble. The Commander of the Squads: Brandimarte.'[94] Piero Brandimarte was famed for his physical strength. He had won medals in the war for valour and 'sporting achievement', before becoming a *squadrista* leader. He also had an appetite for violence. He was not a great speaker, or a theoretician and, like many fascists who rose to prominence, he seemed to be above all an example of brutish mediocrity. He was twenty-nine years old in December 1922. Under the regime he would go on to hold various high-level roles, including that of general.

After the death of Dresda, the bloodshed began before midday on 18 December at the Camera del Lavoro. Fascists easily broke past passive Royal Guards. Neither the prefect nor the police chief were in the city and the streets were left to the *squadristi*, leading some to call this massacre a 'state massacre'.[95]

A socialist deputy, Vincenzo Pagella, was the first to be beaten up, along with two trade unionists, including Pietro Ferrero, anarchist leader of the metalworkers' union, the FIOM. Ferrero escaped with his life.[96] Late on in the night of 18 December, however, Ferrero was on his bike, close to the Camera del Lavoro, when the fascists attacked him for a second time. It was said that Ferrero's eyes were poked out, and that he was dragged from the back of a car attached to a rope. His corpse was left near a monument to the king.[97]

The next target was Carlo Berruti, a communist railway employee, and a well-known and popular trade unionist and local councillor. He was kidnapped in his workplace, driven to a field and shot five times in the back.[98] Not satisfied, the fascists also ransacked his house. At least another ten murders were to follow, many using similar methods. Gunfire was a part of the acoustic memory of those days. A young mechanic called Vincenzo Stratta, who had been stabbed by the fascists and was in hospital, remembered that 'every so often there were shots … *tin tan*'.[99]

Over three days and nights, squads of armed fascists roamed around the city, on trucks, in cars and on foot, killing at will. Some victims were simply executed. Others were beaten to death. Fascists had numerous bottles of castor oil ready for use. Some of the dead had signs hung around their neck indicating that they were communists, or 'subversive' newspapers scattered around their bodies. By the time the killings had finished, at least eleven people had been murdered, but there were rumours that more had died (on both sides). Brandimarte was said to have carried a list with the names of those to be eliminated. At one point, five journalists from *L'Ordine Nuovo* were lined up against a wall. They thought their time had come. But, for some reason, they were saved. Later, Brandimarte would claim this non-execution was an example of his 'mercy'.

A bar owner was stabbed and shot dead in his bedroom (he was also, it was later alleged, a police informer, something of which his murderers were unaware). Another man was killed on his own doorstep; he had been eating dinner with his wife and two-year-old child. A communist was pulled along the street by his hair, beaten savagely, shot and left to die. He had been cleared of killing a fascist in an earlier trial.

Squadristi patrolled the hospitals looking for those who had escaped with injuries. One man was murdered in his office for making critical remarks about previous killings. Some of those who escaped death found that their lives were ruined. One man was thrown in the Po river and shot at while in the water. He spent eight months in hospital recovering from his injuries, and remained a continual target for fascist violence right through to the 1940s. Although a number of those attacked were high-profile socialists, anarchists and trade unionists, others were not, and some seemed to have been selected for personal reasons.

Meanwhile, Turin witnessed, once again, and for the last time as a socialist and free institution, 'the destruction of the magnificent house of the working class'.[100] For the third time the Camera del Lavoro was razed to the ground.[101] It was 'a picture of the apocalypse ... the windows collapsed and the shutters blown open'.[102] A headline from the *Corriere della Sera* summed up the surreal nature of those times. 'A normal morning in Turin. The Camera del Lavoro has been burnt down.'[103] Fascists threw bombs at the burning building. The tower or lookout post, where 'an enormous red flag', which had flown proudly 'in the period of socialist domination', was also set ablaze. The place had been constructed with the contributions of workers over many years. It contained a theatre, a bar, a meeting room and a library. It was all completely destroyed by fire. 'Nothing was saved.'[104] Throughout all this mayhem, according to Italy's leading newspaper at the time, the city went about its business almost as 'normal'. 'The revenge attacks were carried out in silence, without gatherings, without mass meetings, without fear and alarm.'[105]

Later the same week, the fascist victims Dresda and Bazzani received an elaborate, joint 'fascist' funeral at which Brandimarte was present.[106] On 21 December their bodies were transported through the city for over two hours, accompanied by flowers, an abundance of clergy and 'a forest of banners'. Eight fascist railway workers carried Dresda's coffin, which was draped with the Italian flag, while students carried Bazzani. All the shops in the area were closed. Royal Guards on horseback stood at every street corner. Massimo Rocca, a leading fascist at the time, gave one of the eulogies. He referred to 'the two first [fascist] deaths since the triumph of the fascist revolution', and also voiced criticism of the massacre which followed: 'I don't know if what happened afterwards was necessary ... but perhaps it was inevitable.' Rocca was said to be a personal friend of Berruti (one of the victims) and made a rare reference to the 'dead on the other side of the divide': 'I salute the fallen enemy ... because every victim deserves respect. The events that we have seen show that the fascist revolution is untouchable and before it our enemies must give way. I am a human being, and I hope that the terrible lesson inflicted on our adversary is the last and that these victims will spare us further dead.'[107]

Revenge attacks of which Turin was an extreme example were depicted as both a natural, emotional reaction to the deaths of their *camerati*, but also as the work of an army at war. Some were clearly following orders (*kidnap Berruti and shoot him*, for example). Others were acting on a whim, angry, drunk on power, and on alcohol, and enjoying their omnipotence.

Responsibility, justice, forgetting

The ferocity of the Turin massacre seemed to shock some fascists even. A fascist journalist called Piero Belli called the killings 'A kind of pogrom'.[108] He wrote of 'a city which found itself suddenly without order, without authority, without laws'.[109] Mussolini received letters from supporters who were critical of the killings. Manlio Morgagni wrote of his 'disgust', while pointing out: 'There is nothing more persuasive than a cudgel and a revolver.'[110]

There was an official fascist investigation into the massacre, led by the *squadrista* leader Francesco Giunta and Milan's police chief Giovanni Gasti (the supposed target of the Diana bomb in Milan in 1921). The newly formed Gran Consiglio announced its conclusions in mid-January 1923. The fascist report concluded that: 'The police failed and abdicated its powers completely in favour of action squads.'[111] In the aftermath of the massacre the government replaced both the prefect and police chief. Turin's fascist organisations were officially disbanded, but Brandimarte was left in charge of the supposed 'renewal' of the party in Turin. Not a single person went to trial in the 1920s in relation to the massacre, apart from Prato (in absentia). The Turin massacre was an open wound.

In 1922 and 1924, Piero Brandimarte took full 'credit' for the massacre in two separate press interviews. He called the killings an example of: 'Pure revenge, organised and led by me ... we wanted to inflict a terrible lesson on Torinese subversives.'[112] He claimed that the fascists, at the time, had a list of 3,000 such 'subversives' in the city. Twenty-four of these had been selected – 'our best squads' were chosen and 'justice has been done'. Brandimarte insisted that twenty-two had been killed and that the others would eventually be 'rediscovered in the river Po', or in ditches in the countryside and hills around Turin. He also warned that such a massacre could easily be repeated. The interview also confirmed the existence of illegal 'courts martial'.[113]

Turin's massacre was the signal for many anti-fascists to leave Italy altogether. Nobody felt safe anymore, not even in a socialist stronghold. December 1922 marked a definitive defeat, the end of all hope of a revival of the left in the short term. The revolutionary days of 1919 and 1920, the factory councils, the occupations, the strikes, seemed a distant memory. As the historian Brunello Mantelli put it: 'The worker's movement lost a battle which was at the same time material and symbolic.'[114] Turin's once glorious Camera del Lavoro was now in firm fascist control, and was repaired and reused by the regime.

Silence enveloped the workers' movement and the neighbourhoods where socialism and trade unionism had flourished for years: 'Turin was an oppressed city ... it was impossible to speak out.'[115] This silence, and hidden forms of resistance, would replace open opposition to the regime.[116] 'Fascism was the triumph of silence.'[117]

1923

In February 1923, while working as a court lawyer in Livorno, Giuseppe Emanuele Modigliani was beaten up yet again, 'by a group of fascists' who 'roughed him up'. It was said that around 300 fascists and nationalists were involved: Modigliani was chased out of his own city.[1] Once again, his beard was a target: 'Somebody grabbed his long beard and pulled some of it out, and another covered his face with tomato sauce.'[2] There appeared to be an anti-Semitic element to his targeting. One police report stated: 'We should not forget that Modigliani ... is a Jew and like a good Jew, he uses politics in order to serve his own business interests.'[3]

Veteran socialist Anna Kuliscioff expressed dismay at the constant violence in a letter to her socialist comrade and partner, Filippo Turati: 'How horrible, how humiliating, it is so depressing to live in such a terrible moment in the history of our country! I am also worried, because I am afraid of a fascist attack. At the moment, as the newspapers say, at the very mention of Modigliani's name you will be besieged by blackshirts.'[4]

*

During Red Week in 1914, Emaldi Battista had been one of the leaders of the uprising in Fusignano, in the province of Ravenna. Later, he became the socialist mayor of the town. In January 1923 he was assassinated by fascists, in broad daylight, close to the town hall. Unusually, a trial was held of the two fascists (who were brothers). The family of Battista was represented by Genuzio Bentini, the socialist lawyer who had been in the council chamber during the events of Palazzo d'Accursio. At the trial Bentini addressed the jury:

> I am defending a man who was brutally murdered, without motive.
> He was just 44 years old. I am speaking in the name of a widow and
> orphans who have been thrown into trouble, where once there was
> joy, and into a need for everything – bread, love, help – where once
> they were comfortable. Am I representing this situation of damage
> and pain in this case? In the name of damage and pain I would
> be correct in asking you for an exemplary verdict, but the voice of
> justice is stronger than those which remind us of tears or robbery.
> I am asking you for more than I would give myself, if I was in your
> place.[5]

The two fascist murderers were given sentences of ten and eleven years, but they served just a fraction of this time thanks to Mussolini's 1922 amnesty.[6]

Tito Oro Nobili, a well-educated lawyer, dressed elegantly and, in his youth, sported a magnificent moustache. He was one of the leading socialists in the factory town of Terni. In 1920 he was elected as the first socialist mayor of Terni and then to parliament in 1921. Oro Nobili was targeted by the new fascist movement and attacked numerous times – some have said on at least fifteen occasions between 1921 and 1922 – making his life intolerable.[7] In 1923 Oro Nobili's legal office was ransacked and documents burnt by blackshirts in 1923, while his home in Terni was also raided. It reached the point that he could no longer set foot in the entire region of Umbria without being attacked. Often he was most vulnerable while working in law courts. On one occasion in Rieti, he was 'insulted and provoked in the street and, once he was in the [railway] station, he was ferociously attacked and left unconscious in the waiting room'.[8]

Soon, Oro Nobili was finally forced out of Terni for good. Like many other 'refugees' from political violence at the time, he moved to the relative safety of Rome. Writing in *Avanti!*, he addressed his base in Terni:

> By the time that you read this ... I will no longer be a citizen of
> Terni ... this decision, which I have been contemplating for a long

time, and which is entirely in opposition to my own interests, was
the only one which was able to preserve my spirits and a sense
of tranquillity for you – so that the incidents which would have
taken place thanks to my defence of my [socialist] faith would
not disturb your lives. My decision is a sign of affection for you
and the city ... I will continue, as an outsider, to consider myself
as your fellow citizen and I will try and defend your city when
I can.[9]

He was not entirely safe in the capital, however, where he was
persecuted by the police and fascists, and where he was attacked
outside parliament. In 1923 Oro Nobili nonetheless rose to the top of
the Socialist Party (which by then had split yet again) – and was its
secretary until 1925.

THE PALAZZO D'ACCURSIO TRIAL, 1923

In the aftermath of the violent clashes and deaths of 21 November 1920
in Bologna there had been a mass round-up, with some 331 arrests of
whom all but nine were soon released.[10] No fascists were arrested, or
even questioned.[11] This was, from the very beginning, a one-way and
highly politicised investigation, backed by a powerful conspiracy theory.
The conductor of all this was the Prefect of Bologna – Luigi Poli. As
the historian N. S. Onofri has written: 'For Poli, those who were guilty
were all on the left. He organised a witch hunt against the socialists and
invented three charges or crimes from that day: that they wanted to
murder the opposition ... that they had attacked the police, and that
they had tried to start a revolution.'[12]

After a lengthy and difficult investigation, a number of men were
sent for trial. Armando Cocchi, Teodorico Frattini, Vittorio Martelli
and Pio Pizzirani were all absent and on the run, although Frattini was
later captured. Meanwhile, Ettore Bidone, Nerino Dardi, Teodorico
Frattini, Renato Gaiani, Angelo Galli, Alfredo Gelosi, Corrado Pini,
Mauro Raimondi, Abramo Roncaglia and Pietro Venturi all remained
in prison for over two years awaiting trial. Despite the fact that the
violence and deaths all occurred in broad daylight in the central square
of the city and inside the town hall in front of numerous witnesses,
collecting evidence proved to be extremely problematic.

When the police turned up at Vittorio Martelli's house in Bologna in 1920, his wife said that she had no idea where he was. They searched everywhere, seizing money, cheques and other items. The discovery of cheques was immediately splashed across the newspapers and referred to as 'Bolshevik gold'. The *Corriere della Sera* called Martelli: 'One of the most important leaders of local Bolshevism.'[13] Martelli and Cocchi's escape to San Marino was widely seen as proof of their guilt, and they were unable to defend themselves publicly, although Martelli wrote a letter, published in the press, detailing the origins of the money.[14]

Other figures from 20 November were also said to be hiding out in San Marino, or to have passed through there. Armando Cocchi had been secretary of Bologna's Socialist Party at the time of the events in Palazzo d'Accursio. He was sacked from his job in a bank while in San Marino. Cocchi had also been the first secretary of the 'Lega proletaria fra mutilati, invalidi, reduci, orfani e vedove di guerra' in Bologna, a socialist veteran's association which pushed anti-war propaganda and assisted ex-soldiers and their families.[15] Much was made in the press and at the subsequent trial (where Cocchi would be tried in absentia) of this organisation, and it was claimed that Cocchi hated Giordani, the councillor shot dead on 20 November, because of his support for patriotic commemorations and the war. In April 1921 Cocchi left the mountain republic, again secretly, and made the long and difficult journey all the way to the USSR. Pio Pizzirani, the other fugitive, also went into exile in the USSR. Meanwhile, the police claimed that grenades and guns had been found in a room next to the council chamber, conveniently wrapped in anarchist and socialist newspapers, which also, they said, carried Martelli's home address.

The authorities tried to extradite Martelli, Cocchi and others from San Marino, and there were threats of fascist raids on the Republic, but all this was too late – Martelli and Cocchi were long gone. Some said that Martelli had escaped dressed as a priest (or in another version in a 'wooden box').[16] The fact that three of the central figures in the events surrounding the Palazzo d'Accursio massacre had left Italy before the trial, and that two had finished up in the Soviet Union, was proof to many of a 'Bolshevik plot'.

By 1923, when the trial of the events of the Piazzale and Palazzo d'Accursio was held, Mussolini was in power. Fascism was anxious to cement its version of its own rise, and make the 'bestial' and 'violent' label stick to the socialists. The Palazzo d'Accursio – or Giordani trial – was a perfect vehicle for this, although the big socialist names – the two mayors, Gnudi and Zanardi – were only present as witnesses, rather than in the dock.[17]

Prison was particularly difficult for a distinguished surgeon and expert on pregnancy and childbirth, Ettore Bidone, who was already fifty-six years old (but 'looked seventy', according to the *Corriere della Sera*, and was 'trembling' in the dock) by the time the trial began. He denied everything. Giordani had died in Bidone's arms, although there was some debate as to who had, in reality, heard Giordani's final words. Bidone's account of the tragedy brought many to tears. The prosecutor did not call for him to be found guilty in his summing up, asking the jury to allow him to return to his medical work and his family. Bidone cried in the courtroom on hearing this speech. Nonetheless, he was subsequently banned from practising as a doctor, despite being cleared on all charges.[18]

The key daily newspapers ran extensive reports, and there was a long procession of witnesses which included some socialist councillors elected in 1920, opposition councillors, and numerous journalists, as well as many council officials, the ex-police chief and prefect and many others. It was a dramatic trial and those who participated were under extreme pressure. One of the witnesses in the trial attempted to kill himself on New Year's Eve.[19]

The prosecution – both in the investigation documents and during the trial itself – looked to paint a picture of bloodthirsty 'Bolsheviks' who had seized control of democratic institutions through violence and intimidation, in the wake of massive social unrest. Their version of events saw the socialists preparing for 21 November with the stockpiling of bombs and guns. This part of the case was not difficult to prove. It was argued – pushing things further – that there was a pre-conceived plan to fire both on the crowd and to 'eliminate' the minority councillors. The evidence here was much flimsier. The idea of a political motive was a problem for the prosecution, as this could have led to the application of various amnesties the fascists had put in place to protect their own interests. So, the trial itself was used for political propaganda, while the legal aspects were played down. It was, without doubt, a 'political trial'.[20]

The prosecution also looked to omit the fascists from the story altogether. No fascists were on trial, and none testified, although a leading fascist (Dino Grandi) was among the legal team, and gave a famous speech as part of the prosecution summing up which was cited in many future fascist publications.[21] According to the prosecution, the main conspirators were Armando Cocchi, Vittorio Martelli and Pio Passerani – the three men who were still on the run and who were tried in just one day in a second trial – plus Pietro Venturi, who was in the dock.

Gnudi – the 'Mayor for an Hour' in 1920 – was only called to the trial as a witness on 2 February 1923. The atmosphere was, to say the least, intimidating. There were attempts to physically attack him while he waited to give evidence.[22] He backed the theory of an external shooter who had supposedly murdered Giordani, and who had allegedly entered the room during the confused period following the violence in the piazza. Gnudi also said that the shooting in the piazza had come from the bar where the fascists had gathered. A request to read out the posters produced by Gnudi after 21 November was refused by the president of the court, who instead made reference to Gnudi's speech that day, and his support for the Russian Revolution.[23]

But what was lacking was hard evidence, especially with regards to the death of Giordani. Nobody could identify with any certainty the person or persons who shot Giordani, although many appeared to have seen him/them fire a gun/guns. Desperation had set in towards the end of the investigation, with clearly absurd witnesses popping up in prison with prefabricated stories and a strange series of 'overhearings' in cells and on trains.

There was no serious attempt to describe how the other ten people in the piazza died. None of the relatives of the 'other' ten dead were allowed to take the stage at the trial, while Giordani's widow and mother were ever-present, and his children were often mentioned. During the trial, fascist groups from Bologna met Rina Giordani and Giordani's mother, father and a cousin at the station in Milan and accompanied them to the courtroom, 'where they gave fascist salutes'.[24]

In a farcical ending to a long legal process, most of the accused were released, and the prosecutor refused even to ask for guilty verdicts in many cases. Only one person in the first trial was given a relatively long sentence – thirteen years. But the three men on the run had no chance. They had forfeited their chance to any proper defence, and were quickly given life sentences in a second, speedy, closed trial. They were never to serve this time. The men on the run were a gift to the prosecution, and the press, as almost any crime could be laid at their door, and there was no need to produce much evidence against them, as the jury were not involved in their verdict. Ennio Gnudi was never brought to trial although he was accused of being a political ringleader for the violence (along with ex-mayor Zanardi). Gnudi's resignation and that of the council seemed to confirm their collective political guilt.

FASCIST DEMOCRACY

On 21 January 1923, more than two years after the dramatic events in the piazza and the palazzo, new local elections were held in Bologna. The socialists (who had split three ways by then) did not even put up any candidates. They decided to abstain due to the violence and intimidation surrounding the vote. The fascists as part of a 'bloc' swept the board (they had won precisely 0 seats in 1920) and the turnout was high – with over 67 per cent voting, despite the snow that day.[25] Socialist representation had gone from forty-four seats to none. Umberto Puppini (also an opposition councillor in 1920) was elected mayor – the first 'elected' mayor after Gnudi and the last to take power before fascism abolished local democracy altogether.[26]

On the day the new administration took office, Arpinati and other fascists laid a wreath at the bust to Giulio Giordani. The room inside Palazzo D'Accursio was packed, and the crowd included Giordani's mother and his son, who was holding a 'fascist flag'. A further two metal wreaths (one in bronze, from the ex-soldier's association) and one in gold (from the fascists) were placed on the seat where Giordani had been killed in 1920. Oviglio was elected president of the provincial council, which had never taken office after the socialist victory in 1920. In his acceptance speech he 'evoked with emotion the terrible day of 21 November 1920 and the figure of Giordani the martyr'.[27] A letter from Mussolini was read out. At one point Councillor Manaresi, another who had been in the council chamber in 1920, cried out: 'For our unforgettable Giulio Giordani … hip hip hurray.' The minutes then reported that 'everybody there responded with a fascist chant'.[28] After Puppini, there would only be centrally appointed, unelected 'mayors', from 1926 right through until 1945.

1924

THE LAST ELECTIONS, APRIL 1924

A new electoral law was passed in 1923. It was called the Acerbo Law. It guaranteed a huge majority to a list which won the largest share of the vote. With a united fascist bloc and a divided and weakened opposition, the result was a foregone conclusion. By 1924 the electoral system had been reduced to a farce. Violence and intimidation were the order of the day. Many opposition politicians were already in exile, or hiding, including liberals and Catholics. It was impossible to run a normal campaign. Meetings were broken up, a socialist candidate was assassinated, polling booths were surrounded by *squadristi*. It was to be the last chance for Italians to vote for more than twenty years. Mussolini took control of parliament with 374 seats, while the two socialist parties won forty-six seats between them, and the communists elected nineteen deputies.

30 MAY 1924

It was a very different parliamentary chamber in 1924 – dominated by fascists – to that which had taken shape after the previous elections. But, as in 1921, socialist deputy Giacomo Matteotti stood up to make another, equally angry speech. He had not been cowed by the threats, beatings and kidnappings over the last four years, and spoke in great detail of the illegality and violence in which the recent elections had been held. In a break with past practice, there was a proposal on the table to validate every candidate's election en bloc. Previously, each individual case, where there were signs that the rules or the law had been broken, was looked at on its own merits. Matteotti turned this strategy on his head. He claimed that the entire election had been illegitimate.

Throughout his speech, Matteotti was continually interrupted by his fascist opponents, with shouted veiled and explicit threats. The president of the chamber struggled to stay neutral, asking Matteotti not to 'provoke' the deputies, and telling him to speak 'prudently'.[1] Matteotti replied: 'I shall speak neither prudently nor imprudently, but according to parliamentary law.'[2] A number of deputies in the chamber were furious. Edoardo Torre, a fascist, said: 'Enough of this! ... What are we doing here? ... Must we tolerate these insults? You should be under house arrest, not in parliament.' Matteotti was also told to 'Go to Russia!' Matteotti concluded his speech saying: 'We defend the freedom and sovereignty of the Italian people and ... we demand that these elections marked by violence be referred to the election committee.'[3] It was not a long speech, but it had taken him ninety minutes to complete. It was also his last speech. He was thirty-nine years old and was married with three children, all of them under six years old.

10 JUNE 1924

As he sat down in parliament on the 30 May, Matteotti is said to have told a fellow deputy: 'I have made my speech – now you can prepare my funeral oration.'[4] Whether this is true or not, it is certainly a key part of the considerable mythology which surrounds the events that followed.

Eleven days later, Matteotti was walking along the banks of the Tiber in Rome. It was 4.40 in the afternoon. A six-seater black Lancia containing at least five fascists began to follow him. All had fought in the war (one had been convicted of desertion) and all had killed since the conflict ended. One, Albino Volpi, according to some sources, had been Mussolini's bodyguard for a time.[5] All were part of a secret fascist hit-squad known colloquially as the CEKA. The leading member was a *squadrista* named Amerigo Dumini, who was born in the USA and mainly operated in Florence. Dumini was a violent man. It was said – perhaps apocryphally – that he would introduce himself in this way: 'Dumini: 11 murders!' The others were all fascist thugs: violent professionals. Many had spent time in jail.

It was a swelteringly hot day, and the men had been waiting in the vehicle for some time, chain-smoking and sweating. Matteotti hadn't noticed the car. Three of the men jumped out and seized him. He was punched hard in the face and then kicked and bundled into the car. There was a furious struggle and a window was broken. As the Lancia drove off, one of the gang struggled to climb back in.

Soon afterwards, Matteotti was almost certainly stabbed to death. Huge blood stains were later seen across the back of the car. The vehicle drove out of the capital. When darkness came, the men stripped Matteotti down to his underpants and shirt and buried him in a shallow grave in woods twenty kilometres or so out of Rome in a place called Quartarella. They used car tools to dig a hole. His body was stuffed into the ground, folded over. Dumini then drove back to Rome in the blood-stained car, and parked it, somewhat incredibly, in the courtyard of the Interior Ministry. He knew that he could not leave the car in the open. A plan was hatched to move the vehicle to the private garage of the journalist Nello Quilici, friend of Italo Balbo, who apparently knew nothing about what had happened in the car that day. Some claimed afterwards that it had all been an accident; others that the plan was always to kill Matteotti. But the fact was that an elected deputy had been seized and killed, in broad daylight, by fascists, in the centre of Italy's capital city.

It was not long before Matteotti's absence was noted. He had been the subject of violence and threats on numerous occasions during and after the war. His wife, Velia, was distraught. When on 11 June socialist deputy Modigliani went to report Matteotti missing, the police chief apparently told him that he was already aware of Matteotti's 'murder'. Mussolini met briefly with Velia Matteotti days later, on 13 June, and he proceeded to lie to her, claiming that he knew nothing about her husband's disappearance. On that day the Socialist Party newspaper *La Giustizia*, led with the headline: 'Political brigandage in the centre of the capital in broad daylight. The Secretary of the Socialist Unitary Party attacked and kidnapped in a car.'[6]

Spontaneous demonstrations broke out across the country. Velia was photographed kneeling at the spot where her husband had been snatched, her small son placing flowers beside her. Despite the power the fascists held in the country at this point, there was widespread outrage, as news filtered through that Matteotti had been kidnapped and killed. Around 130 socialist and opposition MPs met and decided on their course of action. They agreed they would abandon parliament altogether and gather separately to protest his disappearance.

Matteotti's murderers had been sloppy and there were numerous eyewitnesses to the abduction, with some even noting the car's number plate. Between 12 and 28 June, Dumini and Volpi and two other members of the hit squad were arrested. Cesare Rossi was Mussolini's chief press officer at the time. He had organised some of the political violence in the capital in 1923–24, directed against opposition figures and dissident fascists, and carried out by the CEKA. Many of the connections from the Matteotti gang led to him. He was arrested as part of the investigation and in order to try and save himself he decided to counterattack, issuing and publishing a memorandum blaming Mussolini directly for the murder.

Cesare Rossi's 'declarations' were explosive. 'What we are dealing with here, is a political murder, carried out, obviously, by the State itself.'[7] Rossi was clear: Mussolini was directly responsible for what had happened – 'Everything that happened was thanks to his direct desire: the Duce either approved specific actions, or he was complicit in them.'[8] Rossi's testimony was particularly dangerous for Mussolini, as it came from a senior insider, and it provided evidence of a direct link between the murder and Il Duce.

The search for Matteotti (or his body) continued. It was said that Tito Zaniboni, a socialist who would later plan to assassinate Mussolini, had a number of graves dug up in Rome's Verano cemetery in a fruitless quest for Matteotti's body. It would be two months before his corpse was 'discovered' – on 16 August, when the vast majority of Italians were on holiday. By then the story held Italy transfixed. A famous photo showed Matteotti's body being carried away in a wooden coffin by officials, one of whom was covering his mouth and nose with a handkerchief in order to hold back the stench. Matteotti's wedding ring was missing, and it was not clear what had happened to his passport. The murder had led to the greatest – and only – crisis experienced by Mussolini's regime before the 1940s. Matteotti's assassination turned out to be a tactical error, but it was not a catastrophic one.

*

Matteotti's funeral was a major challenge to the regime, and the fascists did everything they could to stop it becoming a mass protest. 'A huge crowd gathered in Fratta Polesine, Matteotti's home town, while there were incidents between fascists and anti-fascists in many areas.'[9] His grave would be guarded for the next two decades.

Mussolini's authority drained away, for a time, in the spring and summer of 1924. But the opposition was too weak to act decisively; the workers' movement had been crushed, and there was no leadership. As Mack Smith writes: 'the squads had done their job of intimidation only too well'.[10] Mussolini himself noted that there were now seventeen different groups in opposition to his government. In the end, in perhaps his most pivotal act, Mussolini took full control. No other fascists were strong enough or willing to challenge Mussolini's role. He filled his own power vacuum.

It was time to create a dictatorship. In a key speech, reminiscent of the one he delivered after the March on Rome, Mussolini told his audience that *he* was in charge; that *he* took political responsibility for the violence. It is a speech now quoted in every book about Mussolini and fascism. 'Political, moral and historic responsibility,' Mussolini said, 'for what happened is *mine and mine alone* … if a few mangled phrases are enough to hang a man, then get out the gallows and the rope. If fascism was just castor oil and cudgels and not a superb passion shared by the best of Italian youth, it is my fault. If all of the violence was a result of a specific historic, political and moral climate, I have created that climate with propaganda since the intervention.'[11]

There would be no further serious challenge to Mussolini. After every election, traditionally, a popular booklet had been produced with photos and potted biographies of the deputies. In 1924 the communists would not even provide photos to the editor of this volume for fear of police persecution and fascist violence. The parliamentary booklet for 1924 was eventually published, but by then Matteotti was dead. In its introduction the booklet was coy about the facts. It spoke of 'the Matteotti misdeed' and 'the tragic disappearance of Deputy Matteotti', as if he had suffered a heart attack or been run over by a bus.[12] But the individual biographical entry for Matteotti was more hard-hitting, describing the kidnap and murder as an '*L'esecrando delitto*' ('abhorrent murder').[13]

Meanwhile, as fascist power increased, so the past could be moulded to fit the needs of the present. In Florence, a huge and unprecedented trial was about to take place related to the violent events in Empoli in

March 1921. The judicial investigation into the 'Massacre of Empoli' was completed by September 1922 and covered an almost incredible number of accused – some 217 people. Three of these died during the investigation itself (of 'natural causes'), 74 were cleared before trial and 133 were sent to trial – and another death reduced this number to 132.[14] Five leading figures remained on the run. It would be one of the most extraordinary legal events in Italian history; yet today, it is almost completely forgotten.

SHOW TRIAL: THE 'MASSACRE OF EMPOLI' FLORENCE, 1924

'The spectacle of these huge cages full of prisoners is truly extraordinary.'

Ercole Moggi[15]

'Truth was … more or less tolerated. But now it is tolerated no longer.'

Ignazio Silone[16]

It was such a big event that the building itself was too small to host it. There were 132 accused, but where were they to be kept, and how could they even fit inside the courtroom? The 'super-trial' opened in Florence's magnificent Court of Assizes in Palazzo Buonatalenti in May 1924 – some forty months after the events in Empoli. Mussolini's regime wanted to depict events in Empoli as born of wild, uncontrollable fury. But it also needed to paint the aggressors as motivated by political ideology, as cold-blooded 'Bolshevik killers'. These two interpretations were not always compatible, especially in strictly legal terms, but they both served a purpose.

With such a large number of accused, the authorities faced logistical problems. It was decided, given the distance from the city's prison, that a new small, special 'prison' would be created inside the law court building, to house the accused – apart from the only three women on trial.[17] A kitchen was set up in the courtyard of the palace, and the smell of 'prison soup' drifted into the courtroom. Inside, the prison cage designed to hold the accused for normal trials proved far too small. A huge new cage with 'large iron bars'[18] covering the rest of the vast room was constructed. It was, according to the *Corriere della Sera*, the biggest such cage ever built for a Corte d'Assise. There were five rows of steps inside the cage, with numbered sitting places, allowing for the jury to see each person individually, as in a football stadium, or a theatre. The accused were referred to by their number. A complete roll call took two hours. Many were in chains which clanked as they walked. A special cage within a cage was reserved for two men (who also had the 'privilege' of being kept in the main city prison), one of whom had escaped from prison and avoided recapture for two years. These men were under protection, as they had confessed and implicated others. One also had tuberculosis and was dying. His 'raking coughs' were reported in the courtroom, and he was depicted as seeming like a kind of zombie.

103 hearings

It all (finally) began at 8.30 in the morning on 8 May 1924. Ten at a time, chained together in pairs, the accused were brought into the courtroom. Then a 'flock of lawyers' – of all ages, shapes, sizes and experience – appeared; some were famous socialist lawyers (such as Ferdinando Targetti and Dino Lattes), others simple jobbing solicitors who often had a number of defendants to deal with.[19] According to the journalist from *La Stampa*, everyone's gaze immediately fell upon the three women, guarded separately by *carabinieri*, and transported to court from the women's prison every day.

Each jury member was given a booklet with the photos of all the 132 people in the cage, to 'avoid confusion'. Two pages were dedicated to each person. Space was left for taking notes. This, once again, was unique to the trial. These booklets were to be left in the courtroom overnight.

As it opened, one journalist predicted the trial would last two and half months. By day two he had revised this upwards to four months. Some 540 witnesses were eventually heard and 103 hearings eventually took place. It was called: 'The biggest trial ever held in an Assize Court.'[20] The prosecutor's summing up alone took seventeen days. Jury members, each one of which required a vote, had 4,000 or so questions to decide upon – a series of yes or no responses which would decide the fate of the accused.[21]

'La Cinquantaccia': the construction of a monster

By the time the trial started, many of the stories from Empoli in March 1921 had already entered into popular myth. One woman in particular became the most infamous figure of the whole process. She was called Ginevra Innocenti and was often referred to by a supposed sinister nickname (which was hard to decipher) 'La Cinquantaccia'. One of the journalists on the case admitted that he had no idea what this nickname meant, but it certainly sounded bad.[22] It might be roughly translated as the 'bad fifty-year-old one'.

On 28 May 1924 it was Ginevra's turn to testify. Journalists afterwards made much of her physical appearance and clothing. For *La Nazione*, she 'dresses badly, seems slovenly ... and seems not to care [that that] creates in everyone a sense of repugnance'.[23] The *Corriere* described her as: 'A woman with a sinister face and a shrouded expression.'[24] The president of the court greeted her as if she had already been found guilty: 'It is said that you don't just talk too much, but you also use your hands too much,' and referred to her with barely suppressed disdain as '*donnina*' ('little woman'). It was pretty clear that the president of the court was not exactly acting as an impartial arbiter.[25] Innocenti did not fit female stereotypes of the time. She had a criminal record, which included crimes relating to violence and the use of weapons (much was made of this in the courtroom and in the reporting of the case). Moreover, she was accused of having called upon others to cut off one of the ears of one of the dead (or having bitten it off herself) and then to have cooked it for her daughter (who had supposedly eaten it). It later turned out that she didn't even have a daughter. This incredible accusation came from a combination of eye witnesses, and an analysis of the autopsy carried out on the victim. It was a story that quickly captured the public imagination. Who was this monster, this female beast? As Innocenti's short time in the dock came to an end, one jury member enquired: 'Was the ear found?' The president of the court replied: 'It is said that someone ate it...'[26]

Innocenti's lawyer was appointed by the court, and did his best. He described the ear eating story as 'a legend, an invention' and tried to gain sympathy for her by pointing out that one of her sons had fought in the war, and another was a fascist – but it was an impossible task. She was given an extremely long sentence of twenty-eight years and six months in the first instance – from which four years and three months was deducted for an amnesty, as well as the time she had already spent in prison – leaving a final sentence of twenty-one years and six months. There were rumours that she had been beaten and mistreated in prison. One of her sons – who was also arrested – had died in jail in August 1921. Jaurès Busoni, another of the accused, stated that she was innocent, 'that woman ... who had a criminal record ... and a strange nickname ... which perhaps caused her to be found guilty ... "*la Cinquantaccia*" was a hapless person who had never got involved in politics, and wasn't even there when the events she was accused of took place'.[27] She was never released, and died behind bars in Trani, in the south of Italy, in the 1930s.[28]

Exemplary sentences: October 1924

In the end, the jury decided that the murders had *not* been carried out for their own sake (something that the prosecutors had called for – in the legal language of the time 'purely due to an evil impulse' – which would have carried a life sentence) but that they did indeed have a political motive. Yet the prosecutors also tried to exclude the convictions from some of the various amnesties reserved for political crimes; they argued that this was legally appropriate due to the 'level' of the violence carried out and who it was directed at. 'The crimes were not political ones given the violence and the anger which was inflicted on the poor sailors and *carabinieri*.'[29]

On 31 October 1924, after five months, the 'super' trial came to an end. Ninety-two people were found guilty. Hundreds of years of sentences were handed down. A further, speedy trial, without a jury, quickly condemned the five men still on the run, who were all given life sentences on 3 November 1924.[30] Communist Party member Giovanni Morelli was one of the five; he was just twenty-two at the time of the attack. The others were Adolfo Sandonnini, Dario Parri, Raimondo Cioni, and Vasco Ramagli.[31]

REVENGE AND A SOCIALIST MARTYR

In September 1924 a man called Giovanni Corvi shot dead Armando Casalini, a fascist deputy, on a tram in Rome, in front of Casalini's daughter (he had four other children).[32] Illustrated newspapers carried illustrations of Corvi, with a suit and red tie, shooting at Casalini as his daughter clung on to him. Corvi was said to have cried out '*vendetta per Matteotti*' ('revenge for Matteotti') as he fired his gun.

Less than a month had passed since the discovery of Matteotti's body. Corvi knew Casalini personally. He said that he had been offended by Casalini's supposed insult to Matteotti's memory when he had used a broom to 'commemorate' the dead socialist.[33] Casalini was from Forlì, close to where Mussolini grew up, and he had been a republican before moving over to the fascists. During Red Week in 1914, Casalini had spoken to the insurrectionary crowd in Forlì on at least two occasions and had 'incited the crowd to continue with their strike' when it had been called off.[34] On the sixth anniversary of Red Week in 1920 Casalini had made another speech in Ancona.[35] In the traditional book of parliamentary biographies, a page on Casalini appeared despite the fact that he was already dead, and it was stated that he had been murdered in revenge for Matteotti. Two deputies elected in 1924 had been murdered in Rome.

Corvi, who was twenty-six years old at the time of the murder, was described in the press as a 'communist carpenter'. He had fought in one of the bloodiest battles of the First World War. Corvi's lawyer advised a defence that pleaded insanity.[36] Rather surprisingly, this worked, and to the shock of some newspapers, he was cleared at the subsequent trial and then interned in various psychiatric hospitals. But he was still persecuted and tortured. There were reports that he was forced to drink boiling water and his toenails were pulled out.[37] In effect, the Casalini murder helped the fascists to move on from Matteotti. They were able to arrange the usual elaborate funeral and commemorations for their dead colleague. Casalini's murder also led to further violence against anti-fascists and others.

Meanwhile, Italian socialism had found its most powerful and durable martyr in Matteotti. As Silone wrote, 'even a corpse can go on whispering "No! No! No!" with a persistence and obstinacy that only certain corpses are capable of. How can you silence a corpse?'[38] Velia Matteotti became a living personification of martyrdom, a widow whose very presence was testimony to the murder of her husband. The regime was desperate to keep her out of sight. In the end, she was both threatened and paid off. Statues and monuments were dedicated to Matteotti across the world (but not in Italy), as were campaigns for justice, buildings and commemorations.[39] In secret, anti-fascists carried small 'saint-card' photos of Matteotti in their wallets, or built impromptu shrines in their houses. In Genoa, workers wore badges bearing the initials of the company they worked for – 'OM' – which was also a reference to 'Onorevole Matteotti' ('Honourable Matteotti').[40] Many were deeply affected by Matteotti's 'sacrifice'.

Trying to Kill Mussolini
1925–26

Many Italians wanted to see Mussolini face punishment for what they saw as his crimes, and after the Matteotti murder in 1924, some went further and began to put in place plans to kill Italy's prime minister. Avenging Matteotti became something of an obsession for anti-fascists, and not just in Italy. Between 4 November 1925 and 31 October 1926 there were three attempts on Mussolini's life and one foiled plot. Il Duce was shot at on two occasions, and hit once. A bomb was thrown at his car. He escaped from all this with little more than a scratch on his nose.

'WHY WAS THE FATAL AND LIBERATING SHOT NOT FIRED?' – TITO ZANIBONI

On 4 November 1925, at 5 a.m., the seventh anniversary of Italy's victory in the war, a tall, thin, distinguished-looking man with perfect hair and moustache, checked into the Hotel Dragoni in the centre of Rome. He was wearing a uniform adorned with war medals (three silver and two bronze Italian medals and the British Military Cross) and carrying a long thin bag. It was the same hotel that Matteotti's killers had used in June 1924. The man had parked a car with supplies nearby. His name was Tito Zaniboni. He had supported Italy's entry into war in 1915, and had even written for Mussolini's newspaper *Il Popolo d'Italia*. In 1921, he successfully stood for the Socialist Party for parliament. Historian Adrian Lyttelton has called him 'a romantically inclined socialist ex-officer and deputy'.[1] His seven interventions in parliament were all on fairly trivial issues, such as that of frozen meat. Nothing in his past suggested he was a possible assassin.

It was the Matteotti murder which seems to have pushed Zaniboni to the edge. As we have seen, he had some graves dug up in Rome's Verano cemetery in 1924 looking for Matteotti's body. Zaniboni soon began to look for allies in a plot against Mussolini. He was a Freemason, and he found some willing to listen to him among his fellow masons, including a general called Luigi Capello, who had been held responsible by some for the 1917 military disaster at Caporetto. But both men were easy prey for a spy and agent provocateur called Carlo Quaglia, who cleverly encouraged and controlled this 'assassination plot'.

The Hotel Dragoni looked out onto a balcony of Palazzo Chigi, from where Mussolini was due to speak on 4 November 1925. Zaniboni gave a false name and went up to Room 90 on the fifth floor. Mussolini was scheduled for around midday. At 9 a.m. the police arrived. They 'found' a rifle in the cupboard, and saw that Zaniboni had already cut a hole in the window blind through which to shoot. Capello was picked up in Turin. There was never any chance of this non-attempt being successful. Mussolini made his speech, making reference to the 'plot': 'If I had been hit from this balcony, it would not have been a dictator who was shot, but a servant of the Italian people.'[2] Zaniboni was unrepentant. 'In truth I did nothing, but if you had asked me if I was sorry to have done nothing, I would have replied: No.'[3] He was also sure that he would have succeeded in his plan, if given the chance: 'I could not have missed with that shot.'[4] Police chief Guido Leto later described him as 'a nationally famous shot'.[5]

This was not how the story was presented to the Italian public, however. Zaniboni's 'attempt' was depicted as a high-level masonic plot, foiled by brilliant police work. In 1925 Italy's Freemasons had become a major target for fascist violence and repression. A law was passed effectively banning freemasonry: leading masons were arrested and many sent to internal exile. Lodges were closed down. In Florence and elsewhere, *squadristi* attacked the homes of well-known masons, killing a number of people. The war on masonry had been a constant theme of Mussolini's career, before and during fascism, yet many leading fascists had been masons. The accusation of Freemason membership and influence remained a powerful one throughout the period of the regime, and was often tied to other conspiracy theories, including those involving

Jews.[6] In the wake of Zaniboni affair, the reformist Unitary Socialist Party (PSU) (Zaniboni's party) and its newspaper *La Giustizia* were closed down. This was the party Matteotti had led until his murder. *Avanti!*, the other Socialist Party newspaper, was suspended for three weeks. Zaniboni's trial was originally fixed for Siena in an ordinary court in 1926, but the hearings were delayed time and time again.

In the end both Zaniboni and Capello were given thirty-year sentences by an entirely new body – the Tribunale speciale per la difesa dello Stato ('Special Tribunal for the Defence of the State') in 1927. They were the first individuals to be prosecuted by this new institution. Both men were also 'degraded' in terms of their military rank, and Zaniboni's medals were taken away.[7] Zaniboni's charges were a mixture of hyperbole and the prosaic: 'insurrection against the powers of the state', 'attempted murder', 'illegal possession of a rifle'. He admitted full responsibility in front of the court: 'I declare without hesitation that it was my intention on 4 November 1925 to kill the head of government, Benito Mussolini.'[8] Ironically, before November 1925, Zaniboni had been expelled from both the masons and the PSU. In the wake of the various assassination attempts, a secret and mysterious police organisation, with a fake acronym 'OVRA', was set up.

Some claimed that Zaniboni had been working for dissident fascists, in particular the *ras* Roberto Farinacci, who had also been a mason. Yet, despite his ambiguous past, Zaniboni became an anti-fascist hero for many. A number of anti-fascists were sent to prison for expressing 'admiration' for him.[9] Others ended up in internal exile, a form of punishment – *confino* – whereby people were forced to live in remote parts of Italy, usually under harsh conditions. For three years, Zaniboni was kept in solitary confinement on the island of Santo Stefano, the same forbidding place where the regicide Gaetano Bresci was held (and died), as well as one of the Diana bombers, Giuseppe Mariani.[10] Zaniboni was then moved to a prison in Alessandria, in Piedmont. In the 1930s, like many others, he wrote 'submissive' letters to Mussolini, which were later used against him.

FAKE JUSTICE: THE MATTEOTTI TRIAL
CHIETI, MARCH 1926

In the Matteotti case, it was impossible to avoid some sort of trial, but the regime did its best to render any sense of justice as a farce, and to delay proceedings as much as possible. Instead of taking place in Rome, the trial was relegated to the small (and fascist) city of Chieti. The counsel representing the deceased, including the socialist lawyer Modigliani, were threatened, as were his family. Matteotti's wife, Velia, wrote to the court in advance stating: 'I only wanted justice, but this has been denied to me ... I will achieve justice thanks to history, and God.'[11] She was also trying to protect Modigliani and his fellow socialist lawyers from further fascist beatings, or worse. A murder trial had become a 'trivial formality'.[12] Modigliani had accepted the role as *parte civile* lawyer for the Matteotti family, but with the threats and violence the family withdrew and advised Modigliani to do the same. Modigliani suffered yet more beatings in July 1926 in Naples and his house in Rome was later sacked by 'two lorries, full of fascists'.[13]

Roberto Farinacci was appointed as one of five defence lawyers for the killers – his client, Amerigo Dumini, was the leader of the group. Farinacci was not much of a lawyer but he exploited the opportunity to the full. Mussolini wanted to keep the whole thing as quiet as possible, but Farinacci politicised the trial. He argued that Matteotti's death had been necessary to the triumph of fascism. His language was crude and Matteotti was described as a 'a big pig'.[14] 'Was not such a man,' Farinacci asked the jury, rhetorically, 'a permanent provocation to all honest people and those who love and have suffered for the Fatherland?'[15] Farinacci also arranged *squadristi* demonstrations in Chieti, with 'several thousand blackshirts'.[16] Mussolini was furious.[17] Soon afterwards, he sacked Farinacci as the Fascist Party boss and sent him back to the provinces.[18]

The trial was done and dusted in just nine days (the comparison with Empoli was stark); its outcome was inevitable. Only some of the *squadristi* in the car were tried, and none of those who had organised or inspired the attack were ever placed in the dock. Moreover, the death of Matteotti was judged to have been accidental, the unfortunate by-product of over-zealous *squadrista* behaviour. Three of Matteotti's killers were given symbolic sentences (of five years and eleven months each) for involuntary homicide, which were reduced even further by yet another amnesty. Within two months, given the time they had already spent in prison, all the men were free.

Velia Matteotti's requests for the return of some of her husband's clothing and personal effects were in vain. It was said that Matteotti's property was destroyed, and the knife with which he was probably killed was sold at auction. One of Velia's personal lawyers was harassed, forced to leave Chieti and had to work under a false name. The various beatings he suffered affected his eyesight for the rest of his life.[19]

VIOLET GIBSON: A MATTER OF CENTIMETRES
7 APRIL 1926

Violet Gibson was an Irishwoman living in Rome. She was from a privileged background, the daughter of the former Lord Chancellor of Ireland. Like Zaniboni, she had been greatly affected by the Matteotti affair and had attended some of the farcical trial in Chieti.

Gibson became one of the few who attempted to kill Mussolini in the 1920s. Of all those who tried, she came the closest. Her pistol shot – in the Campidoglio Square in central Rome on 7 April 1926 – grazed the Duce's nose.[20] She was also carrying a rock in her pocket, which she said would have been used to smash a car window if necessary. Mussolini was later seen and photographed with a large bandage over the wound. It is said that he only survived a fatal shot by moving his head a matter of centimetres at the last minute by chance. Immediately after the attack, Mussolini was surrounded by doctors (he had just attended a meeting of surgeons) and later quipped that the greatest danger to his life was that he risked 'suffocation' from all the people trying to help him.[21]

Born into a prominent and powerful Anglo-Protestant family in Ireland, Gibson converted to Catholicism at the age of twenty-six and also flirted with the cult of Theosophy. Following this radical break with her family, Gibson drifted between London, France, the English countryside, Switzerland and Italy. She became ill with Paget's disease and had to have her left breast surgically removed. In the early 1920s she was 'treated' in various mental health institutions. It appears that she wrestled with ideas about the moral duty to kill for a higher good. A medical file in 1923 described her as 'homicidal'; although 'she has shown no signs of violence,' the report continued, she 'says she might want to try … to kill someone'.[22]

Violet kept a close eye on the rise of the fascist regime in Italy. She was always on the move, and travelled to Rome in November 1924. While packing, 'she had time enough to include in her luggage a small revolver'.[23] In February 1925, Gibson shot herself in the chest while staying in a convent in Rome but sustained only minor injuries. Fourteen months later, on 7 April 1926, she tried to kill Il Duce, in broad daylight, in the heart of Italy's capital. Her attendance at Matteotti's trial suggests that anti-fascism may well have played a part in her actions.

In the aftermath of the shooting, Mussolini played up to stories that he was 'immortal'. He later said, inventing another personalised slogan: 'shots pass, Mussolini remains', and made a racist joke about his injuries and being able to wear a nose ring 'like the Africans' (his next official trip was a visit to Africa). Meanwhile, the international establishment rallied around the Italian dictator. The British ambassador said that 'happily the bullet only scratched his [Mussolini's] nose' and the Foreign Secretary, Austen Chamberlain, wrote personally to Mussolini: 'My wife joins me in congratulating you on your escape.'[24]

In Rome, the authorities argued over how to deal with the Gibson assassination attempt. Had she acted alone or was she part of a wider political plot? What was to be done with this 'mad' woman? She could not be easily placed within a left-wing conspiracy theory narrative, and her nationality created diplomatic issues. Nobody really wanted a trial. So, it was easier to 'disappear' her after a mental illness diagnosis. A deal was done politically with British state officials, with the full agreement of Gibson's family. The sentence was clear: 'internment for life'.

Some scientific justification was required. Enrico Ferri, the celebrated criminologist who had moved from socialism towards fascism, wrote an official psychological report on Gibson. Ferri, who by 1926 had become a great admirer of Mussolini, produced a long 'character study' of Gibson, meeting with her on a number of occasions.[25] He wrote that he saw her as 'highly intelligent and cultured'. Ferri seems to have spent some time trying to convince Gibson of Mussolini's 'greatness'. His report on Gibson was also full of praise for Il Duce, with phrases such as: 'Benito Mussolini is the man who saved his country from precipitating into the abyss awaiting her.'[26] The report concluded that: 'The deed was not accomplished in an unconscious frenzy of delirium, terror, or hallucination,' and 'she is neither solely "criminal" nor "mad" but is an "insane criminal" ... [and] that on the occasion of the attempt of the 7th of April [she] was mentally infirm and acted consciously but was devoid of her free will power to act.' Ferri recommended: 'That she be considered as a dangerous subject and deprived of her personal liberty.'[27]

Gibson was diagnosed as having acted thanks to a 'morbid, delirious impulse', and was smuggled out of Italy to Britain in May 1927. She was immediately locked up in an asylum in Northampton, where she lived out her days – always hopeful that she would be released, though her family and doctors never contemplated such a course of action. In 1956 she died, at the age of eighty, alone, forgotten and abandoned by the world: powerless until the end against the institutions (including her own family) who had conspired to write her out of history.

GINO LUCETTI: THE ANARCHIST AND THE BOMB

Below the Tuscan hill town of Carrara, on the plain, stands an extensive municipal graveyard – in many ways, no different from others across Italy. Huge temple-like structures house the dead of the rich and powerful families of the area, while small box-like 'loculi' are reserved for most of the others. But Carrara's graveyard has an unusual feature: there is a special section for anarchists. Carrara, with its vast and ancient marble quarries and their almost uniquely harsh working conditions, was a centre of anarchist thought and activity from the nineteenth century onwards. On the way into the cemetery stand two imposing white marble blocks, dedicated to an assassin, Gaetano Bresci, who was an anarchist who shot dead the King of Italy – Umberto I – in Monza on 29 July 1900.

Gino Lucetti was born in Carrara, in August 1900, just after the murder of Umberto I by Bresci. Lucetti, like so many others in Carrara, found work in the marble mines, which still produce some of the finest stone in the world. Getting the marble out of the mines and down into the valley for shipment was back-breaking and dangerous work. Lucetti was a *lizzatore* – one of the workers who had to guide blocks of marble down the mountain side on wooden rails as part of a specialised team.[28] Carrara became one of the most violent parts of Italy during the rise of fascism, with squads led by local *ras* Renato Ricci.[29] Lucetti was an anarchist and an anti-fascist, and had been declared a deserter during the war.[30] In 1925 he shot a fascist after a 'discussion', and was injured in the face by gunfire. Some accounts claim that local doctors refused to treat him.

A trial linked to that shooting incident was about to be held when Lucetti escaped to Marseilles, probably on a boat laden with Carrara marble (this was said to be a common way for marble workers to flee from Italy). In 1926, Lucetti travelled back to Italy from France under a false name with the intention of murdering Benito Mussolini. He decided to launch his attack at a location heavy with symbolism – Porta Pia in Rome, where the final act of the Risorgimento had taken place in September 1870 as Italian troops broke through the city walls and took control of Rome (although it is not clear if Lucetti was aware of this). Porta Pia was close to Mussolini's Rome residence, and was a place where his car passed often, and had to slow down.

It was 10.20 a.m., on 19 September 1926. Lucetti was well armed, and had fortified himself with a glass of Vermouth in a nearby bar. He had with him two small hand grenades, a dagger and a pistol, the bullets of which, it was said later, were dipped in acid to make them more effective. While he waited for the right moment, Lucetti lurked close to a newspaper stall. As Mussolini's car drove past, Lucetti threw his grenade. Some claim he had someone there to help him direct the bomb – a 'pointer'. His aim was accurate, but he was too close and the device bounced off the roof and into the crowd, and only then did it explode, injuring eight people.[31] Mussolini apparently ordered his driver to accelerate, but later stated he would have been able to deal with the bomb in time, given his experience as a soldier.[32]

Lucetti hid in a doorway but was captured, and then beaten up in the police station. He resisted, not giving his real name for some time. Lucetti's two 'accomplices' were soon picked up, as well as members of his family, including his mother. Lucetti then decided to confess. He later said that he had been planning the attempt since the 'massacre of Turin' in 1922. Some claim that there were no accomplices, but two other men were given heavy sentences for the attempt on Mussolini's life, and it is unlikely that Lucetti acted alone. He had logistical backing and, in all probability, support on the day of the attack.[33]

In 1927, Lucetti's trial, like that of Zaniboni, was held in the front of the newly instituted Tribunale Speciale in Rome. He had a lawyer forced upon him (Lucetti wanted to defend himself) and was given thirty years, under exceptionally harsh conditions (with three years of total solitary confinement, like Zaniboni) – although this was later reduced by a series of semi-amnesties conceded by the fascist regime. As the sentence was read out: 'Lucetti cried out "Long live Freedom".'[34]

Lucetti spent over eleven years in the forbidding and remote Santo Stefano prison complex. Others had gone mad in solitary confinement there, and Lucetti's treatment was particularly harsh. He was given further punishments for such petty misdemeanours as 'selling tobacco', 'looking out the window', 'secret communication with other prisoners', 'seditious shouts and a refusal to obey prison officers', as well as 'arrogant behaviour'.[35] Other militants were also caught up in the Lucetti case, directly and indirectly. A man called Vincenzo Baldazzi, for example, was given five years just for giving 300 lire to Lucetti's mother. Soon the death penalty, abolished by liberal Italy, would be reintroduced, and future anarchist plotters would be executed.

In September 1943, Lucetti was finally freed from the Santo Stefano prison by Allied troops as they liberated the country moving north. They left this description of him: 'A creature dressed in white coarse cloth, tall, with a small, lined pale face, close-cropped hair and big, twinkling eyes, calm and serene, [was] standing before me.'[36] Lucetti made his way to the island of Ischia, off the coast of Naples, but there he was mortally injured by shrapnel from a shell fired by the German army. He had only been free for six days. He was buried with a simple ceremony on Ischia, and in 1947 taken back to Carrara to be laid in the 'anarchist section' of the graveyard there.

The Lucetti case led to a revolution in Italy's police and security forces. The police chief and his deputy were sacked, and replaced by a former Prefect of Bologna, Arturo Bocchini, who would remain in charge until his death, in 1940, and become an extremely powerful figure. Some called him the 'vice-Duce'. Bocchini modernised and extended the secret police, political police and other forces. In Bologna he had 'distinguished' himself through his support for fascism and his alleged attempts to – illegally – control voting preferences.

THE ZAMBONI INCIDENT
BOLOGNA, OCTOBER 1926

In late October 1926 in Bologna, instead of a red flag on the Torre degli Asinelli (which had been part of the story since 1920) there was a huge *fascio* symbol, which lit up at night, at the top of the tower. Mussolini spoke in the council chamber where Giordani had been shot dead and from the same balcony where Ennio Gnudi had briefly appeared in November 1920. On the morning of 31 October, a group of *squadristi* put together a kind of macabre carnival exhibit. A rag doll the size of a man was suspended by its neck from a fake gallows, and the *squadristi* brandished signs naming the four potential assassins of Mussolini from 1925/26: Zaniboni, Capello, Gibson and Lucetti. By the end of that day, there would be another name on that list.[37]

Mussolini was in town, in part, to open the new fascistic football stadium, which would eventually be overlooked by an imposing statue of Il Duce himself on a massive horse. A huge crowd (some estimates put the figure at 150,000 people) and a forest of fascist salutes greeted Mussolini in a vast, new stadium which had been constructed in record time. As the extensive multiday celebrations for the fourth anniversary of the March on Rome were coming to an end – which had been seen as a major honour for the city of Bologna – Mussolini was on his way to the station. It was the last day of his visit: 31 October 1926.

Flanked by leading figures in the local fascist hierarchy, including the local *ras*, the ex-anarchist Leandro Arpinati (who was at the wheel), Dino Grandi and the *podestà* of Bologna, Umberto Puppini, Mussolini was in an open-topped car – a red Alfa Romeo. Suddenly someone stepped out of the crowd and fired. At least one shot passed through a sash Mussolini was wearing, and pierced Puppini's top hat, which was resting on his knees, before ending up in the cushioned interior of the car door. Poet, writer and film-maker Pier Paolo Pasolini's father, a policeman, was among the witnesses. Some accounts say Pasolini senior had been able to divert the shot by striking the hand of the assailant, and in so doing, perhaps, saving Mussolini's life. But nothing in this story is certain. Some 2,000 people had been preventatively arrested before Mussolini's visit to protect him, but this did not stop the attack.

Blame in the crowd fell immediately on a thin, small, fifteen-year-old boy called Anteo Zamboni. He was consequently set upon by an angry mob, stabbed, beaten and then strangled to death. His body received fourteen knife wounds.[38] Afterwards, it is claimed, *squadristi* dipped their double-edged knives into Zamboni's blood as a kind of ritual: Antonio Gramsci was on a train later that day when numerous fascists with blood-stained daggers got on board.[39] Within a week, Gramsci himself was arrested. He would spend most of the rest of his life in custody. Mussolini was unharmed in the attack. Later, he sent back the damaged sash 'for display'. It was on show in Bologna for years, although its whereabouts today are unknown.

The child, Anteo Zamboni, was the son of an anarchist printer who was now a supporter of fascism. An automatic Beretta 7.65 pistol was found on Anteo, which his father later recognised as his own. Horrific photos were taken of the boy's beaten body, covered in blood and wounds, and Italo Balbo (who had also been present) took a red-stained

dagger to Mussolini to assure him that 'justice had been done'.⁴⁰ Dino
Grandi remembered that 'the attacker disappeared immediately, grabbed
by a thousand arms in the turmoil … [there was a] terrible cry'.⁴¹ Anteo
Zamboni had not been killed by ordinary *squadristi* – his assailants
included an expert in violence called Arconovaldo Bonaccorsi, who
had offered personally to 'decapitate' oppositionists after the Zaniboni
plot.⁴² Other leading *ras* and *squadristi* on the scene were Renato Ricci,
Balbo and (it seems) Albino Volpi – one of those involved in the
Matteotti murder.

My great-uncle, George Tod, was there that day, in the crowd. He was
eleven years old. In his unpublished memoirs he later left this account:

> We were standing in the crowd along the route … when a large
> open car raced down the road with men in uniform piled, face
> down, on it. A roar from the crowd spread down from the
> main piazza … like a wave of thunder … In the street there was
> pandemonium; we could gather from the shouting that Mussolini
> had been killed, that he had not been killed, that he had been
> wounded, that some of his aides had been killed etc. etc. Finally a
> shout went up from the crowd 'Il Duce è salvo' … women knelt
> and prayed tearing at their hair, men raised their hands to heaven,
> children cried … a young man had shot at Mussolini as his open
> car passed slowly through the crowd … the culprit was lynched on
> the spot by the crowd and only a dark, pink-stained foam remained
> of him.⁴³

The fascists could not accept that a small boy had, on his own, nearly
killed the 'immortal' Duce. It *had* to be a conspiracy. Had dissident
fascists been involved in a plot? Somebody needed to be blamed, and
so – without even a tiny bit of proof – the scapegoats were chosen: Anteo
Zamboni's entire family. Mammolo, his aunt Virginia Tabarroni, and
his brothers Assunto and Lodovico were all arrested, as was his mother
for a time. Another show trial was staged in front of the Tribunale
Speciale, following those of Zaniboni and Lucetti. In a strange turn of
events, the original prosecutor was replaced after calling for the family
to be cleared. Mussolini was said to have directly ordered a guilty
verdict. Anteo Zamboni was buried in unconsecrated land in Bologna
on the so-called Campo dei Traditori ('Traitor's Field'). His family were

not allowed to pay their respects in the normal way, or bury him as they wanted.

*

The series of attempts on Mussolini's life showed how desperate and weak the opposition to fascism had become by the end of 1925. Mussolini's brushes with death and survival reinforced the idea that he was the chosen one, a man of destiny, somehow immortal, a semi-deity. *L'Osservatore Romano*, the official paper of the Vatican, wrote that 'people recognised the hand of God' after one escape.[44] Pope Pius XI himself made reference to 'the almost visible intervention of Divine Providence'.[45]

The failed assassinations prompted further state crackdowns. From 1927 onwards, Mussolini felt pretty safe, and by the 1930s, he was able to drive around on his own, outside Rome. All of these four attempts on Il Duce's life were followed by outbreaks of *squadrista* violence. Following the attack by Violet Gibson, in April 1926, fascists destroyed the offices of the newspaper *Il Mondo* in Rome; after the Zamboni incident in Bologna, violence broke out across Italy. In Naples, the philosopher Benedetto Croce's house was attacked.[46]

In November 1926, leading socialist and lawyer Tito Oro Nobili, who had been forced out of his home town of Terni by *squadristi* three years earlier, was kidnapped by a band of thirteen fascists while visiting family in Pesciano di Todi, Umbria, for the Day of the Dead. He was taken away at midnight in three cars; his family, including his young daughters aged between eight and fourteen, were threatened. Oro Nobili was tortured for hours.[47] According to Francesco Bogliari, 'with refined barbarity the *squadristi* enjoyed themselves by burning his eyelids with cigarette butts'. They then left him 'for dead' – 'his face unrecognisable' – in the road, near Todi hospital in the middle of the night.[48] *Avanti!* wrote that: 'His medical records were an x-ray of a massacre.'[49] It appeared that: 'Fascism wanted to reduce him to silence, for ever.'[50] His wife was prevented from seeing him.

Despite this, Oro Nobili was also arrested – in hospital – on 10 November and sent into internal exile. One of the accusations against him was that he had called for Mussolini to be eliminated. Oro Nobili was despatched to the remote island of Favignana off the Sicilian coast, where medical treatment was difficult to come by. He was soon allowed to return to Rome due to his health, but found it difficult to work. The police continued to harass him at every opportunity. At least one of his children suffered a mental breakdown as a result of the fear and anxiety. The lawyers' guild expelled him, which meant he could no longer work. The violence he endured affected Oro Nobili's eyesight, and he suffered from eye problems for the rest of his life, requiring constant medical treatment. All thirteen fascists (from Todi) involved in his kidnap and torture were cleared during subsequent legal procedings.[51]

Mussolini used these assassination attempts to wipe out the last flimsy vestiges of democracy and rule of law in Italy. He appointed himself Interior Minister on 6 November and on 25 November the opposition was effectively made illegal: 120 deputies were expelled from parliament, which was reduced to an institutional fascist rubber stamp and sounding board for Mussolini.

Regime
1926–27

From 1926 onwards, a regime was installed. Elections were abolished at local and national level. Parliament continued to function, but as a fascist institution. A powerful cult of personality was constructed around Mussolini. There were no further assassination attempts. An efficient and all-encompassing system of spies and informers reported to the political police and to the OVRA. Opposition figures were forced out of Italy, arrested, or silenced. This included a number of leading liberals and Catholics. A variety of punishments were reserved for those who spoke out, or resisted in other ways – prison, forced internal exile, violence, economic sanctions. Italy was a one-party state. Fascism was not all-powerful, however. Authoritative institutions, with deeper and much longer histories, continued to exercise influence – the monarchy, the army and, of course, the Catholic Church. Mussolini left Italy's original constitution in place, while shifting power to new institutions, such as the Fascist Grand Council.

FINAL RESISTANCE: MOLINELLA AND MASSARENTI

The regime set out to crush the last isolated pockets of defiance. In October 1926, over 200 families were forcibly deported from Molinella in Emilia-Romagna in order to break their tenacious resistance to fascist rule. Former mayor Giuseppe Massarenti – the 'Apostle of the Marshes' – had left town after numerous threats and spent the next five years in prison and internal exile, where he suffered frequent beatings and persecution. For a time he was banished to the remote island of

Lampedusa, from where the anarchist Errico Malatesta had escaped way back in 1899, and he was also moved to the islands of Ustica and Ponza. He wrote long elegant letters pleading his case.

After his release back to Rome in 1931 Massarenti was not allowed to return to Molinella, and was continually harassed by the fascist police, even though he was clearly not a threat in any sense. He was reduced to destitution, another repressive tactic used by the regime, telling a friend: 'They have stolen everything from me, the fruit of forty years of work. They have reduced me to extreme poverty and they are stopping any help getting to me from relatives and friends, through significant forms of direct and indirect intimidation.'[1] Massarenti could not pay back his debts, and did not have enough money to eat. 'Often in the evening,' he wrote, 'I don't even have cash for a quarter of a litre of milk.'[2]

Massarenti described a series of 'incredible humiliations' and was followed everywhere by 'lines of policemen and spies'.[3] If he spoke to anybody in the street, those people were questioned. His rooms were searched day and night, randomly raided and his reading matter was frequently examined and seized. He accused the secret police of stealing from him and complained of 'ferocious persecution'.[4] For a time he was effectively rendered homeless, forced to 'live like a tramp on the streets', covered in newspapers, under the *portici* of the Vatican in the centre of Rome. The police argued that he had a 'persecution complex'.[5]

In 1926, fascists attacked the premises of Jewish socialist lawyer, Pio Donati, in Modena for the last time: the offices were 'ransacked, furniture was destroyed, and fire was used to burn papers'. Donati had by then moved to Milan, where he felt safer than in his home town. But even there it wasn't secure: his 'doctors advised him to leave Italy'.[6] He died in Brussels in 1927 from leukaemia, aged just forty-six. Today Pio Donati's remains are part of a unique double tomb in Modena, divided by glass, which unites him with the Catholic anti-fascist Francesco Luigi Ferrari, who also died in exile.

THE 'SUICIDE' OF GASTONE SOZZI

Life was very difficult for communists and socialists after the crackdowns. As Ignazio Silone wrote, "The working masses are cowed, corrupted, intimidated, apathetic, classified, regimented, rubber-stamped, and famished ... How many friends have I seen go to prison? How many have disappeared without trace?'[7] Even clandestine agitation and organisation came to an almost complete halt. Militants were isolated, afraid, and vulnerable. It became nigh on impossible to print or distribute any kind of newspaper that wasn't in full support of Mussolini and fascist rule. Under fascism, prisoners were often 'disappeared' or 'committed suicide' in prison. Torture was common, ritualised and sanctioned from above. This was to some extent in continuity with liberal and pre-fascist Italy, where prisoners were routinely beaten up, prison regimes were harsh and marked by punishing rules and regulations, and confessions were often forced. But under fascism none of this could be tempered or exposed by the work of lawyers and public opinion. There was no escape, or recourse. Prisoners were at the complete mercy of their captors.

Gastone Sozzi was born in Cesena in 1903. His father was a baker and he had childhood memories from Red Week in 1914. Sozzi had been a member of the Communist Party since its formation in 1921.[8] He had been a precocious young militant, writing about his socialism at the age of seventeen: 'I am a socialist because I love peace, I love those who suffer, I love the proletariat who are my brothers, I love truth. And this love leads to hate. I hate injustice, oppression, the rich who crush the poor, the capitalist who gets rich from the sweat of the workers. Love and hate brought together in this way made me into a socialist.'[9] There were some legendary and mythical aspects to many accounts of Sozzi's life. His father was also a socialist, and friend of Mussolini: it was said that the future Duce had once held Gastone in his arms (when he was a baby) and said. 'You will become a revolutionary.'[10]

Sozzi loved classical music: 'Perhaps I was born to be a conductor ... like a general at the key moment of the battle or a revolutionary who leads a revolution.'[11] Fascists tried to burn his house down in 1921, and he was in Turin for the massacre in December 1922. From 1923–25 he lived and worked in the USSR, where he also attended a party school for militants.[12] On his return to Italy in July 1925, he used his time on military service to spread propaganda among the conscripts – an extremely dangerous activity. He also published a socialist newspaper aimed at children. As time wore on, avoiding arrest became harder and harder. Spies were everywhere, and everybody was a potential informer.

Safe houses were rare, and not particularly secure. Sozzi managed for a time to stay out of prison, agitating among soldiers and producing another clandestine, illegal publication called *Caserma* ('Barracks').

Throughout this time he continued to write to his girlfriend, Norma.[13] In October 1926 they married, although Sozzi was late to the ceremony because of a political meeting he was attending. Given Sozzi's vulnerability as a prized asset for the fascists, the couple were rarely together. He was continually on the run, although he had been convicted of no crime. The last time the couple saw each other was in 1927 at Piacenza station, in northern Italy. His wife Norma then discovered she was pregnant. Soon afterwards – between the end of October and the beginning of November 1927 – Sozzi was arrested in Milan but his family were not informed. They discovered eventually that he was being held in Perugia.

The Rocca Paolina prison in Perugia was one of the most forbidding institutions in Italy. *Avanti!* called it: 'The old horrible papal prison where many Italian nationalist prisoners languished,' adding that this particular prison was 'chosen by fascism as their favourite place to torture antifascist youth. The employees and guards there have been recruited from the worst kind of fascist criminality and the thick walls muffle the cries of pain from those poor creatures inside.'[14] Conditions inside fascist prisons were dire, although until the early 1930s the regulations were still those of the liberal era. Prisoners were forced to attend mass, and non-attendance led to punishment. Women were not allowed to wear underwear. Often, their periods would stop altogether in prison due to stress and the conditions in prison. Forced labour was common. A bath was permitted once a month. The food was disgusting and not plentiful, and cells were often infested with rats and insects. Political prisoners organised and managed to protest about these conditions. Resistance was subtle and often symbolic. In one prison a female inmate managed to get permission to display a picture of 'her son' on the wall: the photo she put up was of Lenin.[15]

Avanti! reported that Gastone Sozzi was placed in an underground cell reserved for the worst of the 'ordinary' criminals, and that on arrival he was already weak from the violence that he had received. For the whole of December and January, the paper stated, Sozzi was underfed and 'punches, kicks, beatings with clubs were inflicted on his body'. There is another atrocious detail in the Sozzi case, where it was claimed that he suffered 'injections of iodine into his anus in the vain attempt to get him to speak'.[16] Sozzi's interrogators were desperate for him to give them contacts. They suspected that other members of the army were plotting to kill, or usurp Mussolini. But it seems that Sozzi did not talk, despite the brutal torture he endured.

In February 1928, Sozzi's family travelled to Perugia and were told that he had hanged himself with bedsheets, which he had supposedly tied to the bars of his cell. He had left no note. Sozzi was just twenty-five years old. His body was laid out and his wife noted no signs of hanging around his neck, but heavy bruising to his head. *Avanti!* on the other hand reported that the family were not allowed to see his body, which they said was buried in a sealed coffin. Either way, no autopsy was permitted.

Sozzi soon became a socialist and anti-fascist martyr. There was shock and dismay in the international community at his death.[17] Within Italy, news only travelled by word of mouth as the newspapers refused to discuss the case, but nevertheless nobody within the movement believed the suicide story.[18] Sozzi's death was attributed to a 'state murder'. He was commemorated abroad and remembered, secretly, in Italy. His wife and son Sergio (whom he never met) were also a constant physical reminder of his fate.

1928

THE BOMB AND THE KING

By 1928 the dictatorship was fully bedded in. Opposition consisted of only a few isolated voices. Most leading anti-fascists were in exile, or in some form of confinement. Political conflict only existed at a formal level, between different fascist individuals and factions, and was very often not about politics at all, but power, resources and influence. Despite this, the regime never felt entirely secure, and its extensive political police service and network of spies needed conspiracies and plots to feed and justify its own existence. In April 1928, however, there was something real to deal with, and it saw the mobilisation of the entire repressive apparatus of the Italian fascist state.

Milan's annual trade fair (*fiera*), held every April, was a big deal in the city and traditionally pulled huge crowds – including many families with children – from right across Italy. It usually opened with much pomp and ceremony and in 1928 it was the king, Victor Emmanuel III himself, who was due to do the honours.

The king arrived in town by train, at 9.45 on the morning of 12 April. Just fifteen minutes after his arrival, in the vast square in front of the trade fair's headquarters, at a point where the monarch was due to pass, a huge explosion went off among the gathering crowds. There was carnage. The king was safe, though most assumed he had been the target. A photo of the scene captures the chaos in the minutes after the explosion. A boy is sitting on the ground; there are people milling around amidst the confusion, and the air is thick with smoke. Shrapnel is strewn across the pavement. The police are already in the square.

We still don't know exactly how many people were killed and injured that day, but at least twenty people lost their lives and many others were injured, some very seriously. It was the biggest bomb attack in Italy since the Diana Theatre massacre of 1921 in Milan, and it shook the regime.

The bomb had been placed inside a cast-iron lamppost (a little maintenance door at the base of the structure could be easily opened to allow access). It was designed to cause maximum damage. The explosion created thousands of tiny bullet-like shards of metal, which ripped through the crowd. Police reports decided that it was the work of professionals. Unlike other protests and explosions under the regime, the *fiera* bomb could not be hushed up, and the newspapers, although tightly controlled and censored, carried the news on their front pages.

For Mussolini, it was obvious that this was an *anti-fascist* Bolshevik plot, planned abroad (perhaps in the USSR itself). Hundreds, perhaps thousands, of known, so-called 'subversives' were swiftly rounded up – anarchists, communists, socialists – and interrogated 'vigorously', as the official documents put it. Everyone linked even tangentially to the 1921 Diana massacre (and who wasn't still in custody) was rearrested and tortured. The original police officer from that investigation was brought back to look into this case. But while there were a few linked accounts or connected stories, there was very little in terms of concrete leads or evidence. In fact, there was almost too much second-hand information, as hundreds of anonymous tip-offs flooded into the offices of the various police forces and investigating agencies (of which there were many).

Romolo Tranquilli

On 13 April, the day after the explosion, the investigation seemed to take a big step forward. High above Lake Como, at a place called Brunate, connected by cable car to the city of Como below, a twenty-three-year-old man called Romolo Tranquilli was arrested. His exiled older brother, Secondino Tranquilli – or, as he would later become known, Ignazio Silone – was a key figure in the anti-fascist movement. Crucially, two pencil-drawn maps were found in Romolo's bag, in the left luggage at Genoa station. Some claimed that one of the maps was of the square where the bomb had exploded in Milan. But Romolo denied this, stating that it indicated a meeting place for a future clandestine encounter with a fellow communist. He also had an alibi. But Romolo fitted the bill as the culprit, he was linked to the underground communist movement and to its leadership abroad. He was proof of a plot. Romolo also had some poison in his possession. It was not clear what this was for.

Romolo had lived a difficult life. His father and another brother both died when he was young, and in January 1915 he was orphaned, at the age of ten, by a catastrophic earthquake which wiped out his home in the Abruzzo region in the south of Italy. Adopted by a charismatic priest and taken to Rome to be educated, he failed to finish school. He was never a key part of the communist underground but had, in all probability, been given some basic propaganda tasks to carry out – perhaps by his brother, Secondino. He seemed an unlikely candidate for a bomb attack at this level of sophistication, but the police had little else to go on.

As part of his 'interrogation', Romolo was beaten with sacks of sand, which broke three of his ribs and damaged his lungs. This type of treatment was common practice under the regime. Torture had become institutionalised. The investigative police were often drawn from ex-*squadristi*. It was said that doctors refused to treat him. Despite his suffering he consistently denied having anything to do with the bombing. The investigators were divided as to which line to follow. Many were convinced that the map was unconnected to the massacre in Milan. Some had suspicions that the bomb had not been anti-fascist at all, but part of the deadly and ongoing power games *within* the Fascist Party itself. In a phone call, two of the most important police chiefs in Italy agreed that the investigators should 'look towards Cremona'. This was a coded reference to Roberto Farinacci. Had someone within the fascist movement planted the bomb, and if so, why? Some pointed the finger at dissident or rival fascists – such as Mario Giampaoli, the powerful and eccentric *ras* in Milan.

While Romolo was in prison, his brother Secondino tried to help him, but most of the money and letters he sent were (predictably) seized. Later, Romolo was transferred to the notorious Rocca Paolina prison in Perugia (where Sozzi had died). As Romolo's illness worsened, he was moved again to the island of Procida, off the coast of Naples. In June 1931 he was given a twelve-year sentence by the special tribunal, which included a period of solitary confinement (but not for the 1928 bomb). The injuries to his chest and lungs he received under torture and the lack of medical attention led to severe bronchitis and he died in October 1932, at the age of twenty-eight, and was buried in a common grave.[1] Romolo's arrest, torture and death had a deep impact upon his brother Ignazio Silone.

Despite the lack of any real evidence, in the wake of the 1928 bomb a number of other communists and subversives were tried and convicted in double-quick time by the Special Tribunal. None was directly accused of having planted the 1928 device, and the suspicion remained that the real bombers had not been found.

The spy and the suicide

Despite the convictions, investigations continued. Another target was soon discovered which could be linked to the bomb and – at the same time – allow the regime to further attempt to discredit anti-fascism by connecting it to terrorist methods. The tiny Justice and Liberty (*Giustizia e Libertà*) group were mainly intellectual anti-fascists who produced anti-fascist propaganda inside and outside Italy in the late 1920s and early 1930s. In order to reach them, the secret police (OVRA) recruited a spy and agent provocateur, Carlo Del Re. He was a brilliant lawyer (he had four university degrees), and was physically striking, with a prominent scar and two fingers missing – a character who could easily have been created by a spy novelist. Del Re had crushing debts and was paid well for his work. He was able to infiltrate the group and tried to push them towards carrying out more extreme acts. Del Re managed to persuade leading anti-fascist chemist, Umberto Ceva, who had an international reputation in the science world, to make some incendiary bombs, but Ceva thought they were too dangerous and dumped them in a river.

At this point, in October 1930, Del Re called in the authorities and the Justice and Liberty group were rounded up. Ceva and others from the group were kept in separate cells in Regina Coeli prison in Rome and told stories about their comrades in order to try and get them to talk and implicate others. Attempts were made to link Justice and Liberty back to the 1928 Milan bomb. Ceva was desperate, and he was unaware of Del Re's treachery. He saw no way out of his situation apart from suicide, but that was made almost impossible under the highly controlled fascist prison regime.

Ceva waited until Christmas Day 1930, when the level of guard attention was at its minimum. Using his chemistry knowledge, he collected a 'solid combustible' form of fuel from the small cooker he was allowed to use in his cell, and mixed it with lemon juice and crushed glass from his own spectacles, which he then ingested. It was a deadly combination. He left two notes – one to his wife and one to senior police inspector Francesco Nudi, before drinking the potion.[2] 'I am committing suicide,' he wrote, 'with a clear conscience and clean hands.'[3] His screams were heard by fellow prisoners. Nudi was asked to pass on the news to his wife and family, and to hand over his wedding ring. Ceva died in agony on Boxing Day at 7.26 a.m., leaving behind two very young children.[4] It was not possible to avoid releasing the news, which was done with a press release that made reference to 'personal reasons'.[5]

Ceva's death could not be covered up, and caused widespread shock across the world. There was indignation in the exile community and the press. Del Re was named as the spy who had betrayed Ceva, and other supporters of 'Justice and Liberty' were tried in front of the Tribunale Speciale. Despite its repressive structures, the tribunal did allow those put on trial to provide a written defence and to make a statement. This gave anti-fascists a rare platform, although the press did not report on their statements. Leading anti-fascists Ernesto Rossi and Riccardo Bauer were given twenty years each, with others receiving smaller sentences.

Despite the immense efforts of fascist judicial and police institutions, those who planted the 1928 bomb in Milan were never uncovered or brought to trial. Every clue or possibility ended in a dead end, for different reasons: politics, internal factions, lack of evidence. Nonetheless, all the arrests and trials led to long sentences for many: 'The bomb in Milan helped the regime to attack the entire anti-fascist opposition.'[6] The massacre remains a forgotten tragedy. There is no plaque in Milan, or anywhere else in Italy, commemorating the victims, and we can be pretty sure that the truth will never emerge from the archives.

Secrets and lies

Within the anti-fascist community, there were hundreds of spies. Many activists were persuaded to work for the regime, often through blackmail, bribery or desperation. We left Ignazio Silone in 1928, anxious to help his brother Romolo, after his arrest following the *fiera* bomb. Secondino Tranquilli/Ignazio Silone was born on 1 May 1900 in the tiny village of Pescina dei Marsi, in the Abruzzo region in the south of Italy. Having been orphaned in the earthquake of 1915, he, like his brother, was raised in part by that same charismatic priest, Luigi Orione.

Secondino arrived in Rome as a young boy. He soon became a socialist and rose quickly up the ranks of the youth wing of the movement. It was probably around this time, in the heady days of strikes and protests after the war, that Tranquilli first came into contact with a powerful police officer, Guido Bellone. He was, it appears, recruited at some point as an informer within the socialist movement. In a later novel he depicted a character who was arrested by the police, beaten up – 'for a whole hour my ears were boxed and I was spat upon ... my face and chest were literally covered with spittle' – and offered a way out – as a spy.[7] Silone led a double life, providing information for an official within the fascist regime, but, it seems, remaining an anti-fascist. This subtle and complicated form of duplicity has been the subject of much controversy. Silone's code name was 'Silvestri' (and he also had a code number – 73).

When the Italian socialists split in 1921, Silone joined the Communist Party. He was a frequent visitor to Berlin and Moscow, and organised Italian workers' groups in Spain, France, Belgium and Luxemburg. Within a few years, as fascism consolidated its rule, he became one of the eight top leaders of the PCI in exile, and in 1927 was sent back into Italy as head of the party's underground network. When Moscow imposed sectarian policies on the Communist International at the end of the decade, a line which threatened to tear the Italian party apart, Silone was eventually expelled from the PCI for opposing Moscow.

In 1930 Silone sent a letter addressed to someone called Emilia Bellone in Rome.[8] This was probably a ruse to hide his tracks. Emilia was the sister of Guido Bellone, Silone's handler, who by then was the General Inspector of Public Security, charged with stamping out subversion. In that letter Silone described having entered a period of deep moral and psychological crisis, perhaps connected to the arrest of his brother. He asked Bellone to be released from 'all falsehood, doubt and secrecy' and 'to repair the damage that I have caused, to seek redemption, to help the workers, the peasants (to whom I am bound with every fibre in my body) and my country'.[9] The letter appears to have worked. Silone's collaboration with Bellone stopped.

Withdrawing from active politics after his expulsion from the Communist Party, Silone wrote the novel *Fontamara* (1933), which he dedicated to his brother Romolo. It was one of the most powerful anti-fascist texts to appear in the 1930s. The story was set in a remote southern village, where the local peasants – dubbed '*cafoni*', the lowest of the low – struggle to make sense of social and political change. At every turn, they are outwitted and outmanoeuvred by the authorities and the fascists. Their water is taken away, and their attempts at rebellion are crushed. One scene depicts with horrific detail the moment when the *squadristi* come to the village.

Fontamara became an inspiration to anti-fascists across the world. Silone's follow-up novel, which many see as his masterpiece, was *Bread and Wine* (1936), a book which deals with deception and lying. In that book Silone writes of one of his characters as having a 'divided mind … Was it perhaps impossible to avoid serving two masters?'[10] Was he hiding in plain sight? He also wrote, in the same novel: 'There are wounds that should not be bandaged and hidden, but exposed to the sun.'[11]

Why had Silone become an informer? He was very young when he first met Bellone. From childhood he would have been psychologically fragile; maybe he needed money. Certainly he was paid. His reports reveal little ideological commitment to fascism. What is clear is that at the centre of this story lies his close and mysterious relationship with Bellone. Bellone himself retired in 1936, eventually dying in 1948. He is said to be buried in a Jewish cemetery in Rome. Silone had failed to save his brother, but through his novels he helped to create anger and resentment across the world at the horrors of Mussolini's regime.

THE LAWYER

In 1928 Giuseppe Emanuele Modigliani was thrown out of the lawyers' guild. This meant his livelihood – his ability to work – was taken away. Economic sanctions of this kind were applied to many anti-fascists. Modigliani, however, refused to compromise, or to hide – despite the fact that his life was in constant danger. Eventually he was also forced into exile with his wife Vera – first to Vienna and then to Paris. His passport was cancelled. In exile, Modigliani continued to organise and speak on behalf of the working class and the oppressed, and against Mussolini's regime. In 1928 in Lille he said: 'Our error was not to take fascism seriously from the start, because we could have destroyed it. Now the road to defeating fascism is long and difficult but we will eventually win.' He also said that 'I hope the day that I will see Italy again is not too far away.'[12]

The great Russian revolutionary and writer Victor Serge met Modigliani in Paris. In his classic *Memoirs of a Revolutionary*, he referred to Modigliani as 'an honest old reformist with a keen intellect' and described him as 'stout... with an impressive beard, his manner most patrician, his blue eyes alert and sad, his word measured, always thoughtful and burdened with experience'.[13] While in Paris, Modigliani played his part as a member of the Italian anti-fascist community – the most influential and powerful such grouping in the world. He was a witness at the marriage of fellow anti-fascists Joyce and Emilio Lussu, when, 'with his large and substantial beard, he appeared like a rabbi in a synagogue'.[14]

In exile, Italy's political refugees were often indistinguishable from economic migrants. Legendary anarchist Errico Malatesta had worked as an electrician in London for years. Ercole Bucco was in the building trade, although he listed his occupation as 'architect'. A small number eked out an existence as full-time militants – through writing and help from the communists, socialists or anarchist movements internationally. Support groups for 'victims of fascism' were set up.

The lives of these refugees were often itinerant and unstable. They were separated from their home towns, their families and many of their friends. Letters back and forth were intercepted by the authorities. Rumours of marital infidelity were spread on purpose by fascist spies and agents provocateurs. They were followed everywhere. All movements and activities were monitored. Nobody could be fully trusted.

Exiles were constantly on the move but there were ways to make it back to Italy under the regime. It was possible to publicly renounce your past, and even join the fascist movement (although this was not always effective, since many of these 'conversions' were greeted with caution). Or you could leave politics altogether and some took this route out of conviction, while others did it out of necessity or simply desperation, in order to survive, put food on the table, support their families.

Some tried to re-enter Italy secretly, usually under a false name. A small number of militants did this as part of a political strategy in the

1920s and 1930s, while other refugees returned in order to work or meet their families, and not for political reasons. This was risky as border controls were tightened considerably under the fascist regime. Police files carried up-to-date photos and a series of pseudonyms. The costs of capture were considerable – torture, almost certain conviction with long prison sentences, heavy fines or internal exile. Many preferred to wait and see. Few expected Mussolini to hold power for long.

Exile communities were divided and there were bitter arguments over political strategy and tactics. Above all, these debates affected the socialist and communist organisations, but it was also the case with those linked to Catholic anti-fascism, and to anarchism. Exiles also lived in constant fear of infiltration by informers. Often, there were attempts to push exiles and anti-fascists in Italy into violent action and terrorism, with some success. The 'discovery' of these 'plots' played well to a domestic audience and, as with the 1928 Milan bomb, it created an environment where accusations stuck and heavy sentences against any 'subversive' elements could be passed down.

THE ZAMBONI CASE

In 1928, the Tribunale Speciale handed down thirty-year sentences each to Mammolo Zamboni and Virginia Tabarroni, for their supposed connections to the attempt on Mussolini's life in Bologna in 1926, while the two surviving Zamboni sons were sent into internal exile.

None of the Zambonis would serve their full sentences. A royal pardon, informally requested by Mussolini, was granted to Mammolo and Tabarroni at the end of 1932. Leandro Arpinati, the *ras* from Bologna who had been a friend of Mammolo Zamboni, had pressed for clemency. The Zamboni case would continue to dog Arpinati's career for many years, and was used against him when he fell out with leading fascists in 1934 and was himself arrested and interned.[15] The Zamboni sons, Assunto and Lodovico, were released from the conditions of their exile early. Assunto went on to become a fascist spy.

1929

Italian fascism's effective apparatus of repression was accompanied by policies which engaged with everyday life and looked to win over the population. These included vast public works programmes, welfare policies, and a galaxy of fascist organisations. Fascism was deeply involved in developing and moulding culture, and invested heavily in art, architecture, sport. By the end of the decade, open opposition to the regime was extremely rare. Active anti-fascism was only possible in private, or outside of Italy.

In October 1929, in Brussels, a twenty-one-year-old student called Fernando De Rosa tried to assassinate Umberto, Prince of Piedmont, the heir to the throne (who would later, briefly, become king). In his defence De Rosa claimed: 'I wanted justice ... it is true that I wanted to kill. I wanted to kill the heir to the throne which had destroyed freedom in a great country ... I had heard that this young prince liked to act as a fascist, he wore a fascist uniform, he was in alliance, openly, with the murderers of Matteotti.'[1] As he fired a shot he was said by some to have cried out 'Viva Matteotti'. The student's attempt failed, and he was arrested and tried in Belgium. His trial became an anti-fascist platform, with testimonies by Francesco Nitti and others. He was only given a five-year sentence, released early, and died during the Spanish Civil War.

Fascist repression was all encompassing. It reached far beyond subversives and anti-fascists, taking in their relatives, friends and acquaintances. After Gastone Sozzi died in prison in 1927, the fascists continued to hassle and torment his family. His father was attacked by fascists in 1929 and died in poverty at the age of forty-nine, while his uncle and brother were also the victims of blackshirt violence. In 1930 Gastone's brother, Sigifrido Sozzi, was arrested and accused of distributing anti-fascist leaflets, and sent to internal exile on the island of Ponza, off the west coast of Italy.[2] But Gastone Sozzi also became a symbol of resistance abroad. His name would be given to republican groups in Spain and anti-fascist brigades during the resistance.

THE LATERAN PACTS
FEBRUARY 1929

Church and state in Italy had been in bitter conflict since the unification of the country in 1870, which had taken place with a military assault on Rome itself. Mussolini had been radically anti-clerical in his youth, and during their rise to power fascists attacked leading Catholics, numerous deputies and others from the Catholic Popular Party. Priests were beaten by *squadristi* and, in at least one notorious case, murdered.[3] Yet, as fascism took power, it made a number of concessions to the official Church. Mussolini also remarried his wife in a religious ceremony (the Church did not recognise civil marriages). The Church found in fascism strong ideological affinity, in particular in the anti-socialism and 'return to order' in postwar Italy.

This rapprochement reached its peak in 1929 with the signing of the Lateran Pacts, negotiated agreements with the Vatican which ended the historic conflict between Church and state. The pacts were extremely advantageous to the Church, with generous financial and institutional concessions. They revealed the realist political skills of Mussolini, who by the end of the decade was beginning to create a sense of consensus and a formidable bloc of power among the elites. The pacts were signed in an elaborate ceremony in Rome. A road was blasted through the centre of Rome physically and symbolically linking the Vatican and the centre of the capital – the Via delle Conciliazioni (Conciliation Road).

In the wake of the signing of the pacts, the Vatican put pressure on Mussolini over a key commemoration. Every year, since 1895, the Italian state had celebrated with a national holiday the taking of Rome on 20 September 1870. Now, the pope wanted this holiday abolished and replaced with a new holiday – 11 February – to commemorate the pacts themselves. Mussolini resisted. He did not want to appear to be ordered around by priests and bishops. There were long negotiations and the Vatican had its way. In 1930 the new holiday in February was announced, and the 20 September holiday was removed from the calendar. Another new holiday was also announced: that of the 'Fascist Revolution' – 28 October.[4]

A price was paid by the Catholic Church for its pact with fascism. Mussolini's cult of personality became so powerful that it challenged, for a time, that of the pope himself. There was an attempt, no less, to construct a new political religion – pumped out through official and unofficial propaganda channels, newsreels, radio, murals, photography and publications – focused on Il Duce. Numerous biographies were published, both in Italy and abroad. Mussolini was presented as both a man of the people and a kind of god, at the same time.

Il Duce's double image was also translated into his home life, where he was presented as the perfect family man, happily married to Rachele with their five children, born between 1910 and 1929. Yet, he had sex with numerous women, as well as taking long-term lovers; both these facts were well known to the general public. Pithy slogans covered walls across the country – 'Mussolini is Always Right, Many Enemies: A Lot of Honour'. Often, a simple M was enough. In one of the new towns built across the reclaimed marshlands to the south of Rome, a huge building was constructed simply in the form of an M. Thousands of statues of Mussolini went up, and even when they weren't of him, they looked like him. Italo Calvino, the great Italian novelist, who was born in 1923, later wrote: 'You could say I spent the first twenty years of my life with Mussolini's face always in view, in the sense that his portrait hung in every classroom as well as in every public building or office I entered.'[5] Smaller cults also surrounded leading fascists below Mussolini – especially his only serious rival, Italo Balbo.

Predappio is a small town ninety kilometres or so east of Bologna by road. Mussolini was born there and this fact alone led to a focus on the town throughout the period of the regime. When Mussolini was alive an entirely new town was constructed and he kept a holiday home nearby. Predappio became a key part of the geography and topography connected to the cult of personality constructed around Il Duce; a huge fascist building dominated the new town centre and people visited on 'pilgrimages'.

From 1928 to 1933, a cycling race was organised annually which began in Predappio and ended in Rome. It was known as 'La Coppa del Duce'. This was an incredibly long race which usually took place in just one day. In 1930, it was won by the legendary cyclist Learco Guerra, who took 18 hours, 56 minutes and 30 seconds to complete the route. After all that cycling, he eventually only won in a tight sprint against the equally famous Alberto Binda. In 1931 the distance had risen to 580 kilometres, and of the thirty-five cyclists who started, only twenty-three finished. A year later, another five kilometres was added to the route, and Guerra won again. In its last edition, 1933, the race was run in two stages, over a distance of nearly 630 kilometres.[6] Under the regime, sport was seen as an epic activity for heroes – the new fascist man.

STADIO DEL LITTORIALE, 27 OCTOBER 1929

The Stadio del Littoriale in Bologna was one of the world's first modern football stadiums, opened officially in 1927. On 27 October 1929 an extra piece of the complex building was to be completed. Seven tons of bronze, said by some to be repurposed from melted down Austrian cannons, went into building a 42-metre high 'Marathon Tower', which overlooked the centre of the pitch. The tower hosted a huge statue of Mussolini on a horse, celebrating and commemorating the day when Il Duce addressed a huge crowd of blackshirts and others at the (as yet unfinished) stadium in October 1926. Later that same day he had survived an assassination attempt, the fourth in less than a year, in the centre of Bologna.

Sculptor Giuseppe Graziosi had sat with Mussolini on a number of occasions in Rome in order to sculpt an accurate likeness of his face. So heavy was the monument that it was transported in sections to Bologna, with the bronze horse arriving before Il Duce's head and body. On 27 October 1929 the tower itself was officially opened in the presence of leading fascists. Mussolini was represented as himself, but also as a deity, an emperor, a man of power – human and mythical at the same time, dynamic but also, it seemed, built very much to last.

HISTORY OF THE FASCIST REVOLUTION

Giorgio Alberto Chiurco, while a medical student, had also been a leading *squadrista* in Siena, responsible for murders and beatings. He almost certainly killed people and took part in attacks on many others before going on to become a university professor and doctor. When fascism decided to write its own history, well in advance of the tenth anniversary of the March on Rome in 1932, it was decided to entrust the entire project to Chiurco. It is not clear how he got the job, but it was a huge undertaking, and the results were immense: five hefty volumes of the *Storia della rivoluzione fascista*, covering the 1919–22 period, which all appeared in 1929.[7]

These books are lavishly illustrated, with dozens of photos. Many of the images are of dead bodies reproduced in grim, gruesome detail – almost always of young fascists or nationalists, the 'martyrs' of the movement, the revolution. It is an almost absurdly one-sided historical representation. In Chiurco's version of the past, only fascists had died, and only socialists had killed. The volumes were dedicated, of course, to Mussolini, and carried a perfunctory two-page introduction by Il Duce, as well as a reproduction of his signature. Many thousands of copies were printed and are still to be found in numerous libraries across Italy.

Chiurco referred to the books as 'the history of our salvation'. Often, there were long and dull lists of names, running for pages and pages. Many lobbied to be included. It was a question of status, but also of economic gain. 'Martyrs of the revolution', officially registered participants in the March on Rome, and their families, had access to welfare payments and other tangible benefits. After the war, when Chiurco was imprisoned and placed on trial for collaborationism and other crimes, his authorship of the *Storia della rivoluzione fascista* was used against him. He was accused of the glorification of violence. After an initial guilty verdict, he was eventually cleared in the early 1950s.[8]

The 1930s

By the 1930s, public resistance to fascism was becoming more and more desperate. On 3 October 1931 an intellectual anti-fascist called Lauro De Bosis took off from Marseilles in a wooden plane. It was effectively a suicide mission. He was carrying a cargo of anti-fascist leaflets. The leaflets were dated '*anno VII dal delitto Matteotti*' ('Year VII since the Matteotti Murder') in a parody of fascist dating reaching back to 1922. Anti-fascism now also had its own alternative calendar. De Bosis dropped the leaflets over Rome, but was killed when his plane, probably having run out of fuel, crashed into the sea on his attempted return, creating another anti-fascist martyr.[1] Neither any part of the plane nor his body was ever found. De Bosis left behind a written testament entitled 'The Story of My Death'. He was a brilliant scholar and translator and author of a poetic drama called, appropriately, *Icaro*. The leaflets he distributed were unusual, containing advice such as 'Never buy a newspaper; they contain nothing but lies', and 'Accept nothing from fascism. All that it can give you, is but the price of your prostitution.'[2]

In Ignazio Silone's novel, *Bread and Wine*, a communist militant returns to Italy from exile, disguised as a priest. He struggles to recognise Italy. It has become, in Silone's words, the 'Land of Propaganda'.[3] Resistance has been reduced to almost nothing, to scratched slogans on walls, or the occasional remark in a bar (which could get you into deep trouble). 'The Land of Propaganda,' wrote Silone, 'is built on unanimity ... if one man says, "No", the spell is broken and public order is endangered.'[4] But Silone was wrong. De Bosis's action did not break the spell. It was a glorious, symbolic, individual act of anti-fascist heroism, which had no political impact whatsoever.

1932: FACISM CELEBRATES ITSELF – A DECADE IN POWER

By 1932, fascism seemed impregnable. Ignazio Silone wrote bitterly that "The truth is officially as follows … Bolshevism reigned here, and religion, morality and private property were being trampled underfoot. Then came Etcetera Etcetera, and religion, morality and private property were restored.'[5] All opposition in Italy had been more or less wiped out and Mussolini now felt so safe that he could go out for car trips and walks on the beach by himself, with no obvious bodyguards (although he was always monitored, supposedly for his own protection, everywhere he went). In keeping with this confidence and strength, a huge, imposing celebration of the March on Rome and the rise of fascism was staged in the capital.[6] The series of events and commemorations were known collectively as the *decennale*, and were accompanied by publications, film screenings and a vast celebratory exhibition visited by millions of Italians. Mussolini made sure that Chiurco's propagandist five-volume history of the 'Fascist Revolution' was distributed in vast numbers, underlining his power, generosity and confidence. An extensive amnesty in which thousands of prisoners and internees were released, emphasised his apparent sense of clemency.[7]

Italian fascism was neither entirely nostalgic nor exclusively modern.[8] Representations of the march in 1932 made frequent reference to ancient Rome. It had not just been a march on a political capital, with its almost insignificant, fifty-or-so-year history. It was also a march back towards ancient greatness, to a place which symbolised a former magnificent empire: the past was being revived and reinvented, fascism claimed, through a new and glorious future. A photo of 'the deserter' Francesco Misiano was also included in the exhibition, staged to celebrate the first decade since the 'Fascist Revolution' in October 1932. Fascism wanted to keep the memory of the recent past, and of who they had supposedly 'defeated', very much alive. There were images and 'relics' from Palazzo d'Accursio, Empoli, the Diana Theatre bombing and the 'Renzino ambush'. Fascism's 'martyrs' were a key part of the exhibition. Many were reburied with elaborate ceremonies in special crypts across Italy, often below or next to major churches.

Nineteen twenty-three had seen the first celebration of the March on Rome. From 1927 onwards, the year 1922 was posthumously recast as Year Zero. Across Italy, you can still see buildings with year markings on them which correspond to this fascist, supposedly 'revolutionary', calendar – Year X of the Fascist Era, for example, was 1932 (*Anno X E.F.*). From 1930 onwards, 28 October became a national holiday, with all public offices closed.[9] It was said that on 28 October, in Terni prison, anti-fascist prisoners would always be beaten up: 'you could hear the blows, the lashings, we heard the screams from here. From inside the jail.'[10]

Over time, laborious official lists were drawn up of the 'participants' in the march: for example, 230 Italian Jews officially took part.[11] Participation was interpreted elastically; not everyone who was said to have taken part even made it to the capital. But official recognition was important, bringing prestige and even special housing. In Bologna a whole neighbourhood was built for 'fascist martyrs' and their families.

THE DEFEATED: ODYSSEYS AND JOURNEYS – ANTI-FASCIST FUGITIVES AND OTHERS UNDER THE REGIME

What happened to those involved on the 'wrong' side of the civil war in 1919–22? Having been forced to give up his seat in parliament, 'the deserter' Francesco Misiano hid for a time with comrades in the industrial town of Piombino, where it was thought that the local left was strong enough to protect him. For his final place of exile, he chose the USSR, where he remained until his premature death in 1936. His early demise probably saved him from being purged by the Stalinist regime. There he was able to reinvent himself once again, working in the cinema industry, producing numerous films and inviting stars to the Soviet Union from Hollywood. He sometimes told people that his entire life 'had been like a film'.

Other exiles disappeared altogether. Vittorio Martelli, who had been convicted in absentia for his supposed role in the Palazzo d'Accursio massacre in Bologna in 1920, was never seen again in Italy, or noted abroad. Every year after 1920 it was dutifully reported in his police file that: 'He is still missing.' He had no contact with his family that could be detected by the police, and they noticed at one point that: 'His elderly mother mourns for him as if he was dead. In his house, according to our enquiries, there is a photo of Martelli which is constantly lit up, with an oil lamp, with flowers around it.'[12] In official files he was described as a 'Communist ... Dangerous ... Exile ... Capable of Terrorist Acts' – hitting the jackpot of epithets for the political police; he was the target of twenty-six arrest warrants. He left behind his wife and a son (Minos) who went on to be a fascist war hero.[13]

The other two men who had successfully evaded arrest and avoided the D'Accursio trial (in person, but they were still convicted in absentia) both ended up in the USSR. Pio Pizzirani worked in a cushion factory in the Soviet Union. He died there, it seems, of typhoid in 1932, after being joined by his wife and two sons, who travelled via Germany. One of his sons, Galileo, would later be another victim of Stalin's purges. In 1938 Armando Cocchi, the third fugitive, was arrested there and ended up in Stalin's gulag, but he was not executed.[14] After a period in semi-internal exile, Pietro Farini, the socialist deputy from Terni who had been driven out of his home town and seen his pharmacy burnt to the ground by the fascists, fled to Paris and then on to the USSR. He died there in 1940, in a home for 'veterans of the revolution'. Communist Party member Giovanni Morelli was one of the five who disappeared after the 'massacre in Empoli' in 1921, and who were all given long sentences after the 1924 trial. He was just twenty-two at the time of the attack. After escaping to France he also reached the USSR around 1934. In 1937 he also fell victim to Stalin's purges, dying in a gulag in 1943.[15] It was a tragedy within the tragedy.

Bernardo Melacci, the anarchist who was given thirty years after the trial for the 'ambush of Renzino' in Tuscany in 1921 was finally released thanks to an amnesty in 1935. But he was then rearrested and almost immediately sent to internal exile. Eventually, in order to silence him once and for all, he was confined in a psychiatric hospital, where he died in 1943, more than two decades after the events in Foiano and Renzino.[16]

Fascism adapted its repressive methods for those it wanted to suppress. After the Diana bomb disaster, the veteran anarchist Errico Malatesta was released but the regime made sure he did not slip out of Italy again: he was kept under strict 'undeclared house arrest' in Rome for a decade until his death in 1932.[17] As the historian Maurizio Antonioli has written, Malatesta was a 'prisoner in his own house … a guard was permanently stationed on the pavement outside his house and another two in the doorway'.[18] Fascism was so worried about Malatesta that even his tomb was guarded and watched, and all those who visited were asked to give their names.

Argentina Altobelli, the reformist trade union leader who had led an organisation of over a million landworkers after the war, was threatened, followed and intimidated by fascists. Eventually, like so many other activists, she chose to 'withdraw into the private sphere' – code for a 'choice' which was really just a means of surviving. Some, however, saw this kind of 'withdrawal' as a passive act of submission to the regime. Altobelli moved to Rome, working in a number of jobs, including teaching French, in order to get by. Under fascism, Altobelli described her situation as that of 'the defeated' – she added that 'it is like we have been shipwrecked … and we no longer have the right to speak'.[19] She scratched a living writing unsigned technical articles for very low pay. In private, 'the final phase of her life saw her protect and remain faithful to the values which had ruled her life, and which were outside of those preached by the regime'.[20]

In the 1930s Altobelli looked back on her life, and the demands of being a mother and a militant: 'It was an incredible, gigantic effort to try and be a different kind of woman … my life as a political woman had been led by a sense of love towards humanity, and by a sincere and deep sense of thought and conscience.'[21] She died, forgotten, in Rome. Years earlier, she had written: 'You cannot defeat ideas with a cudgel, or a revolver, or with arson … an idea lives forever!'[22]

Others moved in a kind of grey zone, drifting between submission and desperation. Ercole Bucco, the forceful maximalist revolutionary leader who had experienced a dramatic rise to prominence and swift fall from grace in 1919–21, fled to France in 1922, leaving his five children behind. In exile, he looked to find work as an architect. Another – obscure – phase of his life began to take shape. In 1926 Bucco expressed a desire to return to Italy and it was reported that 'he does not want to have … political problems'. This was a forlorn hope. His political past would follow him like a shadow as long as fascism was in power. In the 1930s, still in France, Bucco appeared to move towards fascism. He expressed admiration for Mussolini and in November 1935 joined the Fascist Party and formally renounced 'his political past'. It was claimed that he had 'finally understood all the false nature of his previous political ideas and was repentant. He admires the Duce and expresses his reverence for him.' 'He,' it was reported, 'only desires to be pardoned, and to be freed from what weighs on his conscience, he knows he is hated in his own country and that nothing can be done about his family situation, which is the outcome of his disgraceful political past.'[23] This was quite the turnaround from one of the highest profile radicals active in postwar Italy.

These acts of contrition were common under fascism, and were often insincere, as people formally expressed fascist ideas or love for Mussolini with the hope of being able to work and live without harassment and, if they had been exiled, move back to Italy.[24] Bucco was perhaps playing a game: his letters always ended with the stock phrase 'With a friendly fascist greeting.'

Bucco's embrace of fascism cut him off definitively from the anti-fascist exile community. Not only was he still seen as a notorious 'coward' linked to his activities in 1920, he was also now seen as a 'traitor'. Many believed him to be a spy, or a double agent. Meanwhile, he had a new partner, and had fathered another (it seems) four children *adulterina* (in the official language of the time; or 'out of wedlock'). But his strategy failed; his political conversion was not seen to be credible. After finally returning to Italy in the late 1930s he was arrested, and convicted by the Tribunale Speciale per la Difesa dello Stato of 'fraud', corruption, spying and anti-fascist statements (overheard in prison, allegedly) and given a fourteen-year sentence in April 1939. He was also accused of 'insulting the nation'.

Direct appeals to Mussolini were common, and Il Duce received hundreds of thousands of letters and personal entreaties during the 1920s and 1930s. He replied to many of them and took a direct interest in numerous individual cases. Tito Oro Nobili, the socialist from Terni who suffered torture and beatings in 1926, and who, like Modigliani, had been barred from working as a lawyer, eventually wrote to Mussolini and other leading fascists in the 1930s seeking some form of forgiveness or clemency so that he could return to his work. By doing so, he had broken a moral code, causing other socialists to look upon him with suspicion. The long letters are conserved in the state archives in Rome. Letters of this kind were often copied by the regime to be used later for blackmail. In some of them, Oro Nobili describes the violence he had suffered at the hands of *squadristi* in 1926, which he connected to personal and local feuds, rather than fascist political strategies.[25]

Oro Nobili knew this version of his own past was untrue – it was a desperate attempt to simply get back on his feet and earn a living. The letters seem to have had some effect and Oro Nobili was re-admitted to the lawyers' guild in 1934. They were classic 'letters of subjugation', both humiliating and politically problematic.[26] It was a new literary genre, the public documentation of a complete personal and political defeat. Even the language had to be 'fascist'. Mussolini would read these letters out in parliament on occasion, revelling in his victory and power. Oro Nobili was criticised from within the anti-fascist exile community, but the letters were quietly forgotten about after the war.

Ennio Gnudi's story was a true odyssey. Having been forced into exile, Bologna's tragic 'Mayor for an Hour' of November 1920 was constantly followed across the world by the antennae of the fascist secret police. Spies reported on his every speech and each move. Gnudi lived for nineteen years or so in a series of modest rooms and flats in Switzerland, Belgium, the USA, France, Canada, Argentina, the USSR, Spain and Mexico. He changed his name often and used fake identification cards and passports. He had very little money and survived day to day on handouts from comrades and support associations. He had left his family behind in Italy (he never married, and fascist spies tried to imply he was a paedophile)[27] and tried to keep in touch by letter, but his post was opened by the police who also hassled his family and friends, bringing them in for questioning. Gnudi never saw his mother again.

Gnudi's letters, kept in the archives in Rome and Bologna, are intensely sad. Fascism had forcibly separated him from those he loved, who waited for scraps of news about his life and wellbeing. In 1934, he wrote to a family member saying he had 'never forgotten' his family and asking after his 'poor mother'. He apologised that he 'couldn't' send any money which was a 'great misfortune'. All money sent to his mother had been 'seized' and their correspondence read, copied and filed, leading to further interrogations and harassment. He was ashamed that he couldn't help his family in Italy financially, but wrote that they were still 'a part of me'.[28]

All of these stories were indicative of the absolute defeat suffered by the anarchists, socialists and communists of Italy. These movements had not merely suffered a political reversal; they had been eliminated from the scene entirely. Fascism pursued them without pity across the globe, rarely closing its files, or halting its attempts to find them. They had no voice in their own country. It was as if they had never existed, except as walk-on parts in propaganda about the 'red years'. Even the heaven on earth of the Soviet Union turned out to be a terrible illusion. For many, it was a double tragedy. The USSR was as repressive as the country they had fled from. Resistance was reduced to individual acts of defiance, which often led to arrest and punishment. Archives and reports are full of incidents of people detained for 'insulting Il Duce' or 'singing subversive songs', especially in bars, late at night, after a few drinks. The regime, meanwhile, set out to create alternative heroes, and claim credit for the success of others.

1933

SUPERMAN: THE RISE AND FALL OF PRIMO CARNERA

He was already a giant at birth. Some stories put his weight as a newborn, in October 1906, at 10 kilos.[1] Primo Carnera was from a desperately poor mountain village called Sequals, in Friuli, north-east Italy. Like so many others from this region he was forced to emigrate in his teens, and left for France at the age of fourteen in 1920.

As he grew, and grew (there is some dispute over his final height, but it was close to two metres; his feet were 32 centimetres long) Primo was first picked up by a circus as a kind of freak. Then a wily entrepreneur saw some potential there, and Carnera began a long and successful boxing career. Most of the first part of his boxing life was in the USA, and there were frequent claims that many of his bouts were fixed by the Mob. But he rose through the ranks, and in 1933 he had his big break. In New York, he fought Jack Sharkey for the title of Heavyweight Champion of the World, winning by a knock-out.

Carnera's first successful defence of the title was staged in Rome in October 1933. Mussolini attended the fight with all three of his sons, along with his spin doctor, Achille Starace, his son-in-law and future leading fascist Galeazzo Ciano and others. The crowd was huge – between 60,000 and 70,000 people were said to be there that day. Carnera leant his immense fame to the needs of the regime, wearing a black shirt on many occasions (including before that 1933 fight) and giving the fascist salute when required. It was an extraordinary event, and fascism made the most of this new hero – this superman, with his enormous muscles and incredible body. Some said that shaking his hand was like trying to grasp a water melon.[2] Carnera was usually quoted, when he was winning, in terms which connected his victories with those of Il Duce, and with the regime in general. After he became world champion he said: 'When I saw [his opponent] on the canvas my thoughts went immediately to Italy, to Il Duce.'[3] One newspaper claimed that Carnera's punch to win the title contained 'the force of all 43 million Italians'.[4]

Carnera's usefulness for fascist propaganda was short-lived, though for a time his popularity had seemed to rival that of Mussolini himself. In 1934 Carnera was humiliated by the US fighter Max Baer in New York, who knocked him down on numerous occasions. Heavy subsequent losses to boxers, including the great Joe Louis, were embarrassing for the regime. Newspapers in Italy were banned from printing images of Carnera on the canvas. Soon, fascist publications stopped talking about him altogether. He fought on for years, in part to pay his bills, as he had lost all of his winnings due to unscrupulous hangers-on and bad business deals. In the end, seventy-two of his fights were won by knockout, a record.

Yet Carnera remained popular among ordinary people, who thronged to greet him whenever he appeared on Italian soil. His fame went beyond fascism – almost as he if were a film star (and he did make movies) – beyond the political use which fascism saw in him. *Carnera* even became a word in itself, meaning a strong man, or a giant. In his later years, he became a figure of fun and ridicule (attracting nicknames such as 'The Ambling Alp', 'The Walking Mountain', or even 'The Colossus of Clay') and earned money by taking part in numerous wrestling matches. Many were happy to pay for tickets just to see him. Carnera had entered the hearts of Italians in deeper and more emotional ways, going beyond the role of a simple propagandistic puppet.

*

In power, fascism continued to construct a heroic version of Italy's past, centred around itself. Huge fascist-style war memorials were inaugurated. Fascism wrote and rewrote history both backwards and forwards. Italy's war had been a *fascist war*, and Mussolini and the blackshirts had saved the country from the socialists and chaos after 1918. Fascism's martyrs from the postwar period were celebrated through football stadiums, streets, squares, schools and numerous monuments, which were the sites for annual commemorations. In 1933, for example, a huge granite monument was built to the two young fascists whose deaths had sparked off the 'massacre of Turin' in 1922. The monument was close to the place where the shootings were alleged to have taken place. It carried this inscription, with a classic combination of religious language and demonisation of the enemy:

The blackshirts
Dresda Giuseppe Railway worker
Bazzani Lucio Student
Unaware of the cowardly attack
Here they fell victim
Of their faith in the *duce*
Of their love for the Fatherland
Preparing with their generous
Sacrifice a new spring
And the Fascist rebirth
       The night of 17/18 December 1922

The architect was Gino Levi-Montalcini, a Jewish-Italian whose sister was the future Nobel Prize in Medicine-winner, Rita Levi-Montalcini. Gino later suffered discrimination under fascist anti-Semitic laws and decrees.[5] A road was also named after Bazzani. No monuments were erected under fascism to the numerous victims of the massacre of Turin which followed the deaths of the two fascists in 1922. Their memory lived on in private, or among exile communities.

1934

RAS IN CONTROL

Fascist power put down deep roots at a local level, which was often transmitted through family and friendship ties. Political, economic and cultural power were fused and leading fascists became very rich. Italo Balbo's nephew, Lino, was appointed *federale* (the leading local fascist position) in Ferrara in 1934 (the year Italo left for Libya, where Mussolini had appointed him as governor, in part to get rid of his most serious rival) and remained in that post until 1940. Balbo himself ran the influential *Corriere Padano* newspaper, based in Ferrara, from 1925–40. Local power was often absolute, and personalised: 'Ferrara and Balbo are indistinguishable ... these two names are united in every country in the world.'[1] Italo Balbo was a 'rich man by 1924'.[2]

In Livorno, the Ciano family were in control politically, economically and culturally.[3] Cremona was effectively the fiefdom of Roberto Farinacci, who also managed his own heavily subsidised and widely distributed daily newspaper. Giuseppe Bottai later purchased a forty-two-room villa, for example, for a huge amount of money at the time. Clientelist structures were reinforced. *Ras* became a combination of Mafia bosses, small-town dictators, business leaders and gatekeepers for resources. Another lie that fascism told was that it was different from the corrupt politicians of the liberal period.

Yet, there were limits to these powers. There was no danger of being voted out, of course, but *ras* could be removed from above – sidelined, hit by real or manufactured scandals, or sent into internal exile. Moreover, the fact that this influence was largely *local* was a limit in itself. Mussolini never allowed the *ras* to become too powerful. He often neutralised his rivals by sending them to the colonies, as with Balbo, or by allowing them free rein in the provinces, far away from Rome. Power struggles also developed *within* fascism – over resources, jobs, prestige. These were often connected to long-standing regional and local conflicts. In 1923 Mussolini claimed that: 'Everywhere the Fascist Party appears to be marked by divisions and personal quarrels.'[4] It was back to politics as usual, once revolution (and democracy) had been safely suppressed. There was no further need even to bother with the fixing and policing of elections: they had been abolished.

Many *ras* thus became (unelected) politicians, with their *squadrista* past conveniently forgotten, apart from when it was required for ritual celebrations, or was needed as political capital. Some who drew on such capital had never been *squadristi* at all, like Costanzo Ciano in Livorno.[5] The fact that the *ras* had often murdered and beaten numerous people – or had ordered others to do so – was played down, or ignored. Once squadrism had achieved its aims of violently rooting out the socialist menace, the *ras* settled down to a life of opulence and prestige. By the 1920s and 1930s many were embedded deep inside a political system they had once railed against.

Giuseppe Caradonna from Apulia, for example, became under-secretary in the Department of Postal Services – a classic clientelist position, as well as vice-president of the Lower House of parliament. He presented only three laws in a parliamentary career which lasted twenty-two years. Two were linked to charity lotteries. After coming to power, Mussolini did try on occasion to remove Caradonna from office and from Italy, but he resisted a transfer to Cuba and in the end he was paid off with various administrative and corporate positions. At a local level Caradonna continued to draw local prestige from his connections with the popular friar known as Padre Pio, who became his confessor during the 1920s and the 1930s. Rumours of miracles linked to the fascist regime began to spread. It was said that Padre Pio had helped Caradonna to recover from a serious illness.[6] Some even claimed that Padre Pio later 'appeared' and protected Caradonna from a partisan firing squad in Milan in 1945.[7]

IL DUCE ON TOUR

While the defeated socialists, communists and anarchists eked out a living in exile, or were forced to compromise with the regime to be allowed to work, the cult of personality around Il Duce continued to grow. Mussolini visited Apulia in 1934 amidst great pomp and ceremony (it was his first visit to the region since 1923). The trip lasted five days. Il Duce visited schools, public works, new towns under construction, factories, a new trade fair and modern farms. It was said that 150,000 people travelled from the surrounding areas to greet him in Foggia. He was presented on every stage-managed occasion with medals, trophies and commemorative items. All of this was covered in triumphant tones by the national and local press, and in newsreels which were shown in cinemas, depicting Mussolini speaking at big rallies flanked by blackshirts, including his spin doctor, Achille Starace, who had started out on his glorious fascist career in the same region.

A documentary was made and a whole book published by a local fascist about this Mussolini 'tour', which described Il Duce as: 'A prodigious sower who left Rome from time to time, in order to visit those places where he had spread seeds with his hand, to admire the first flowerings or the new fruits.' It was more like the visit of a monarch, or even a semi-deity, than that of a prime minister, but Mussolini also presented himself as a man of the people, who could communicate with anyone.[8]

BORDERLANDS AND EMPIRE: GENOCIDE AND INVASION

Italy's borderlands saw the *squadristi* at their most violent, often in conflict with non-Italian speaking peoples. Once in power, fascism constructed hostile policies towards what it saw as 'others' especially on the north-eastern frontier, and around Alto Adige. *Squadristi* burned Slovenian institutions to the ground during the rise of fascism in Trieste. On the Carso plain above Trieste, where the language and people were mainly Slovenian, Italian was imposed with force in schools, Slovenian organisations were repressed, 'foreign' surnames were changed by law (even, it is said, in graveyards) and Slovenian teachers were sacked en masse.[9]

Italian fascism was desperate for a new empire abroad, and violence and military power were directed at seizing new land. Italy had to become a great power. This would be both a new, fascist empire, and an attempt to make Italy (and specifically Rome) great *again*, through reference to the glories of the past. All means necessary were used to achieve these aims. Local resistance in the territory later known as Libya, an Italian colony since 1912 (after a war Mussolini had served a jail sentence for opposing) was 'pacified' with extreme forms of repression and genocidal massacres.[10] In 1930 one of the key army officers involved in this campaign, Pietro Badoglio, wrote that Italian tactics 'will spell the ruin of the so-called subjected population. But the path has been set, and we must follow it to the end, even if it entails the death of the entire population.'[11] Local people were forced to march across vast swathes of desert and herded into camps. Thousands died or were executed. 'Overnight, an entire society that had survived and adapted with extraordinary resilience in an unforgiving environment for centuries was almost entirely destroyed.'[12] A consensus has since emerged that the actions carried out by the Italians in Libya constituted a genocide. Libya was finally declared as 'conquered' in 1934.[13]

But there was a bigger prize: the land Italians called Ethiopia (but which was known by others as Abyssinia). Liberal Italy had suffered a humiliating defeat at the hands of the Abyssinian army in 1896 at a place called Adua. Mussolini's new imperial wars and expansion aimed to wipe out that moment of national shame. In October 1935, close to 500,000 Italian troops were mobilised to invade Ethiopia from bases in Italian Eritrea, and 110,000 men were on the ground as the war began. Mussolini's speech announcing the declaration of war against Ethiopia lasted just thirteen minutes and contained 425 seconds of pauses, which were filled by wild applause in Rome and by those listening via loud speakers in *piazze* across Italy. It is estimated that ten million Italians heard this speech on the radio. Margherita Sarfatti, Mussolini's former lover and hagiographer, was listening from another balcony. It is claimed that she described Il Duce's speech as 'the beginning of the end ... we will win it [she predicted] and he will lose his head'.[14]

Early progress was swift: it took just three days for the Italians to reach Adua. *La Gazzetta del Popolo* led with a huge banner headline: 'Il Duce has avenged the dead from 1896. The Italian flag flies at Adua.'[15] An enormous 5-metre-tall head of Mussolini was sculptured in rock in

Adua. General De Bono later inaugurated a further small monument to the fallen from 1896.

The rest of the war was much more complicated and bloody, but with relatively few losses on the Italian side. Italian propaganda even exaggerated their own casualties upwards to increase the impact of the war back home.[16] Addis Ababa, the capital, was occupied by Italy's fascist army in May 1936 and was seen as the jewel in the crown of Mussolini's quest for a glorious new 'Roman Empire'. Emperor Haile Selassie was forced into exile, much of which he spent in Bath, England. Italy had gained control of a rich country consisting of 3.5 million square kilometres and 13 million inhabitants. International protests at the invasion led to sanctions being imposed on Italy, but the conquest seemed popular at home. A racist campaign accompanied the military endeavours, including the popularisation of one of Italian fascism's most popular songs, '*Faccetta Nera*' ('Little Black Face').

Mussolini called Ethiopia a 'a barbarian country … unfit to remain amongst civilised people'.[17] On 9 May 1936, Mussolini gave another triumphant speech from his favourite balcony in Rome: 'Finally, Italy has its empire … a fascist empire, an empire of civilisation and of humanity for all the peoples of Ethiopia.' Italy, he claimed, was a great power once again, hailing the return 'after fifteen centuries … of the empire on the fatal hills of Rome'. Mussolini was presenting himself as a new, modern and triumphant emperor. Fascism appeared unstoppable.

Poison gas dropped via hundreds of bombs was used to destroy the Ethiopian resistance, and was in particular used against civilians. Mustard gas 'rained down corrosive drops that penetrated through clothing and produced potentially fatal internal lesions'.[18] On the ground 'this rain … burned and killed'.[19] This illegal weapon was utilised both before and after the official 'end' of the colonial war. Although there were reports and discussions of poison gas deployment after the fall of fascism, the Italian state did not officially admit to this war crime until 1996, six decades later. Ethiopian losses were sixty times greater than those in the Italian army.

Many of fascism's hierarchs joined up and fought in the war. Mussolini's second son, Vittorio, wrote about the burning of villages as 'a job which was great fun … you needed to hit the thatched roofs in the middle … and those wretches who were inside and saw the fire rushed outside as if they were possessed by the devil'.[20] Indro Montanelli, who would go on to become one of Italy's most famous journalists after 1945, and has a statue dedicated to him in Milan, wrote in 1936: 'This war is like a long and happy holiday given to us by the Great Father as a prize after thirteen years of school. And, speaking amongst ourselves, it was about time.'[21] Montanelli purchased a twelve-year-old local 'wife' in Ethiopia. He later claimed, somewhat unbelievably, to have met this woman again in 1952, and that she had called her son by him 'Indro'. Squadrism was reborn and celebrated in Italy's colonial wars. Fascism's empire was a new playground for the ex-*squadristi*. Extreme racist violence was the way Italy pacified its colonies.

Other figures enjoyed the reflected power of this new empire. The king was given yet another title – Emperor of Ethiopia, and Ethiopia was united to Somalia to create Italian East Africa. Leading Church figures supported the colonial wars. Many ordinary Italians were connected to the new empire, beyond the army itself. Although a relatively small number of Italians settled in Ethiopia, it has been estimated that up to a million Italians visited one of the countries in the empire in the second half of the 1930s. Racial laws were applied in the colonies in legal experiments which would later be used back home. 'Mixed' marriages were outlawed. Children of relationships between Italians and the colonised were afforded a lesser status to white offspring, and segregation policies were introduced. In short, the "civilising mission" was never more than an ideological veneer'.[22]

Massacre in Africa

On 19 September 1937, the 'Viceroy of Ethiopia', fascist general Rodolfo Graziani, was hosting a ceremonial 'alms-giving' event in Addis Ababa. Suddenly, at about 11.40 a.m., a series of explosions rang out. It was an audacious attempt on Graziani's life by a handful of members of the Ethiopian resistance. Graziani himself was wounded. Nine grenades had been thrown.

Immediately, a reprisal began. Italian soldiers and *carabinieri* and other officials (alongside Eritrean and other Askari troops, although some of these refused to take part) killed every Ethiopian they could find in the vicinity, using machine guns, hand grenades and other weapons.[23] Nearly all the Ethiopians present in the area, some 3,000

Figure 1. Alfonsine, June 1914. A monarchist club after being sacked by demonstrators during Red Week. The slogan on the wall reads: LONG LIVE MASETTI, DOWN WITH THE ARMY. The men with the horses are *carabinieri*. On the ground are the remains of the billiard table which stood inside the club, and of the portraits of the King and Queen which had been thrown from the first-floor window. Some locals are posing on the right.

Figure 2. A plaque to the victims of Red Week, Ancona, date of photograph unknown. The plaque reads: HERE KILLED BY ROYAL LEAD FELL NELLO BUDINI, ANTONIO CASACCA, ATTILIO GIAMBRIGIONI, RED WEEK, 7 JUNE 1914. DESTROYED BY THE FLOOD OF 5 SEPTEMBER 1959, THE ANARCHISTS AND REPUBLICANS OF ANCONA PUT THIS UP AGAIN ON 5 JUNE 1960.

Figure 3. Florence, 1920. The workers of the factory and foundary of the Pignone in occupation for the great struggles of the proletariat. Presumably red flags are on show, plus a banner which reads: FIOM [THE METALWORKERS' UNION] 2 SEPTEMBER 1920.

Figure 5. Teatro Carlo Goldoni, Livorno, January 1921. The Seventeenth Italian Socialist Party Congress. The banner behind the huge image of Karl Marx reads: WORKERS OF THE WORLD UNITE.

Figure 4. Nicola Bombacci, 1920s.

Figure 6. Exhibition on the Fascist Revolution, Rome Exposition Palace, 1932. A reconstruction of Mussolini's office (also referred to as a *covo*, or 'haunt') in Milan's Via Paolo da Cannobio. Note the grenades and gun on the desk, and the Arditi banner on the wall.

Figure 7. A photograph by Ulderico David titled *Squadristi di Cervia in assetto di combattimento.* ('*Squadristi* from the town of Cervia near Ravenna in full battle dress').

Figure 8. A photograph by Ulderico David titled *Tipo di squadrista di questi giorni: 'Pugnale fra i denti, le bombe a mano'* ('*Squadrista* with a grenade and gun in hand, a knife between the teeth').

Figure 9. Rome, probably 1921. Francesco Misiano is marched through the streets by fascists and others, his head having been partially shaved. The banner around his neck reads: YOU MUST SERVE THE FATHERLAND AND I AM A DESERTER.

Adolfo Porry Pastorel, Istituto Luce

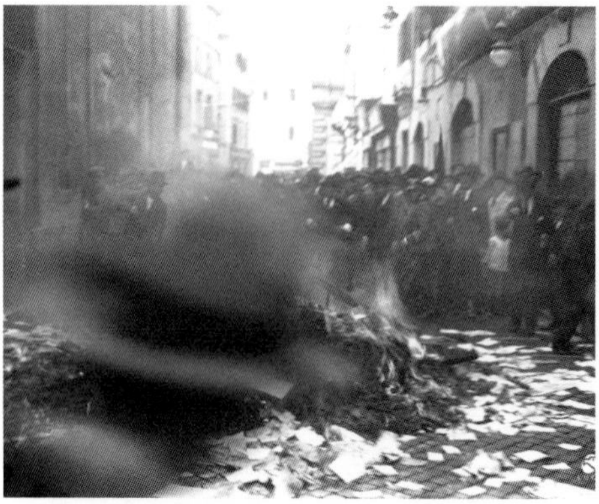

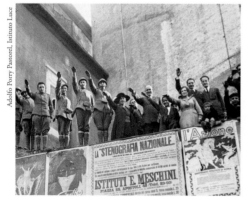

Figure 10. The March on Rome, October 1922. Papers and books are burned by fascists.

Adolfo Porry Pastorel, Istituto Luce

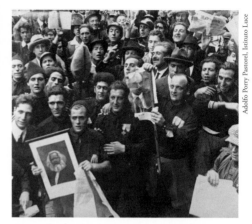

Figure 11. The March on Rome, October 1922. Blackshirts with 'trophies' seized from Socialist and Trade Union buildings, including a portrait of Marx, a poster of Lenin and left-wing newspapers.

Adolfo Porry Pastorel, Istituto Luce

Figure 12. The March on Rome, October 1922. Citizens and soldiers give the fascist salute.

Adolfo Porry Pastorel, Istituto Luce

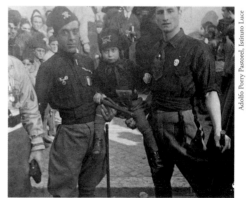

Figure 13. The March on Rome, October 1922. Blackshirts with a 'blackshirt' baby.

Figure 14. The March on Rome, October 1922. Benito Mussolini in Naples before the march commences. Other fascists present include Achille Starace (with medals, to the far right of the photo), Italo Balbo (back to us, next to Mussolini), Emilio De Bono (white beard), Attilio Teruzzi (black beard and medals, to de Bono's right), Michele Bianchi (no beard, to the left of De Bono) and Cesare Maria De Vecchi (with the moustache and medals, to Mussolini's left).

Figure 15. Riano, June 1924. Giacomo Matteotti's body is carried away in a coffin for the autopsy at the cemetery after being discovered outside Rome.

Figure 16. Rome, 1944. The graffiti reads: MURDERER OF MATTEOTTI.

Figure 17. Statue of Mussolini in the 'Littoriale' Football Stadium, Bologna, 1929. Statue designed by Giuseppe Graziosi (1879-1942).

Figure 18. Head of Mussolini carved from rock, Tenbien (close to Adua), Ethiopia, March 1936. It seems that this head was later destroyed by explosives.

Figure 19. Naples, date unknown. The boxer Primo Carnera gives a fascist salute in front of the Vesuvius volcano.

Figure 20. World Cup, Rome, 1934. The Italian national football team is photographed while performing the fascist salute before a match. Note the sparse crowd.

Figure 21. A fascist gathering in Piazza del Duomo, Milan, 1933. Note the Fasci lights around the statue of King Vittorio Emanuele II in the foreground.

Figure 22. Mussolini's rally in Piazza del Duomo, Trento, 31 August 1935. Mussolini is speaking on the left in front of the city cathedral. A temporary stage has been erected in the form of an axe.

Figure 23. In this close-up from Trento, Mussolini can be seen on the temporary stage with his hands on his hips.

Figure 24. A fascist family, circa 1935. Seven children was the minimum requirement for welfare benefits afforded to those with 'extra births'.

Figure 25. Fascist militia hold their daggers out towards Benito Mussolini at Palazzo d'Accursio in Piazza Maggiore, Bologna, 30 October 1936. This gathering marked the fourteenth anniversary of the March on Rome, and the tenth anniversary of the assassination attempt on Mussolini, which occurred nearby.

Figure 26. An individual jumping through a burning hoop, Stadio dei Marmi at the Foro Italico, Rome, 1938. Achille Starace (at that time President of CONI, the national Italian sports body) is waiting his turn, behind the hoop, in a vest. Benito Mussolini is next to him, dressed in a white suit and hat.

Figure 27. Palazzo delle Esposizioni, Rome, 6 May 1938. Mussolini and Adolf Hitler with Police Chief Arturo Bocchini. Those forming the guard of honour are the 'Musketeers of Il Duce'.

Figure 28. This official poster from the Council of Ministers reads: JEWS CANNOT BE (EMPLOYED IN OR MEMBERS OF) ... THE MILITARY AND CIVIL BUREAUCRACY, THE (FASCIST) PARTY, IN PROVINCIAL AND LOCAL GOVERNMENT BODIES, IN PARA-STATE BODIES, IN BANKS, IN INSURANCE COMPANIES. At the bottom of the poster there is a university building similar to that in Rome and the phrase THE JEWS ARE EXCLUDED FROM ITALIAN SCHOOLS. Note also the anti-semitic caricatures.

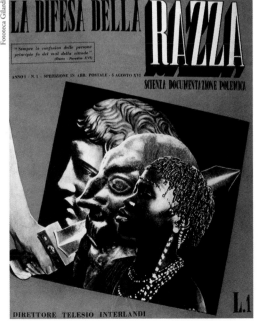

Figure 29. The front cover of the first issue of the official state-sponsored, fortnightly magazine *La Difesa della Razza: Scienza, Documentazione, Polemica* (*The Defence of the Race: Science, Documentation, Polemics*), 1938.

Figure 30. Demonstrators with the head of a (knocked-down) statue of Mussolini, Rome, 25-26 July 1943.

Figure 31. Milan, 26 July 1943. Demonstrators knock down fascist symbols. Note the war propaganda poster below.

Figure 32. A football game at Stadio Comunale, Bologna, 1949. The Mussolini statue can be seen in the background, minus Mussolini's body, which was removed on 25 July 1943. His legs are still attached to the horse.

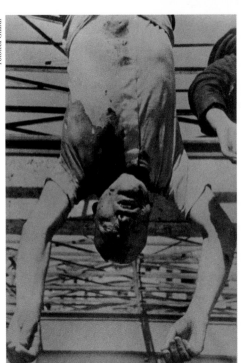

Figure 33. Piazzale Loreto, Milan, 29 April 1945. Bodies of Fascist Hierarchs and Clara Petacci hang from a garage. Mussolini is fourth from the right, Petacci fifth from the right. Former Communist Nicola Bombacci is third from the right. Two other bodies lie on the ground. Note the bombed out buildings in the background.

Figure 34. Piazzale Loreto, Milan, 29 April 1945. Mussolini's body is hung from its feet.

Figure 35. Piazzale Loreto, Milan, 29 April 1945. Achille Starace, Mussolini's right-hand man and spin doctor for much of the regime, is about to be shot in the back by partisans after a rapid 'trial'. The writing on the wall says: NO SMOKING.

Figure 36. The tomb of Ennio Gnudi, Certosa Cemetery, Bologna.

people, were murdered in the immediate aftermath of the attack on Graziani. As the massacre spread to the rest of the city, the violence became even more extreme. The 6th Division of Fascist Blackshirts based in the city, rampaged through the streets. Heads of victims were smashed to pieces, bystanders were beaten with shovels, pickaxes, iron bars or sticks or stabbed to death. Many were run over by trucks. Women were raped and then killed; children were not spared. Houses were burnt to the ground, often with their residents still inside them: 'as children came running out of the burning houses, the Italians lifted them up and threw them back into the flames'.[24] Thousands of prisoners were taken, many of whom were summarily executed, while others died later from torture, ill treatment, illness or lack of food. Death was accompanied by the theft of private property, from jewellery to livestock. A beautiful cathedral was looted and damaged.

The massacre continued for at least three days (19–21 February 1937), spreading right across the city to the outskirts (and beyond) where thousands more dwellings were destroyed. Vehicles roamed around full of bodies while dragging live locals tied by their feet or hands. It became apparent that this was not just a spontaneous reaction to the attempt on Graziani's life, but that it had been ordered by the fascist regime in place in Ethiopia and it was encouraged directly from Rome. Once the butchery was finally called off, the city was literally in ruins. Most residents had either left, or were dead. It is estimated that over 19,000 people were killed in the massacre (20 per cent of the population of the city at the time).

Nobody was ever prosecuted for what happened in Addis Ababa in September 1937.[25] There was no war crimes trial, or indeed criminal proceedings of any kind. A combination of the convenience of international geopolitics and internal pacification led to numerous leading members of the regime getting off scot-free – including Graziani himself, but also key perpetrators such as Guido Cortese (federal secretary of the Fascist Party) – a central figure in ordering and organising the massacre. Mussolini's invasion, war and occupation of Ethiopia cost the lives of some 750,000 Ethiopians – an extraordinary figure over a period of just six years.[26]

*

Mussolini also sent more than 40,000 troops and equipment to fight with Franco in Spain during the civil war in the 1930s. Many of the troops were violent members of the *squadristi* militia. Leading *squadristi*, such as Arconovaldo Bonaccorsi, took part in massacres of republican soldiers and civilians.[27] Italian aircraft, supplies and other support forces proved crucial in Franco's eventual victory against the republicans.

On the republican side, many anti-fascist Italians rallied to the cause and travelled to Spain to volunteer. This was in some ways a dress rehearsal for the civil war in Italy to come. Divisions on the left were also mirrored in Spain. Carlo Rosselli, a leading anti-fascist who had escaped from internal exile on the island of Lipari in 1929, was in Spain for a time, as was Palmiro Togliatti with the Communist Party and a number of Italian anarchists. Some of the violence in Spain was also *between* these groups.[28]

SOLDIERS OF SPORT

'They are rare, the rarest of matches in which you see the metamorphosis of the players, no longer little ... boys who go about their work, with the ball at their feet, but little, gallant soldiers that fight for an idea that is greater than them but who work for the divine unknown, that is the genius of the soldier on the charge. They are the matches, in other words, where not one squad of eleven men but a race shows itself with its feelings and instincts, its anger and its ecstasy, its character and attitude. The game that the Italians won at the stadium was this type of match.'
           Bruno Roghi, *Soldati dello Sport* ('Soldiers of Sport')[29]

Fascism, from the beginning, understood the power and reach of sport. The regime invested heavily in infrastructure and talent. Five hundred stadiums were officially opened on one day in 1929. Huge new stadia were built in Bologna, Florence, Milan, Naples, Trieste, Genoa, Turin and Rome. One, in Florence, was named after a 'fascist martyr', Giuseppe Berta, others after Mussolini or linked to fascist language. Most carried statues and fascist symbols.

In May–June 1934 Italy hosted the FIFA World Cup.[30] It was a perfectly stage-managed event, supported by numerous journalists and the patriotic tones and commentary of legendary broadcaster Nicolo Carosio.[31] Many Italians read about their team's successes, but most heard the games on the radio. Ticket prices had been set high to recoup losses on the tournament, leading to empty spaces in the stands. Very few saw the games live, but highlights were shown via newsreels in cinemas. Large numbers of posters, postcards and stamps were produced for the tournament. Fascist symbols were a constant presence. At the draw in Rome, for example, there was an enormous bronze bust of Il Duce in the centre of the room. The World Cup was officially opened at the Campidoglio in the Julius Caesar Room on 24 May, the anniversary of Italy's entry into the First World War, with Mussolini's spin doctor and right-hand man Achille Starace and Jules Rimet, the president of FIFA, present. Almost every speech contained a 'salute' to Mussolini.

The Italy team's manager was Vittorio Pozzo, who had served as an officer with the Alpini mountain troops in the First World War. He had played for FC Torino and also worked as a journalist for *La Stampa*, and had long experience as a club manager. Pozzo saw football as a form of war, and his players as his foot soldiers. He liked to use war metaphors when discussing football tactics and took his players to see a war memorial before one important game. Journalists at the time also used warlike metaphors to describe football matches and other sporting events. Pozzo's team rarely lost, being defeated just six times during the 1930–38 period (when Italy played sixty-two games). He has a claim to have been the most successful international manager of all time.

In 1934, however, Italy's progress to the final was not easy. A replay (the day after the original game) was required to get past Spain (Italy played 220 minutes of football in two days to get through this round) in the quarter-final. On Sunday 10 June 1934 – a fateful date for Italy and fascism and for Rome, being the day in 1924 when Matteotti was murdered, and when Mussolini would declare war in 1940 – the final was held in Rome's Fascist National Party Stadium. It was a global event, with 2,000 fans from the opposing team attending and 277 foreign journalists, as well as dignitaries. Mussolini was present at the final, and his appearance was underlined in reports on the match, including the fact that for one game he had apparently queued up and paid for his own tickets, and for those of his sons who accompanied him. People waved their handkerchiefs and hats when he entered the stadium.

Italy's opponent was Czechoslovakia. Italy won 2–1 after extra time, coming from behind. '*Giovinezza*', the fascist hymn, was played and sung by the crowd of 50,000 or so, along with the Royal March. The squad gave a fascist salute from the pitch towards Il Duce and Mussolini himself handed the cup to the Italian captain, Giampiero Combi. Starace framed the victory (and the entire tournament) around Mussolini even further through a special, enormous, Coppa del Duce (an extra cup created for the occasion) which was also awarded that day. It was so heavy that four people were required to carry it.[32] Journalists and commentators made constant connections between fascism, Mussolini, the victory and the superiority of the Italian 'race'. A reception followed at the Circolo della Stampa in Rome. The next day the team visited the headquarters of the National Fascist Party. Extra medals were handed over as well as a signed photograph of Mussolini. Il Duce did not take part in the post-match celebrations and commemorations. It was 'Mussolini's shadow', Achille Starace, who displayed the cup from a balcony to crowds below that evening.

Four of the Italian squad were so-called *oriundi* – Argentinians who were connected to Italy via emigration. The rules had been interpreted loosely to allow them to play for Italy. Two of the *oriundi* were central to the Italian victory: Raimundo Orsi opened the scoring in the final, while Enrico Guaita, who was known as the 'black pirate' and played for Roma, scored the only and winning goal in the semi-final, and provided the assist for the goal which won the World Cup itself. Orsi had been the subject of intense controversy between Argentina and Italy. He had played for Argentina in the 1928 Olympics, and his transfer to Italy was held up for a year by the Argentinian Football Federation.[33] The 'hybrid' status of the *oriundi* was glossed over by the regime, who celebrated them as the glorious 'repatriated'.

Ever since that victory there have been persistent stories of match-fixing. The great Italian journalist Gianni Brera wrote of the referee in the quarter final against Spain, that he 'behaved as if he was well aware [as to] where the game was taking place'.[34] There were complaints from Spain and letters to Mussolini calling him a 'bandit'. The Spanish newspaper *El Liberal* described the match as 'the Italian–Spanish war', but there is evidence that their interpretation was also influenced by politics. The article in question ended with the cry 'Viva Matteotti!'[35] Some have claimed that the ambitious young Swedish referee, Ivan Eklind, was bribed to favour Italy. Eklind refereed Italy in both the semi-final and final, and was something of a surprise choice. It has been argued that he was 'a referee willing to do anything to get ahead'.[36]

But the proof for any of this is, at best, anecdotal, and often involves the reviewing of past games through modern football eyes. Fouls on goalkeepers were common in football at the time. Moreover, favouritism towards home teams in world cups does not seem to be an exclusively fascist phenomenon, as even a cursory analysis of the 1966, 1978 and 1998 World Cups would reveal. As David Goldblatt has written about the stories surrounding Eklind, 'delightful though this conspiracy is, there is not a single shred of documentary evidence to support it'.[37] Nonetheless, alternative opinions are available. 'These countless clues mean a historian can only come to one verdict: guilty' wrote the sports historian Marco Impiglia. 'In the history of the World Cup, no other year has ever been manipulated with such contempt for sportsmanship as that of 1934.'[38]

Football's influence in Italy in the interwar period should not be exaggerated. Cycling was still by far the most popular sport in the country, and the second billing given to the World Cup victory the next day in the main sports paper, *La Gazzetta dello Sport*, behind the Giro d'Italia was telling. Nonetheless, many of the major newspapers of the day led with the triumph in Rome, with banner headlines. Germany finished third in the World Cup, and the closing ceremony included Nazi salutes. Just four days after the end of the tournament, Hitler and Mussolini met for the first time, at a golf course in Venice. What has been called a 'fatal alliance' was taking shape.[39]

Battle of Highbury: footballing war

Italy could claim that it was the greatest footballing nation in the world, although the absence of the teams from Uruguay, the holders, and of England, the supposed 'home of football', made such a statement problematic. Soon after the 1934 victory, in November, a 'friendly' match was organised at Highbury, in North London, between Italy and England. Many saw it as an unofficial playoff to decide the best team on the planet. The battle for title of best team in the world was also an ideological one, pitting democracies against dictatorships, fascism against liberalism.

More was at stake than mere footballing pride. The British Foreign Office argued that if the Italians were to beat England, 'it merely proves to a vast assembly of people, including perhaps Il Duce and his supermen, that the Fascist system produces a finer type of homo sapiens that the decaying system of [parliamentary] Govt. Football becomes a subsection of the creed.'[40] Il Duce himself agreed. On the twelfth anniversary of the March on Rome – 28 October 1934 – he said this to athletes: 'Remember that when you take part in contests beyond our borders, there is then entrusted to your muscles, and above all to your spirit, the honour and the prestige of national sport. You must hence make use of all your energy and of your willpower in order to obtain primacy in all struggles on the earth, on the sea and in the sky.'[41]

It was a violent match, with broken bones and cuts. England, led by Arsenal's captain Eddie Hapgood, stormed to a 3–0 lead. Italy had only ten men after one of their players broke a bone in his foot. Hapgood, whose nose was smashed, wrote that 'the Italians had gone berserk, and were kicking everything in sight', adding: 'it's a bit hard to play like a gentleman when somebody closely resembling an enthusiastic member of the Mafia is wiping his studs down your legs, or kicking you up in the air from behind'.[42] Then Italy's superstar forward, Giuseppe Meazza, stepped up with two goals, and came close to a sensational hat-trick. Enrique Guaita seemed to miss a great chance towards the end. Carosio's biased rhetoric via the radio reached fever pitch. It was almost an incredible comeback and Italy's journalists were able to depict the match as a glorious defeat, and the team as 'lions'. Patriotic journalist Bruno Roghi wrote that 'the Italian squad returns to the Motherland with a defeat that is worth twice as much as a victory'.[43]

British journalists, on the other hand, called the Italian players thugs and one signed his match report as from a 'war correspondent'. Hapgood wrote after the match that the dressing room at Highbury resembled a 'casualty clearing station'.[44] Later that evening there was a tense dinner, where Dino Grandi, the ex-*squadrista* who was now Italian ambassador in London, handed out medals to the players. Hapgood was incensed: 'I thought then that I never wanted to see another Italian in my life', claiming that it was 'the dirtiest game I ever played in'.[45]

DIVIDED LOYALTIES

In 1935 the ambiguities of the *oriundi* who had played for Italy in the 1934 World Cup exploded into major scandal. The details were largely kept out of the press, but the incident itself was much discussed, especially as it involved some very famous and popular footballers. With the invasion of Ethiopia looming, Enrique Guaita and two other *oriundi* (Alessandro Scopelli and Andrea Stagnaro) faced the possibility of being called up and sent to fight for Italy. They had already been ordered to attend a barracks in Rome and been cleared for military service.

The three players decided to slip out of Italy. Given the choice of fighting in a war for Italy, they decided they would rather be Argentinian. Yet, when the choice had been a footballing one, they had opted for Italy. It was towards the end of September 1935 – the eve of the Italian offensive, and just days before the beginning of the football championship. The escape attempt was by taxi, train and boat. Their wives followed with large amounts of cash (the press stated that it was a whopping, and improbable, 2,800,000 lire) in a suitcase. The escape was apprehended at the border with France at Ventimiglia. Small articles in the press mentioned the wives but not the actual players, and the scandal was quickly hushed up. The players were accused of contraband.[46]

Fascist journalists quickly dismissed the three players as opportunistic traitors. The fascist sports magazine *Il Littoriale* wrote on 23 September 1935: 'We have no need of sheep dressed up as Sunday lions [football was played on a Sunday]. This gesture feels to us like a liberation … They [the players] were not Italian. Cowardice has no right to citizenship in our country.'[47] The headline of the article was in capitals: 'SCHIFO' ('DISGUSTING'). Another fascist journal called Guaita and the others: 'Heroes on Sunday, cowards for their whole lives.'[48] But if the players were *not* Italians, surely the recent World Cup victory was 'tainted', and why were other *oriundi* still playing for the national team?

Guaita was not just a major star with the national team who had been a key player in the World Cup (he had been described as one of the 'heroes' of that 1934 victory) but a very popular player with Roma, scoring a record twenty-eight goals (in twenty-nine games) and finishing as Serie A's top scorer in the 1934–35 season. Ever since, there have been dark rumours about plots involving Lazio, Roma's great city rivals, or power struggles within the club.[49] Guaita returned to Argentina and the residence rules over the *oriundi* were tightened. A short item on 22 October 1935 announced that Guaita and another three players were to have their playing permits removed 'as unworthy'.[50] A Lazio player was included in the ban. Raimundo Orsi also returned to Argentina. No details were given as to what they had done to deserve this ban. Guaita never played for, or visited, Italy again. His career quickly fizzled out, he became a director of a prison and died at the age of just forty-nine.

Roma's president at the time the *oriundi* were signed was a financier called Renato Sacerdoti, who was Jewish, although also baptised. He paid a high price for the Guaita scandal. Accused of financial crimes linked to these player transfers, he was sent to internal exile for five months. He later only escaped deportation during the Second World War by disguising himself as a Catholic priest.[51]

*

Italy's victory in 1934 was not a one-off. Pozzo took a young student team to the Berlin Olympics in 1936 where they won the football gold medal, beating Austria in the final. He was also in charge for the June 1938 World Cup in France. It was another triumph, this time away from home and in front of hostile and often anti-fascist crowds, including exiled Italians, in particular in Marseilles for the semi-final. As that game began, 'the Italians were howled at as soon as they emerged from the tunnel, and their national anthem was booed. The Italian coach Vittorio Pozzo recalled how his players' fascist salute on that occasion provoked "a chorus of whistles" among the crowd.'[52] Pozzo supposedly made the team hold their fascist salutes before one game until the whistles of the crowd had died down. Black shirts were worn by the national team – for the first and only time – for the quarter-final against France.[53]

This time Mussolini hosted the players personally on their return and held a reception in the map room in Palazzo Venezia, as well as attending a mass outdoor celebration in Rome. In 1934 he had not taken part in the post-match celebrations. A celebratory photo was taken with the team in semi-military uniform, plus Pozzo. Mussolini was in the centre, in a white suit, with Starace, ever present, to his left, also in white. The team's success masked some darker aspects of the regime. There was only one *oriundo* in the Italian team this time round, and one of their key players had his name 'Italianised' – all signs of the times. Italy had been triumphant in the footballing wars.

FASCISM AND THE MEDIA

'Every village should have a radio.'

Benito Mussolini[54]

Italy's sporting triumphs underlined the power over the media exercised by the regime. Press control was tightened considerably by 1925–26, with the substitution of liberal journalists and editors and the continued (and final) forced suppression of opposition publications. Many newspapers moved spontaneously to pro-fascist positions. Journalists wrote articles to order, often containing opinions and 'facts' they did not agree with. Books and other media were carefully and systematically censored. Meanwhile, new fascist publications were launched in a myriad of areas, from sport to popular culture to architecture to cinema.

Radio was a key part of the regime's reach, given still-high levels of illiteracy. By the end of the 1930s there were around 1.2 million radio licences in Italy, and it was estimated that there were six or so listeners per licence. The birth of mass radio ownership was 'one of the key moments in the history of contemporary society'.[55] But radio worked both ways. Listeners could also pick up anti-fascist stations, such as Radio Mosca (organised by the Italian Communist Party). This subversive listening was a dangerous activity, which could lead to a prison sentence or internal exile.[56] Newsreels pushed propaganda into cinemas – and were screened before all feature films. These short films covered all areas of life, and often concentrated on speeches or actions by Mussolini himself, who was 'fascism's leading film star'.[57] Fascism also produced epic cinema, including films about itself, depicting *squadristi* as conquering heroes.

Between the lines, and in the gaps, other opinions were available. Mainstream newspapers always outsold fascist publications, including Mussolini's own *Il Popolo d'Italia*. Consumers preferred journalism to propaganda. Catholic publications continued to influence a wide audience and the Vatican daily newspaper, *L'Osservatore Romano*, was not censored. Internal dissent within fascism also emerged, often through allusion and gossip, and in provincial fascist publications. Dossiers circulated directed at certain individuals and there were intense rivalries. Radical opinions could emerge and even flourish, usually within cultural practice and debate, such as architecture or literature.

Mussolini's journalistic past never left him: he was said to read up to 350 newspapers a day, and would frequently phone up editors and journalists. Access to the journalistic profession was tightly controlled. A system of notes called *veline* were sent to newspapers to encourage the promotion of a certain kind of news, and the suppression of inconvenient truths. Here is an example from 28 June 1935 relating to the boxer Primo Carnera: 'Photographs of Carnera on the canvas must not be published.' Joe Louis had just defeated Carnera in New York, knocking him out three times in the sixth round. Only authorised photos of Mussolini were permitted. Images which seemed to make him look old, or tired, or short, or pale, were suppressed.[58]

There was an official, and highly fascist, news agency (which had been set up in liberal Italy, and was then controlled by the regime from 1924 onwards) – the Agenzia Stefani, run by a fascist 'of the first hour', Manlio Morgagni. This was an agency with huge resources, and it also could boast its own radio stations.[59] By 1937 controls were being exercised over 81 dailies, 132 political journals, 7,000 parish bulletins and nearly 3,900 magazines – every day.[60] Newspapers were ordered to be 'optimistic'. Lists of banned authors were produced and distributed, including Franz Kafka and Virginia Woolf. In this climate, a number of leading or aspirant journalists lent their pens to the racist campaigns pushed by the regime, which intensified with imperial war, and the rise of Hitler in Germany. As fascism entered its second decade in power, the regime began to target a small internal subsection of the population – Jews.

War on Italy's Jews
1938

By the late 1930s, Mussolini required a new internal enemy (socialism was non-existent, the masons had largely been crushed) and Il Duce also wanted to please his new and powerful ally, Adolf Hitler. Preparations for a war on Italian Jews began in the mid-1930s, as anti-Semitic views and tropes were pushed by leading fascists in a series of official publications. Racial laws had already been drawn up and implemented in Italy's colonies, paving the way for domestic legislation. The decision was then made by Mussolini to discriminate, through a new series of laws, against Italian Jewish (and foreign Jewish) communities. As a scapegoat, Italian Jews were an easy target. They were relatively few in number, and economic and political discrimination would cause minimal damage. The political rewards, at home and abroad, however, could well be significant.

ITALIANS AND JEWS

Fascism often claimed that it, and Italy, was neither racist nor anti-Semitic. In 1920 Mussolini wrote in *Il Popolo d'Italia* that 'In Italy no distinction whatsoever is made between Jews and non-Jews.'[1] Jews in Italy had been liberated by national unification in the nineteenth century. The ghettoes which had enclosed the community physically and economically within Italian cities were swept away, and the last to fall was in Rome in 1870.

As a result of these new freedoms and equalities, which coincided with the creation of the nation itself, Italian Jews felt a deep attachment to the Italian state and the monarchy. Despite their tiny numbers – there were approximately

35,000 Jews in Italy in 1900 – many rose to positions of great prominence. Ernesto Nathan, a Jew, became Mayor of Rome in 1907 and stayed in post until 1913. Alessandro Forti, a Jew from Forlì, was prime minister from 1905–06. Sidney Sonnino (raised as a Protestant with a Jewish banker father from Livorno, and a British mother) was a minister on various occasions and prime minister in 1906 and 1910, while Luigi Luzzatti, a Jew from Venice, was prime minister in 1910. It seemed that anything was possible. Integration and even assimilation appeared complete and unproblematic. Numerous Italian Jews also became leading figures in the Italian army.

When Italy's entry into the war was announced in 1915, Italian Jews rushed to sign up. War cemeteries and synagogues across Italy are dotted with memorials to those Jews who gave their lives 'for the nation'. Others, a minority, were opposed to the conflict, particular those within the socialist movement. In the social and political conflicts of the postwar period, Jews were to be found on both sides of the political divide. Many of the leading socialists were of Jewish origin – Modigliani from Livorno, Treves from Milan, Donati from Modena. Other Jews joined the fascists, and some played a major role in that movement. There were Jewish 'fascist martyrs', and Jewish prefects.

Some 4,920 Jews signed up to the Fascist Party (PNF) between 1928 and 1933. In 1938, PNF members were approximately 26.9 per cent of the entire Jewish adult population with Italian citizenship. According to the historian Michele Sarfatti, Jews were more likely to join the Fascist Party than non-Jews. But these figures should be treated cautiously. Sarfatti also stresses the historical tendency towards political engagement of Italy's Jewish population, rather than any extra tendency towards 'being fascist'.[2] Party membership was often necessary to obtain certain jobs or privileges. Many Jews did not 'break' with their 'Jewish identity' to join the fascists, as at the time they saw no contradiction in their position. There had been between six and eight Jews at San Sepolcro, at the founding moment of fascism, and 230 or so officially took part in the March on Rome. Yet, while Jews were not excluded from the party or positions of power, many people within the party and the movement, including key leadership figures, were actively anti-Semitic and made their views known well before 1938. Jews in the party were *tolerated* as Jews, but frequent references were still made to their 'Jewishness'.

Leading fascist figures were openly and consistently anti-Semitic, both before and after 1938. Roberto Farinacci ran an extensive anti-Semitic campaign in *Il Regime Fascista*, his Cremona-based paper, which continually questioned the loyalty of Italian Jews. This paper, with its 150,000 copies a day, was second only to Mussolini's *Il Popolo d'Italia* in terms of reach and influence. Farinacci built strong and durable links to the Nazis, attending congresses in Germany. By 1938 his references to anti-Semitism were 'almost daily'.[3] Much of this campaign was made up of barely disguised threats: 'at the proper time,' he wrote, 'we will publish names, surnames, and details of positions held'.[4]

In private, however, Farinacci was happy to intervene to help Jewish associates or friends. He tried to protect a Jewish secretary in his office, writing to Mussolini: 'I am fully agreeable even to exterminate all Jews, but before we reach the humble and innocent ones we must hit the powerful ones.'[5] But the reply was emphatic: 'One cannot pose as the paladin of anti-Semitism and keep a Jewish secretary hanging around. Let him give her even fifty thousand lire and get rid of her.'[6] Farinacci also appears to have profited personally from the business which developed among those who thought that they could occasionally be 'saved' from the effects of discrimination.[7]

Farinacci used Catholic publications to justify anti-Semitism, while at the same time attacking the Church for being 'soft on Jews'. Many within the Church were happy to support these anti-Semitic campaigns. The Bishop of Cremona, for example, argued in favour of the right of the state 'to limit or suppress the economic, social, and moral influence of the Jews, when noxious to the tranquillity and welfare of the nation'.[8]

The Protocols of the Elder of Zion, a classic hoax anti-Semitic conspiracy text, had first been published in Italy in 1921 by Giovanni Preziosi, a notorious Italian anti-Semite.[9] A new edition appeared in 1937 and the following year, 60,000 copies of a special new third edition were distributed, to accompany a new campaign against the Jews, containing a list of surnames of the supposed 9,800 'Jewish families' in Italy.

MANIFESTO DELLA RAZZA, 1938

'It is time that Italians proclaim themselves genuinely racist.
There is today a pure "Italian race".
The Jews do not belong to the Italian race.'

'Manifesto of Race', 14 July 1938

Pseudo-science was weaponised thanks to the willing contribution of a series of 'experts' and academics, who provided an official veneer of legitimacy for the idea of an 'Italian race'.[10] In 1938 the laws themselves were preceded by a 'Manifesto of Race' which called on Italians to be 'racist' and stated, starkly, that 'the Jews do not belong to the Italian race'. It was also argued that there was such a thing as 'a pure Italian race'. The text of the manifesto was complemented by anti-Semitic visual propaganda, depicting grotesque visions of hook-nosed and bearded figures, sucking the blood out of dead children. All this was accompanied by a violent anti-Semitic campaign in the mainstream press. Celebrated journalists penned anti-Semitic pieces. Photos, lies and conspiracy theories were all pushed out to the Italian people. This propaganda also drew on anti-Semitic prejudices which ran deep in Italian society.[11]

The manifesto contained ten points. It was first published in the newspaper *Il Giornale d'Italia* in July 1938 and then on 5 August 1938 in the first edition of *La difesa della razza*, an official glossy fortnightly newspaper/magazine which dealt exclusively in racial theories and racism. One hundred and eighteen editions of *La difesa della razza* were eventually published, running up to 1943.[12] Fascism felt the need not just to issue anti-Semitic laws and measures, but also to provide a 'scientific' basis for its racist decisions.

Some of the manifesto consisted simply of a series of statements of what the scientists claimed to be fact, such as Article 7 which stated:

> A pure Italian 'race' exists. This statement is not based around
> a confusion between the biological concept of races and the
> historic-linguistic idea of a people and a nation, but on the pure
> blood relationship which unites Italians of today with those
> generations who have inhabited Italy for generations. This ancient
> purity of blood is the greatest sign of nobility of the Italian
> nation.

But the first mention of the Jews was in Article 9:

> The Jews are not part of the Italian race. Nothing has generally
> remained of the Semites who over the centuries have appeared
> on the holy soil of our Fatherland. Even the Arab occupation of

Sicily left nothing behind apart from a few names: and in any case assimilation has always been very quick in Italy. The Jews represent the only population who have never been assimilated in Italy because they are made up of non-European racial elements, different in an absolute way from the elements which provided the origins of the Italians.[13]

TRIESTE, 18 SEPTEMBER 1938

Trieste was a city with a sizeable Jewish population – one of the biggest in Italy – and a huge and beautiful synagogue. Mussolini's whistle-stop tour of the Friuli region in the summer of 1938 was essentially a series of propagandistic events and photo opportunities. Il Duce was pictured opening new fascist buildings, running in a virile way with other military-uniformed individuals, unveiling the first stone of the new university, visiting a local grotto, kissing children.

Enrico Paolo Salem was *podestà* of Trieste from 1933 to 1938. His father was of Jewish origin, and it is said that Salem was both circumcised and baptised. He organised and promoted Benito Mussolini's three-day visit to Trieste and surrounding areas in September 1938, a trip on which Il Duce publicly announced the introduction of anti-Semitic legislation. However, Salem was no longer in the post at this time, despite having been reappointed in 1937. Two weeks before the visit he had been effectively sacked, although the official story was that he had 'resigned'. Salem was probably one of the first Jewish officials to lose his post in the purges that followed, before Mussolini's decrees had officially been issued.

Mussolini arrived in the city on a destroyer, the *Camicia Nera* ('Black Shirt'). On 18 September 1938, he made explicit the 'racial politics' of the regime, in front of an enormous crowd (150,000 people were said to be there) in the central Piazza Unita d'Italia. Hailed as 'Italy's largest square',[14] with one side open to the sea, the piazza was a key site for Italian (and fascist) history, with strong links to the victory in the First World War. In 1918 an Italian ship landing here signalled the 'liberation' of Trieste from Austrian rule.[15] An entire fountain had been moved to accommodate Il Duce. Mussolini spoke from a special stage shaped like a boat, below which was written in enormous letters 'DUX'. His speech, as ever, was frequently interrupted by wild applause and cheering.

Mussolini's address was a statement of intent. The Jews were to be subject to a 'politics of separation'. The 'prestige of the empire' required a:

> clear, severe, racial conscience which lays out not only differences, but clear superiorities ... world Jewry has been, for sixteen years, despite our politics, an irreconcilable enemy of fascism. Nonetheless Jews with Italian citizenship, who have made a clear military and civil contribution to Italy and the regime, will be treated with a sense of justice and understanding ... as for the others, *a politics of separation* [my emphasis] will follow. In the end, the world will, perhaps, be surprised by our generosity and our sense of rigour, unless enemies from abroad and those within, and their unexpected and impromptu friends, who defend them [the Jews] from too many pulpits, do not force us to radically change our approach.[16]

Once again, there was a mixture of threat and ambiguity. It was an ominous sign, especially given the increasing connections between Italy and the Nazi regime in Germany.

DRAFTING THE RACIAL LAWS

In the autumn of 1938 the discrimination and prejudice against Jews took legal form in a series of decrees issued by the government. Mussolini and Guido Buffarini Guidi, undersecretary in the Interior Ministry, drafted the decrees. There was then a discussion in the Gran Consiglio. It is often claimed that Italo Balbo expressed 'vigorous' opposition to the racial laws in that meeting. However, he made no public statements on the matter. Moreover, in 1938 alone the *Corriere Padano*, Balbo's newspaper, published 172 pieces which made reference to Jews.[17] These included 'an article lavishing praise on the "Protocols of the Elders of Zion"'.[18] The *Corriere Padano* also ran the *Manifesto della Razza* on its front page. No minutes have survived of the Consiglio meeting, and we are forced to rely on second-hand reports and 'diaries'.

Balbo's supposed 'vigorous' opposition to the laws appears to be linked to an attempt to secure exceptions for some groups (or simply arguing in favour of these exceptions). Balbo's criticisms, as Sarfatti points out, were 'within the logic of decisions around persecution and not against them'.[19] The law itself passed into legislation with no public opposition from any leading fascist. Yet the myth of Balbo's dissent survives. His biographer, Segrè, concludes that 'Balbo argued bravely and honestly against the racial laws'.[20] But the evidence for such a claim is not particularly convincing. As Rabbi Dante Lattes stated: 'How can we say that Balbo was a friend of the Jews? He was only a friend of Renzo Ravenna [the Jewish *podestà* of Ferrara].'[21]

There was little open opposition to the laws themselves, not from within fascism, or society as a whole, although Mussolini complained privately about what he saw as hostility to the measures. Some leading fascists (including Farinacci) did try to save or procure preferential treatment for individual friends and colleagues, as did the king (who still officially supported the discrimination). Tepid protests came from the Catholic Church. Other fascists, especially those closer to the ideas of Hitler, such as the hypocritical Farinacci, urged Mussolini to go further. Countries across the world – such as Hungary in May 1938 – were passing anti-Semitic legislation. Many others would follow in 1939, 1940 and 1941.

THE KING SIGNS

All the key decrees were signed by the king in 1938. It was early September, and the king was still on holiday in his huge 4,800-hectare estate – a place called San Rossore, near Pisa – bordered on one side by the sea. The estate contained some magnificent avenues and sets of trees. When the Savoy dynasty took over the land they used it mainly for hunting. Dromedaries were even kept there and used for agricultural work.[22] Vittorio Emanuele II and his family would usually stay in the estate from June to October, arriving and leaving in a special royal train. Part of the estate was a beach for exclusive use of the royals. Laws which needed signing in those months were taken to him there. The first racial decree was signed at ten in the morning on 5 September 1938, in a large palazzo called the Villa delle Cascine Vecchie, after the king returned from his seaside walk.

The signing was perhaps the most shameful act in the history of united Italy. It was seen as a particular betrayal that the king signed off on these decrees, as Italian Jews were often fervent monarchists, going right back to 1848 and the emancipation brought in by the Savoy dynasty. There was a cult of the monarchy within many Jewish families.[23] Vittorio Emanuele's seeming indifference to what he was agreeing to contrasted starkly with his refusal to sign the proposed martial law decree during the March on Rome in 1922. Without that non-signing, this signing would not have been possible. The racial decrees and laws were all then passed by the Lower House (unanimously) and in the Senate (where most of the 'Jewish' senators at the time were absent), where there were just ten votes against the first law. There were no speeches against the measures.

DEFINING AND COUNTING JEWS

An entire new legal apparatus was constructed to apply these laws. First, a new census of all Italian Jews was ordered. Legislators had to decide exactly who was a Jew, and who wasn't. A 'blood' definition was required to impose the discrimination, since many Italian Jews were not particularly religious and some had converted to Catholicism, or tried to do so when the laws were issued. Jews, it was decided, were a 'race' – and as such, if you had a 'Jewish' father or mother you were yourself automatically Jewish. But of course, this was a circular argument. How were the 'Jewish' mother and father to be defined and categorised? In the end it came down to the grandparents. People were defined by law as part of a 'Jewish race' if they had two parents who were 'part of the Jewish race' (who were defined in the same way) even if they 'belonged to religions which were different to those of the Jewish race ... those who were born from parents of the Jewish race belong to the Jewish race, even if they practise a different religion'.[24] In line with this bizarre logic, those who practised the Jewish religion were defined as 'Aryans', if their parents were (defined as) 'Aryans'.

All of this, of course, was absolute nonsense. There is no such thing as 'Jewish blood'. Nonetheless, the consequences of these classifications were deadly, and very real. Sometimes, these definitions were tweaked, and these decisions were crucial to people's actual lives. Definitions were also applied to dead people – sometimes going right back to the eighteenth century. All people 'of the Jewish race' in Italy were counted, officially, in 1938–39 – and the regime decided that there were around 55,000 Jews on Italian soil (some were Italian, some were foreign).[25] These imprecise and incomplete and dangerous lists would later be utilised by the Nazis to round up and deport Jews, or simply to murder them.

Following these complicated definitions, what actually happened to Italy's 'Jews' (foreign and Italian) after 1938? Foreign Jews were officially ordered out of the country that year, and given six months to leave. In November 1938, leading fascist Jews were removed from positions of power and authority and all Jews who could be identified as such were also kicked out of the Fascist Party (PNF). All Jews progressively lost status, jobs, income, property and businesses. They suffered open, sometimes violent, and daily discrimination. Later, some were subjected to forced labour. A few individuals decided to protest.

THE TOWER: ANGELO FORTUNATO FORMIGGINI

'Once upon a time there was a Modenese publisher of seven generations, who was thus Italian seven times, and who lived in Rome. When they said to him: you are not Italian, he wanted to show that he was Modenese of seven generations and he threw himself off the top of his Ghirlandina tower.'

Angelo Fortunato Formiggini[26]

On 28 November 1938, a bald, elegantly dressed Jewish man with a white beard and moustache, checked into a hotel in Modena, central Italy. He was well known in the city. His family had roots there going back generations. He had travelled with a one-way train ticket from Rome. The next morning, the man walked into the central city square, with a suitcase in hand and – despite the heavy fog, typical of that time of year – bought a ticket to visit the city's tower.

A guard wanted to accompany him, but he asked him to run a fake errand, which left him alone. He climbed the 200 steps to the top of the Torre Ghirlandina, symbol of the city, 86 metres above Modena, and from there, he threw himself from a window, shouting, it is said: 'Italia, Italia, Italia.' Today, that window is closed by a metal grille. The man was sixty, and he left behind his wife, Emilia Santamaria, and an adopted son, Fernando Cecilia, known as Nando.[27]

The death was hushed up. Nobody was allowed to attend his funeral, and the few people who did, in defiance of the authorities, were all arrested. There was a heavy police presence at the cemetery.

No Italian paper reported the suicide, although the foreign press did pick up on it. Locally, the news spread in secret and by word of mouth, but we have little evidence that it had much of a political impact. The spot where he hit the ground became referred to as 'Formiggini's handkerchief'.

The man was called Angelo Fortunato Formiggini and he was an extraordinary cultural figure of the time. When he was eighteen, and at school, he published a parody of Dante's *Inferno*, with real teachers among the characters he invented.[28] He completed two degrees and the second, in philosophy, included a thesis entitled: 'The philosophy of laughing.' He became a tireless reader, writer and critic, and wrote over 13,000 book reviews, founding the Formiggini publishing house in 1908. His publication *L'Italia che scrive* ('Italy that writes') was highly influential. After Formiggini had volunteered and fought in the First World War, he became a supporter of Mussolini and collaborated with fascist institutions and intellectuals, accompanying Il Duce at book fairs and other events in the 1930s.

Formiggini envisaged his spectacular death as a protest against the anti-Semitic laws of which he had been a prominent victim. He left behind a number of letters, a selection of which were later published. In some of them he joked about his impending suicide, and pointed out that his family went back seven generations, 'and because of this [he was] seven times Italian', or, as he underlined, his Italian heritage stretched back at least '309 years' into the past. In a letter he left to the people of Modena, he was still able to joke about his destiny, right to the last. 'With an extreme act of discipline I raise my brief salute to the Duce – the "sign of the umbrella" [a gesture which essentially signalled *fuck you*] – and then I throw out a loud shout from on high: Italy! Italy! Italy! And I also throw myself: *bumf!*'[29]

Formiggini argued that Mussolini had clearly gone mad and compared the events of 1938 with those of 1924, and the murder of Giacomo Matteotti: 'In 1924 you had one person killed with a knife … in 1938 you have treacherously attacked 50,000 completely innocent citizens.'[30] Mussolini's racial laws were applied to publishers, and in September 1938 the Ministry of Popular Culture had written to Formiggini with a request for information about the 'race' of those working for and running the company. Formiggini's business was already in financial difficulty and this had been the final straw.

In letters to leading fascists, Formiggini attacked the anti-Semitic legislation and campaigns. He claimed (and perhaps hoped) that his suicide would free his family from oppression. With his death, he wrote: 'They will become Aryan again and will no longer have any problems.'[31] By law, the deaths of Jews could no longer be publicly announced. As one of the few public displays of dissent against the racial laws in Italy after 1938, Formiggini's demise was clearly best kept hidden.

EXCEPTIONS, 'DISCRIMINATION' AND 'ARYANISATION'

The surreal and horrible legislative corpus which became known as the 'racial laws' was backed up by legal structures set up to adjudicate on 'test cases'. It was decided that some categories of Jews could apply to be classified as *'discriminati'* ('the discriminated'), which created a kind of hybrid status. Intermediate or special groupings – such as those linked to victims from the war, or 'fascist martyrs' – could ask to be officially 'discriminated' (which meant the opposite of what we would mean by the term today). This allowed them access to privileges not allowed for other Jews as defined by various decrees and measures.

Some 8,512 people applied for *discriminazione*. A case had to be made, backed by documents and testimonies. It took some time for a decision to be made. The tactic of those who applied for discrimination was often to present oneself as a fervent fascist, and to claim presence or participation in past fascist acts. Presence during the March on Rome was a powerful piece of evidence, and any documentation in this regard was extremely valuable.[32] Statements of fascist faith were common and necessary. Any hint of anti-fascism would be fatal to any claim. Many were desperate, having lost their jobs almost overnight.

Decisions on 'Aryanisation' were handed over to another new institution, set up specifically for this purpose. In 1939, a tiny notice in the press announced the beginning of the work of the Tribunale della Razza ('Race Court'). This organisation, based physically inside the Interior Ministry in Rome, had been set up to adjudicate – under the racial laws – as to whether certain Italians were Jewish or not. The *tribunale* was presided over by five institutional figures and a secretary. Its first and only president was an illustrious magistrate called Gaetano Azzariti, who had been born in 1881 in Naples and had graduated in law at the age of twenty.[33] In the press release it was said that Tribunale della Razza already had fifty cases to adjudicate on.[34] Very little public information was released around the cases looked at by the *tribunale*, and most of the records relating to its operations have been 'lost'.[35]

The procedure was relatively simple. Individuals applied to be 'Aryanised' with documentation, which was sent to their local prefect, who then prepared a report and passed on the material to the Tribunale della Razza. A decision was then given and, if the 'Aryanisation' was accepted, the documents of the individual or family of the person in question were altered. If the change was not accepted, the documents remained the same.[36] In general, it appears that the most popular way to 'become Aryan' was to provide evidence which proved that you were an illegitimate child, but another route was to send documents showing Catholic or Protestant lineage. By mid-1942, the *tribunale* had looked at 143 cases, and accepted 104 of them.[37] There is anecdotal evidence that the *tribunale*, and the whole process surrounding it, was open to corruption. But there were other routes to relative salvation. Mussolini himself could also decide to change someone's 'race', with the flick of his pen.

Enrico Paolo Salem, who had organised Benito Mussolini's fateful propaganda tour of Trieste in September 1938 (but had been sacked just before the visit itself) refused to accept his fate. He appealed to the Interior Ministry and was officially designated as an 'Aryan'.[38] Salem had joined the Fascist Party in 1921. In December 1938 he set out his case, with thirteen certificates. 'I was born in Trieste,' he wrote,

> and baptised in accordance with the Catholic ritual … My father
> Vittorio Salem was a Jew from a family which has lived in Trieste
> for more than two centuries. My mother was Aryan Catholic …
> and born under Italian nationality in Vienna. My father received
> the Italian citizenship officially on 18th of August 1881 … I am
> asking for the recognition of my Aryan and Italian race.[39]

He was confirmed as 'Aryan' in March 1939, and later that year Salem moved away from Trieste.

FERRARA: THE FASCIST *PODESTÀ* AND THE NOVELIST

Near the centre of Ferrara, in the gently curving Via Mazzini, was the Jewish ghetto, a series of small streets fanning out from the city's synagogues. There is evidence of a Jewish presence in the city from at least the thirteenth century onwards. Ferrara was under papal rule until 1859, when the ghetto was opened up, and the main piazza today has a number of anti-clerical plaques celebrating the fall of that domination, and the unification of Italy. In Via Mazzini there were three different working synagogues, which served its relatively sizeable Jewish community.

Ferrara's Jews felt secure under fascism. Institutionally, they were represented at a high level. The unelected mayor of the town under the regime, Renzo Ravenna, was Jewish, and a close friend of local *ras*, Italo Balbo. Ravenna was *podestà* from 1926 to 1938, and as such he accompanied kings, queens and princes on official visits, and was often to be seen alongside Balbo. According to some statistics, 90 per cent of Jews in Ferrara were signed up members of the PNF. Fascism hardly affected the community at all throughout the 1920s and most of the 1930s; in fact many of the city's Jews appear to have been enthusiastic supporters.

Yet, Ravenna's time as *podestà* had not been without tensions. In 1934, Guido Buffarini Guidi, who would play a key part in drafting the racial laws from his role within the Interior Ministry, wrote, on behalf of Mussolini, to the prefect of the city. He claimed that the citizens of Ferrara were 'unhappy' with their Jewish *podestà*, and that they wanted him replaced with a Catholic.[40] A further request came from Rome for a list of Jews (or, as the telegram said, 'non-Catholics') holding leading positions in the city, such as school heads, charity administrators and so on.[41] This request for 'information' was not confined to Ferrara, but extended to the whole of Italy, and took place in the wake of the discovery and arrest of a group of young anti-fascists, a number of whom were Jews, in 1934. One of those picked up was Renzo Ravenna's cousin. As a result of pressure from Rome, two Jewish unelected councillors were relieved of their posts in Ferrara.

It was a small sign of what was to come, later, for Ravenna and the entire Jewish community. However, in 1934, the Prefect of Ferrara did manage to protect Ravenna. In a letter to the ministry, the prefect played the Balbo card, writing that Balbo's 'political faith in Ravenna is unwavering despite the fact he belongs ... to the Jewish religion'.[42] He described Ravenna as a 'good fascist' (which he was).[43] Ravenna was not moved on, for now. Nonetheless, further warning signals were seen after 1934. In 1936 anti-Semitic graffiti was daubed on walls in the city. The prefect, while defending Ravenna, also reported in 1937 that he had removed fourteen Jews from senior positions in the city.[44] But in March 1938 more pressure came from Rome. Soon afterwards. Ravenna resigned for 'health reasons'. Ravenna's close friends suspected that, instead, the real explanation was more to do with Mussolini's increasingly close collaboration with the Nazis.[45]

*

Giorgio Bassani was born in Bologna in 1916, but he grew up in Ferrara and his parents and other relatives were Ferrarese.[46] Both his mother and father were Jewish. Bassani's celebrated novel *The Garden of the Finzi Continis* is set in a fictional garden in a real place – Ferrara. It revolves around a series of languid summer tennis matches and encounters within the vast grounds of a house owned by wealthy Ferrarese Jews in the late 1930s. Slowly, the net of the racial laws draws in around the community, but they carry on more or less as normal. They feel secure, although cut off, enveloped. But they were not safe: none of them were. It is a novel in part about fascism. As Bassani later said: The 'bourgeoisie was all made up of fascists'.[47] The census of 1938 identified 733 people in Ferrara as officially 'belonging to the Jewish race'. The drip drip drip of racial decrees led to a process whereby rights were taken away, and humiliations piled up day by day, month by month.

Like many other Jews from Ferrara, Bassani embraced fascism for a time, participating in cultural events organised by the regime. Much later, in 1961, he dealt with this charge of hypocrisy, of having 'been a fascist', in a lecture he gave in Bologna (in a series which also included Primo Levi). In that lecture, Bassani read out a letter he had received identifying him as having written for Italo Balbo's newspaper and participated in fascist events in 1937. Bassani was clear: these 'accusations' were all true. But, unlike other writers and journalists in postwar Italy, instead of trying to hide this 'fascist' past, he turned the question on its head. He said that he was 'amazed' to be accused of 'no longer being a fascist!' and noted that he had been thrown out of the Fascist Party as a Jew and had been arrested as an anti-fascist.[48]

During his studies in Bologna, Bassani had become an anti-fascist. 'The first anti-Semitic persecutions, which consolidated my political ideas, started while I was in my third year at university ... I was an anti-fascist before fascism started to attack me because I was a Jew.'[49]

SHOCK, RESIGNATION, EXILE: 1938–40

For Italian Jews, most of whom hadn't seen the anti-Semitic campaign coming, and who had a strong sense of loyalty to Italian institutions, it was a deeply traumatic time. In a single day they found that their children were suddenly excluded from school. An article in the *Corriere della Sera* stated: 'it is natural that the government looks to protect schools from Jewish contamination'.[50]

Rossana Rossanda, who would later become a resistance fighter, and then a leading communist and left-wing intellectual in postwar Italy, remembered her Jewish classmate 'disappearing' from the desk next to her in her school in Venice: 'The girl sitting next to me said "from tomorrow I won't be at school any more", why? "Because I am Jewish." She was called Georgina Moll, she had a nice calm face, and was slightly older than me ... brown-haired, a nice girl ... I never saw Georgina Moll again.'[51] Special Jewish-only schools were set up, at first with some state funding. Giorgio Bassani taught in Ferrara's Jewish school for a time.

A series of other separations, humiliations and discriminations followed. Jewish soldiers were removed from the army. This set up a stark contrast with the First World War, when many Italian Jews volunteered as a sign of their loyalty to king and country. Progressively, Italian Jews had their status, rights and livelihoods taken away. A succession of measures excluded, separated and banished them. No Jews could teach in Italian schools and university students and professors were kicked out.[52] Only one professor refused to take up a post made vacant by the removal of a Jewish person. Something like 5,600 school and university students were removed from educational institutions. The list of measures grew longer and longer. Jews could no longer marry anybody who was not defined as a Jew. Mussolini's laws penetrated deep into family life. A form of apartheid was instituted.

At the end of 1938 all 'Jewish' public employees were sacked. In 1939 they were banned from practising as lawyers, doctors and other professions.

Welfare payments were taken away. Property of all kinds was effectively seized from those defined as 'Jews'. Sometimes these bans verged on the surreal, such as those relating to fishing rights, or the sale of radios, or the upkeep of racing pigeons. 'Jews' were not allowed to have 'non-Jewish' domestic servants. Personal documents were marked with the phrase 'Of Jewish race'. So, for example, if a person defined as Jewish stayed in a hotel, this 'racial characteristic' was registered (and the information passed routinely to the police). Later, holidays were effectively ruled out for Italian 'Jews'. Books by Jewish authors could not be borrowed from libraries, and Jewish scholars or readers could not even visit libraries to study.

What choices did Italian Jews have? Some took the road of exile, such as the brilliant historian Arnaldo Momigliano, who had been a supporter of fascism, and had, it seems, also joined the Italian fascist militia for a time.[53] Momigliano graduated in his early twenties and in 1932, before he was thirty, he took over as Chair in Greek history in the University of Rome. In that same year he joined the PNF. He replaced one of the few professors – his 'maestro', Gaetano De Sanctis – who had been sacked (and lost his pension) for being one of only a handful of academics in Italy (twelve out a total of over 1,200) to refuse to swear an oath of loyalty to the regime. Momigliano pronounced the oath. It read as follows:

> I swear fidelity to the King, his heirs and to the Fascist Regime, to
> observe faithfully the Statute and the other laws of the state, and
> to carry out all my duties as a teacher with the aim of forming
> hard-working and principled men, devoted to the Fatherland and
> to the Fascist Regime. I swear that I do not belong nor will I join
> associations or parties whose activity is not consistent with the
> duties of my office.[54]

Momigliano then moved to another chair in Turin, but the racial laws soon led to his expulsion from the university system. In 1939 he left Italy for Paris and then for Oxford. His father and mother would both die in Auschwitz.[55] He would work in British universities for much of the rest of his career.

In the early twenty-first century, Momigliano (who died in 1987) was at the centre of a public and academic debate concerning his previous commitment to fascism, as documents emerged including a letter he had written to fascist hierarch Giuseppe Bottai in 1938. This kind of 'scandal' often affected leading Italian intellectuals in postwar Italy, many of whom had in some way been linked to fascism, either through conviction, or necessity, or a combination of both.[56] Individual journeys through and beyond fascism were very rarely linear or without moments of compromise. Reinvention was common, including that of one's own past.

In the late 1930s many Italian Jews stayed on in Italy, hoping that things would not get worse, or because they did not have the resources or connections to escape. As time went on, the possibilities for exile narrowed. Some Jews avoided capture, some hid, some changed their names and identities. Success in these ventures depended on chance, influential friends and the help or otherwise of the community. A number of Jews were betrayed; some were protected and saved. Each story was different, but many of them ended in tragedy.

JEWISH FASCIST MARTYR

The racial laws of 1938 created problems for the status of Modena's Jewish 'fascist martyr' from 1921, Duilio Sinigaglia, who had been shot dead in clashes with the Royal Guards in the city. In the wake of the laws, the secretary of the PNF in Modena wrote to the national party secretary, Achille Starace, pointing out that that 'the *squadristi* ... venerate the martyr Sinigaglia'.[57]

What was to be done? Sinigaglia's parents and six children still lived in the city. They were all fervent fascists. An exception was made. Sinigaglia's family were not excluded, and did not lose their jobs. In 1939, Sinigaglia's mother made an official request to be 'discriminated', which was accepted. In this request it was noted that her son had fought against those from the same religion, 'because of his fascist faith'.[58] The local fascist section carried his name right up to the end of the Second World War. It was another sign that the law did not apply to all Jews in the same way. There were, however, small changes to ceremonies and commemorations for Sinigaglia. His name was no longer cited first, for example, and the commemoration no longer involved a visit to the Jewish cemetery. With the end of the war, the memory of the fascist martyrs went underground, connected only to those tiny groups of militant neo-fascists who continued to operate politically. Duilio Sinigaglia's tomb is still in the Jewish cemetery of Modena, as is that of Pio Donati, the Jewish socialist lawyer who had been a victim of fascist violence.

Fatal Alliance and the Pact of Steel

Italy invaded Albania in April 1939. The king, strutting on his horse, was proclaimed emperor. It was another title to add to a growing list, but there were signs that things were about to change.

In May that year Mussolini gave a speech at the opening of the gigantic Fiat Mirafiori factory in Turin – which covered an area of a million square metres, and had a canteen with space for 11,000 people. His audience was made up overwhelmingly of workers, in their overalls. Mussolini's reception was not what he was used to – the seemingly adoring, lively and responsive 'oceanic' crowds which had greeted him across Italy for seventeen years. A police report analysed what happened that day:

> There was none of the welcome that there should have been on the part of the 50,000 assembled workers. The Duce began his speech (with which you are familiar), and towards the end, speaking of what would have been the regime's policy for the working classes – [he] asked: *'Do you remember it?'* But of the 50,000 who were present only 400 answered YES![1]

It had been a long wait, outside, in the rain, for the thousands of workers forced to attend. Official propaganda ignored the silence, talking of a 'roar of hurrahs'.[2] In the later telling and the retelling, the non-response of the Torinese working class was framed as the beginning of the antifascist resistance to come. History was read backwards. But even at the time, it was an ominous sign for Mussolini, who was well aware of the silence, and commented on it in real time. Had fascism ever won over the working class? There is considerable evidence that fascist rule was already in crisis in 1939.[3] Many Italians were tired of the Fascist Party, of the constant mobilisation, of the obvious corruption.

In the same month, May 1939, Italy signed the 'Pact of Steel' – Mussolini's name for Italy's alliance with Nazi Germany. It was an agreement which tied Italy to Hitler's coat-tails, formalising the informal coalition of the Rome–Berlin Axis agreed in 1936. Italy was a minor partner, and would remain so for the duration of the inevitable war to come. Article 3 was the key clause:

> If it should happen, against the wishes and hopes of the Contracting Parties, that one of them becomes involved in military complications with another power or other Powers, the other Contracting Party will immediately step to its side as an ally and will support it with all its military might on land, at sea and in the air.

This clearly was an offensive alliance. After September 1939, Italy lost control of its own destiny.

FASCIST NON-BELLIGERENCE AND WAR: 1939–40

'*Vincere, e vinceremo.*' ('Win, and we will win.')
                                        Benito Mussolini, Rome, 10 June 1940

When Hitler invaded Poland in September 1939, Mussolini waited (violating the pact he had just signed). He knew that the '8 million bayonets' which had been a key part of fascist propaganda were just that – propaganda. This was an uncomfortable position given fascism's past and its origins in the 1915 intervention. A new term was used – non-belligerence – avoiding that of 'neutrality', which smacked of the old liberal position which fascism had railed against for so long. But it was clear that, sooner or later, Italy would have to join Hitler's war. Italy waited until France had nearly fallen.

On 10 June 1940 Mussolini gave another set-piece speech in Rome, in line with those linked to the conquest of Ethiopia; it was also the anniversary of Giacomo Matteotti's kidnapping and murder in 1924. Mussolini came straight to the point:

Combatants on the land, the sea and in the air! Blackshirts and Legionnaires of the revolution! Men and women of Italy, of the Empire and of the Kingdom of Albania! Listen! The hour of destiny has sounded in the sky of our fatherland. The time for irrevocable decisions. The declaration of war has already been handed over to the Ambassadors of Great Britain and France.

Italy was at war against 'plutocratic and reactionary democracies'. It was a battle of rich against poor, Mussolini claimed. He also praised Hitler and the 'Emperor King' of Italy. The soundbite came towards the end: 'There is only one slogan – categorical and challenging for all. It has already flown over the Alps and lit up hearts from the Alps to the Indian Ocean: win – and we will win! In order to finally bring a long period of peace and justice for Italy, for Europe, for the world. Italians, rush and take up arms! And show your courage, your tenacity, your valour!' The whole speech was precisely 600 words long.

Leading fascists were well aware that the huge, cheering crowds, were not an accurate indicator of public opinion. Mussolini's Foreign Minister, Ciano, wrote in his diaries of the speech that it did not 'arouse very much enthusiasm'.[4] An informer in Milan wrote in May 1940 that: 'a fairly sizeable mass, composed especially of elements of the lower-middle classes, does not make a mystery of the fact that it is against the war' and that only 'the most rabid fascists' were enthusiastic.[5] Well before the Second World War started to go wrong for Italy, it was clear that 'people were just waiting for the conflict to end and wanted it over as soon as possible'.[6]

The Italians' initial 'French campaign', if it could be called that at all, was an immediate (and easy) success: victory came in just four days. But every other invasion and theatre proved to be a disaster for Italy. On 28 June 1940, just two weeks or so into the war, an aircraft carrying leading fascist Italo Balbo was shot down by friendly fire over Libya. Four months later, on 28 October (the anniversary of the March on Rome) Italy attacked Greece through Albania, but the Italian invasion was forced back in mid-November. Hitler's armies came to the rescue, forcing Greece into submission in April 1941. Italian East Africa also fell swiftly. Less than six years after the triumphant seizure of Addis Ababa, the Italians left the city in April 1941, although Italian military resistance continued until November.

In perhaps the most tragic decision of all, Mussolini sent a total of nearly 230,000 troops to support Hitler's invasion of the USSR in July 1941. This campaign would end in a horrific retreat in the extreme cold, with heavy casualties and high numbers of POWs in Soviet hands. It was a desperate time. 'Men who were very near the end of their tether threw away their weapons ... and drank the anti-freeze from Russian lorries in the belief that it was alcohol.'[7] During the retreat, life was reduced to its bare bones, with starvation and almost unimaginable scenes of violence and pain – frostbitten limbs were cut off without anaesthetic and soldiers collapsed barefoot in the snow. There were countless sad and silent deaths. Survival seemed almost impossible, and only luck, immense strength, or a crucial skill (such as the ability to speak or understand Russian) meant that some of these men finally made it home.[8] Losses were extremely high. A mere 1,200 soldiers from the 11,000-strong Torino division survived. Overall over 50 per cent of the Italian forces were lost; 70,000 were captured, and many died in 'death marches'.

Italians, however, should not be presented only as victims. The occupying Italian armies in Albania, the Balkans and Greece carried out massacres of civilians and partisans and used concentration camps. In the USSR, the Italians were both victims and perpetrators: Italian troops plundered farms and murdered civilians. Italy's entire African campaign finally ended in total defeat in May 1943, with huge numbers of Italian soldiers taken prisoner.

Total War

At home, Italy and Italians experienced 'total war' – bombings, deportations, hunger, occupation. The consequences would be traumatic for every corner of the country, and for every single citizen. Morale quickly dropped. Bombs rained down on Italy, flattening cities. 'Between 1940 and 1945 the Allies dropped some 370,000 tons of bombs on Italy, killing over 60,000 civilians and causing massive destruction, particularly to industrial and port cities.'[1] Naples was the most bombed city in Italy (there were twelve night-time raids in November 1942 alone, and things would soon get worse) and the nightly experience in makeshift shelters (where people often died in the crush and panic) marked many young Italians for years afterwards. At one point, Benevento, a town fifty kilometres or so to the east of Naples, was reduced to rubble, leading to 'the complete collapse of all public institutions'.[2]

Everywhere, food shortages, rationing and high prices began to hit home early in the war. Transport first became difficult and then almost impossible. Train journeys of fifty minutes in peacetime were now taking up to six hours. Thousands fled to the countryside to escape the bombings. Outward signs of support for the regime were useless in judging the real feelings of Italians. 'Even if,' wrote one informer from Florence, 'he [Mussolini] is still greeted with applause ... and demonstrations for him are well attended ... [these] are not spontaneous and are not indications of the real feelings of the people ... nobody can refuse to go to the demonstrations and to applaud for fear of beatings and of reprisals of various types.'[3]

War saw an increase in anti-Semitism and an intensification of the internal war on Jews. Those foreign Jews who were still in Italy were interned in camps by the Italian government almost immediately following the entry into war in June 1940.[4] In September 1941 there was an attack on two of the synagogues in Ferrara and the city's chief rabbi was 'slapped' by a 'fascist official'. Ferrara's prefect wrote a report on the incident:

> The [patriotic] demonstration having broken up, a group of fascists, moving suddenly into Via Mazzini, succeeded in penetrating the building in which are located the Italian, German, and French rite Jewish temples and the residence of the rabbi, Leone Leoni, damaging, amidst hostile shouts at the Jews, the furnishings of two of the said temples. The public [police] forces quickly intervened and obtained the orderly breakup of the said fascists, preventing the burning of several sacred objects [*arredi sacri*] brought by them into the piazza for that purpose ... the population which witnessed the incident *remained indifferent* [emphasis mine].[5]

Signs were placed outside shops stating 'Aryan', and Jewish stores were boycotted. On the night of 14/15 October 1941 a fire was started on the steps of the synagogue in Turin. On 16 October a young Jewish student called Emanuele Artom wrote in his diary that he had come across two posters in the centre of Turin, one of which read: 'These are all Jews: Da Verona, Pitigrilli, Moravia, Loria, Segre, Momigliano, Terracini, Franco, Levi Montalcini, Einstein, Blum, ... Carlo Marx ... Lenin, ... Modigliani, Maestro, Roosevelt, Jachia, Bombacci, Artom, il Negus, De Benedetti, Dario Disegni.' It was a strange list. Some were socialists, some were international figures, some were fascists, one was a fascist spy. 'All the heads of masonry are Jews,' the poster continued, 'and all the accomplices of the stock exchange ... all homosexuals are Jews, as are those who have never worked, those who have always betrayed the fatherland ... shall we end all this once and for all ... no to concentration camps ... up against the wall with a flamethrower ... Long live Il Duce! Long live Hitler!'[6]

Synagogues and other Jewish buildings were also attacked by fascists in Casale Monferrato and Trieste in that same year, where religious structures were ransacked and looted. It was, purely and simply, daylight robbery. In Ferrara, for example, numerous items were stolen, including invaluable relics, books and entire archives. Individuals were also beaten. Further and similar incidents took place in 1942 and 1943 – before and after Nazi occupation.

Fascism, which had appeared impregnable in 1940, quickly began to crumble. Despite the cheering crowds who appeared to hail Mussolini's declaration of war, public opinion was tepid at best, and soon turned hostile. Violent protests broke out, for example, in Genoa in December 1942. Demonstrators 'pelted the shelters of the rich with stones, forcing their way inside. Scenes of panic turned to angry demonstrations against the war, the fascist authorities and the government.'[7] There were many dress rehearsals for the outpouring of anger to come. Leading fascists, and the king, but not, it seems, Mussolini, were well aware of the deep hostility towards the party and regime. By 1943 this anger had been translated into mass, organised class action.

1943

THE BEGINNING OF THE END: SPRING 1943

Turin's working class rose up in early March 1943. It all began in the Fiat Mirafiori complex, where those workers gathered had only weakly applauded Mussolini in 1939. The action moved from factory to factory, and was also backed by tram drivers. Over 100,000 workers were said to be involved. It was an extraordinary moment, and almost unique – a moment of mass opposition to a fascist regime. Although these strikes have been mythologised, they were a clear sign of support ebbing away, symbolically and in reality. It was a decisive break in the supposed but fragile 'consensus' which had marked the twenty or so years since the factory occupations and the disastrous anti-fascist strikes of 1922. As the historian Tim Mason wrote: 'The wave of strikes in March–April 1943 was in every way the most important act of mass resistance ... an action by a vanguard which persevered in spite of initial setbacks ... which issued some shrewd propaganda; and which managed to win huge popular support and harvest a great political success without sacrificing a single human life.'[1]

On 5 May 1943 Mussolini made his last 'balcony speech', from Palazzo Venezia in Rome. It was the anniversary of the conquest of Addis Ababa in 1936. Two days later, the empire was lost with the surrender of the Axis powers in Tunisia. On 27 May Mussolini ordered that his old 'Red Week' comrade, Pietro Nenni, who was now a leading anti-fascist, be transferred from Rome's Regina Coeli prison to internal exile on the island of Ponza.

Italian territory was now under direct threat. Pantelleria and Lampedusa, two Italian islands off the coast of Sicily, fell to the Allies on 1 June. During the night of 9 July the invasion of the island of Sicily began, under the command of General Eisenhower. On the ground, there were indications that not all troops were fully behind Mussolini's war. 'Soldiers manning an armoured train tore up railway tracks to ensure that it could not get into position.'[2] Nenni wrote in his diary that 'the recent speech by Mussolini, with his lame joke about the fact that the enemies would never have reached the shoreline unless they were horizontal – dead – now appears as a tragic farce'.[3] It was a rapid campaign. By 24 July 'the whole of western Sicily was in enemy hands'.[4] Mussolini's bombastic promises were falling apart.

Leading fascists had been plotting for the removal of their once beloved Duce for some time. Crucially, the king, who was still head of state, began to look for an exit strategy. Italy was divided and weakened. Mussolini's alliance with Hitler had proved to be a 'fatal embrace'. His failure to galvanise more than a minority of Italians for a fascist war was a sign that the 'new fascist man' had perhaps been an illusion, all along. Had the regime really been no more than speeches and parades?

On 19 July 1943 Allied bombers hit Rome for the first time in a raid that used 662 planes and lasted for three hours. Their target was ostensibly the railway connections into the centre of the city, but most of the bombs fell on San Lorenzo, the working-class and 'red' neighbourhood close to the central station that had seen frequent clashes between fascists and socialists after the First World War and during the March on Rome. It was an inferno. Around 3,000 residents of San Lorenzo were killed in the attack.[5] Survivors later recalled the bodies of animals lying in the street and the overpowering smell of burning human flesh.

Pope Pius XII left the Vatican to view the damage. A famous photograph (from a later visit in August) depicted him in front of a crowd, his arms spread wide. Rome had been designated as an 'Open City' – somehow outside of the conflict – but it was not spared. Many Italians did not blame these deaths on the Allies, but on Mussolini himself. The bombings were described by some as being carried out by 'liberating guns'. Constant defeat, bombings, the loss of empire, hunger, strikes, and the invasion of Italy itself heralded the imminent end of Mussolini's reign. Public support had melted away. Now, the fascists themselves would turn against their leader.

ENDGAME
GRAND COUNCIL, 24–25 JULY 1943

Bizarrely, the Gran Consiglio, set up and run by Benito Mussolini as a kind of rubber stamp on his decisions, and his power, was to play a key role in his downfall, and bring about the end of fascism itself. Mussolini had unwittingly created an instrument for his own defenestration. Only once did the Grand Council act in this way, and in doing so it destroyed itself. Its last act was one of suicide. Unexpectedly, democracy of a sort had broken out from within the heart of the regime.

The crucial Grand Council meeting began at 5.15 p.m. on 24 July 1943. It ran right through until 2.30 in the morning. No minutes were kept and notes were only published in 1965, although diaries later emerged and individual accounts were provided by various protagonists. It was a dramatic moment, and one subsequently cloaked in rumour, conspiracy theories and divided memories. There was a lengthy debate, accompanied by dark accusations of betrayal. Twenty-eight people were present in the Sala del Pappagallo in Palazzo Venezia. Mussolini's desk, as usual, was raised up, above the others. Two of the original four leaders of the March on Rome were there (Italo Balbo and Michele Bianchi had both died in the meantime). Mussolini spoke first. It is said that he delivered a rambling tirade for at least two hours, offering little of substance to placate his critics, apart from some changes in personnel.[6]

Dino Grandi, the ex-*squadrista* from Bologna who had been ambassador in London for most of the 1930s, put a motion, which had been agreed with the connivance of the king, before the Grand Council at 9 p.m. The atmosphere was tense. Grandi later claimed that he had hidden two grenades in his bag and was worried that he might not get out alive. There were large numbers of blackshirts inside and outside the building. He spoke for an hour, calling on Mussolini to pass all power to the king, and for the return of some form of democracy. It is said that Grandi accused Mussolini of having 'engulfed us in a war that is against honour, and against the interests and the sentiments of the Italian people'.[7]

A loyalist counter-motion was presented by Farinacci and others. Then, surprisingly, Mussolini called for a vote on Grandi's motion first, at 2.30 a.m. He was astonished when nineteen members voted for the motion, and thus against him, including historic and leading fascists such as De Bono, Bottai, Federzoni, Ciano, De Vecchi and Grandi.

Depending on different accounts, seven or eight voted against the motion, and one or two abstained. Farinacci was said to have walked out of the room before the vote.

Mussolini carried on with his daily routine, despite the vote. He was in denial. On 25 July the king, who had basked in the regime's success for so long, told Mussolini that he was being replaced with an elderly general – Marshal Badoglio – as prime minister. It was a meeting which took no more than twenty minutes. Mussolini was then surrounded and arrested by *carabinieri* loyal to the king in the courtyard of the Villa Savoia in Rome, and driven away.

There were surreal aspects to this fall – as there had been with the initial rise to power in October 1922. How could a dictator, a semi-deity, a man 'who was always right', be arrested by humble officials of the state? Instantly, the aura which had surrounded Il Duce, and his regime, fell away. He was just a normal man, weak, ageing, ill, indecisive – and now in custody. Fascism had never bothered to remove the powers of the monarchy. The king was still head of state, and, for the first time in twenty years, he had exercised these powers against Mussolini himself. The ex-*duce* was taken away in a Red Cross ambulance, and held in barracks in Rome. Badoglio later took over Mussolini's official Alfa Romeo car.

At 10.45 that night the news was announced to the nation on the radio, sending shock waves through Italy and across the world. Many Italians were already in bed. But those who tuned in were met with some moments of silence. Then the classic 'fascist voice' which was so familiar to radio listeners under the regime, piped up again with an announcement. It was an almost total shock to the audience:

> Attention, Attention. His Majesty the King and Emperor has
> accepted the resignation of the Head of Government, the Prime
> Minister, His Excellency *Benito Mussolini*, and has nominated as
> Head of the Government and Prime Minister, Pietro Badoglio.

It was a brief statement – just forty-five words long – the initial announcement taking less than a minute to read out. There was no mention of the fact that Mussolini had been arrested, just that he had resigned – most listeners heard only this part, before taking to the streets to celebrate. The rest of the announcement was something of a damp squib in comparison.

Next were the words of the king himself, read out by the same announcer. Italy's monarch was taking control of the armed forces. It was time for unity, but the Italians should be careful: 'No deviation will be tolerated, no recriminations will be allowed.' Italy's 'sacred soil' needed to be defended. Finally, it was Badoglio's turn. His language was not particularly anti-fascist and he was assuming 'full powers', as had Mussolini in 1922. Above all, the war was not over. He also laid out an explicit warning: 'Those who are under the illusion that they can disturb the peace, or public order, will be squashed ... Italy will keep its word.'

Badoglio was hardly a new face and was deeply compromised by his activities under the regime, including his brutal role in the suppression of resistance in Libya and the Ethiopian war. German soldiers poured into Italy as the news filtered through. Italy was being invaded twice. It was about to become a major battleground.

25–26 JULY 1943

The speed of the collapse took almost everyone by surprise. On the streets of Italy, there was sheer joy, and anger. As news spread of Mussolini's arrest in Rome on 25 July 1943, anti-fascists in Bologna headed straight for the stadium, which at that time was being used for the fire service and to house those made homeless by wartime bombing. Their target was Bologna stadium's imposing statue of Mussolini on a horse that had stood for less than fourteen years. Ropes and sticks were used to snap the body and head off, which was then pushed down the terraces and onto the pitch. Mussolini's horse resisted the crowd and Il Duce's legs remained attached to the bronze animal's flanks. His metal head was paraded around town, before being abandoned in the street. The emperor had fallen, and so had many of his icons and symbols. Some Bolognese remembered stories of a previous case of statue desecration, way back in 1511, when the people of the city had chucked a statue of Pope Julius II down the stairs of the central Basilica.

ONE ISLAND, THREE MEN

When he was in charge, Mussolini had banished many of his opponents to internal exile. One of the sites of exile was the island of Ponza, off the Lazio coast. After prison, Tito Zaniboni, the ex-war hero who had planned to assassinate Mussolini in 1925, was interned on Ponza; Pietro Nenni, who had stood alongside Mussolini against the Libyan war and during Red Week, was also there. In July 1943 another unexpected prisoner turned up on that small island – Benito Mussolini himself. On the 27th the ex-*duce* was taken to Gaeta and then by boat to Ponza, arriving the next day. Mussolini, Zaniboni and Nenni did not meet on Ponza.[8] Nenni later said that he had seen Mussolini from afar through binoculars. According to some accounts, the ex-*duce* was kept in a dwelling which had once housed the Ethiopian, Ras Imru, Haile Selassie's cousin, in another symbolic overturning of power.[9] By then, Mussolini's glorious empire was no more. He would stay on Ponza for just ten days. The old regime had fallen, but the new Italy had not yet been born. It was an interregnum.

LONG MEMORIES

Fascism's fall overturned power hierarchies in a few hours. After 25 July 1943, Piero Brandimarte, the architect of the 'Turin massacre' of December 1922, became the first name on lists – of the *anti-fascists*. Memories of the 1922 massacre were still fresh, despite the years that had passed. On 26 July 1943, in Turin, a group of demonstrators attacked Brandimarte's house and a storeroom, ransacking the property. They found a large amount of food which was taken and handed out to the poor. Despite rationing, it was said that Brandimarte had accumulated 150 kilos of oil, 200 litres of alcoholic drinks, 10 kilos of salami and the same amount of coffee, canned meat and five fur coats 'for women'. There were also boxes of soap. He was reported to the authorities for black-market trading and hoarding.[10] It seems that Brandimarte had enriched himself, like many other leading fascists, under the regime. When a deposit box of his was opened it was found to contain numerous share and bond certificates for considerable amounts of money.[11] He quickly fled, heading for the border town of Ventimiglia, taking his wife and children with him. On 28 August 1943, Brandimarte was arrested, but, like Mussolini himself, he would not be behind bars for long.[12]

Giovanni Roveda was, at the time of the massacre in 1922, secretary of the Camera del Lavoro in Turin. In the wake of those events, he had carried out his own private inquest, through his lawyers. He would attempt on numerous occasions in subsequent years to bring the perpetrators to justice. It was a kind of mission for him, something both personal and political. In July 1943 Roveda gave a speech in Milan's Piazza del Duomo – one of the first openly anti-fascist speeches to be heard in Italy since the 1920s (during which time Roveda had spent time in prison, in internal exile, had escaped from incarceration, and been shot)[13] – and called again for justice for the victims of the Turin massacre. He felt, he said: 'A duty towards those poor people who were so brutally murdered.'[14]

On the morning of 26 July, a shopkeeper called Ebe – who traded on a road towards Livorno – left some excrement on the doorstep of the secretary of the local Fascist Party. ' "Here's my shit" – she cried – "I've been holding on to it for twenty years, and now it's your turn to eat it." ' In 1921, Ebe, a socialist, had been forced to drink castor oil at the hands of the local fascists and now, more than two decades later, it was payback time.[15] 'Grudges that had sometimes been nursed for over twenty years could now be aired, and scores settled.'[16]

AUGUSTO MASETTI
IMOLA, 1943

Augusto Masetti was finally released, having been given a dubious psychiatric diagnosis in 1936, twenty-five years after he had shot at his commanding officer in a barracks in Bologna in protest at being sent to war. In 1940 he moved to Imola in central Italy. On or around 25 July 1943, the former bricklayer was spotted on the streets carrying a bag of tools and a ladder. Masetti headed straight for the local fascist party headquarters where, in front of a growing crowd, he was said to have chiselled off the heads and hands of soldiers on the bas-relief on a pillar on the front of the building. One of these figures with a missing head can still be seen in Imola today, perhaps the one Masetti himself resculpted.[17]

Fascism was over, and squares across Italy were packed with joyous crowds, looking for blackshirts (who had seemingly disappeared overnight) and pulling down symbols and statues. Mussolini, as Il Duce, was finished. The National Fascist Party was no more.

But all the parties and celebrations were premature. Italian fascism would soon be resuscitated by the ongoing war and by the Nazis. Italy was entering a period of deep uncertainty and transition – a phase from 25 July to 8 September 1943 – which would become known by its length: the '45 Days'.

Forty Five Days

Mussolini was under arrest, and the Fascist Party had been banned, but who was in charge? Badoglio appointed a cabinet and a government; his authority, however, was uncertain. It was a 'technical' and not a political government. There was no mention of elections and there were deep continuities with the recent past. The first Minister of Justice, for example, was Gaetano Azzariti, who had been president of the Tribunale della Razza, a key body in the application of the racial laws. Later, in January 1944, this government would abrogate some parts of those racial laws which, until recently, Azzariti had been central to applying and interpreting. It would also abolish the Tribunale della Razza itself. Ironically, Azzariti was also the architect of 'Decrees for the Punishment of Illegal Enrichments'. One of the accusations often levelled against that institution was that it was open to all kinds of corruption.[1]

REPRESSION: REGGIO EMILIA

On 26 July 1943, General Mario Roatta, Army Chief of Staff, issued an extraordinary order. 'Any minor disturbance to public order, of any kind,' he declared, 'will be treated as betrayal: a little blood spilt will save a lot of blood later on ... the army ... should open fire ... without any kind of warning, *as if they were acting against enemy troops* ... there should be no shooting in the air. You should shoot as if you were in battle... any [troops] who ... rebel ... will be immediately executed.'[2]

In Reggio Emilia, central Italy, on 28 July – just three days after the arrest of Mussolini – workers in the huge Reggiane tractor factory complex, where over 12,000 workers were employed, staged a demonstration calling for an end to the conflict. Badoglio had issued orders that any demonstration with more than three people involved was to be fired upon, and Roatta's repressive orders were to be put to the test. Some claim that around 5,000 workers took part and there were Italian flags flourished by those on the protest. It is unclear who opened fire first – the security guards at the factory or an army unit. Nine workers were killed, including a pregnant woman.[3] In some accounts, the commanding officer of the army unit forced reluctant soldiers to aim at the unarmed protesters.[4]

In other areas, however, Badoglio's government acted swiftly to disband the fascist state. On 2 August the Partito Nazionale Fascista was dissolved, with a decree which became operational four days later. Soon afterwards a further decree got rid of the Gran Consiglio. Political parties were legalised and the fascist parliament was also abolished. Formally, fascism appeared to be over – but this was an illusion. It would be a long and bloody denouement.

War was coming closer to home. Sicily fell to the Allies on 15 August 1943, with the overall loss of nearly 41,000 Italians; 116,000 prisoners were taken into Allied hands. Frantic (secret) negotiations took place with the Allies. But Italy had no room for manoeuvre, and was forced to accept whatever terms were offered to them. It was such a bad deal that it was kept secret until after the war. On 3 September 1943, the humiliating peace agreement was signed in a tent in a field in Sicily, in a nondescript place called Cassibile.[5] Harold Macmillan, an army officer, and future British prime minister, was present to witness the historic moment. Italy was officially out of the war, but nobody had told the Italian people, or the Italian army. Badoglio and the king delayed the announcement of this surrender as long as they could.

8 September 1943

Italy's fascist war had been a total disaster.[1] If he had stayed out of the conflict, Mussolini might well have died in his own bed, at a good age, like Franco in Spain. On 8 September, five days after the signing of the peace agreement in the tent in Sicily, Eisenhower announced the armistice, via radio, forcing Italy's hand. Less than an hour later, Badoglio himself read out this proclamation on the radio. It was under a hundred words long:

> The Italian Government, recognising the impossibility of continuing this unfair battle against the overwhelming force of the adversary, and with the desire of sparing further and more serious disasters for the nation, has asked General Eisenhower for a peace agreement ... the request has been accepted. As a result, every act of hostility against the Anglo-American forces on behalf of the Italian forces, in every place, will cease. They will, however, react to eventual attacks from whatever quarter.

Hitler was furious at what he saw as Italian betrayal. Plans were already in place for a full-scale Nazi occupation of Italy, which would become a battleground between the German army and the Allies. As the Nazis began to take total control of Italian cities and entire regions, the king fled to the south, already liberated by the Allies. Italy's capital city had been abandoned by its own head of state. Badoglio and the king wanted to save their own lives, but did little or nothing to warn the Italian army, or his own people, as to the next step. In short, they prioritised themselves over the fate of the nation. At around 5 a.m. on 9 September the king and Badoglio and other military officials were driven in a five-car convoy to Ortona on the coast, a journey that took around seven hours. They then travelled by sea to Brindisi, where they set up a self-styled 'Kingdom of the South'.

After having reigned supreme in Rome for so long, both King Victor Emmanuel III and Mussolini were in exile, and both had effectively renounced all claim to be in control. Badoglio and the king's squalid 'escape' from Rome was later immortalised in a trenchant non-comme-morative plaque in Ortona. It reads:

> From this port
> On the night of 9th September 1943
> The last King of Italy escaped
> With his court and with Badoglio
> Consigning the martyred fatherland to the anger of the Germans
> Republican Ortona
> With its ruins and its pain
> Cries eternal damnation
> Against the betrayals of the Monarchy
> Against Fascism and the ruins of Italy
> With a yearning for justice by the people and by history
> In the Holy Name of the Republic

> 9-9-1945

It was unclear even whether the nation of Italy existed in any meaningful form anymore. Without the king, or any leadership, and with the army in disarray, only a small minority of Italians took up arms to try to repel the German army in Rome. Fighting on the edge of the city marked the official beginning of the anti-fascist resistance, but Rome was quickly brought under Nazi occupation. By 10 September 1943, Italy had already lost control of its capital.

Across the world, Italy's army was abandoned. Where they had been serving alongside their old German allies, something like 800,000 Italian soldiers refused to fight for the Nazis and were deported to work camps in Germany and elsewhere. In some isolated cases, such as on the island of Kefalonia in Greece, the Italians fought back against the

Germany army, and were massacred as a result. Many others deserted and tried to get home, throwing off their uniforms. A number kept their arms and joined up with the nascent anti-fascist resistance, while a minority stayed loyal to Italian fascism. Italy's army had fallen apart, splitting into numerous factions. Meanwhile, the Italian peninsula became a stage for 'total war'. Allied troops fought their way slowly up the country, taking heavy losses against the German occupiers. Towns, cities and regions were liberated and reoccupied by the Allies at the same time.

IL DUCE RETURNS

After Ponza, Mussolini was held in the Maddalena archipelago off northern Sardinia, and then in a hotel in a mountain ski resort, at a place called Campo Imperatore, in the Abruzzo region in the south of Italy. In the armistice agreement signed by Italy, Mussolini had been mentioned by name and a promise was made to put him before the League of Nations to face charges, presumably for war crimes. But as they escaped south, the king and Badoglio decided not to take Mussolini with them. On 12 September, German SS and paratroopers freed the ex-*duce* in a dramatic operation, using gliders flown down from Rome. It is said that not a shot was fired, although two Italians were killed during the ground operations. A propaganda film was made of the raid.

Mussolini was taken to Germany via Austria, where Hitler was able to dictate terms. Mussolini then returned to Italy as head of a puppet state, whose official birth was 23 September 1943. This entity had an official name: the Italian Social Republic (RSI); the king was now a hated traitor and the fascists had rediscovered their (long forgotten) republican roots. But this entity was also quickly given a humiliating joke title by its opponents: the 'Republic of Salò'. Mussolini's government had set up their ministries in a series of buildings around Lake Garda, near a small town called Salò. The RSI was allowed some autonomy in the areas still under Axis control. Italian fascism was not finished yet. Vichy France was the model – a weak, collaborationist administration with little real power, which attracted the most fanatical and most racist elements, and which practised extreme violence against Italian civilians and the resistance.

Nonetheless, Mussolini was back in Italy. The twenty-fifth of July had proved to be an illusion. Fascism was taking a long time to die. Blackshirts were back and operating with brutality across large areas that were now under Nazi control. The RSI claimed that it was taking an improbable shift to the left, while unleashing further waves of bloodshed and enthusiastically supporting the Nazis in their own endeavours. One of Mussolini's first acts was to put on trial and execute some of the 'traitors' from 25 July, or at least those who had not yet fled.

A swift three-day show trial was held in Verona in January 1944, and five men were then executed by being shot in the back by a thirty-man firing squad. The leading fascists were tied to chairs in a field at a shooting range. They included one of the original leaders of the March on Rome and a key player in the Ethiopian invasion, General Emilio De Bono, and Mussolini's former Foreign Minister (and son-in-law) Galeazzo Ciano. A film was made of the executions. Many of the other leading fascists who had voted against Mussolini were also condemned to death, but managed to avoid arrest.

*

War continued and intensified. As the bombs rained down, the Nazi occupiers terrorised civilians with lootings and mass deportation. In the town of Teano near Naples, for example, nearly all men of working age were rounded up. Basic infrastructure was destroyed or collapsed. A malaria epidemic was deliberately triggered. Much of this was met by various kinds of resistance. During the 'four days of Naples' at the end of September 1943, armed civilians took on the Nazi occupiers. It was women who suffered the most as total war passed through their communities. Women played a key part in daily resistance and survival, and were often the first and most dramatic victims of war.

As the Nazis dug in and then retreated northwards, they carried out atrocities against civilians and partisans. In March 1944 in Rome, 335 civilians were taken to the dark caves of the Fosse Ardeatine, and executed in revenge for an anti-fascist bomb attack which had killed thirty-three members of the German occupying force in the centre of the city in March 1944. Other horrific massacres decimated the hamlet of Sant'Anna di Stazzema high up in the Tuscan mountains in August 1944, with over 500 dead, and the hill-top town of Civitella Val di Chiana near Arezzo. Italy's German occupiers used repressive tactics developed from the Eastern front to attempt to pacify the Italian people, and annihilate all resistance. In the area around Marzabotto in central Italy hundreds of people – nearly 800 – were executed in a series of operations covering a large area between September and October 1944.[2] Other violent and scorched earth actions took place right across Italy.[3]

CHOICES

'It was a question, at that time, of working out which side you were on.'

Ruggero Zangrandi[4]

All Italians were faced with choices. Should they join the resistance – heading for the mountains and taking up arms, or working secretly in the cities and countryside – or could they try and make it home, and simply survive the war, waiting to see how things turned out? There was also the option of fighting on with the Nazis, and joining Mussolini's Italian Social Republic. For thousands of Italian soldiers, sailors and airmen across the world, these choices were more limited. Many were simply disarmed by the German army.

It is beyond the scope of this book to provide a history of the Italian resistance between 1943–45. Many of those involved had experienced the rise of fascism, and almost all had witnessed the repressions of the regime itself. For others, their main enemy was not fascism at all, but the occupying Nazis. For a minority, their aim was nothing short of a social revolution.[5] Few could avoid some confrontation with what remained of Italian fascism, especially in the north and centre of the country. A bitter civil war raged alongside a war of liberation. Liberation was a double or triple moment – from Mussolini, from the Nazis and, some hoped, from class oppression.

Liberation could also be violent and oppressive. There were mass rapes of women in Campania and Lazio, largely at the hands of Moroccan soldiers fighting with the French army. These women often suffered from the humiliation of rape well after the war was over, but, largely ignored in their quest for some sort of compensation or help, were condemned to remain in silence.[6]

The ambiguous and unique position of Italy in 1940–44, as it moved from aggressor to 'semi-ally', left the civilian population vulnerable to revenge and violence from all sides. The French army were 'liberating' a country which had invaded France in 1940, on the coat-tails of the Nazis, and had little pity for locals. Nazis saw the Italians as traitors, and treated them as such. Partisans taken prisoner were tortured and executed; described as 'bandits', their bodies were hung from trees in parks or in public squares. It was a dirty, bitter war. Many died lonely deaths, on hillsides or mountain tops.

Italy's Holocaust:
Deportation and Slaughter, 1943–45

With the Nazis in control of much of Italy, the writing was on the wall for those Jews who had remained. Round-ups of Jews took place across the country under Nazi occupation, with the often willing participation of the Italian authorities. The lives of Jews were now in real danger. Anti-fascists were also constantly arrested and many were simply shot. Thousands were deported to death- or work-camps. Italy's shameful racial laws had paved the way for an Italian holocaust.

HOTEL MEINA: THE FIRST MASSACRE

Despite the internment policy, until 1943 foreign Jews often took refuge in Italy; they thought it was safer there. Some came from Greece, and in particular from Salonica, where mass deportations had taken place.

On 15 September 1943, SS officers from the elite Adolf Hitler Regiment turned up at the Hotel Meina, on the banks of Lago Maggiore in the north of Italy, having received a tip-off about the guests hiding out there. The soldiers rounded up sixteen Jews, many of whom had escaped from persecution in Greece, and locked them in one of the hotel rooms.

It then appeared that 'orders from on high' came through. The Jews were subsequently taken away in small groups by car, and shot dead. Their bodies were dumped in the lake. The corpses of three children were never found. According to Giuseppe Mayda: 'The SS tied the children together with barbed wire, hand to hand, feet to feet, and after throwing them into the water from a boat ... they pushed them under with their oars.'[1] Becky Behar, who was thirteen at the time, survived a similar fate in another hotel on the lake thanks to the intervention of the Turkish consulate. Hotel Meina was the first massacre of Jews inside Italy, but it would not be the last.

In the Nazi-occupied city of Ferrara, arrests and deportations began from 7 October 1943, with the round-up of five Jews and anti-fascists (people, of course, could be both of these things) and the rabbi, Leone Leoni. More followed, including Eugenio, the nephew of former *podestà* Renzo Ravenna. All these detentions were carried out by Italians. Many decided to flee. Some left for other cities, others tried to cross the border to what they thought was safety. Renzo Ravenna, his wife and their three children managed to get to Switzerland. Many others did not make it. Two of Renzo's sisters and his brother, plus other family members, would be deported to Auschwitz. Of his relatives, only Eugenio made it home to Ferrara.[2]

ROME, 16 OCTOBER 1943

In 1943, seventy-three years had passed since Rome had become Italy's capital. That moment had seen the final emancipation of the Roman Jewish population, whose history went back thousands of years. Many of Rome's Jews still lived in the area where the ghetto had once been, not far from the city centre. Within a week of the Nazi occupation, at dawn on 16 October 1943, the streets of the Jewish neighbourhood close to the Tiber river were blocked by German troops (an SS division) in trucks. Italian police were also involved in the round-up. Many of the men tried to escape over rooftops or by merging in with the crowds. They had not thought that women and children would also be arrested. Jews were picked up elsewhere across the city.

Over 1,200 Jews were detained over a period of nine hours. Those from 'mixed marriages' were released. On 18 October 1943 a train left Rome with around a thousand Jews on board. In her sweeping novel *History*, Elsa Morante describes the events from that day: 'At the bottom of the ramp, on an unused platform, there was a train ... there were perhaps twenty cattle trucks, some open and empty, others closed with long iron bars.... As with other deportations the wagons had no windows, apart from a tiny, slatted opening in the roof. From some of those openings there were two hands sticking out, or a pair of eyes could be seen inside.'³ The destination was Auschwitz. It took five days to get there. Only a small number – sixteen – survived, including just one woman. It was the biggest round-up and mass deportation to take place on Italian territory. At a stroke, something like 2 per cent of the entire Jewish population in Italy had been removed; 828 were killed immediately on their arrival in Auschwitz.⁴

THE LUSENA FAMILY: PRIVATE TRAGEDIES AND SECRETS

Aldo Lusena was a successful businessman with a shop in Florence which dealt in cloth and other materials. He was Jewish. After 8 September 1943 he decided to go into hiding, in rural Tuscany, with his wife, Alda, and their two-year-old daughter, Bianca. The couple had met in Turkey in 1939.

Lusena devised a strategy for his escape. He would pretend to sell up and instead, store his stock until it was safe to return to Florence. He moved his family to a remote part of Tuscany, north of Arezzo, and there befriended a trader called Giuseppe Ferroni, who was also effectively in hiding, avoiding a military call-up. Using false receipts, Lusena 'sold' material to Ferroni, and then found somewhere to store his wares in a small hamlet called Biforco, in the Casentino region. But the arrival of the family in this tiny and remote settlement caught the attention of locals. Ferroni betrayed his trust. Lusena had brought with him a considerable amount of cash and other valuables. One night, after a meeting with Giuseppe Ferroni, the Lusena family appeared shocked and worried. The next morning, 7 December, they failed to turn up for breakfast in the house in which they were staying. By then, they had been in hiding for around a hundred days.

The three were discovered the next day together on their bed, in a death embrace. Both Aldo and Alda had taken their own lives, using a razor, having suffocated their daughter with a pillow. Not all of the letters they left behind were found, and a box with valuables disappeared. The stock which had been carefully transported from Florence was cleared out by Ferroni. Aldo left a note for the local priest, and a considerable sum for the family's funeral. However the priest only used a tiny amount, giving them a pauper's ceremony instead. Nobody emerges well from this story: it is a kind of counter-narrative to the 'good Italian' narrative.

Overnight Ferroni seemed to become very rich, purchasing property, a pedigree horse, a shop and vehicles. His shop was known locally as the 'Jewish store', even though he was not Jewish. Suspicion also fell upon the family who had rented accommodation to the Lusenas. After the war, a lawyer carried out an investigation and an official complaint was made. The police and judiciary got involved. Giuseppe Ferroni was arrested and charged, and a trial took place. He was eventually convicted of theft, along with his two brothers (but not of 'instigation to suicide', which was one of the charges) after a long and complicated legal process. The most likely version of events was that Ferroni had led the Lusena family to believe that they were about to be discovered and he then stole and sold everything they left behind.[5] After the war, the Lusena family moved their loved ones' remains to a cemetery in Florence, where they are now found buried with the inscription: 'Innocent victims of Nazi fascist persecution.'

ITALY'S SHOAH

Italy's prisons in occupied cities were taken over by the Nazis who held Jews in separate wings. A large flat space at Fossoli, in the countryside outside Carpi in the centre of Italy, was used as a holding centre, while a rice store on the edge of Trieste was repurposed as a death camp with an oven for burning bodies. Not all of those who passed through these camps were Jews; many thousands of political prisoners were also arrested and deported (there were also political prisoners who were Jews, and vice versa). Primo Levi, a Turinese chemist at the time and future writer, was arrested for being a partisan, not rounded up as a Jew. Other 'categories' were also included in Italy's Shoah, including Roma communities.

Most Italian Jews who were deported from Italy were taken to, and died in, Auschwitz. Trains took deportees there directly, from cities such as Trieste, Bolzano, Florence, Milan, Rome. The majority of Italian political prisoners who were deported were taken to, and died in, Mauthausen. Some Italians risked their lives to save Jews. The vast majority did not. Betrayals were common. A number profited directly from the discrimination. Jewish property was seized and stolen.

Shame and indignities piled up. Forced labour was imposed on some Jews. More synagogues across Italy were sacked and emptied.

Sometime between the summer and autumn of 1944, Ferrara's synagogues were 'looted', again. This was an official act of 'seizure' of 'assets', ordered by fascist administrators in the name of Mussolini's puppet republic in January 1944.[6] In March 1944, four cases of silver religious objects and other material from the synagogues were taken to the central police station. 'And from that moment on this material was never seen again.'[7] Almost nothing remained: 'Everything was destroyed, devastated, torn apart ... it was a form of ferocious vandalism and uncontrolled theft.'[8] One of the synagogues was also used as a holding centre for Jews before deportation.

In Ferrara, Jews were picked up on various occasions between October 1943 and October 1944. Just one of these round-ups was carried out by the Nazis. On 26 February 1944 the first group of forty-seven Jews from Ferrara reached Auschwitz. Forty were killed immediately, in the gas chambers. Only one person from this group returned home. The prefect at the time was Enrico Vezzalini. He arrived in Ferrara as an enforcer, and called for the arrest of 'all Jewish males' in the city, playing a key part in the long night of November 1943. On 6 December 1944 the local newspaper, *Ferrara Repubblicana*, called for the city to be 'completely "freed" from the Jews and their property'.[9] In September 1945, with the war over, Vezzalini was shot (in the back) by a firing squad after a trial in Novara.[10]

'GOOD ITALIANS' AND SAVING JEWS

Italian officials (either in Italy or elsewhere) sometimes went out of their way to rescue Jews. Local priests and others were involved in creating fake documents. Some hid Jews in their own houses. Often, survival as a Jew in Italy was a matter of luck, or money, especially in terms of crossing the frontier into Switzerland. Timing was also important and friends in high places helped.

A false identity card was required to obtain ration cards. In Florence, for example, Jews would be routinely arrested if they used their real ID, which carried a reference to their 'race'. A prominent role in this traffic in illegal documents has been assigned to the great cyclist Gino Bartali. Although he rarely discussed his wartime activities during his life, books published mainly after his death have described how he carried fake documents in his bicycle frame, from Florence to Assisi and back again, on numerous occasions. This activity has also been the subject of a TV special, a number of books and at least one plaque. Bartali died in 2000. In 2013 he was officially given the title of 'Righteous Among the Nations' by the State of Israel and he was also awarded a medal by the Italian state.[11]

However, one of the most respected experts on the Italian racial laws and the Shoah, Michele Sarfatti, has recently cast doubt on this version of the facts. One of the main sources for the Bartali story was a priest called Padre Rufino Niccacci, who had been interviewed for a book published in the 1970s by a Polish writer and film director called Alexander Ramati (which is described as a novel, and was first published in English). According to Sarfatti: 'Ramati-Niccacci invented the story about Bartali as a carrier [of documents].'[12] The numbers of those Bartali supposedly 'saved' has also been inflated over time, reaching the improbable figure of 'nearly 1,000' in some recent accounts.[13] In 2021 a book by sports historian and expert on Bartali, Stefano Pivato, who had previously supported the heroic tale of the salvation of Jews by the great cyclist, debunked the entire story, causing a sensation.[14]

Many other stories of Italians saving Jews have also turned out subsequently to be problematic or exaggerated, as in the extraordinary story of Giovanni Palatucci, whose supposed role in the war has also been called into question by recent research. Palatucci was praised as a hero who saved hundreds (if not thousands) of Jews while working for the police service in Fiume. Streets and squares were named after him. A process of canonisation was begun by the Church. But the Primo Levi Centre argued that not only were these claims untrue, but that Palatucci appeared to have played a major part in the *deportation* of Jews from Fiume.[15] Other historians disagree. The debate over Palatucci is ongoing.

Italy's Shoah has often been played down, or excused. A powerful myth emerged which claimed that Italians were fundamentally 'good people' who could never have committed such hideous crimes as those perpetrated by the Nazis. Italy and Mussolini, it was argued, were 'forced' into passing the discriminatory decrees.[16] At the end of the day, it was often said, the Italian holocaust was 'not as bad' as that which hit the Jews in many other countries. Stories of 'Good Italians' were often magnified and exaggerated. Mussolini, many claimed, aside from passing anti-Semitic laws, 'did lots of good things'. Italy, a leading historian argued, was outside of the 'shadow cast' by the Holocaust.[17]

Most of these myths and stereotypes have been comprehensively demolished by historical research over the last twenty years or so. They remain as powerful tropes within popular culture, both within and outside Italy. Captain Antonio Corelli, the mandolin-playing fictional Italian-occupier created by Louis de Bernières and played by Nicolas Cage in the subsequent film, is a common and familiar depiction of Italian soldiers. We rarely encounter those Italian soldiers and fascists who massacred Ethiopians, Greeks and Italian partisans and obediently arrested Jews on behalf of the Nazis.

JEWISH PARTISAN

Emanuele Artom was born in Aosta in 1915, just a month after Italy's entry into the war. His father was Emilio Artom, a teacher and a contributor to Italy's national encyclopaedia. Emanuele grew up in a bookish and intellectual household, where his Jewish family felt very much at home in the Italian state.

As one of the most prominent and numerous Jewish families in Italy, the Artom were torn apart by the racial laws and the Shoah that followed. The name Artom can now be found on memorials across Italy, and elsewhere. Four people with the Artom surname died in Auschwitz, while others named Artom fell as partisans.

Emanuele Artom joined the resistance, and kept an extraordinary diary which was later published.[18] Primo Levi said of Artom that he 'endured discomforts and dangers with cheerful pride'.[19] He mainly operated in the area around the Pellice and Germanesca valleys to the west of Turin. Captured by an Italian SS group in March 1944, he was brutally tortured and humiliated as a 'Jewish bandit', dying in Turin prison on 7 April 1944, aged twenty-nine. His body, hidden it seems in woods, has never been found.

JUDENFREI

It is often assumed that Italy's holocaust was historically insignificant because of the low numbers involved. Yet Italy's fascists and the Nazis rendered many places in Italy, with a history of a Jewish presence going back centuries, free of Jews – *Judenfrei*. Often, the community has simply not recovered, and never will. Jews, who had played such a significant part in Italy's history, culture and politics, were expunged from the streets, the landscape, the institutions. All who could be found were deported. As such, any historical judgement cannot be in any way connected to bare numbers, percentages and statistics.

An example of such a place is that of Lugo – a small town in the Romagna region, west of Ravenna. During Red Week in 1914 a general strike 'paralysed' all activity there for a time. In 1922, Giovanni Foschini, the socialist mayor, was forced out of office by the fascists. There had been a Jewish community in Lugo since the sixteenth century.[20] Twenty-six Jews from Lugo were deported and died during the Second World War, including two entire families, and the synagogue was destroyed by bombing. A plaque in the memory of these Jews was unveiled in Lugo in 1960, after a proposal by a Social Democrat councillor called Vasco Costa, who lost nine members of his family in the Shoah.[21]

Liliana Picciotto, who in a series of publications and studies has documented the fate of Jews in Italy after 1938, believes that 8,529 Jews were arrested in Italy purely because they were Jews. Some 322 were murdered in Italy itself, mainly at three locations: Lake Maggiore; in Rome in March 1944 (the Fosse Ardeatine massacre); and in Trieste. A further 6,806 were deported, of whom 837 survived. Other Italian Jews were deported from France and Greece – 1,819 Jews were arrested in the Aegean Islands on one day in 1944, and were all deported to Auschwitz. Only 180 returned.[22]

ATTENDISTI: WAITING FOR THE END OF THE WAR

Gaetano Azzariti, the illustrious magistrate who had been president of the Tribunale della Razza under Mussolini's regime, was made Italy's first post-fascist Justice Minister by Badoglio in July 1943. Trapped in Rome under Nazi occupation in 1943–44, he took refuge in convents and other religious institutions until the liberation of the city in June 1944.

As part of the official 'de-fascistisation' of the Italian state, in the autumn of 1944, Azzariti, like many others, was investigated by a 'Purging Committee' with regard to his fascist past. He was asked if he had ever been part of 'racial bodies or commissions', a question to which he replied (falsely) in the negative. He claimed that his work on the Tribunale della Razza had been largely technical – and he had *saved Jews* by taking part. The very idea that the *tribunale* had 'saved' Jews is offensive. Its very existence was grotesque and horrific. Nonetheless, Azzariti was cleared. Nor was he the only high-level official to carry on as if nothing had happened. Many of those who had worked at the upper echelons of the regime became part of the democratic state, exercising power and influence. Azzariti would rise even further in post-war Italy.

SURVIVAL, FREEDOM, RETURN

Exiled socialists Giuseppe and Vera Modigliani finally saw Italy again in October 1944. They had felt relatively safe in France, but the Nazi occupation there in 1940 changed everything. As socialists and Jews, the Modiglianis were in mortal danger again, and had to prepare for a new exile.

In Paris, Giuseppe Modigliani had got to know US journalist Varian Fry, who helped many Jews and others (some 4,000 people, it is claimed) escape from Vichy France. Fry was central, it seems, to the Modiglianis' attempted journey to Switzerland, but the two clashed over the use of illegal documents and disguise. In his account of those years, *Surrender on Demand*, Fry wrote that Modigliani 'wanted to leave France, but refused to do anything illegal'. He also reports the following exchange between Vera and Giuseppe: ' "If only he would shave off his beard and leave his fur coat behind," she sighed, "he could go as easily as the others. But every time I mention it he begins to shout: 'Shave off my beard indeed. No, my dear, I have always worn a beard and I always shall'." '[23]

Joyce Lussu, wife of the leading anti-fascist Emilio Lussu, who had escaped with Carlo Rosselli to France in 1929, told the dramatic story of the escape of the Modiglianis in her diaries, later published as *Fronti e frontiere*. 'In the whole of France,' after the defeat in 1940, she wrote, 'Italian antifascists were arrested and handed over to the Germans or to OVRA ... [Pietro] Nenni's son-in-law was shot by the Germans, and his daughter [Vittoria, born in 1915] was deported to Auschwitz. Old Modigliani, who was also Jewish, was in serious danger ... We had already advised him more than once to move to a safe place, but he hated any kind of illegality and false papers. We decided to try again.'[24]

They had a plan. Joyce Lussu met Giuseppe and Vera in the countryside in the Garonne region in southern France. They were ready to attempt the dangerous crossing to Switzerland. The first part of the escape was by train, they would then use taxis and the last part would be by foot. During the long and complicated journey, they were stopped numerous times, and there were many false trails and moments of desperation and fear. Modigliani's beard and distinctive appearance remained a worry on every occasion he left the house. As Lussu wrote: 'The problem was when Modigliani and his prophet-like beard was outside on the streets.'[25]

After one arrest, Modigliani lost patience and declared his true identity: 'Here is who I am. The lawyer Emanuele Modigliani, deputy in the Italian parliament for nine legislatures … arrest me if you wish, I have been ready for some time.'[26] Lussu reported how Modigliani's very body was testimony to his importance: ' "Look at him!" Vera said as if the appearance of her husband was, on its own, a convincing argument. And in fact he had a venerable head, with a wide forehead and white beard … "look what the fascists did to him?" And she pointed to a long scar on his head, which was a sign of an old injury.'[27]

In the end, Lussu sacrificed her own freedom to save Vera and Giuseppe Modigliani. The couple walked hand in hand across the frontier. Lussu was arrested, and later released. It was something of a miracle that the Modiglianis got out at all.

Over four years later, in October 1944, the Modiglianis took a US military plane back to Italy from Switzerland. Ignazio Silone was with them. They had been in exile since the late 1920s. After touchdown in Naples, Modigliani first touched Italian soil with his hand and then bent down to kiss the ground.[28] Silone described what happened next: 'Modigliani, with his imposing beard evoking an Old Testament prophet,' was tired, sitting at the side of the road, when a woman recognised him and 'practically knelt in front of him'. According to Silone, 'we had not fully understood the significance of what was happening. In that old man with the great beard, she had seen *padreterno* [god] defeated, humiliated, a power dispossessed.'[29]

Tito Oro Nobili, the socialist deputy from Terni who had been driven out of his home town, beaten to the point of death and virtually blinded in 1926, and forced out of his work as a lawyer, continued to live in Rome in the 1930s. In 1943 he underwent operations in order to save a little of his eyesight. In March 1944 he and his wife Olina were caught in a bomb and strafing attack on a train. Olina was killed and Oro Nobili survived with injuries.[30] Meanwhile, anti-fascists were being released from prison and internal exile, and others were finally returning to Italy after long periods of exile.

Liberation
1944

With liberation, power relationships were quickly overturned. Ravenna, the city which experienced uprisings during Red Week in 1914, was liberated by partisans and Canadian troops early in the afternoon of 4 December 1944. The Piazza Vittorio Emanuele II was immediately renamed Piazza del Popolo. Partisan leaders spoke from the balcony of the town hall, brandishing their weapons and flying a number of flags, including one carrying a hammer and sickle symbol. Ancona, where Red Week began, was liberated on 18 July 1944 by Polish troops and partisans, just over thirty years after that short-lived anti-militarist insurrection. Oddo Marinelli, a republican who had been forced into exile after Red Week in 1914, was appointed as prefect of the city. He had been one of the founding members of the anti-fascist Action Party.

Alfonsine, which had attempted a revolution during Red Week in June 1914, had to wait until 10 April 1945 for liberation, given its location right on the front line (the so-called 'Gothic Line'). The town had suffered heavy bombing, with large parts reduced to rubble. In June 1946, 96.63 per cent of those who voted in the referendum on the monarchy in Alfonsine chose the option of the republic, making it the most republican place in the whole of Italy. Something had remained of those days during Red Week, when the monarchist circle had been sacked and the Republic proclaimed.

SETTLING OF ACCOUNTS

Liberation from fascism, which took place at different times across Italy, led to mass reprisals against fascists. Thousands were killed, sometimes after summary trials, whose result was inevitable. It was a mixture of revenge – for *squadristi* violence in the 1920s, for the Second World War – and social revolution. In Terni, where social and political rage was hard to separate, testimonies from that period remembered that 'anger, fury, wrath was in the air'. Pitchforks were used. As one witness recalled: 'We wanted the skin of the fascists.' The reprisals were described as 'savage, a frightful scene'. There were stories of 'children knocking out the eyes of fascists with sticks ... Boys, children, who know nothing about fascism.'[1]

There was a thirst for instant justice. Memories went back to the rise of squadrism in the 1920s, and these were overlaid, and sometimes replaced, with events from the more recent civil war.[2] Often, those killed or humiliated in 1944–46 after liberation, locally or nationally, had been responsible for fascist violence in the early 1920s. Scars had not healed. Children wanted to avenge their fathers and mothers; siblings their brothers and sisters; socialists and trade unionists their comrades. The violence was rarely random.[3]

The conflict was long and complicated and only ended with the final liberation of the north in April 1945. It was a very dangerous time for leading fascists whose faces were familiar – they had been seen in numerous photographs and newsreels under the regime. Arpinati and Farinacci were both killed by partisans in April 1945. Roberto Farinacci's end, when it came, was inglorious. Captured by partisans while trying to escape, he was summarily tried and shot against a wall in the nondescript peripheral town of Vimercate near Milan. The biggest prize of all, however, was still at large.

Mussolini Between Life and Death:
a Story in Fragments

On 27 April 1945, Benito Mussolini was travelling in a truck as part
of a large convoy of vehicles, including German soldiers and officers,
which was making its way north – perhaps to Switzerland – via the
western shore of Lake Como. After the cars and lorries were stopped
at a partisan roadblock, negotiations took place via an interpreter. The
convoy was allowed to proceed to a lakeside place called Dongo, where
every vehicle was fully searched.

Mussolini was in the fourth vehicle, loosely disguised as a German
soldier, complete with helmet, but was recognised by a cobbler and
ex-sailor called Giovanni Negri. The ex-*duce* was then arrested by a
partisan – Urbano Lazzaro – and taken to the local town hall. Later,
the partisans moved Mussolini to a barracks about six kilometres away,
in the hills above the lake (he was later moved again). There he was
reunited with his mistress, Claretta Petacci, who had followed him with
her brother, Marcello.

After being held for a night, Mussolini was executed at a roadside –
by communist partisans led by Walter Audisio – at around 4.10 on
the afternoon of Saturday 28 April. Claretta Petacci, who would not
leave Il Duce's side, was also shot dead. Audisio always claimed that
he personally carried out the orders given to him by the Committee
for National Liberation – the coordinating body of the resistance – to
execute Mussolini. It is said that Hitler decided to kill himself once he
had heard of Mussolini's fate. Fifteen leading fascists and figures from
the Italian Social Republic, captured at the same time as Mussolini,

were executed on the western shore of the lake itself in Dongo just before 6 p.m. that same day. Petacci's brother, Marcello, threw himself into the water in a vain attempt to escape before being mown down by partisan machine-gun fire.

MEMORY AND REVENGE

Late on 28 April 1945, the sixteen bodies from the lakeside executions were loaded onto a truck, which then began to make its way back to Milan. One further stop was made, but it was an important one. Two more bodies were picked up – those of Mussolini and Claretta Petacci. The drivers had a clear idea of their destination: Piazzale Loreto – a wide square to the north-east of the city. It was between three and four in the morning of Sunday 29 April when the lorry reached the city. Here the bodies were tipped onto the ground, with no ceremony.[1]

8 AUGUST 1944

'There were many bodies on the pavement, against the fence ...
All around there were people standing in silence, in the baking
sun. When I turned up to see them it made me dizzy – shoes,
hands, arms, dirty socks – to my child's eyes it was something
unheard of, men thrown onto the pavement like rubbish
and other young men, dressed in black, who seemed to be
guarding them!'

Franco Loi[2]

Piazzale Loreto had been chosen for a precise reason. Two previous moments from the war had led to 29 April 1945. On 8 August 1944 a bomb placed by the resistance (not far from the square) and aimed at the German occupiers had killed six people.[3] In reprisal, and as a warning to others, fifteen anti-fascists were taken from the 'political' section of Milan's San Vittore prison and executed by Italian fascists, following Nazi orders. Their bodies were piled up and left in the heat, in the open, for an entire day. Piazzale Loreto was a place of transition into and out of the city. The Nazis had not chosen it by chance. Anything or anyone left there would be highly visible.[4]

Resistance groups immediately vowed that these men would be avenged. Mussolini's body was thus taken to the *piazzale* as a way of cancelling out those images of dead anti-fascists. Since August 1944, Piazzale Loreto had become a place of memory, and of infamy. It was now about to become something else, with further layers of meaning.

SCOOP OF THE CENTURY

'The brains which took fascist Italy into the war ooze onto the filth of a dirt plot in the centre of Milan.'

James Roper, *United Press*, 29 April 1945[5]

'Benito Mussolini came back last night to the city where his fascism was born. He came back on the floor of a closed moving van, his dead body flung on the bodies of his mistress and twelve men shot with him.'

Milton Bracker, *New York Times*, 30 April 1945[6]

Rita Hume was a rarity – a female journalist covering the war as a foreign correspondent. It appears that she had volunteered for the Red Cross in Naples and had then begun to work for the *International News Service*, having previously written for the *Seattle Times*. She was in Piazzale Loreto on 29 April 1945.[7] It was said that she was the first to report the death of Mussolini.

As well as Rita Hume, there were numerous foreign journalists in the *piazzale* that day. James Roper of the United Press claimed that he had been pushed on top of Mussolini's body. Another journalist wondered about the fate of the corpse, in real time: 'There is no way of telling how long the gruesome show will go on. But if many more misguided young men leap through the circle, aiming their boots at what is left of Mussolini there will be hardly enough left for burial.'[8]

Milton Bracker was a 'restless, high-strung, energetic man', who dabbled in poetry. He often wore a beret and worked as a reporter for the *New York Times*.[9] In April 1945 he was one of the first journalists to see Mussolini's dead body in Milan. His piece written that day became famous, his signature article, and is often quoted.[10] Ten years after that day – in 1955 – he reflected on what he had witnessed, a decade earlier, in Milan's morgue. 'When I last saw Mussolini there at 6 o'clock, he was a shrunken, ruined, virtually shapeless thing, lying in a pre-autopsy tray numbered 167.'[11]

Bracker got right up close to Mussolini. In the 1945 piece he described parts of the ex-dictator's brain emerging from his skull, and the mud on his boots. Bracker wrote of 'a hideous crunch' as somebody kicked Mussolini's famously large head while the body was still on the ground.[12] He added, in 1955, that 'I have never ceased to hear it.' In one of the films we have of the *piazzale* that day, a journalist can be seen right next to the bodies, taking notes, asking questions. One of them seems to be Bracker himself. Piazzale Loreto made careers. Howard Norton of the *Baltimore Sun* also claimed to be either the first to see the body, or break the news, in subsequent years. It was said that Norton 'scooped the world'.[13] His famous piece started like this:

> With Italian Partisans in Milan, April 29 – The body of Benito Mussolini lies in the mud in the Piazza Loreto here this morning and thousands of Milanese are fighting their way through crushing crowds for an opportunity to spit on it. The enormous, shaved head and loose meaty jowls of the fallen *duce* are resting on the breast of his mistress, Clara Petacci, twenty-five-year-old daughter of a Milan doctor, who, with Mussolini and about twelve other high fascists, was given a hasty trial and shot by Partisans near the town of Dongo yesterday. Lying in grotesque positions, in a mass of blood and gore around their leader, are other Fascists shot with him. They were all dumped there without ceremony after dark yesterday by Partisans who brought them to Milan in a moving van from the town where they were tried and executed. This particular spot was chosen by the Partisans to display the bodies for sentimental reasons. It was there that fifteen innocent victims were executed by the Fascists and their bodies left exposed for a full day.[14]

In films and images we have, the crowd seems mixed, with men and women, soldiers, partisans, and an array of weapons on show. Shots can be seen being fired into the air, and many people are laughing and cheering. There is water everywhere – firefighters used hoses to keep the crowds back. Vans and lorries with armed partisans on board pass through the square, as spaces open for them, and then close up again. It seems both frightening and exhilarating. The crowd is swaying. Some are carrying photos of the dead or missing. The partisans and others appear to be losing control.

During the first period of the morning, the corpses of Mussolini, Petacci and the others were on the ground, and people in the crowd picked their way through and often trod on the bodies. Some even fell on top of the corpses. Journalists straddled the bodies with difficulty, taking notes. Photographers and film-makers tried to get space to capture the perfect image. They were aware of the historical significance of what they were witnessing.[15] Armed partisans and others pushed the crowd back, with difficulty.[16] A few had shinned up lamp posts, and many were standing on top of buses in order to get a proper look. Milanese poet Franco Loi, who was fourteen at the time, and was in the *piazzale* that day, called the period when the bodies were on the ground 'the most violent and disgusting part'.[17]

Some in the crowd seemed angry. Word had got around. There were, quite simply, too many people, and more were arriving by the minute. Everyone wanted to see. Was *he* really dead? Was it possible? Was *he*, in the end, mortal after all? But there he was, besides his lover (not his wife, Rachele) on the ground, crumpled up, his head grotesquely swollen and beaten – and clearly no longer alive.[18] Mussolini's caustic biographer Paolo Monelli described him in the *piazzale* as having 'the gloomy air of a theatrical king who had tumbled off his throne'.[19]

This was not a passive crowd. 'The crowd did not just look on; it became a protagonist.'[20] Some cleared their throats and spat at the corpse. Others kicked it. Shots were fired into dead bodies, and into the air. The autopsy found twenty-five bullet holes in Mussolini's body.[21] Another man was said to have screamed at Mussolini: 'Make a speech now, make a speech!' The tables had been turned. Under the regime, you could be sent to jail or internal exile for merely criticising Mussolini, making a joke about him, or singing a song which belittled him.

On the ground, in the sweltering heat, the situation was chaotic, risking further and pointless casualties. Someone, nobody knows who, took a decision. It was *his* body they wanted to see, so it should be lifted up – in full view. But where? To the side of the square, opposite a department store, was a bombed-out petrol station, with a metal skeleton frame in front of it. It seemed like the perfect place. It was also close to the spot where the partisan bodies had been dumped eight months earlier. At some point, the corpses were lifted and tied up feet first. 'It was ... a symbolic ritual and the foundation of a new political order.'[22]

According to Monelli, 'a tall, fat, bare-armed man in shirtsleeves, covered in blood, started to lift up the bodies and show them to the crowd'.[23] Armed men sat on top of the frame of the garage, guarding the corpses. Photographs were taken, some of which were later reproduced as postcards. It was a revolution, a restoration, and a literal and symbolic overturning. In the official words of the resistance at the time, it represented a 'a clear break with a past full of shame and murders'.[24] Phase one of this ending had taken place in July 1943. Then, statues and fascist symbols had been attacked and removed across the country. Many had wished death upon Mussolini for years. Now their dreams had come true: 'Mussolini died and died again on many occasions.'[25]

There were children in the *piazzale* that day, and not by chance. Alberto Scerbanenco was just six years old. He had been taken to see Mussolini's dead body by his nanny, and she held him on her shoulders in order to 'take part in this terrible spectacle'.[26] Later, he wrote that she clearly thought that this was something he should be seeing. Oreste Del Buono, the future intellectual and critic, who was also in the square that day, remembered 'the smallest children on their parents' shoulders'.[27] Children were raised up to see Mussolini, himself lifted up, by rope.

In the city where he had founded and built his movement, where he had edited his daily newspaper for so many years, and from where he had taken a train to seize national power in Rome in 1922, Benito Mussolini's life, and dictatorship, were finally – and unequi vocally – over. Some thirty years had passed since the first issue of *Il Popolo d'Italia* ('*un giornale socialista*' – 'a socialist newspaper') had hit the newsstands, with its twin by-lines: 'Revolution is an idea which has found bayonets' (Napoleon), and: 'Who has iron, has bread' (Blanqui).

Soon the bodies were cut down and carted off, making their separate ways to morgues and cemeteries. Strange forms of legality and due process were duly carried out, amidst the general sense that the rule of law itself had broken down (while at the same moment, democracy itself was being restored, and expanded). An autopsy on Mussolini's body was performed, and filmed, and a meticulous report prepared. This did not prevent conspiracy theories, political polemics and endless discussions over Mussolini's last few days. There is even a book dedicated to Il Duce's 'last five seconds'.[28]

Under Nazi occupation, captured partisans had often been hung in public, as a warning to others, or had their bodies displayed in piles – as had happened in Piazzale Loreto – often with signs around their necks saying 'bandit' or 'partisan'. These terrifying images traumatised the general population. In the last, beautiful, scene of Roberto Rossellini's film *Paisà*, released in 1946, partisan bodies float down the Po river with similar signs attached to them.[29]

Mussolini's body in Piazzale Loreto was a riposte to these previous exhibitions of the dead, but it was also significantly different. With the hung bodies in places like Bassano and Trieste, people tended to look away, to avert their eyes from the horror. In the case of Piazzale Loreto, they were all looking *towards* Mussolini, or trying desperately to climb up to a higher point in order to do so. The hanging up itself had been to allow more people to see the dead dictator. There were similarities, however, between Mussolini's command of the *piazzale* under the regime and his centrality in Piazzale Loreto. He was still the main attraction. As Oreste Del Buono wrote: 'In a certain sense, this was an event created by Him. Maybe not exactly created. This isn't the right word. If it had been up to him, he would have happily not been there, I'm sure of that.'[30] Moreover, In hanging up the bodies, by their feet, and not by their necks, the partisans and fire fighters in the square that day (unknowingly) turned a practical decision into an image with deep symbolic significance.

People wanted to be there, whatever the cost. Maria Conti Cafasso, a Turin resident, told the oral historian Luisa Passerini a story in the 1970s about 'the uncle of my neighbour' who took a train to see Mussolini in Piazzale Loreto. Images of the dead dictator were widely shared. Another person, Lucia, remembered sending a postcard of the garage and the bodies in Piazzale Loreto to her brother who had been forced out of Italy under the regime. Only then did her brother feel it was safe to return.[31]

IMAGINING REVENGE

Many imaginary stories emerged from that morning and afternoon, and some of these tales came straight from fiction. Almost every account of the events of that day mention a woman who shot Mussolini three, or five, or six times, in revenge for the deaths of her children, allegedly (in some versions) killed in a botched US bombing of a school in Gorla on the edge of Milan in October 1944.

Did this really happen? Who knows? George Orwell was sceptical: 'It is said that when Mussolini's corpse was exhibited in public, an old woman drew a revolver and fired five shots into it, exclaiming, "These are for my five sons!" It is the kind of story that the newspapers make up, but it might be true. I wonder how much satisfaction she got out of those five shots, which, doubtless, she had dreamt years earlier of firing. The condition of her being able to get near enough to Mussolini to shoot at him was that he should be a corpse.'[32] Here, memories also went back to 1925/26 and the failed or botched assassination attempts by Zaniboni, Gibson, Lucetti and Zamboni. This time, Mussolini was an easy target.

The Gorla bomb in 1944 had killed 204 people in an elementary school, including 184 children. In the list of names of the victims from that bomb, there are just two surnames which are cited three times but other information points to the fact that in both of these cases one of the victims was a cousin of the other two. So, it looks like no mother lost either three or five children in the bomb in Gorla. Perhaps the witnesses had misheard the woman, or the number of shots, or perhaps this had not happened at all.[33]

But maybe it doesn't matter. It is a powerful story, which ticked a number of boxes at the time: revenge, symmetry, fascist responsibility for the horrors of war (including US bombs). Did a woman really urinate on Il Duce's face?[34] This seemed even more unlikely. It was, however, an image straight from peasant Italy, a sign of barbarity, an almost bestial reduction of a god to an animal. 'Hacking, cursing, swaying, the people were trampling the corpses, blind with the hatred of years.'[35] It was a public execution without the execution (although one fascist was executed later in the *piazzale*). It was a kind of 'ritual revenge ... a real overturning ... full of ritual meaning, with references to ancient traditions and forms of symbolic violence'.[36]

There were other stories from that day, as Luisa Passerini writes:

Some women had put vegetables and black bread into Mussolini's hands on his corpse (a typical reversal of positions, doing to him what had been done to them). Someone had allegedly tried to put a dead rat in his mouth (the animal symbolising, par excellence, 'baseness' and a sign of contempt).[37]

Once again, did these events really happen? Or were they imagined – examples of wishful thinking, perhaps, of things that people had dreamt might happen, thought should have happened, had wanted to happen, for twenty years? Mussolini's smashed body was overloaded with meaning and possibility.

*

There was clearly hatred and rage, but there was also a carnival atmosphere.[38] When Mussolini's body was first lifted up – and he was the first to be lifted up – a strange noise rose up from those massed around.[39] It was a sound that was hard to describe. 'An immense cry rose up.'[40] It wasn't applause, or cheering, but rather 'a huge roar' – and it happened again when a leading fascist was executed in the *piazzale* later that day.[41] This soundscape can only be recreated from the words of the witnesses and journalists who were there. The film we have has no sound.

It was a classic *colpo di scena*. Everyone's eyes were drawn one way. Monelli takes up the details of what happened next. 'A noose knot was tied around the feet of the corpses, bound together, and someone up on the scaffolding started to pull the rope.' Mussolini 'was dressed in a shirt drenched in blood … you could see his underwear … his boots were broken, falling apart … His mouth was open in a grimace.'[42]

The metal skeleton of the bombed-out Esso petrol station acted as a stage, as did the wide *piazzale* surrounded by ruins and half-standing walls. It was the hottest ticket in town, and it was free. At some point, somebody decided to write the names of those below on the garage above the swinging corpses, across the structure of the petrol station, with an arrow pointing downwards. This was a kind of guide to who was there, an unofficial cast list. Most in the crowd were wearing hats, and they were all looking one way. It was a play where the fourth wall had been decisively removed.

Revenge was necessary. There was much to avenge. One man was not enough, though he was more than one man. A place of sacrifice was chosen as the place for a new sacrifice. As Luigi Meneghello put it: 'It was important to bring an end to fascism in a clear way, which could be seen … interpreting in a literal way those toponomastic criteria for revenge which had been used by partisan justice during the days of the insurrection.'[43]

Perhaps the partisans had learnt more from the fascists, and fascism, than they dared to admit – summary trials, swift executions, mockery. It had a horribly familiar ring to it all, although to say so would have been taboo. As the historian Claudio Fogu has written: 'In 1945 Mussolini's dead body was exposed to the gaze of the Milanese people in Piazzale Loreto, first with a mock sceptre in his right arm and then hanging from an electric pole head down … many levels of intellectual confrontation and iconic collusion between fascist and anti-fascist imaginaries may suggest more than a family resemblance.'[44]

A MOB?

The Italians in the *piazzale* that day have often been presented as brutal avengers, lacking in basic humanity, 'a pushing mob', a 'howling mob, kicking and spitting'.[45] It was said that this was a terrible way for Italy to become a democracy. Shouldn't Mussolini have been put on trial, made to pay for his crimes in a legal sense, forced to stand in the dock? Once again, counterfactual history has played a large part here. What if Il Duce had been captured instead of shot? Would Italy have become a better place, a more humane society? Would Italy have made peace with its past? The lack of an 'Italian Nuremberg' was – it is claimed – a factor in the seeming lack of debate and reckoning with the entire fascist period. When Mussolini's granddaughter, Alessandra, became a politician in the 1990s, she frequently made reference to what she called the 'disgrace' of Piazzale Loreto. She was still complaining about the event on national television in 2019.[46]

For the Socialist Party newspaper *Avanti!*, which Mussolini had both edited and destroyed, Piazzale Loreto represented an act that was both 'horrible' and 'necessary'.[47] Other anti-fascists depicted the execution in much more positive terms. Carlo Levi wrote that it was a democratic act. The day after Piazzale Loreto he argued, in the resistance journal *La Nazione del Popolo*, that the killing of Il Duce had been neither 'an act of revenge, nor the self-righteous application of a right' but rather 'the first example of the Italian people's ability to govern itself'.[48]

Another obvious feature of that day was the very clear sense of total defeat. Mussolini could not defend himself, he was not just dead, but also humiliated. The gap between the bombast and power of the regime, its boasts of '8 million bayonets' and a 'new Italian empire' was palpable. Nothing beside remained. For many fascists, this was a trauma which they struggled to deal with. Mussolini was not a demigod, he was mortal. Fascism was no longer loved by more than a tiny minority. It was, by then, almost universally hated. And Mussolini's was just one death among many, especially in those days of the 'settling of accounts'. There was also an obvious sense of shame. Mussolini's death was sad, pitiful, without any sense of dignity.

RHETORIC

Much rhetoric has been devoted to Piazzale Loreto. Often, it is said that the 'oceanic' crowds in the square that day were the mirror image of those who had applauded Mussolini for years. How many were indulging, almost immediately, in that ancient and supposedly Italian art of *trasformismo* – changing sides for political advantage?[49] This rhetorical trope is based on no evidence – it is above all a statement – as in the claim that, in the words of partisan leader Bruno Cerasi: 'many had changed sides from one day to another'.[50] Some were said to be making these comparisons that very day. Leo Valiani was one of those involved in the decision to execute Mussolini. It is said that he was worried that 'the people now execrating the fallen in the piazza were not resistants … but the Fascists who a few weeks ago had fawned on him.'[51]

POLITICS: ANTI-FASCISTS, AFASCISTS, FASCISTS, NEO-FASCISTS

'The Italians were forced to execute their own tyrant in order to free themselves from the nightmare of an irreversible insult.'

Avanti![52]

People projected their political positions, their fears and their prejudices onto the backdrop of Piazzale Loreto. Cynics who believed that 'all the Italians had been fascist' saw the entire event as an act, a moment of theatre – 'a spectacle'.[53] Revolutionaries saw it as a revolution. Fascists saw it as yet another example of left-wing barbarism. It felt like an ending, and a beginning, at the same time. But it was also overloaded with meaning. Mussolini's death, in itself, changed nothing. Fascists and ex-fascists remained in place, deep within the country's institutions, all over Italy.

WITNESSES

'Unfortunately, I was there.'

Franco Loi[54]

'A revolution has happened … a clear break with the past. The blood of fascist leaders, the petrol station in Piazzale Loreto was a beneficial and unforgettable symbol of this break.'

Carlo Levi[55]

Rossana Rossanda – future communist, New Left militant and journalist – said she was there:

I saw the bodies, Mussolini, Clara Petacci and the others, strung up by their feet in Piazzale Loreto. They looked done for, their faces swollen and anonymous as if they had never lived. Someone had tied Petacci's skirt up around her knees, out of pity. In front of them there thronged a furious mass of people, women shouting, men white-faced with indignation, screaming out their anger and their impotence: justice had been done by somebody else, on their behalf. There was some derision, but mostly rage. I turned away; it was a necessary ritual, perhaps, but terrible.

There. Again. That formula: terrible, horrible, but *necessary*. 'The Italian tricolour was flying everywhere,' Rossanda continued, 'and people that you would have avoided the month before now had red scarves around their necks. It was the end of an epoch. Everything would start again.'[56]

*

Twenty-four-year-old Franca Valeri was also there. She would go on to become a famous actress in the postwar period. She said that she had finally understood 'it was all, really, *over*'.[57] Valeri had only escaped persecution under the anti-Semitic laws thanks to fake documents.

Many, many other people said they were there. One of these was the celebrated journalist Indro Montanelli, but his presence that day has been called into doubt. Why would he pretend to be there? Montanelli used Piazzale Loreto to push a kind of *a*fascist version of the past. 'Everybody – more or less – was a fascist', he wrote later; 'either through passion or because they had no choice.'[58] Having been there, physically present, in the square that day, added authenticity to any future statements. It provided lustre.

A PHOTOGRAPHER

Christian Schiefer was a Swiss photographer who somehow made it down to Milan when news came through of Mussolini's death.[59] At the age of 100, in 1996, he was interviewed by Mario Chiodetti for the daily newspaper *L'Unità*. Asked about the Mussolini photos, he replied that 'too much has already been written and said about those events'.[60]

The vehicle he'd been travelling in that April of 1945 was stopped on numerous occasions on the way to Milan but always allowed to pass through. His first port of call had been the Diana Theatre, the site of the 1921 bomb, which had become the headquarters of the Red Cross. Someone there had told him to go to Piazzale Loreto. On the way, he was first taken to the Politecnico (the city's scientific university), where leading fascist Achille Starace was 'on trial'. There he took a series of extraordinary photographs. He arrived in the *piazzale* just before the bodies were lifted up. The Swiss paper *Schweizer Illustrierte* refused to publish the images due to their graphic nature, but many other British and European newspapers did. Schiefer returned to his shop in Switzerland, and his bread-and-butter wedding photos, but, like so many other journalists and photographers, those images defined his career.

ACHILLE STARACE AND THE FATAL JOG: 29 APRIL 1945

It was not the right time to go for a jog, but that is what Achille Starace, Il Duce's right-hand man for years, his 'spin-doctor', decided to do that day, in Milan. Fascists were still being put against walls and executed all over the city. Perhaps he thought he was safe, that he had been forgotten completely. If he did, he was wrong. He had even gone for a run on liberation day, 25 April, itself. And so, on Sunday 29 April, as Mussolini's body was lying on the ground in Piazzale Loreto, Starace left his flat for another – this time fatal – jog.

So often he had stood beside Il Duce at official ceremonies, or signed absurd orders which were then handed down to the people. He was instantly recognisable. He had been photographed jumping through burning hoops, or running alongside Mussolini. True, he had fallen from favour, and no longer had an official role within the regime. But this did not save him. That Sunday he left his home 'in a blue jogging kit with cloth boots'.[61] Recognised, the following strange conversation then allegedly took place:

'Starace, where are you going?'
'To have a coffee.'[62]

The partisans who picked him up could not believe their luck.

Starace was 'tried' in a building in Piazza Leonardo da Vinci – not far from Piazzale Loreto – the improvised HQ of the 6th Sector Committee for National Liberation, in a lecture room of the Politecnico. It is said that he played down his role, saying: 'I was merely the imperial functionary who organised the circus for the people.'[63] He was then paraded around town and asked to make a clenched fist and a fascist salute, in an aping of or a homage to previous fascist humiliation of socialists.[64] Next he was taken to Piazzale Loreto, and shot in the back, right in front of the spot where the partisan bodies had been left in 1944, and which was now a mass of flowers, and close to the Esso petrol station where Mussolini and the others were swinging in the wind. It was all done quickly, to avoid the crowds getting hold of him.[65]

Starace was fifty-six years old. He had been a *squadrista*, and it was said that he enjoyed violence. His fellow fascist, Giuseppe Bottai, wrote in his diaries that Starace, while he was in the colonies, derived pleasure from inflicting pain on prisoners and those about to be executed.[66] Starace now took his place, alongside Il Duce, up in the air. So often in life he had been at Mussolini's side, as his 'shadow', and now, in a kind of grotesque joke and another overturning, he was also there in death.

*

Victor Serge, the great Russian revolutionary, writer and rebel, heard the news on 1 May in Mexico City. His reaction was as follows:

> Mussolini shot. The last fascist government leaders shot. I felt a
> satisfaction for having written in 1932 ... 'The Gramscis and the
> Terracinis [Italian communists imprisoned under fascism] know
> that they are almost nothing at this moment, that they can be
> assassinated tomorrow, that they will perhaps never see the light of
> day again; but they understand the inexorable laws of history, they
> know where all the parades will end up.[67]

George Orwell had also thought about how dictatorships end, and what happens to dictators. 'When tyrants are put to death,' he wrote, 'it should be by their own subjects.'[68] But he would have avoided the creation of new martyrs: 'not death, unless it is inflicted in some hurried unspectacular way. If the Germans and Italians feel like giving them [their dictators] a summary court-martial and then a firing-squad, let them do it. Or better still, let the pair of them escape with a suitcase full of bearer securities and settle down as accredited bores of some Swiss *pension*. But no martyrising...'[69]

THE COMMUNIST

There is one more bizarre story from that day that connects right back to the socialist opposition, the First World War, and the formation of the Communist Party. One of the bodies hanging alongside Benito Mussolini at Piazzale Loreto was a bearded, stocky individual. He had been with Mussolini almost until the last. His name was Nicola Bombacci, he was sixty-five years old and he had first met Il Duce when they were both school teachers in Romagna, and socialists, in the early twentieth century.

If we go back twenty-four years we find Bombacci in Livorno, speaking to the Socialist Party congress held in that city in January 1921. At one point he brandished a pistol during a debate. Bombacci was a hate figure for the nascent fascist movement. He had been imprisoned for 'defeatism' in 1918 and was the target of numerous attacks – so much so that he had to live more or less in hiding. His house was ransacked during the March on Rome and he was a frequent visitor to the USSR. Fascists sang about cutting off his beard and using it to polish Mussolini's shoes.

Bombacci was sometimes referred to as the 'Lenin of Romagna'.[70] The journalist Ugo Ojetti left this description of him: 'dressed in black, with a fine head of hair and a large brown beard ... and his beard and hair seem to come closer and closer, every minute, to taking over his face, his prominent cheekbones, his sad eyes, his sharp nose ... the honourable Bombacci is angelic'.[71] He was 'a passionate and incendiary speaker'.[72] When Lenin died in 1924, Bombacci attended his funeral.

There is a photo of Bombacci addressing a crowd, inside a factory. It could easily have been from one of his powerful meetings during the red years of 1914, or 1919–21. Yet, there is something strange about this image. Right behind Bombacci there appears to be a man in uniform. Why? This would not have been a feature of those early meetings. But we are in *1945*, not 1914, or 1919. Bombacci is addressing workers, inside a factory, but on behalf of Mussolini's puppet Italian Social Republic. This was a fascist demonstration, not a socialist one.

Under the regime, Bombacci had gone on his own, long, and often lonely, journey. After 'leaving politics' in the 1920s he fell on hard times. He was expelled from the Communist Party. Mussolini set him up with a newspaper to run, *La Verità*, which attracted interest from other ex-socialists. In the end, this journey took Bombacci to the Republic of Salò, where he became one of Mussolini's closest advisers. In that speech, in 1945, Bombacci claimed that he had not changed, he was the same 'Bolshevik' as he had been in 1919. 'Let us speak freely,' he said:

You ask if I am the same socialist, communist agitator, a friend
of Lenin, from twenty years ago ... yes ... I am the same person,
I have never renounced the ideas I fought for and if God allows me
to live for a little longer, I will continue to fight forever. The reason

I have adhered to the Italian Social Republic is that this time I think that action will truly be taken and the rights of the workers will be satisfied.[73]

Few were convinced. Italy was in the middle of a civil war. Bombacci became the ultimate symbol of betrayal, a turncoat, a renegade, even more than Mussolini himself. His presence among those bodies was another form of exorcism, a cutting out of a wound. According to the historian R. W. Johnson:

When Mussolini was making his last desperate exit from Milan in April 1945, Nicola Bombacci, his old comrade – the two men had been revolutionary socialist schoolteachers together thirty years before – climbed into the *duce*'s car carrying only a small suitcase. 'What else would I need?' he said. 'I am an expert in such matters. I was in Lenin's office in Petersburg when the White troops ... were advancing on the city and we were preparing to leave, as we are doing today' ... In the space of a quarter-century Bombacci, an old communist and Comintern hand, had progressed right across the ideological spectrum, beginning as an intimate of Lenin's and ending as an adviser to Mussolini: by fluke he stood next to both men in their supreme hour of crisis.[74]

Bombacci was hated. Jaurès Busoni, who had been at Empoli in 1921, and had spent years in prison and in exile, wrote of him after the war:

Bombacci returned to the scene again at the time of the Republic of Salò ... when his sense of abjection had become worthy of the mud into which he fell under the bullets which struck him in the back alongside all the other unworthy traitors. The partisan firing squad had brought justice to someone who was a representative of one of the worst categories of human beings, lacking in character, sentiment, dignity, who was marked by servility and illegality, an example of those who helped to corrupt the moral fibre of the Italians with their activities and the example they set.[75]

In 1945, on hearing the news of Mussolini's and Bombacci's deaths, Victor Serge shared this memory of Bombacci:

I saw him once ... at Petrograd and Moscow (in '20 or '21), tall, thin, sporting a magnificent beard below a bony face, with gentle and lively eyes – enthusiastic, aggressive, cheerful, believing with all his soul in communism. An uncomplicated mind more warm than penetrating, a faith mingled with naïveté ... But what in those times foreshadowed the sombre, sinister complications of the twenty years to come?[76]

Bombacci is buried in the 'fascist section' of the Cimitero Maggiore in Milan – Campo X. Every year, neo-fascists visit the cemetery to 'pay their respects' to the dead fascists there.

Post-fascist Italy: Ghosts and Memories

THE 'MAYOR FOR AN HOUR' RETURNS TO BOLOGNA

Ennio Gnudi, the 'Mayor for an Hour' from Bologna in November 1920, was only able to return to Italy in November 1945. He had been in exile for two and a half decades. Back in his city at last, he was given a warm welcome by the new communist Mayor of Bologna, Giuseppe Dozza. Memories of Palazzo d'Accursio were still strong in the city, although Gnudi's account seemed confused about what happened that day. He also argued that the socialists should have fought back with more force, and taken on fascism right from the start. Italy's railways took Gnudi back as an employee and he became a leading national figure in the union. But he seemed out of place in postwar Italy.

Gnudi died in 1949. He was just fifty-six and had spent nearly half of his life in political exile. The democratic institutions in his city gave him an impressive send-off. Over 2,000 people turned out for his funeral. Dozza said of him that he was 'perhaps tired of the very tough life which he had lived, and the work he had been forced to carry out'.[1] It was perhaps ironic that his coffin stood, for a time, in Palazzo d'Accursio. He had only recently been able to re-enter the space which had cost him so much pain and disappointment twenty-six years earlier.

Gnudi's tomb – in the Certosa cemetery in Bologna – is beautiful. Six figures are carrying a coffin, on which he lies. The figures are metaphors for peasants and workers, complete with hats and, in some cases, moustaches. There is a railway worker, a female rice picker, complete with hat, and a blacksmith; one figure carries a sickle, another a hammer. The inscription is simple: To Ennio Gnudi/ Italy's Railway Workers/ to whom he was a leader/ in their struggles in the workplace. In the same cemetery are the graves of Francesco Zanardi – mayor of the city from 1914–20; Libero Zanardi, his son who was beaten to death by fascists; and Giulio, Francesco's brother who took his own life in front of Libero's grave.

GIACOMO MATTEOTTI: MARTYRDOM AND RETRIAL

Giacomo Matteotti and his 1924 'martyrdom' at the hands of the fascists remained an inspiration for anti-fascists before, during and after the war. Numerous partisan groups had been named after Matteotti. In 1945, rumours circulated that Mussolini had actually been killed by Matteotti's son.[2] Almost immediately, after liberation, streets and piazzas were renamed in honour of Matteotti. This was at first often done by hand – with a scribbled 'Matteotti' cancelling out a 'Mussolini', or the name of a fascist martyr – before being officially ratified. Usually, these spaces were the most important ones in each city, the most prominent, the biggest – such as Piazza Matteotti in Genoa. Piazza Matteotti had previously been named after the fascist Ettore Muti. This was a way of honouring Matteotti, but also of saying: *We* are in control now. *You* are finished.

Historic wrongs needed to be corrected. In 1944, the so-called Sforza law annulled numerous judicial sentences passed under fascism. After the war, a new investigation and trial into the Matteotti murder was one of the first to take place. By 1944, Amerigo Dumini, who had been part of the gang which murdered Matteotti, was on the run again, complete with a false identity and documents. He managed to avoid any danger to himself in the 'settling of accounts' in 1944–5 and even attended a commemoration ceremony for Matteotti.[3] But he was recognised and arrested in July 1945 and taken to the island of Procida, where he remained for a year, along with a number of other ex-fascists.

Finally, the new trial began – it was 22 January 1947 – this time in Rome. There was a sense of overturning around the whole event: 'The room was that which had been used for the Special Fascist Tribunal and on the wall a new slogan on a plaque stated that "after the gloomy period of the dictatorship" the room had been "re-dedicated to Justice".'[4] Of the men in the car when Matteotti was kidnapped in 1924, two had since died and one was on the run. Only Dumini and Poveromo were in the courtroom. In the end, in April 1947, Dumini,

Poveromo and Viola (in absentia) were given life sentences – reversing, to some extent, the outrageous outcome of the earlier trial. Justice, it seemed, and at last, had been done. In March 1956 Dumini was released, for the last time, from prison (although he had already spent eleven months as a free man in 1953–54 due to another judicial error, before being re-arrested). Since then, the debate over that murder has passed to the historians.

JUSTICE DENIED: GIUSEPPE DI VAGNO

With the end of fascism and the liberation of Puglia, as with many other cases of fascist violence, the Di Vagno murder case was also reopened. In 1946, six of the original group arrested in 1921 were condemned for the murder of the socialist deputy, and for connected crimes. But the Corte di Cassazione (High Court) quashed their sentences in 1948, arguing that the killing was, in fact, involuntary manslaughter ('*omicidio preterintenzionale*'). Another sweeping amnesty, this time passed by leading communist and anti-fascist Palmiro Togliatti, was also applied. Once again, the killers from 1921 were free men.

How was Di Vagno remembered (or forgotten)? Soon after his murder, a plaque had been unveiled describing him as a: '*Tribuno Apostolo Martire dell'ideale socialista*' – 'Tribune Apostle [and] Martyr of the socialist ideal'. Obviously, this wasn't to the liking of local fascists, who twice smashed the plaque down. In 1947, the same plaque was put up again with an added phrase recording its own history: 'Twice destroyed by the cowardly regime, twice rebuilt by the people.' Under fascism, anti-fascist memories were passed down within families, as all non-fascist official commemorations were forbidden. Locally, Di Vagno remained a potent symbol: 'A moving form of devotion was carried forward in the houses of the poor where, alongside religious symbols, there was often a yellowed photograph of the "Good Giant".'[5]

Giuseppe Di Vagno's death never became part of Italian *national* memory, unlike that of Giacomo Matteotti. There are roads and squares named after Di Vagno in Bologna, Bari and Brindisi and across Puglia, but the numbers of these places is far below the Piazze Matteottis which are found in every corner of Italy. Why? It is difficult to say. Perhaps because the murder took place in the south, perhaps because of the context – at a time when murder and violence were everyday occurrences – perhaps because Di Vagno had been a relatively obscure national figure.

ENDLESS PROCESS: PIERO BRANDIMARTE, JUSTICE AND THE TURIN MASSACRE, 1945–53

Unlike many of his fascist *camerata*, Piero Brandimarte managed to escape summary justice, at its peak just after the liberation in 1945. He hid in the northern city of Brescia, where he was arrested again in May 1945. He then began to make a series of defence statements that he would later use in all his trials: he had 'helped partisans' and 'saved the lives of socialists in 1922'. The massacre in Turin, he claimed, improbably, was 'nothing to do with him', although crimes were of course committed. These were familiar claims, used by many 'ex' fascists after 1945. Brandimarte's conciliatory and self-justificatory tone was in stark contrast with interviews he had given in the 1930s, where he had happily taken responsibility for violence and even said that there were further victims whose bodies had not been found. In 1945, Giovanni Roveda became the first mayor of post-fascist Turin, a position he used to continue to campaign around the 1922 massacre. Roveda called publicly, once again for justice to be done.

From the time that Turin was liberated there were those who wanted to avenge the 1922 massacre and called for Brandimarte's immediate execution. Brandimarte did not feel safe in Turin, and with good reason. He had been struck around the face by an anti-fascist and shouted at by another citizen on his way to the city's huge Le Nuove prison complex, where partisans and others had been executed before the liberation.[6]

A judicial decision was made to move the trial away from Turin, to Florence – for 'public order reasons'. This caused outrage and demonstrations of protest. It seems that angry articles in the left-wing press in Turin had led the authorities to shift the trial. Then, everything seemed to stop. Progress was glacial. Turin's judicial investigation into the 1922 massacre took an unusually long amount of time, even by the standards of Italian justice. It was not until 1950 that the Brandimarte trial finally began. By then, many of the relatives of the victims had given up hope. Only a few were able to testify.

Cesare De Vecchi, the other key *squadrista* leader in Turin in 1922, was put on trial in 1947 for 'crimes' linked to the March on Rome, and was eventually cleared. De Vecchi had been on his own odyssey. After taking control of an army unit in September 1943, he was part of resistance against the Nazi occupation, but after surrendering to the Germans he moved north, where he hid with Salesians and in a convent. As one of those who had voted against Mussolini at the famous Gran Consiglio meeting in July 1943, he had also been condemned to death under the puppet 'Salò' regime, in absentia, in Verona in 1944. With the help of the Church he was moved to Rome and in 1947 took a boat to Argentina, travelling with a false Paraguay passport. After returning to Italy in 1949, De Vecchi was then bedridden after a brain haemorrhage until his death nearly ten years later. The contrast between the trials of socialists and communists on the run in the 1920s and 1930s, when the accused were almost always convicted, often in absentia, and given long sentences, was clear. De Vecchi – and many others from the upper echelons of the regime – were free men.

The Brandimarte trial

Brandimarte's trial eventually opened in July 1950 in Florence, twenty-seven years and four months after the Turin massacre.[7] The trial took place in suffocating heat, in the same courtroom used for the 'big' Empoli trial in 1924. Then 132 people had been in the dock for nine murders. Here there were ten murders, and although Brandimarte was on trial with a few other minor fascists, he was the key figure. There had been false rumours that Brandimarte had escaped from prison.[8] In addition to the ten murders, he was also accused of two attempted murders. Three of his co-accused had died in the meantime. In both the Empoli and Brandimarte trials, there were claims of evil, brutality and unimaginable violence. But beyond that, the differences were many. Public interest, for example, beyond Turin, was low. Journalists noted only thirty or so people in the public gallery, a mixture of relatives and so-called *nostalgici* (supporters of Brandimarte). Very few journalists attended in person. The whole thing was over and done with very quickly.

Brandimarte was described at the trial as 'stocky, elegant, arrogant'.[9] He was dressed 'in a well-tailored double-breasted suit, with a white handkerchief in the top pocket, clean shaven ... clearly well fed ... his strong voice seems to have come back to him'.[10] Under the regime he had been known for his ample waistline, and a love of grand uniforms. He was unrepentant about his support for fascism in court, referring to the March on Rome as a revolution.[11]

Yet in terms of the crimes of which he was accused, Brandimarte was happy to reinvent his past, like many fascists after the war (powerful, and not). He presented himself as a moderating force, holding back *squadristi* from further excess: 'How many more dead and injured would there have been without my pacifying image?'[12] The interviews which had appeared in the press and were read out as evidence, were, he said, fake (yet he had not complained about them at the time). In court, he was sweating and his testimony was unconvincing. *La Stampa* wrote that: 'Brandimarte's face was drawn, he was pale, and he didn't seem as fearless as in the past, nor did he smile all the time as he used to.'[13]

The 1950 trial was poorly organised. Too many years had passed and many of the witnesses failed to turn up. But at least this time the relatives of the victims achieved what they had been fighting for since 1922. Brandimarte was found guilty on all the murder and attempted murder charges, and given a sentence of twenty-six years and three months.[14] It seemed like a long sentence, but with amnesties and time already spent in prison taken into account, he would be free in just three years or so. The case went to appeal in Bologna, in April 1952. Even less interest was created by this further trial.

In 1952, Brandimarte gave evidence again. He described the massacre as the work of out-of-control fascists, acting without any leadership. But this time, he was cleared due to 'insufficient evidence'.[15] For many, particularly in Turin, it was a shocking outcome: nobody was guilty of the 1922 massacre. The Italian state had failed twice, first during the original massacre, and now in its haphazard and weak attempts to bring those responsible to justice. The news came through to Turin on May Day, the workers' holiday, in 1952. A protest demonstration was organised and Renato Battistini from the Social Democratic Party told the crowd that: 'Turin waited 23 years for justice. Now we have had an answer: the criminal has been cleared!'[16] A further appeal was made by the prosecution to the High Court in Rome, but it came to nothing.[17] Brandimarte was free to return to Turin. Fascism's crimes were being whitewashed. A pact of forgetting seemed to have taken root.

Brandimarte's case was not unique. Postwar trials of fascists were often difficult and harrowing. Original investigations had been botched, and usually biased, when they had been carried out at all. Evidence was hard or impossible to obtain; witnesses had died or were missing; new information was not available; and many of the presiding judges, especially in the appeal and high courts, had faithfully served the regime. A series of amnesties seemed to favour ex-fascists, especially highly prominent ones. Records had 'disappeared' from the archives and investigations. Retrials or new trials thus often ended without resolution, or with fascists being cleared on technicalities or for 'lack of evidence'. Trauma was piled upon trauma – for victims, relatives, comrades.

Ex-*squadristi* walked the streets, wrote for newspapers, did their shopping, drank coffee in bars, or even remained in positions of power and influence. In one of Giorgio Bassani's most bitter short stories, he recounts the return of *squadristi* from the regime to public spaces in Ferrara after the war.[18] All of this felt like a smack in the face for many anti-fascists, and those with memories of 1919–22, and more recent experiences during the 1943–45 civil war. Violent and murderous fascists had got away with it. Many had even prospered and a legacy of bitterness, and then resignation, was created.

As a free man, in 1950s Turin, Brandimarte was still a worrying presence. In 1955, just as there were signs of a rapprochement at a national level between the neo-fascist right and the governing Christian Democrats, there were rumours that he would address a fascist event in the city on the anniversary of the foundation of the fascist militia in 1923. This was national news, and questions were asked in parliament. In the end the event was cancelled.[19] Brandimarte lived out the rest of his life in Turin in relative peace and quiet. He was occasionally accosted or shouted at in the street, and there was a bomb attack on his house, but he did not hide away, or, it seems, feel ashamed, continuing to draw his military pension. When he died in 1971, he was given military honours.

WHERE IS MASSARENTI?

Giuseppe Massarenti, the reformist socialist, had been driven out of his stronghold in Molinella in the 1920s, forced into poverty, and then finally interned in Rome's psychiatric hospital with a false diagnosis in the 1930s. But he had not been entirely forgotten. In July 1943 there were attempts to release him from where 'he was being held due to a mental illness which he has never suffered from'.[20] Yet, he remained in the asylum despite strong evidence of his sanity.[21] Massarenti campaigned to have his diagnosis overturned but this proved to be impossible.[22] He complained that 'ten years of his life' had been taken away from him.[23]

In 1947 a committee was formed to restore all civil rights to Massarenti, who finally returned to Molinella in triumph in 1948. He was by then in his eighties, thin, grey and gaunt. A huge crowd turned out to hear him speak, once again from that town-hall balcony – *his* balcony, and an alternative one to that of Mussolini. He was still alive and had survived everything fascism had thrown at him. A photo of that day became a model for a later statue. He had refused to accept any charity, and had continued to live in relative poverty. He was made a candidate in parliamentary elections. but sectarian divisions amongst the socialists probably prevented his election.

Massarenti died in 1950 at the age of eighty-three and his funeral was attended by Luigi Einaudi, the president of Italy at the time. His body lay for forty-eight hours in the town hall in Molinella, where thousands of people paid tribute in an 'uninterrupted' flow where a number were said to have made the sign of the cross. Many were rural day-labourers, or rice workers. Einaudi kissed the corpse on the forehead and described Massarenti as a 'saint', a 'constructor', and a 'poet', whose reforms had helped raise the peasants out of poverty and ignorance. Eulogies were made from the town-hall balcony to a crowd of over 10,000. Massarenti's coffin was followed by thousands of Italian flags and marked by dozens of mourners holding 'mostly red' wreaths.[24] It was one of the last great funerals linked to Italian socialism.

In 1953 a bronze statue of Massarenti was erected in Molinella in front of the town hall. It was by the artist Luciano Minguzzi.[25] It is a simple likeness of Massarenti, dressed in a type of coat known as a *paletot* and wearing a hat. His finger raised, he seems about to give a speech. The inscription is simple: '*A Giuseppe Massarenti, i lavoratori. 1867–1950*' – 'To Giuseppe Massarenti: the workers, 1867–1950'. His ashes were placed inside the monument, an unusual location for them. On one side is a quote attributed to Massarenti: 'I am working for the birth of a society where my goodness is your goodness, my evil is your evil.'

AFTERLIVES: IMPRISONMENT, DEPORTATION, 'DEATH' AND REBIRTH

Giuseppe Mariani, one of the Diana bombers from Milan in 1921, was not released from the forbidding Santo Stefano island prison in 1943, but was part of a prison riot in that year. In 1946 he was freed due to a presidential pardon. Mariani remained an anarchist after the war and wrote an autobiography entitled *Memories of an Ex-terrorist*. The other Diana bombers did not make it to the postwar period. Ettore Aguggini perished in prison in Sardinia in 1929 aged twenty-six. It is said that he died as a result of beatings and violence while in custody. In the only photograph we have of him he still appears as a fresh-faced young man. The other convicted Diana bomber, Giuseppe Boldrini, also remained in prison throughout the 1920s and 1930s, and served sixteen years in solitary confinement. After being deported as a political prisoner during the war, he died at Mauthausen concentration camp in Austria sometime in 1945.

Ercole Bucco, the former socialist and communist who had also been expelled from the Fascist Party in the 1930s, had been tried and arrested on his return to Italy. From prison in Sulmona in southern Italy he was deported to Dachau concentration camp near Munich in October 1943.[26] He arrived in the camp on 13 October as one of 166 Italians on that train (there were also a number of deportees from Italy of other nationalities) and was classified as a political prisoner.[27] Many sources claim that he died in Dachau. Yet, in reality, he was freed on an unknown date (the camp was liberated on 29 April 1945) and returned to Italy in either 1945 or 1946, living on until 1964 in relative obscurity.

In September 1943, Ponza was liberated by the British Army, and Tito Zaniboni, the man who had wanted to kill Mussolini in 1925, and who had been in prison or internal exile ever since, was appointed – briefly – as governor of the island. In 1945 Zaniboni published an interview-based book which carried the subtitle 'Why was the fatal and liberating bullet not fired?'[28] He stood for parliament again in 1948, after forming his own social democratic fringe grouping, but failed to get elected. One of his opponents in that election was the communist ex-partisan Walter Audisio, who actually had shot Mussolini dead in 1945.[29] Zaniboni was eventually given his military rank back (in 1951) and his wartime medals, taken away by fascism, were returned. In December

1960 he fell from a bus in Rome on his way to a meeting, and died a few days later. The Hotel Dragoni – from where he had planned to murder Mussolini – closed its doors in 1963.[30]

PIAZZALE LORETO AND DEMOCRATIC ITALY

In 1945, a year after the killing of the fifteen partisans, a simple stone monument was placed right in front of the famous petrol station in Piazzale Loreto, and Milan's mayor took part in a commemorative ceremony. In 1948, the metal gantry from which Mussolini and the others were hung was removed.[31] Ceremonies continued in front of the petrol station until 1961, when the original inscribed stone block was replaced, in a different part of the square, with a larger bronze monument.[32] Occasionally, neo-fascists would also hold small commemorations in Piazzale Loreto itself.

Theodor Saevecke, who ordered the execution of the fifteen anti-fascist 'martyrs' of Piazzale Loreto in 1944, returned to Germany after the war. For many years he worked at a senior level in the West German police force. In 1999 a trial was held in Turin, following the discovery of numerous documents relating to war crimes carried out in Italy – documents which had been deliberately concealed. Saevecke was convicted in 1999 of 'crimes of violence and murder against Italian citizens', but the German authorities refused to agree to his extradition. He died in 2004.[33]

Mussolini's body, meanwhile, went on its own journey. It was hidden, stolen by neo-fascists, hidden again, and then finally released to the family in 1957. The whole story has been brilliantly told and analysed by the historian Sergio Luzzatto.[34] In August of that year Mussolini's corpse was finally interned in the family crypt in Predappio, amidst a forest of fascist salutes surrounding his widow, Rachele, dressed in black. '*Mussolini riposa a Predappio*' ('Mussolini laid to rest in Predappio') was the headline in the neo-fascist daily, *Il Secolo d'Italia*. This new funeral was front-page news in the national press.

MELTING IL DUCE

Football matches continued after the war in Bologna's vast fascist-built stadium. The de-Mussolinised horse still stood up above the stands, but now as a symbol of anti-fascism rather than fascism. After a debate, bronze from the remaining statue in the stadium was eventually removed in 1947, melted down in Verona, and used by the sculptor Luciano Minguzzi for two new figures, representing a male and female partisan. These can still be seen today, standing in Porta Lame, a zone of Bologna where there was a major battle between Italian and German fascists and resistance fighters in 1944.

EX-*SQUADRISTI* AND EX-HIERARCHS AFTER 1945

Ferruccio Vecchi's life took many twists and turns after his career as an early *squadrista* and fascist, and his key role in the pioneering violent raid on the Socialist Party paper *Avanti!* in April 1919. He spent time in prison, fell out with his colleagues, and produced plays and novels of dubious quality, roaming around the world looking for work and fortune. Expelled from Switzerland and France, and possibly from the US, he also lived in Belgium for a time. Throughout, he was constantly monitored by the Italian police.

In the end he settled on an artistic career, producing unimaginably hideous bronze works of Mussolini and Hitler. In his 'sculpture' 'The Empire jumps from the mind of Il Duce', for example, a nude, muscled Mussolini emerges from the large head of another, more pensive Mussolini, with a sword in one hand and fasces (rods) in another. Vecchi seemed to have been able to tap into generous funds to finance his artist's studio and he had powerful patrons. One of his shows in the 1930s was opened by leading fascist hierarch Giuseppe Bottai, and Mussolini himself attended.

After the Second World War, Vecchi attempted to reinvent himself again. He even went as far as offering a partisan monument to *Avanti!* itself. But his past had not been forgotten. On 6 June 1945 the trade union daily *Il lavoro* published a front-page article with this headline: 'That hooligan from 1919 Ferruccio Vecchi is living like a sultan in Piazza Sallustiana. Nobody can be bothered to purge him.' The article accused Vecchi of being 'responsible for sadistic attacks against the workers' and 'the instigator of fascism's violent methods'.[35]

Following this article, 'research' was carried out by the police. In a surreal twist, they consulted the fascist propaganda publications produced by the ex-*squadrista* Giorgio Chiurco in 1929, which celebrated fascist violence, as 'evidence'. Vecchi was arrested in his home on 4 July

1945, and taken to the Regina Coeli prison in Rome, before being released. He was then rearrested. Clearly, there were forms of political interference here. Vecchi had been a high-profile fascist. His name had not been forgotten. But the events he was accused of taking part in were twenty-six years in the past.

Vecchi decided to go on the attack. His target was very high profile: Pietro Nenni, the republican rebel of Red Week in 1914, who had been an interventionist, an early fascist, and then a leading anti-fascist. Vecchi noted and highlighted Nenni's fascist past, and the socialist, who was by now a key figure in the purging process, was forced to defend himself publicly. Vecchi also looked back at his own 'squadrista' past. Some of the attacks he had taken part in were described by him as 'a bit of fun' and even tried to claim that his 'Empire' sculpture of Mussolini was, in some sense, anti-fascist. Vecchi was eventually cleared. He died in 1960 'in total solitude'.[36]

Giuseppe Caradonna, the once powerful *squadrista* and *ras* from Apulia in the south, escaped a violent end after the Second World War. He was in Milan's San Vittore prison during dramatic riots there in April 1946.[37] After avoiding prosecution linked to events in 1922 he lived until 1963. His political career had been undistinguished at a national level under the regime, but he had exercised local power with impunity. There is no serious biography of Caradonna and he is barely mentioned in histories of fascism, even those which concentrate on Puglia. His speeches have not been preserved for posterity, but he did create a dynasty. His son, Giulio, became a deputy for the postwar neo-fascist party, the MSI (the Italian Social Movement). In 1968 Giulio Caradonna was one of the organisers of neo-fascist squads who fought with left-wing students on the campus of the University of Rome.[38] Fascist hierarch Giuseppe Bottai, who also had a death sentence hanging over his head after 25 July 1943 and the Verona trial, fled to Algeria and joined the foreign legion, with whom he fought against the German army. In postwar Italy he was able to work as a university professor and a journalist, and he died in 1959.[39]

Renato Ricci, the violent *capo squadrista* from Carrara, managed to escape from Milan in 1945. Arrested rather than shot, he was helped by the postwar amnesty (which mainly benefited ex-fascists) and released from prison in 1950. Dino Grandi escaped to Portugal in 1943, and was also sentenced to death in absentia at the Verona trial in 1944. He moved to Brazil where he worked in business, building up a large fortune, before returning to Italy in the 1950s and laying down his version of the past in a series of books. His personal archive was donated to historian Renzo De Felice, who would write a huge, unfinished and highly controversial biography of Mussolini from the 1960s onwards.

Right to the end, in April 1945, Rodolfo Graziani was alongside Mussolini in Milan. Yet when Il Duce's entourage and convoy headed north, Graziani made a smart move, surrendering to the Allies. If he had stayed close to Mussolini he would also have been shot and his body would have been displayed at Piazzale Loreto. International judicial proceedings were mooted around his role in mass genocidal murder in Ethiopia, but Italian and Allied opposition prevented any war crimes trial. Convicted of collaborationism in 1948, he served just four months of a nineteen-year sentence. A huge crowd turned out for his funeral in Rome in 1954, as his coffin was carried through the streets surrounded by fascist salutes.

Graziani today is still exalted by many and often celebrated as a war hero. In Affile, near Rome (where Graziani lived for part of his later years), a repugnant monument was constructed in his honour in 2012, with public funding. It remains in place, seventy-one years after the terrifying events of Addis Ababa in 1937. The Mayor of Affile at the time called Graziani 'an example for the young'.[40]

JEWISH CEMETERY, FERRARA

Giorgio Bassani's most famous novel, *Il Giardino dei Finzi-Contini*, takes its cue from the Jewish cemetery in Ferrara, which covers an extensive walled area on the edge of town. It is often closed to visitors. As you go in, the custodian of the cemetery assumes you want to see Bassani's tomb, designed by the artist and sculptor Arnaldo Pomodoro. Elsewhere in the cemetery are the tombs of Bassani's parents, his grandparents and an uncle. The first area of land for the cemetery was purchased by the Jewish community of Ferrara in 1626. It is a beautiful and peaceful place. There are dedications to Jews who 'gave their lives for the fatherland' in the First World War. That same 'fatherland' which would discriminate against them so openly and brutally after 1938.

Ferrara and Renzo Ravenna, 1946

Renzo Ravenna's return to Ferrara had not been easy. Despite the fact that he was *podestà* of the city from 1926–38, he was persecuted as a Jew and then forced into exile. His house in the city was destroyed by bombing, and he had to go through a political purging process, which cleared him. He was the only one of six siblings from before the war to return to live in Ferrara, a fact which symbolised the decline of the community in the town. In autumn 1946 he settled back in the city for good. Fascism's racist and racially based census from 1938 had estimated there were 700 Jews in Ferrara.[41] After the war, only 200 or so were still present in the city. Around 102 had been deported to camps, of whom only five survived. Many others had emigrated.[42] The prefect reported on the community after the war with these words: 'They no longer have anything.'[43] Ravenna's nephew Eugenio's traumatic return from the camps in September 1945 was the basis for a celebrated and caustic short story by Bassani.[44]

Ferrara's first postwar mayor was an anti-fascist called Michele Tortora, who made serious criticisms of the past regime, and of Ravenna himself. Ravenna was moved to protest in a letter to Tortora, but he then stayed out of political debate. In the referendum on the monarchy of June 1946, Renzo Ravenna supported the Republic, and he was friendly with a number of people on the left and anti-fascists. But Bassani was not kind to him in his writings, referring to his 'pathetic greying goatee' and describing him as 'that old fascist lawyer ... who was seen as so meritorious by the regime that he succeeded, for at least two years after 1938, in being able to go, now and then, to the Shopkeeper's club'.[45] Ravenna continued to work as a lawyer until his death in 1961. He was also buried in the Jewish cemetery in Ferrara, where his tomb describes him as a 'lawyer', making no reference to his role as *podestà*.

IL DUCE'S BODY TODAY

Since 1957, when Mussolini's body was interred in the family crypt, his birthplace Predappio has been contested territory, a place of divided memory, fascist kitsch and political controversy.[46] It has been a site of fascism, neo-fascism and anti-fascism. In the 2000s a proposal to set up a museum or study centre dedicated to the history of fascism in the town, in the huge, empty space of the ex-Casa del Fascio, caused controversy among historians and a public debate. The election of a mayor from the centre-right of the political spectrum in May 2019 (the first non-left-wing mayor in the town for seventy years) led to doubts as to whether the proposed museum would ever be opened. The new mayor argued that Mussolini's crypt should be open throughout the year – previously it had been accessible only at certain times – in order to bring 'more tourists' to Predappio. There were even calls for the state to fund the upkeep of the ex-dictator's mausoleum. Comparisons were made with the debates in Spain concerning Franco's enormous Valley of the Fallen monument; Franco's body was moved away from that site in October 2019.[47]

FASCISM, ANTI-SEMITISM, SILENCE AND LIES

In the postwar period the press made no mention of the magistrate Gaetano Azzariti's fascist past, despite the fact that he had been an integral part of the regime's legal system, playing a role in both legal reform and practice. Azzariti had been president of the Tribunale della Razza, a body specifically set up to decide whether specific Italians were Jewish, or not, in line with the notorious racial laws. Azzariti went on to work with postwar Justice Minister, the communist Palmiro Togliatti, and was for a time consultant for the purging process. Azzariti's past was both forgotten and re-invented.

Azzariti's nomination as a constitutional judge in 1955 saw the same gloss put on his career.[48] In April 1957, when he was appointed President of the Court, after the resignation of the previous president, Enrico De Nicola, he said: 'I have always modestly lived in the background.'[49] He now occupied one of Italy's most prestigious and most powerful judicial positions. In 1957, the Communist Party daily paper L'Unità described him in this way: 'He has been part of the judiciary for 46 years … and he is well known for a series of judicial publications. A Minister of Justice in the Badoglio government [in 1943] he began the revision of fascist legislation.'[50] Azzariti was a perfect example of what some called 'the continuity of the state'.[51]

At the time of his death in 1961, when he was seventy-nine, Azzariti's loyal service to fascism was again absent from all accounts of his career.

There was not a word on this subject, in either the left-wing or the mainstream press. Published obituaries chose their dates carefully, passing seamlessly from 1919 to 1943, glossing over his activities in the 1930s, and writing only that he had 'passed through all levels of the judiciary'.[52] In its obituary, *La Stampa* also spoke of his 'modesty' and of the fact that in terms of 'the [work in the] posts he was entrusted with during his long career as a magistrate he never moved away from the criteria which had governed his own life'.[53] His funeral was attended by numerous dignitaries, including the Italian head of state at the time, the president of the republic (Giovanni Gronchi) and other key figures from Italy's parliament, such as Giulio Andreotti, Prime Minister Amintore Fanfani, and the Mayor of Rome.

In March 1965 a bust was unveiled in Azzarriti's honour inside the Constitutional Court building in Rome, again in the presence of the President of the Republic, senators, deputies, the mayor of Rome, the Prefect of Rome, members of the Constitutional Court and others. It depicts Azzariti in his judicial robes, and glasses, with a severe look. A speech was given by the President of the Court at the ceremony. The President of Italy at that time was Giuseppe Saragat, socialist and anti-fascist.[54] Of Azzariti's fascist activities, both under the regime and as president of the Tribunale della Razza, there was, again, total silence.

It took until the twenty-first century for historians to dig into this past and for Azzariti's strange journey to the top of the tree in postwar Italy to be finally noted.[55] In 2014 an article was published which revealed more of the lies and half-truths around the purging process as applied to Azzariti. It caused a sensation, and opened up debates over how Azzariti had been remembered.[56] In Naples, in 2017, a road named after Azzariti was changed to the name of a young Holocaust victim. There were then attempts to have the bust inside the court building removed, and there were highly critical articles in the *Corriere della Sera*. Protests also came from the Jewish community. One of the judges on the court at the time, Paolo Maria Napolitano, officially asked for the bust to be taken down. But the request was rejected and no reason was given for the decision.[57] Napolitano died in 2016. Azzariti was defended by his grandson.[58] At the time of the controversy, the bust was conveniently 'being restored', and had been replaced by a plant.[59] As I write in 2021 the bust, by the artist Lello Scorzelli, is still to be found in Palazzo della Consulta, on the second floor, in the corridor.[60]

1964: RED WEEK, FIFTY YEARS ON

In 1964 celebrations took place in Ancona and elsewhere for the fiftieth anniversary of Red Week. Augusto Masetti, the soldier who had shot at his own commanding officer in 1911, attended and was warmly greeted by many of those present.[61] He was interviewed for television, while standing on the balcony of his house in the town of Imola. His memory of the controversy from fifty-three years earlier was still strong. But he still claimed, as he had at times after the shooting, that he remembered little or nothing of the actual moment which had made him famous, or infamous. He stuck to his story of temporary amnesia. Within two years Masetti was dead, run over accidentally by traffic police in 1966. Since 2011, the site of the barracks in Bologna has a plaque dedicated to: 'Augusto Masetti the soldier who said no to war – Bologna 30 October 1911 – [placed by the] Antimilitarists.'

The forbidding Ergastolo ('Life Sentence') prison complex on the island of Santo Stefano was only finally closed in 1965. It had held one of the Diana bombers, two failed assassins of Mussolini – Zaniboni and Lucetti – and many leading anti-fascists, including the future President of Italy, Sandro Pertini. It is now a crumbling ruin.

Epilogue

'Liberty is something you have to take for yourself. It's no use begging it from others.'

Ignazio Silone, *Bread and Wine*[1]

The legacy of the regime that fell in July 1943, and then again in April 1945, is still very much present in Italy – in popular culture, in the built environment, and within institutions. The spectre of Italian fascism has returned time and again to haunt the postwar, democratic Italian nation, as well as influence fascists and regimes way beyond Italy. Fascism affected democratic Italy in lasting ways. Italy's 1948 constitution was so preoccupied with guarding against a return of fascism that it almost paralysed its own political system, often making it very difficult for laws to be passed at all.

For most of the postwar period, a neo-fascist party – the Italian Social Movement (MSI) – was deliberately kept out of central power. So strong was popular feeling that in 1960, national riots followed the external support given by the MSI to a Christian Democratic government. Neo-fascist extremists planted numerous bombs and attracted militants in the 1960s and 1970s, but neo-fascism was largely kept out of the mainstream, beyond the pale. But after the end of the Cold War this all changed. The re-legitimisation of neo-fascism in the 1990s led to their participation in national government and numerous local administrations. Was Italy still an anti-fascist republic, or was it *anti-anti-fascist*? Were the former admirers of Mussolini 'post-fascist'? What did all of this mean so many years after the end of the regime? An unexpected political shift led to a widespread and passionate debate within and outside academia about the meaning of fascism and anti-fascism. It was a moment of traumatic change.

Today, many flock to Mussolini's home town and final resting place in Predappio. There, souvenir-traders hawk toy cudgels, Il Duce calendars, Mussolini-branded bottles of wine, and other trinkets. Leading politicians use slogans from the regime and neo-fascists occupy positions of political power. Fascism is enjoying a revival, with large numbers of young people attracted to its ideas and its symbols. The 'CasaPound' network of social centres across Italy have reinvented fascist ideas, and have been hugely influential. Fascism also enjoys popular appeal amongst many police officers, and football fans. Fascist tattoos are common, fascist songs are used as ring tones. Mussolini died over seventy-five years ago, but fascist buildings with fascist symbols are still prominent across the country, and fascist murals have been restored without too much controversy. Some were even *completed* in the 1950s.

Mussolini's movement and time in power has been a constant reference point. Silvio Berlusconi, who had brought the neo-fascists back into the political fold in the 1990s and 2000s, was frequently compared to Il Duce. The media magnate's concentration of political and business power, use of censorship and the cult of personality which grew around him, bore comparison with the fascist past, and his governing of Italy was often called a 'regime'. Berlusconi's speeches, and his clothes, seemed sometimes to be modelled on those of Mussolini, and in many controversial statements he played down the crimes of the fascist regime of the 1920s and 1930s, painting it as a benign dictatorship when compared to Stalinism in the USSR. His was a revisionism perfectly suited to a generation raised on consumerist television. Berlusconi was fond of using the classic clichés: 'Mussolini also did good things', and: 'It wasn't all bad under fascism.'[2]

More recently, Donald Trump has often been compared to Mussolini. His speaking style and – in this case, more than with Berlusconi – his policies (nationalism, racism, autarchy, a corporate state, a distaste for democracy itself) – have led to associations with Il Duce. Some of those on the 'alt-right' have been inspired by Julius Evola, an enigmatic Italian neo-fascist who achieved a significant following in Italy and elsewhere in the postwar period (including in the important Russian Eurasianism movement). Links have also been made between Putin and Mussolini (in both style – the shirtless horse-riding – and substance – the creation of a near-dictatorships from above, the use of violence, special courts, assassinations) and many other populist dictators or those who aspired to be dictators. Democracy does not last forever. Indeed, it is often extremely fragile. Italian fascism showed how democracy, and its institutions, can quickly crumble in the face of violence, disaffection and rage. Some of this was seen in the USA after 2016, and not just in the armed attack on the Capitol in January 2021. When the 'forces of law and order' are also on board, things can quickly disintegrate. Collusion between parts of the state and the fascists was a key factor in Mussolini's victory.

Questions have been asked about the connections between the past and the present.[3] Was Mussolini himself the first populist to create an authoritarian regime? On social media, the word fascism is bandied about on a daily basis by millions of people. Yet many are unclear about what fascism actually was, and why it remained in power for so long. Did the appeal of 'fake news' have its origins in Italian fascism? The use of falsehoods – not for their own sake but as part of a political tragedy – was a classic trait of Italian fascism.[4] Fascism's historic attempt to 'deliberately … transform its lies into reality' certainly chimes with much of what is happening today on the far right, and more widely on social media.[5] Fascism will not return in the same form; yet it may still make a comeback in some way. It could be argued that this might have already happened, in different times and various places.

Italy in 1919 was a society which was deeply and radically divided. Conspiracy theories quickly had taken hold about 'traitors' and 'patriots'. Italy's victory, which had cost 600,000 lives, was 'mutilated'. The country had been stabbed in the back at the negotiating table. Its leaders were feckless and corrupt liberals. Prices were rising and jobs were scarce. Trauma was everywhere. In this context, the demonisation of the enemy was the norm. Individual and collective violence became commonplace. Politics and violence became inseparable. A new way of doing politics was invented, and it was highly effective. Within four years of that first meeting in Milan in 1919, the fascists had managed to organise a nationwide insurrection, and terrify the state itself into submission. In power, the violence was institutionalised, its victims driven out of the country altogether, murdered, or forced into humiliation and silence. Fascism ruled in this way for twenty long years, leaving its mark on every corner of the country, and beyond.

*

Three times a year, in Predappio, the door to a crypt is usually opened.[6] Those dates are: 28 April (Mussolini's death), 29 July (his birth), and 28 October (the March on Rome). On these occasions, thousands of people descend on the town. Once there, some march, some give the fascist salute, many go for lunch or a drink, or buy souvenirs. Many express love for Il Duce in interviews. For others, it just seems like a fun day out, with the whole family. Mussolini died over seven decades ago, but his memory, and his legacy, live on.

For many years, a bust of Mussolini stood on a plinth in a nondescript room in Bologna. Its head was the very same one that could once be found on top of Mussolini's body, on a huge bronze horse in the city's stadium, witnessing football matches and parades, and which was partially destroyed in July 1943. His metal head was paraded around town, before being abandoned in the street. It was then supposedly 'saved' by a fascist and buried in his garden, before, by a roundabout route, it ended up on a plinth in an unofficial 'museum'. Mussolini's bust was an object of veneration for those – young and old – who still believed in the greatness of Il Duce: 'a disquieting reminder, as well as an uncanny, almost physical embodiment, of the persistence of a cult that, in clandestine or authoritarian forms, still persisted in Italy'.[7]

By studying fascism, do we perhaps give it too much dignity? Was it really just 'the cudgel and the bottle of castor oil'? Was the anti-fascist intellectual Gaetano Salvemini right to say that: 'A fascist lacking in ideas but with a gun will always defeat ten anti-fascists with ideas but without guns'?[8] In October 2021 far-right activists at the fringes of an anti-vax demonstration in Rome attacked the main offices of the biggest trade union federation in Italy and ransacked the building. It was difficult to ignore the parallels with events one hundred years earlier across Italy. Was *squadrismo* back?

Violence was central to fascism's rise to power in Italy, and it wrought brutal trauma on the bodies and lives of individuals. In Ignazio Silone's *Bread and Wine*, published outside of Italy in the 1930s, he describes one minor, forgotten incident of fascist violence:

> About a dozen students of my faculty started beating a young
> workman in the middle of the street, till the blood flowed.

I remember the scene very well. The workman lay on the ground, in the roadway, with his bleeding head on the tram line, while the students stood all around him and kicked him and beat him with sticks. 'He didn't salute the flag,' they shouted. Some policemen arrived and congratulated them on their patriotic action and arrested the injured man.[9]

Silone's account ends with the sentence: 'A big crowd gathered but kept completely silent.'[10]

Many Italians, as in that story often told by my father about my great-grandmother, did indeed think of the era of fascism in Italy as a 'wonderful' time. Others stood by, allowing violence to spread and remain unpunished. As one historian has written: 'For Mussolini, violence is power without restraints.'[11] The bystanders, the onlookers, those who watched 'with indifference' – perhaps they were even the 'silent majority'? – were central to the rise of the blackshirts. A lesson, perhaps, that can be applied to today's world.

Notes

1 George Tod, 'From Pillar to Post: the Family and Autobiography of George Tod', unpublished manuscript.

PROLOGUE

1 A phrase influenced by Raul Hillberg, *Perpetrators Victims Bystanders: The Jewish Catastrophe 1933–1945*, Harper, London, 1993.
2 I have been greatly influenced by the everyday life school of history, by micro-history and oral history. See for example: Joshua Arthurs et al. (eds), *The Politics of Everyday Life in Fascist Italy*, Palgrave, New York, 2017; Michael Ebner, *Ordinary Violence in Mussolini's Italy*, CUP, Cambridge, 2011; Kate Ferris, *Everyday Life in Fascist Venice, 1929–1940*, Palgrave, London, 2012; Carlo Ginzburg, *Miti, emblemi, spie. Morfologia e storia*, Einaudi, Turin, 1986; *The Cheese and the Worms: the Cosmos of a Sixteenth-Century Miller*, Johns Hopkins University Press, Baltimore, 1992; Alf Lüdtke (ed.), *The History of Everyday Life: Reconstructing Historical Experiences and Ways of Life*, Princeton University Press, Princeton, 1995; and Luisa Passerini, *Fascism in Popular Memory. The Cultural Experience of the Turin Working Class*, CUP, Cambridge, 1987.
3 Matteo Millan, 'Origins', in Arthurs et al. (eds), *The Politics of Everyday Life*, p. 29.
4 Richard Evans, 'Why Trump isn't a Fascist', *New Statesman*, 13 November 2021, https://www.newstatesman.com/world/2021/01/why-trump-isnt-fascist; Jason Stanley et al., 'Will Fascism Win the US Election?', Project Syndicate, 30 October 2020.
5 Ruth Ben-Ghiat, *Strongmen: How They Rise. Why They Succeed. How They Fail*, Profile Books, London, 2020.

6 Richard Bosworth, *Mussolini's Italy: Life under the Dictatorship, 1915–1945*, Penguin, London, 2007, p. 4.

1911

1 Cited in Elena Iorio, 'Il riconoscimento tardivo. Idee, pratiche e immagini dell'obiezione di coscienza al servizio militare in Italia con una comparazione con la Repubblica Federale Tedesca (1945–1972)', PhD, European University Institute, 2014, p. 81: https://cadmus.eui.eu/bitstr eam/handle/1814/33885/2014_Iorio.pdf?sequence=1.

2 Roberto Zani, 'Intervento alla giornata di studi su Augusto Masetti e l'invasione della Libia Bologna del 30 ottobre 2011: "La sovversione antimilitarista di Augusto Masetti"', http://circoloberneri.indivia.net/ wp-content/uploads/intervento_zani_masetti.pdf; https://www.wumin gfoundation.com/giap/2011/05/augusto-masetti-luomo-che-sparo-al-bersaglio-giusto/; 'L'arabo di Bologna', *Corriere della Sera*, 31 October 1911.

3 For a book-length account of Masetti's life see Laura De Marco, *Il soldato che disse no alla guerra. Storia dell'anarchico Augusto Masetti (1888–1966)*, Edizioni Spartaco, Santa Maria Capua Vetere, 2003.

4 https://www.aspi.unimib.it/collections/entity/detail/418/. The psychiatrists were Pietro Petrazzani and Augusto Saccozzi.

5 De Marco, *Il soldato che disse no alla guerra*, p. 77.

6 See also: https://giuseppearagno.wordpress.com/2015/05/30/proletari-con tro-la-guerra-dalla-campagna-per-masetti-alla-settimana-rossa/.

1914

1 'La rivoluzione in Italia', *Volontà*, 23, 17 June 1914, cited in *Gino Cerrito, Dall'insurrezionalismo alla Settimana rossa: per una storia dell'anarchismo in Italia (1881–1914)*, Cp Editrice, Florence, 1977, p. 237.

2 *Utopia*, II, July 1914, cited in Mario Visani, *La Settimana rossa*, Le fonti della storia/46, La Nuova Italia editrice, Florence, 1978, p. 1.

3 Cited in *Utopia*, II, July 1914, p. 1.

4 http://dati.acs.beniculturali.it/CPC/.

5 Maurizio Antonioli, 'Prefazione', in Paolo Finzi, *La nota persona. Errico Malatesta in Italia dicembre 1919–luglio 1920*, La Fiaccola, Ragusa, 1990, p. 8.

6 See Pietro di Paola, 'Italian Anarchists in London (1870–1914)', PhD, Goldsmiths, University of London, 2004, p. 88.

7 Marco Severini 'Introduzione' to Severini (ed.), *La Settimana rossa*, Aracne, Rome, 2014, p. 11.

8 Cited in Luigi Lotti, *La Settimana rossa con documenti inediti*, Felice Le Monnier, Florence, 1965, pp. 59–60.

9 See the detailed description of these events in Lotti, *La Settimana rossa*, pp. 61–9.

10 'Una rivoluzione senza programma', *L'Unità*, 19 June 1914.

11 Descriptions and citations from Lotti, *La Settimana rossa*, pp. 86–7.

12 *Avanti!*, 8 June 1914, cited in Lotti, *La Settimana rossa*, p. 72.

13 The use of the phrase 'premeditated murder' and the title of the report and editorial harked back to a famous piece Mussolini had written in 1913 after another 'proletarian massacre': see 'Assassinio di Stato', *Avanti!*, 7 January 1913. On that occasion seven people had been shot dead in a small town called Roccagorga after a demonstration.

14 For the death of Miniago see T. Dalla Valle, '1914: i "giorni rossi" nelle speranze e nelle illusioni dei rivoltosi', *Studi Romagnoli*, XLIV, 1993, pp. 449–50.

15 For the Agliardi incident see Samori, 'La Romagna e l'Emilia', in Severini (ed.), *La Settimana rossa*, p. 201, and Silvia Serini, 'Le deuteragonisti', pp. 357–8.

16 Manuela Martini, 'Giugno 1914. Folle romagnole in azione', *Rivista di storia contemporanea*, 4, XVIII, October 1989, p. 522.

17 Cited in http://alfonsinemonamour.racine.ra.it/alfonsine/Alfonsine/doc2 _sett_rossa_parroco.htm. For the Catholic reaction see Ilaria Biagioli, 'I cattolici e i moti della Settimana rossa', in Severini (ed.), *La Settimana rossa*, p. 177.

18 Alessandro Portelli, *Biography of an Industrial Town: Terni, Italy, 1831–2014*, Palgrave, London, 2017, p. 95.

19 Portelli, *Biography of an Industrial Town*, p. 95.

20 https://umbriasud.altervista.org/settimana-rossa-38-operai-tribunale/.

21 Martini, 'Giugno 1914', p. 517.

22 Fausto Butta, *Living Like Nomads: The Milanese Anarchist Movement Before Fascism*, Cambridge Scholars Publishing, Cambridge, 2015, p. 152.

23 Scuola Media Statale 'Bice Zona', Giuseppe Aragno (ed.), *La Settimana rossa a Napoli: Giugno 1914: due ragazzi caduti per noi*, La Città del Sole, Naples, 2000, p. 29.

24 In the aftermath of Red Week, in general, the repression was relatively mild, and a royal pardon (30 December 1914) led to amnesties for many of those who were arrested. Some of the leaders (if Red Week had leaders) or most prominent figures involved were, however, forced into exile, or brought to trial.

25 On 9 June, a general strike with no time limit was called by the Confederazione generale del lavoro, the Socialist Party, the Republican Party and the Unione Sindacale.

26 'Brutta giornata ad Ancona', *La Stampa*, 9 June 1914.

27 Ibid.

28 Errico Malatesta, 'E ora?', *Volontà*, 20 June 1914, cited in Cerrito, *Dall'insurrezionalismo alla Settimana rossa*, p. 242.

29 'La rivoluzione in Italia', cited in Cerrito, *Dall'insurrezionalismo alla Settimana rossa*, p. 237.

30 'Intervista concessa da E. Malatesta a C. Calza Bedolo', *Il Giornale d'Italia*, 1 July 1914, cited in Cerrito, *Dall'insurrezionalismo alla Settimana rossa*, p. 243.

31 https://www.avvenire.it/agora/pagine/settimana-rossa-rivoluzione-manc ata; A. Varni et al. (eds), *Storia di Cesena*, Vol. 4, Pt 2, Bruno Ghigi Editore, Cesena, 1991, p. 512. Comandini had been Mayor of Cesena on a number of occasions and was a well-loved local figure. A bust in a local town park is dedicated to him. See also: Renzo De Felice, *Mussolini*, Vol. 1, Einaudi, Turin, 1965, p. 204. For Italy and the tradition of declarations of a republic going back to 1848, see Piero Brunello, *Colpi di scena. La rivoluzione del Quarantotto a Venezia*, Cierre, Verona, 2018.

32 When war was declared in 1914 Comandini initially backed a neutral position for Italy, before moving towards support for intervention. He was a minister in war cabinets in 1916 and 1918–19.

33 'Echi dei tumulti di Romagna. "La repubblica nei fatti" secondo l'on. Comandini', *Corriere della Sera*, 19 June 1914. See also: 'Echi della rivolta', *La Stampa*, 20 June 1914.

34 Marco Severini, *Nenni il sovversivo. L'esperienza a Jesi e nelle Marche (1912–1915)*, Marsilio, Venice, 2007, p. 97. Under fascism, the Chambers of Labour became one of the key targets of the fascist squads.

35 'La rivoluzione in Italia', cited in Cerrito, *Dall'insurrezionalismo alla Settimana rossa*, pp. 238–9.

36 Lotti, *La Settimana rossa*, p. 244.

37 Gaetano Salvemini, 'Una rivoluzione senza programma', *L'Unità*, 19 June 1914.

38 Cited in Lotti, *La Settimana rossa*, p. 153.

39 'Claudio Treves, 'Cause ed effetti', *Critica Sociale*, XXIV, 12, 16–30 June 1914, pp. 177–9; 'La teppa e la rivoluzione socialista', *Critica Sociale*, XXIV, 13, 1–15, June 1914, pp. 193–5, cited in Martini, 'Giugno 1914', p. 518.

40 *Utopia*, II, July 1914, cited in Visani, *La Settimana rossa*, p. 1. See also: G. Fanoli, 'Teppa e proletariato', *Utopia*, II, 9–10, 15–31 July 1914, pp. 253–6, cited in Martini, 'Giugno 1914', p. 519.

41 See Malatesta's own description of his escape in 'Intervista concessa da E. Malatesta a C. Calza Bedolo', *Il Giornale d'Italia*, 1 July 1914, cited in Cerrito, *Dall'insurrezionalismo alla Settimana rossa*, p. 237.

42 Errico Malatesta, 'Movimenti stroncati', in *Umanità Nova*, 28 June 1922, cited in Cerrito, *Dall'insurrezionalismo alla Settimana rossa*, pp. 245, 247.

43 Severini, *Nenni il sovversivo*, p. 96.

1915–18

1 Cited in Leonardo Paggi, 'Gramsci's General Theory of Marxism', in Chantal Mouffe (ed.), *Gramsci and Marxist Theory*, Routledge, London, 2014, p. 152, and Q. Hoare and G. Nowell-Smith (eds), *Selections from the Prison Notebooks of Antonio Gramsci*, Lawrence and Wishart, London, 1973, p. 106.

2 Speech to parliament, 'Ente per la storia del socialismo e del movimento operaio italiano', Fondazione Giuseppe Emanuele e Vera Modigliani, ESSMOI, *Attività parlamentare dei socialisti italiani, volume sesto, 1919–1921*, Edizioni ESSMOI, Rome, 1989, p. 21.

3 Eric Leed, *No Man's Land: Combat and Identity in World War One*, CUP, Cambridge, 1979, p. 21.

4 The literature on the Italian war is vast: see Vanda Wilcox (ed.), *Italy in the Era of the Great War*, Brill, Leiden and Boston, 2018; Mario Isnenghi and Giorgio Rochat, *La Grande Guerra. 1914–1918*, Il Mulino, Bologna, 2014; Antonio Gibelli, *La Grande Guerra degli italiani, 1915–1918*, Rizzoli, Milan, 2014.

5 Paul Fussell, 'La grande guerra: tante storie', *Passato e Presente*, 1986–7, 1, 2, pp. 9–22.

6 Rosalia Muci, 'Produrre armi, domandare pace: Le operaie milanesi durante la Prima guerra mondiale', *Storia in Lombardia*, 3, 1985, p. 36. See also: John Foot, 'Socialist-Catholic Alliances and Gender. Work, War and the Family in Milan and Lombardy, 1914–21', *Social History*, 21, 1, 1996, pp. 37–53.

7 For May 1917 in Milan see: R. De Felice, 'Ordine pubblico e orientamenti delle masse popolari italiane nella prima metà del 1917', *Rivista Storica del Socialismo*, xx, 1963, pp. 467–504. Other accounts include Muci, 'Produrre armi, domandare pace', and Mario Isnenghi, *I vinti di Caporetto nella letteratura di guerra*, Marsilio, Padua, 1967; see also the contemporary description in L. Albertini in *Epistolario*, iii, edited by O. Barie, Mondadori, Milan, 1968, pp. 715–16.

8 Martini (6 May 1917), cited in in G. Procacci (ed.), *Stato e classe operaia in Italia durante la Prima guerra mondiale*, FrancoAngeli, Milan, 1983, p. 91.

9   See De Felice, 'Ordine pubblico'.

10 Giancarlo Carcano, *Cronaca di una rivolta. I moti torinesi del '17*, Stampatori nuovasocietà, Turin, 1977, p. 213.

11 Teresa Noce, *Rivoluzionaria professionale. Autobiografia di una partigiana comunista*, La Pietra, Milan, 1974, p. 22. For an account of the revolt in one neighbourhood of Turin, see Angelo Castrovilli and Carmelo Seminara, *Storia della barriera di Milano, 1852–1945*, Stargrafica, Grugliasco, 2004, pp. 93–102.

12 'Allora mangeremo i biscotti', cited in Carcano, *Cronaca di una rivolta*, p. 52.

13 'Questa volta i biscotti li mangiamo anche noi, non solo i signori', cited in ibid.

14 Noce, *Rivoluzionaria professionale*, p. 23.

15 Cited in Palmiro Togliatti, 'Antonio Gramsci capo della classe operaia italiana', *Lo Stato operaio*, n.5–6, May–June 1937.

16 Noce, *Rivoluzionaria professionale*, p. 24.

17 Ibid., p. 22.

18 My emphasis. Paolo Spriano, *Torino operaia nella grande guerra (1914–1918)*, Einaudi, Turin, 1960, p. 261.

19 Paride Rugafiori, 'Nella Grande Guerra', in Nicola Tranfaglia (ed.), *Storia di Torino*, VIII, *Dalla Grande guerra alla Liberazione (1915–1945)*, Einaudi, Turin, p. 72.

20 Giovanna Savant, 'Intransigenti e collaborazionisti. Serrati e Treves davanti alla Grande Guerra', *Quaderni della Fondazione Luigi Salvatorelli Marsciano*, 14, Aracne, Rome, 2013.

21 Spriano, *Torino operaia*, p. 260.

22 Carcano, *Cronaca di una rivolta*, p. 255.

23 Ibid., p. 71.

24 On this see http://storieinmovimento.org/wp-content/uploads/2017/06/Zap-39_13-StoriaAlLavoro1.pdf

25 Carcano, *Cronaca di una rivolta*, pp. 35–6.

26 Noce, *Rivoluzionaria professionale*, p. 23.

27 Spriano, *Torino operaia*, pp. 228, 302. See also Palmiro Togliatti's version in: 'Antonio Gramsci capo della classe operaia italiana', *Lo Stato operaio*, n.5–6, May–June 1937.

28 'I rappresentanti social-rivoluzionari e menscevichi dei Soviet hanno parlato a Torino, il 13 agosto 1917, ascoltati da 40.000 manifestanti, nell'infiammata e libera traduzione in chiave leninista di Giacinto Menotti Serrati', cited in P. Rugafiori, 'Nella Grande Guerra', in Tranfaglia (ed.), *Storia di Torino*, VIII, p. 76.

29 Carcano, *Cronaca di una rivolta*, p. 246.

30 Ibid., pp. 35–6.

31 'Fateci impiccare, ma non condannateci per tradimento', *Avanti!*, 2 August 1918, cited in Stefano Merli, *Autodifese di militanti operai e democratici italiani davanti ai tribunali*, Comune di Venezia, Avanti!, Milan-Rome, 1958, p. 146.

32 'Fateci impiccare, ma non condannateci per tradimento', in Merli, *Autodifese*, p. 149.

33 Merli, *Autodifese*, p. 148.

34 Ibid.

35 Ibid.

36 Cited in Mario Isnenghi, *L'Italia in piazza. I luoghi della vita pubblica dal 1848 ai giorni nostri*, Il Mulino, Bologna, 1994, p. 169.

37 'Il testamento politico di Serrati, 1926', cited in Tommaso Detti, *Serrati e la formazione del Partito comunista italiano. Storia della frazione terzinternazionalista, 1921–1924*, Riuniti, Rome, 1972, p. 528; Savant, 'Intransigenti e collaborazionisti', p. 74.

38 See the seminal work of Alessandro Portelli, 'Uchronic Dreams: Working Class Memory and Possible Worlds', *Oral History*, 16, 2, 1988, pp. 46–56.

39 Cited in August Simonin, *Il linguaggio di Mussolini*, Bompiani, Milan, 1978, p. 136.

40 Ernest Hemingway, *A Farewell to Arms*, Scribner, New York, p. 52.

41 https://web.vittoriale.it/wp-content/uploads/2016/12/d-Annunzio-e-il-Garda.pdf; https://ricerca.repubblica.it/repubblica/archivio/repubblica/1991/11/24/il-diario-del-guerriero-gadda.html.

42 Mark Thompson, *The White War: Life and Death on the Italian Front 1915–1919*, Faber and Faber, London, 2008, pp. 236, 311.

43 https://www.pensalibero.it/la-parabola-del-generale-luigi-capello-da-comandante-della-ii-armata-a-trentanni-di-carcere/.

44 Thompson, *The White War*, p. 129.

45 Ibid., p. 170.

46 Ibid., p. 236.

47 Ibid., p. 267.

48 Ibid., p. 268.

49 Cited in Massimiliano Magli, *Fucilazioni di guerra: testimonianze ed episodi di giustizia militare dal fronte italo-austriaco, 1915–1918*, Nordpress, 2007, p. 41; see also: John Foot, *Fratture d'Italia*, Rizzoli, Milan, 2009, pp. 74–7.

50 Isnenghi, *L'Italia in piazza*, p. 254.

51 Giulia Belletti and Saturno Carnoli, *L'Ardito: Vita provocatoria di Ferruccio Vecchi, Ravennate, fondatore del fascismo*, Edizioni Moderna, Ravenna, 2013, p. 23.

52 'Il gen. Andrea Graziani muore cadendo dal treno', *Corriere della Sera*, 28 February 1931.

53 'Fatale concatenazione di circostanze nel drama del gen. Graziani', *Corriere della Sera*, 2 March 1931.

54 'Gli imponenti funerali di Verona', *Corriere della Sera*, 3 March 1931.

55 Giovanna Procacci, 'The Disaster of Caporetto', in John Dickie et al. (eds), *Disastro! Disasters in Italy since 1860: Culture, Politics and Society*, Palgrave, New York, 2002, pp. 141–65.

56 Franca Pieroni Bortolotti, *Francesco Misiano: Vita di un internazionalista*, Riuniti, Rome, 1972, p. 107 (7 December 1919).

57 Atti Parlamentari: Camera dei Deputati, Tornata di sabato 10 luglio 1920, https://storia.camera.it/regno/lavori/leg25/sed053.pdf; Ente per la storia del socialismo e del movimento operaio italiano, Fondazione Giuseppe Emanuele e Vera Modigliani, ESSMOI, *Attività parlamentare dei socialisti italiani*, volume sesto, 1919–21, Edizioni ESSMOI, Rome, 1989, p. 144.

58 Gaetano Arfé in D. Cherubini et al. (eds), *Giuseppe Emanuele l'altro Modigliani. Pace, Europa e Libertà. Mostra storico documentaria, Roma-Livorno (Ottobre-Dicembre 1997)*, Fratelli Palombi Editori, Rome, 1997, p. 12.

59 Antonio Casali, 'Il "marchese di Caporetto", Claudio Treves e l'interventismo di sinistra', *Italia contemporanea*, September 1990, 180, pp. 481–504.

60 Giuseppe Modigliani, Archivio Centrale dello Stato, Casellario Politico Centrale (ACS, CPC), 3327.

61 Ibid. See also the account in Paul O'Brien, *Mussolini in the First World War: the Journalist, the Soldier, the Fascist*, Berg, Oxford, 2005, p. 181, and the article by Benito Mussolini in Edoardo and Duilio Susmel (eds), *Opera Omnia*, X, La Fenice, Florence, 1955, pp. 137–9.

62 Francesco Ciccotti, 'L'estrema socialista, profili ed episodi', *Avanti!*, 6 January 1914, in *Giuseppe Emanuele l'altro Modigliani*, p. 83.

63 ACS, CPC, 800.

64 Ibid.

65 Ercole Bucco, *Le ragioni dell'opposizione socialista alla guerra*, CdL di Cento, Cento, 1914.

66 Tommaso Detti, 'Bucco Ercole', in T. Detti, F. Andreucci (eds), *Il movimento operaio italiano. Dizionario biografico 1853–1943*, Riuniti, Rome, 1975, p. 409.

67 Portelli, *Biography of an Industrial Town*, p. 98.

68 In ibid.

69 Mario Isnenghi, 'L'esposizione della morte', in Gabriele Ranzato (ed.), *Guerre fratricide: Le guerre civili in età contemporanea*, Bollati Boringhieri,

Turin, 1994, p. 332; https://sicilians.it/il-confino-messinese-di-giacomo-matteotti-18031.

70 Richard Collier, *Duce! The Rise and Fall of Benito Mussolini*, Collins, London, 1971, p. 72.

71 http://www.treccani.it/enciclopedia/giacomo-matteotti_(Dizionario-Biografico)/ (ACS, CPC 3157).

72 Cited in Benito Mussolini, *My Autobiography*, Paternoster Library, London, 1936, p. 203.

73 *Lotta di Classe*, 2 July 1910; Gaudens Megaro, *Mussolini in the Making*, Houghton and Mifflin Company, Boston and New York, 1938, p. 253.

74 See O'Brien, *Mussolini in the First World War*.

75 Harry Fornari, *Mussolini's Gadfly. Roberto Farinacci*, Vanderbilt UP, Nashville, 1971, p. 3.

76 Fornari, *Mussolini's Gadfly*, p. 19.

1919

1 'Fasci d'azione fra interventisti', *Corriere della Sera*, 24 March 1919.

2 *L'Ardito*, 11 May 1919, cited in Belletti and Carnoli, *L'Ardito*, p. 19.

3 Ibid., p. 22.

4 Vincenzo Mantovani, *Mazurka blu: La strage di Diana*, Rusconi, Milan, 1979, p. 62; Filippo Tommaso Marinetti, *Taccuini. 1915–1921*, Il Mulino, Bologna, 1987, p. 415.

5 Belletti and Carnoli, *L'Ardito*, p. 29.

6 Jonathan Dunnage, *The Italian Police and the Rise of Fascism: a case study of the province of Bologna, 1897–1925*, Praeger, Westport/London, 1997; *Mussolini's Policemen: Behaviour, ideology and institutional culture in representation and practice*, Manchester University Press, Manchester, 2012.

7 Paolo Valera, *Giacinto Menotti Serrati, direttore dell'Avanti!*, La Folla, Milan, 1920: http://www.intratext.com/IXT/ITA3216/_P3.HTM.

8 Ibid.

9 *Storia di quattro anni. 1919–1922. Crisi del dopoguerra e avvento del fascismo al potere*, Einaudi, Turin, 1946, p. 28.

10 Antonio Gramsci, 'Il compagno G. M. Serrati e le generazioni del socialismo italiano', *L'Unità*, 14 May 1926, cited in Tommaso Detti, *Serrati e la formazione del Partito comunista italiano: Storia della frazione terzinternazionalista, 1921–1924*, Riuniti, Rome, 1972, p. xxii.

11 Angelo Rossi, *The Rise of Italian Fascism 1918–1922*, Methuen and Co. Ltd, London, 1938, pp. 17, 19.

12 Unpublished manuscript, no date, p. 68.

13 'La cronaca degli avvenimenti', *Avanti!*, 7 July 1919.

14 'L'affermazione socialista di fronte al monarca. Il Proletariato, a mezzo dei suoi rappresentanti, grida: Viva il Socialismo!', *Avanti!*, 2 December 1919.

15 'Il Re inaugura la nuova Legislatura tra imponenti dimostrazioni. I problemi dell'ora prospettati nel discorso della Corina. Il gesto dei socialisti', *Corriere della Sera*, 2 December 1919: 'L'affermazione socialista di fronte al monarca'.

16 Carlo Longhini, *Le giornate rosse: 1919 a Mantova. Storia di una sollevazione popolare e storie di rivoluzionari senza rivoluzione*, Editoriale Sometti, Cremona, 2009.

17 For the memory wars around the First World War in Italy, see John Foot, *Italy's Divided Memory*, Palgrave Macmillan, New York, 2011; 'Guerre delle memorie nelle esperienze europee. Italia, Gran Bretagna e Irlanda a confronto', in Adolf Mignemi (ed.), *'Nessuno potrà tenersi in disparte'*, *La Grande Guerra: Memoria, territorio, documentazione*, interlinea edizioni, Novara, 2009, pp. 85–114.

18 For his life see http://www.treccani.it/enciclopedia/giuseppe-massarenti_(Dizionario-Biografico)/; and Matteo Poli, *Giuseppe Massarenti. Una vita per i più deboli*, Marsilio, Venice, 2008; Giorgio Vecchietti, 'Gli scioperi del "Diavolo"', *La Stampa*, 3 December 1948.

19 Lucilla Antonelli, *Il santo della palude. Biografia di Giuseppe Massarenti*, dall'Oglio editore, Varese, 1953, p. 17.

20 Gianna Mazzoni, *Un uomo, una città. Giuseppe Massarenti a Molinella*, Bologna: Coop Il Nove, 1990, p. 76. See also: *Molinella. Alle fonti della fede con lettera di G. Massarenti*, Ufficio stampa del Partito Socialista Unitario, Rome, Morara, 1924; Anthony Cardoza, *Agrarian Elites and Italian Fascism: the Province of Bologna, 1901–1926*, Princeton University Press, Princeton, 2014, pp. 214–16.

21 *Molinella, Alle fonti della fede*, p. 18.

22 On the strikes and demands in this period, and the role of Massarenti see: Cardoza, *Agrarian Elites and Italian Fascism*, pp. 275–7.

23 Mario Missiroli, *La repubblica dei accattoni*, Bologna, 1916. Missiroli later wrote a letter to Massarenti apologising for this book, see N. S. Onofri, *Il triangolo rosso: La guerra degli liberazione e la sconfitta del fascismo (1943–1947)*, Sapere, Rome, 2000, pp. 152–3.

24 *Il fascismo e la crisi italiana*, Bologna, 1921, p. 28, cited in Renzo De Felice, *Mussolini il rivoluzionario: 1883–1920*, Einaudi, Turin, 1965, p. 613.

25 For Altobelli see Silvia Bianciardi, *Argentina Altobelli e 'la buona battaglia'*, FrancoAngeli, Milan, 2013; Nadia Ciani, *Fuori da un secolare servaggio: Vita di Argentina Altobelli*, Ediesse, 2011; A. Albertazzi, L. Arbizzani, N. S. Onofri (eds), *Gli antifascisti, i partigiani e le vittime*

del fascismo nel bolognese (1919–1945): http://www.iperbole.bologna.it/ iperbole/isrebo/strumenti/strumenti.php.

26 http://www.enciclopediadelledonne.it/biografie/argentina-bonetti-altobelli/.

27 Bologna, Camera di Lavoro di Cento, 1919. For Bucco see: Steven Forti, 'L'operaio ha fatto tutto; e l'operaio può distruggere tutto, perché tutto può rifare', *Storicamente*, 2, 2006: http://storicamente.org/02forti.

28 *Chi non lavora non mangi*, Bologna, Camera del Lavoro di Cento, 1919.

29 Cited in Mimmo Franzinelli, *Squadristi: Protagonisti e tecniche della violenza fascista*, Mondadori, Milan, 2003, p. 64.

30 Forti, 'L'operaio ha fatto tutto', p. 17; see also: Steven Forti, ' "Tutto il potere ai Soviet!" Il dibattito sulla costituzione dei Soviet nel socialismo italiano del biennio rosso: una lettura critica dei testi', *Storicamente*, 4 (2008).

31 Ercole Bucco, 'I consigli a Bologna', *L'Ordine Nuovo*, 21 February 1920.

32 Cited in Giampietro Berti, *Errico Malatesta e il movimento anarchico italiano e internazionale, 1872–1932*, FrancoAngeli, Milan, 2003, p. 649.

33 Armando Borghi, cited in Mantovani, *Mazurka blu*, p. 156.

34 In Merli, *Autodifese*, p. 160.

35 Portelli, *Biography of an Industrial Town*, p. 96.

36 Ibid.

37 For Malatesta as a speaker see: Giovanni Contini, 'Il comizio', in Mario Isnenghi (ed.), *I luoghi della memoria. Strutture ed eventi dell'Italia unita*, Laterza, Rome, 1997, pp. 180–1, and Carl Levy, 'Errico Malatesta and Charismatic Leadership', in J.-W. Stutje (ed.), *Charisma and Emergent Social Movements*, Berghahn: Oxford/New York, 2012, pp. 89–90.

38 23 April 1920, cited in Philip V. Cannistraro, 'Mussolini, Sacco-Vanzetti, and the Anarchists: the Transatlantic Context', *Journal of Modern History*, 68, 1, 1996, p. 37.

39 Finzi, *La nota persona: Errico Malatesta*, p. 65.

A SECOND RED YEAR: 1920

1 Giorgio Alberto Chiurco, *Storia della rivoluzione fascista: 1919–1922*, Vol. II (1920), Vallecchi Editore, Florence, 1929, p. 168, vol 1, p. 111. See also: Pietro Alberghi, *Il fascismo in Emilia-Romagna: Dalle origini alla marcia su Roma*, Mucchi, Modena, pp. 170–3. The Catholic newspaper *L'Avvenire d'Italia* referred ironically to 'His Majesty Bucco the 1st', p. 171.

2 Portelli, *Biography of an Industrial Town*, p. 104.

3 Riziero Montesi in ibid. These words, however, are not to be found in the official version of the parliamentary debates around the massacre where Farini spoke: https://storia.camera.it/regno/lavori/leg25/sed047.pdf.

4 Paolo Spriano, *The Occupation of the Factories: Italy 1920*, Pluto Press, London, 1975.

5 Ercole Bucco, 'Giolitti', *La Squilla*, 19 June 1920, cited in Forti, 'L'operaio', p. 16.

6 'Uomini in carne e ossa', *L'Ordine Nuovo*, 8 May 1921, cited in Gwyn Williams, *Proletarian Order: Antonio Gramsci, Factory Councils and the Origins of Communism in Italy 1911–1921*, Pluto Press, London, 1975, p. 308.

BLACK YEARS: 1920–21

1 Belletti and Carnoli, *L'Ardito*, p. 31.

2 Marco Fincardi, 'Contro il "nemico interno": la gioventù squadrista', in Mario Isnenghi and Giulia Albanese (eds), *Gli italiani in guerra: Conflitti, identità, memorie dal Risorgimento ai nostri giorni*, Vol. IV, Tomo 1, *Il Ventennio fascista. Dall'impresa di Fiume alla Seconda guerra mondiale (1919–1940)*, UTET, Turin, 2008, pp. 94–101.

3 See also: Victoria De Grazia, *The Perfect Fascist. A Story of Love, Power and Morality in Mussolini's Italy*, Harvard University Press, Cambridge MA, 2020, pp. 67–8.

4 Simona Colarizi, *Dopoguerra e fascismo in Puglia (1919–1926)*, Laterza, Bari, 1971, p. 28.

5 Colarizi, *Dopoguerra e fascismo in Puglia (1919–1926)*, p. 16.

6 Frank Snowden, *Violence and Great Estates in the South of Italy. Apulia, 1900–1922*, CUP, Cambridge, 1986, p. 175.

7 Ibid., p. 3.

8 Ibid., p. 167.

9 Ibid., p. 182.

10 Ibid., p. 178.

11 Colarizi, *Dopoguerra e fascismo*, p. 141.

12 He was the 'sole fascist deputy elected in the entire south of Italy' in 1921: Luzzatto, *Padre Pio: Miracoli e politica nell'Italia del Novecento*, Einaudi, Turin, 2007, p. 116.

13 Balbo 'pioneered the tactics of agrarian *squadrismo* (squad violence): selective murder, beatings, force-feeding of castor oil to political opponents, ritual humiliation, and arson', Ebner, *Ordinary Violence*, p. 9.

14 Pieroni Bortolotti, *Francesco Misiano*, p. 107.

15 'La Camera approva la domanda a procedere per diserzione contro l'on. Misiano', *La Stampa*, 11 July 1920.

16 *Atti Parlamentari, Tornata di sabato 10 luglio 1920*: https://storia.camera.it/regno/lavori/leg25/sed053.pdf.

17 Francesco Misiano, *Il Disertore: Discorso pronunziato alla Camera dei Deputati da Francesco Misiano*, a cura del Partito Comunista d'Italia, Milan, 1921.

18 *Atti Parlamentari, Tornata di sabato 10 luglio 1920*, pp. 3146–7: https://storia.camera.it/regno/lavori/leg25/sed053.pdf.

19 Ibid.

20 In an appeal to his private circumstances, Misiano also described how he had been separated from his young children: 'I am your victim. You haven't taken my body, but you have crushed my soul, you have separated me from my children for three years and nine months, with your impositions and your laws … I found one who was four years old who did not know me and who I did not know.'

21 https://storia.camera.it/regno/lavori/leg25/sed053.pdf p. 3157.

22 *Atti Parlamentari, Tornata di sabato 10 luglio 1920*, p. 3158.

23 Pieroni Bortolotti, *Francesco Misiano*, p. 113.

24 Ibid., p. 109.

25 This declaration was celebrated by fascism, Mussolini and D'Annunzio himself under the regime. D'Annunzio later (9 January 1923) wrote to Mussolini claiming that he had created 'what is best in the movement called "Fascist" … are my concise orders dealing with the deserter Misiano and my painful sacrifice during Bloody Christmas', cited in Fernando Esposito, *Fascism, Aviation and Mythical Modernity*, Springer, New York, 2015, p. 82.

26 Pieroni Bortolotti, *Francesco Misiano*, p. 113; see also: D'Annunzio on Misiano in Chiurco, *Storia*, Vol. II, p. 101.

27 Mussolini, *Opera Omnia*, Vol. XVI, p. 274.

28 'La persecuzione di Francesco Misiano', *Incontri meridionali*, 5 (No. 1), 1985, now in Nando Marzano, Fortunato Nocera, *Francesco Misiano: Il pacifista che portava in valigia la Corazzata Potemkin*, Città del sole, Reggio Calabria, 2009, p. 109.

29 However, in one of the photos the sign appears to have a different slogan, ending with the word 'Bombacci' (another communist, and colleague of Misiano). This attack was captured in a series of photos taken by Adolfo Porry-Pastorel, a pioneer of newspaper photography and an inspiration to Rome's paparazzi, who became world famous in the 1950s and 1960s: Vania Colasanti, *Scatto matto: La stravagante vita di Adolfo Porry-Pastorel, il padre dei fotoreporter italiani*, Marsilio, Venice, 2013. Stefano Mannucci identifies

these photos as taken in via del Corso in Rome in June 1921: 'La fotografia dell'Istituto Luce. Storia e critica', 2014, p. 3; see also: http://senato.archi violuce.it/senato-luce/scheda/foto/IL0000009926/10/Il-deputato-comuni sta-Francesco-Misiano-messo-alla-berlina-dagli-squadristi.html; Massimo Firpo and Pier Giorgio Zunino, *La storia e le sue immagini: Istituzioni, società, costume*, Garzanti, Milan, 2003, p. 121.

30   http://www.treccani.it/vocabolario/berlina1/.

31   Renzo De Felice (ed.), *Dino Grandi. Il mio paese. Ricordi autobiografici*, Il Mulino, Bologna, 1985, p. 119.

32   Parlamento, 22 July 1920, https://storia.camera.it/regno/lavori/leg25/sed 063.pdf; Franzinelli, *Squadristi*, p. 293.

33   'Il coraggio e la paura. Emozioni e violenza politica nell'Italia del primo dopoguerra', in Penelope Morris, Francesco Ricatti and Mark Seymour (eds), *Politica ed emozioni nella storia d'Italia dal 1848 ad oggi*, Viella, Rome, 2012, p. 102.

34   See 'Depositi di armi e esplosivi sequestrati a Bologna', *La Stampa*, 6 November 1920; 'Un vero arsenale sequestrato alla Camera del Lavoro di Bologna', *Corriere della Sera*, 6 November 1920. It seems the police also took part in this destruction, which was not as complete as that linked to later attacks in 1921 and afterwards; see for one version: *Fascismo: Inchiesta Socialista sulle gesta dei fascisti in Italia*, Edizione Avanti, Milan, 1963, pp. 266–8.

35   Cited in Giacomo De Marzi, *I canti del fascismo*, Fratelli Frilli, Genoa, 2009, p. 112.

36   Nazario Sauro Onofri, 'L'eccidio di Palazzo d'Accursio il 21 novembre 1920', *Avanti!*, 20 November 1970.

37   Federico Saladini Pilastri, *L'eccidio di Palazzo d'Accursio (21 novembre 1920)*, PhD, University of Bologna, 2014–15, p. 51.

38   He was not the candidate who had received the highest number of votes in the election (he won 19,661 preference votes, coming twenty-first out of those socialists elected).

39   Enrico Pontieri, *Piccole sovversioni quotidiane. Strategie di controllo del territorio e tattiche di resistenza in un quartiere popolare bolognese durante il fascismo*, PhD, University of Bologna, 2018, p. 79. There is some confusion as to Gnudi's name – Enio or Ennio? The latter is used in many accounts, although the former seems to be the most accurate in terms of birth certificates and the like, p. 79, n.249. Sometimes contemporary newspapers also referred to him as Enrico.

40   *Atti del Consiglio Comunale di Bologna Anno 1920*, Bologna, Cooperative Tipografica Azzoguidi, 1925, p. 664.

41 'My thoughts, at this time, are with the memory of a man who is no longer with us: Erminio Zucchini', https://www.bibliotecasalaborsa.it/cronologia/bologna/1920/gli_incidenti_del_casermone; http://www.comune.bologna.it/storiaamministrativa/documenti/oggetti/338584/1; *Atti del Consiglio Comunale di Bologna Anno 1920*, p. 664.

42 Cited in Brunella dalla Casa, 'Il movimento operaio e socialista a Bologna dall'occupazione delle fabbriche al Patto di pacificazione', *La Squilla*, 4 September, 1920, in Luciano Casali et al., *Movimento operaio e fascismo nell'Emilia-Romagna 1919–1923*, Editori Riuniti, Rome, 1973, p. 20.

43 *Atti del Consiglio Comunale di Bologna Anno 1920*, p. 664.

44 'Numerous white doves were freed from the main balcony of the town hall with small red flags attached to their tails', N. S. Onofri, *La strage di palazzo d'Accursio: Origine e nascita del socialismo bolognese*, Feltrinelli, Milan, 1980, p. 274.

45 'Nuovo rinvio di due settimane del processo per l'eccidio di Bologna', *Corriere della Sera*, 14 January 1923.

46 There is some debate as to who performed this removal. Some versions claim that it was a fascist called Giovanni Battista Berardi who would later be appointed as the unelected appointed mayor of the city in 1930. The symmetry of this reversal of roles is perhaps too neat.

47 These descriptions are based on the minutes, which are not entirely reliable (to say the least) given that they were written up some time after the events in question, and after fascism had come to power, http://www.comune.bologna.it/storiaamministrativa/documenti/oggetti/338584/3; *Atti del Consiglio Comunale, Anno 1920*. The volume (published in 1925, but the notes are dated 1 December 1922) called 21 November 1920 'ominous' and 'tragic' and demanded 'exemplary punishment for [Giordani's] disgraceful murderers', p. 667. The minutes were compiled from 'notes' and 'newspaper reports'.

48 Saladini Pilastri, *L'eccidio di palazzo d'Accursio 1920*, p. 63.

49 'La scena dell'eccidio a Palazzo d'Accursio', *Corriere della Sera*, 6 February 1923. Bentini was critical of both Martelli and Cocchi in his testimony to the court in Milan.

50 Ibid.

51 *Il Resto del Carlino*, 22 November 1920; for the legend of the 'missing copies', see: Onofri, *La strage*, p. 287.

52 See for example the account in Dunnage, *The Italian Police and the Rise of Fascism*, pp. 104–8.

53 Sergio Zavoli, *Nascita di una dittatura*, Società editrice internazionale, Turin, 1973, p. 88.

54 Onofri, *La strage*, p. 290.

55 Masetti today has a street named after him. Biographical information from http://www.iperbole.bologna.it/iperbole/isrebo/strumenti/strume nti.php.

56 Francesco Berti Arnoladi, 'Prefazione', in Luciano Casali, *Bologna 1920: le origini del fascismo*, nuova universale cappelli, Bologna, 1982, p. 5.

57 Saldini Pilastri, *L'eccidio di Palazzo d'Accursio*, p. 61.

58 *Padre Pio: Miracles and Politics in a Secular Age*, Henry Holt and Company, New York, 2010, p. 84.

59 Luigi Federzoni, *Presagi alla nazione: discorsi politica a cura del Fascio romano di combattimento*, Imperia, Milan, 1924, p. 175.

60 Antonio Scurati, *M. Il figlio del secolo*, Bompiani, Milan, 2018, p. 270.

61 For the exhibition see: *Guida della Mostra della Rivoluzione Fascista*, Stabilimenti Grafici Vallecchi, Florence, 1932; PNF, Dino Alfieri and Luigi Freddi (eds), *Mostra della Rivoluzione Fascista, Guida storica, 1 Decennale della Marcia su Roma*, Officine dell'Istituto Italiano d'Arti Grafiche di Bergamo, Rome, 1933; Jeffrey Schnapp, *Anno X: La Mostra della Rivoluzione Fascista del 1932*, Istituti Editoriali e Poligrafici Internazionali, Pisa-Rome, 2003. Photos of the sections dedicated to Giordani can be seen online at: http://dati.acs.beniculturali.it/MRF/. Giordani's 'relics' had already been donated to a local museum in Bologna by his wife, in 1926: Andrea Spicciarelli, https://www.storiaememoriadibologna.it/giordani-giulio-519 509-persona.

62 Rossi, *The Rise of Italian Fascism*: 'The era of violence, reprisals and "punitive expeditions" had begun', p. 101.

63 'Il corteo fascista in onore della vedova Giordani', *Corriere della Sera*, 29 January 1923.

64 De Felice (ed.), *Dino Grandi. Il mio paese*, p. 112.

65 https://www.bibliotecasalaborsa.it/cronologia/bologna/1920/leccidio_d i_palazzo_daccursio#top.

66 Between May and December 1923, 368 councils were dissolved, plus ten provincial councils: Alberto Aquarone, *L'organizzazione dello Stato totalitario*, Einaudi, Turin, 1965, pp. 35–6.

67 Scurati, *M. Il figlio del secolo*, p. 269.

68 'Arresti di socialisti a Bologna', *Corriere della Sera*, 23 November 1920.

69 'L'inchiesta per i fatti di Bologna', *Corriere della Sera*, 26 November 1920.

70 'Further credence was given to the theory of a socialist attack when a number of reformist socialists resigned from the council in order to dissociate themselves from Giordani's murder', Dunnage, *The Italian Police and the Rise of Fascism*, p. 104.

71 Luciano Casali, 'Fascisti, Repubblicani e Socialisti in Romagna nel 1922. La "conquista" di Ravenna', in *Movimento di Liberazione in Italia*, 93, October–December 1968, p. 12.

72 Onofri, *La strage*, pp. 292, 313.

73 See, for example, the similar events in nearby Ferrara in December 1920, Paul Corner, *Fascism in Ferrara 1915–1925*, OUP, Oxford, 1975, pp. 116–22.

74 'Discorso pronunciato a Bologna il 3 aprile 1921', *Il Popolo d'Italia*, 5–6 April 1921.

75 'L'on. Bucco assediato in un bar a Bologna', *Corriere della Sera*, 18 January 1921.

76 'L'on. Bucco bloccato dai fascisti', *Il Resto del Carlino*, 18 January 1921. For Arpinati's cellar see Onofri, *La strage*, p. 257.

77 *Atti Parlamentari, Camera dei Deputati*, 21 December 1920, p. 6880.

78 Onofri, *La strage*, p. 303. This label of the 'moral killer' or 'moral instigator' linked to Giulio Giordani and his death followed Zanardi right through to the 1930s and 1940s. Official reports claimed that the ex-mayor, Zanardi, 'moved to Rome after the rise of fascism, given the difficulties he had to stay in Bologna, especially after the martyrdom of Giulio Giordani, the mere memory of which offended fascist sentiment[;] an event in which Zanardi was not a protagonist but the main actor [sic]', 'Zanardi, Francesco', 'Sovversivi', Archivio di Stato di Bologna, *Questura di Bologna, Gabinetto, Sovversivi*, Il prefetto al Ministero del'interno, 21 January 1938.

79 Onofri, *La strage*, p. 303.

1921

1 Cited in Angelica Balabanoff, *My Life as a Rebel*, Hamish Hamilton, London, 1938, p. 341.

2 *L'Assalto*, 19 March 1921.

3 De Felice (ed.), *Dino Grandi*, p. 119.

4 See Pontieri, *Piccole sovversioni quotidiane*, p. 199.

5 In October 1922 the Socialist Party split again after the expulsion of the leading reformist Turati.

6 Gnudi was elected but his election could not be confirmed as he was below the legal age for a deputy at the time.

7 http://www.pertini.it/turati/Matteotti90_antologia_Fascismo.pdf. For fascism in the Polesine, see Michelangelo Bellinetti, *Squadrismo di provincia. Nascista dei fasci di combattimento in Polesine (1920–1921)*, Minelliana, Rovigo, 1985; Valentino Zaghi, *L'eroica viltà. Socialismo e fascismo nelle campagne del Polesine, 1919–1926*, FrancoAngeli, Milan, 1989;

Lorenzo Pavanello, *Il processo Burletta. Un omicidio impunito*, Ilmiolibro, (self-publication), 2016.

8   Gino Beri, 'Tipi del mondo "rosso"', *Corriere della Sera*, 11 February 1921; Antonio Spinosa, *Mussolini: Il fascino di un dittatore*, Mondadori, Milan, 2017, Kindle location 2456.

9   'Comica avventura dell'on. Misiano', *Corriere della Sera*, 30 March 1921.

10 Only two weeks earlier, Lavagnini had been present at the setting up of the Communist Party in Empoli. Now, he was dead – executed while working on his newspaper in the centre of Florence. For more details see Pier Vittorio Orlandini (ed.), *Vita ed attività politica di Spartaco Lavagnini: nel quadro dei drammatici avvenimenti degli anni 1920–1921. Raccolta di articoli pubblicati in vari giornali degli anni 1920, 1921, 1981, e di alcune pagine tratte dal romano 'Lo scialo' di Vasco Pratolini*, n.p., 2014.

11 It appears as if the whole operation had already been called off, but nobody managed to get the message through to the sailors: see the account in 'I fatti del '21 dividono la città', *Il Tirreno*, 2 March 2008.

12 Paolo Pezzino, 'I fatti del 1 Marzo 1921', in Paolo Pezzino (ed.), *Empoli antifascista. I fatti del 1 marzo 1921: La clandestinità e la Resistenza*, Pacini, Comune di Empoli, Pisa, 2007, p. 53.

13 This seemed to be true of Renzino as well.

14 Pezzino, 'I fatti del 1 Marzo 1921', p. 53.

15 Rossi, *The Rise of Italian Fascism*, p. 115.

16 https://empolinostra.wordpress.com.

17 If we exclude the bombing of the Diana Theatre.

18 Speech to parliament, 8 March 1921, https://storia.camera.it/regno/lavori/leg25/sed171.pdf.

19 Similar tropes could be seen in the reporting, the investigation and trial with regard to the facts of Renzino in 1921.

20 This chimed with similar (and presumably also mythical) stories of cannibalism from Renzino.

21 'I fatti del '21 dividono le città', *Il Tirreno*, 3 February 2008.

22 See John Foot, *Pedalare! Pedalare! A History of Italian Cycling*, Bloomsbury, London, 2011, pp. 24–31; Lucio Fabi, *Enrico Toti: Una storia tra mito e realtà*, Persico, Cremona, 2005.

23 Federico Ciavattone, 'L'eccidio di Empoli nella pubblicistica fascista', in Pezzino (ed.), *Empoli antifascista*, p. 286.

24 Ibid.

25 Roberto Cantagalli, *Storia del fascismo fiorentino, 1919–1925*, Vallecchi Editore, Florence, 1972, p. 190.

26 Jaurès Busoni, *Confinati a Lipari*, Vangelista, Milan, 1980, pp. 76–7.

27 *L'Umanità Nova*, 10 August 1920, cited in Mantovani, *Mazurka blu*, p. 258; for the Cova and Milan's fascists, see also: De Grazia, *The Perfect Fascist*, for example: pp. 95, 113, 115, 121, 122, and Ernest Hemingway's account of the Cova, 'In Another Country', in *Hemingway on War*, Simon & Schuster, New York, 2012, p. 33.

28 For the history of this tactic in Italy see Carl Levy, 'The Anarchist Assassin and Italian History, 1870s to 1930s', in Stephen Gundle and Lucia Rinaldi (eds), *Assassinations and Murder in Modern Italy: Transformations in Society and Culture*, Palgrave, London, 2007, pp. 207–23.

29 See Marco Albeltaro, *29 luglio 1900*, Laterza, Rome, 2019, and John Foot, 'Quando l'anarchico uccise il re', *Internazionale*, 717, 2/8 November 2007.

30 10 August 1920 cited in Mantovani, *Mazurka blu*, p. 258.

31 'Una bomba in piazza della Scala a Milano', *La Stampa*, 26 June 1920.

32 Mantovani, *Mazurka blu*, p. 259.

33 He had been arrested in February 1920 in Tombolo near Livorno while on a train, and released almost immediately (workers in that area had immediately gone on strike in protest).

34 'Il caso Malatesta' (March 23, 1921) in Mussolini, *Opera Omnia*, Vol. 1, pp. 252–3; Mantovani, *Mazurka blu*, p. 388.

35 Fabrizio Giulietti, *Gli anarchici italiani dalla grande guerra al fascismo*, FrancoAngeli, Milan, 2015, p. 151.

36 Comitato Anarchico Pro Vittime Politiche (ed.), *Il processo agli anarchici nell'Assise di Milano. 9 maggio-1 giugno 1922*, G. Zingales, Milan, 1922, p. 20.

37 Butta, *Living Like Nomads*, p. 222, http://ebookcentral.proquest.com/lib/bristol/detail.action?docID=4534713.

38 Bruno Filippi was just nineteen at the time; see Mantovani, *Mazurka blu*, pp. 107–13.

39 Comitato Anarchico Pro Vittime Politiche (ed.), *Il processo agli anarchici nell'assise di Milano*, p. 36.

40 An extraordinary book was based upon the Diana bombing and the events surrounding it: Vincenzo Mantovani's *Mazurka blu*, first published in 1979 and reissued in almost identical form in 2007. Mantovani's narrative style and deep research combined to extraordinary effect in this text which remains an inspiration to this author and a model of narrative history to this day. A TV film, *L'ultima Mazurka* (1986), was also produced based upon the Diana events (but is unavailable today). See also: *L'attentato al Diana: Processo agli anarchici nell'assise di Milano*, Napoleone, Rome, 1973; Giuseppe Mariani, *Memorie di un ex-terrorista. Dall'attentato al "Diana" all'ergastolo di Santo Stefano*, Ultima Spiaggia, Genoa, 2009; Giuseppe Mariani, *Nel mondo degli*

ergastoli, Arti Grafiche F.lli Garino, Turin, 1954; Giuseppe Galzerano (ed.), *Il processo agli anarchici nell'assise di Milano. 9 maggio-1 giugno 1922*, Napoleone, Rome, 1973; Comitato Anarchico Pro Vittime Politiche (ed.), *Il processo agli anarchici nell'Assise di Milano.*

41 Mantovani, *Mazurka blu*, pp. 552–3.

42 Vincenzo Mantovani, *Anarchici alla sbarra. La strage del Diana tra primo dopoguerra e fascismo*, Il Saggiatore, Milan, 2007 p. 456.

43 Mantovani, *Anarchici alla sbarra*, p. 456

44 'Tra la civiltà e la barbarie', *Corriere della Sera*, 25 March 1921; see also: 'Malatesta e i suoi compagni riprendono il cibo', *Corriere della Sera*, 25 March 1921.

45 Cited in Mantovani, *Mazurka blu*, p. 448; see also: Antonio Orlando, 'L'attentato al "Diana" del marzo 1921. Gramsci, gli anarchici e gli esordi politico-forensi di Leonida Répaci', *Studi e ricerche, Rivista calabrese di storia del '900*, 1–2, 2009, pp. 61–2.

46 'Le dodici salme al Monumentale', *Corriere della Sera*, 25 March 1921, 'Scoppio di una bomba e orrenda strage al Teatro Diana di Milano', *Corrierodella Sera*, 24 March 1921. A second edition was brought out that evening of the *Corriere*, with a slightly different title: 'L'orrenda strage al Teatro Diana', *Corriere della Sera*, 24 March 1921. See also: 'Attorno alle salme martoriate', *Corriere della Sera*, 26 March 1921.

47 See also: De Grazia, *The Perfect Fascist*, pp. 23–4.

48 'Il popolo di Milano in un impeto di pietà rende imponenti onoranze alle vittime del "Diana"', *La Stampa*, 29 March 1921. For the debates and the ceremony, see also: 'I funerali fissati per domenica', *Corriere della Sera*, 27 March 1921; 'Il solenne pietoso omaggio di Milano alle vittime dell'attentato', *Corriere della Sera*, 29 March 1921; 'I grandiosi funerali alle vittime del delitto anarchico', *Corriere della Sera*, 28 March 1921.

49 For descriptions of the funeral, see: Mantovani, *Mazurka blu*, and the press of the time, for example: 'Il popolo di Milano in un impeto di pietà', *La Stampa*, 29 March 1921.

50 'La morale', cited in Salvatore Mannino, *Una domenica di sangue. I "fatti di Renzino" fra storia e mito*, Il Mulino, Bologna, 2011, p. 50 (originally in *Il Popolo d'Italia*, 19 April 1921).

51 Cited in Mannino, *Una domenica di sangue*, p. 142.

52 For the *spedizioni*, see: Marco Fincardi, 'I riti della conquista', in *Regime e società civile a Reggio Emilia 1920–1946*, Mucchi, Modena, 1988, pp. 7–137, and 'La spedizione punitiva: conquista e sottomissione del territorio', in Mario Isnenghi, Giulia Albanese, *Gli italiani in guerra. Conflitti, identità, memorie dal Risorgimento ai nostri giorni*, Vol. IV, Tomo 1, UTET, Turin,

2008, pp. 310–17; Matteo Millan, *Squadrismo e squadristi nella dittatura fascista*, Viella, Rome, 2014.

53 *La Giustizia* cited in Fincardi, 'I riti della conquista', p. 31.

54 For these events, and their interpretation, see Mannino, *Una domenica di sangue* and Giorgio Sacchetti, *L'imboscata Foiano della Chiana 1921: un episodio di guerriglia sociale*, Arti tipografiche toscane, Cortona, 2000 and *Sovversivi e squadristi. 1921: alle origini della guerra civile in provincia di Arezzo*, Aracne, Rome, 2010. This section is based largely on the analysis of Mannino and Sacchetti.

55 'Undici morti nelle tragiche giornate di Foiano', *La Stampa*, 20 April 1921.

56 http://www.societastoricaretina.org/biografie/GGRoselliAldo17705 081.pdf.

57 See Sacchetti, *Sovversivi e squadristi*, pp. 135–48 for the fascist violence in response to the Renzino attack.

58 'Imboscate di comuniste contro fascisti', *La Stampa*, 18 April 1921.

59 Cited in Mannino, *Una domenica di sangue*, p. 41.

60 *La Nazione* in Florence was solidly behind Il Duce by January 1922, referring to his 'magnificent' ability to synthesise: 'Il "secondo tempo" della rivoluzione fascista in una magnifica sintesi dell'on. Mussolini', *La Nazione*, 9 January 1922.

61 'I sanguinosi episodi in Toscana', *La Stampa*, 19 April 1921.

62 Annalisa Galasso, *La violenza politica alle origini del fascismo nel Mezzogiorno*, http://www.sissco.it/download/attivita/Galasso.pdf.

63 Colarizi, *Dopoguerra e fascismo*, p. 156.

64 Official report cited in ibid., p. 160.

65 On 16 April 1921, see: Mimmo Franzinelli, *Squadristi. Protagonisti e tecniche della violenza fascista. 1919–1922*, Mondadori, Milan, 2003, p. 197; Mario Dilio, *Puglia antifascista*, Adda, Bari, 1971, p. 63. Vella had also been attacked outside parliament in Rome on 1 December 1919.

66 Colarizi, *Dopoguerra e fascismo*, p. 191.

67 Vera Modigliani cited in Aldo Santini, 'Quando le barbe erano antifasciste. Quella del livornese Modigliani venne considerata "eroica"', *Il Tirreno*, 15 December 1999. In 1920 the socialist deputy Giuseppe Reina told parliament what he had seen: 'I tried to get through to reach my friends thanks to the protection of the Royal Guards, and in the meantime Modigliani had been taken to a restaurant ... his head pouring with blood,' Franzinelli, *Squadristi*, p. 325. In other versions the train was stopped in the station during the attack.

68 Santini, 'Quando le barbe erano antifasciste'. See also the official fascist version: 'In Pisa station ... Modigliani was given a severe lesson,' Chiurco,

Storia, III, p. 247; Fabio Fabbri, *Le origini della guerra civile. L'Italia dalla Grande Guerra al fascismo*, UTET, Turin, 2009, p. 576; 'L'aggressione a Modigliani', *L'Ordine Nuovo*, 4 May 1921 and 'On the Pisa–Viareggio line the 19-year-old *squadrista* was shot (he would die the next day) and in revenge Modigliani, who was on the same train, was attacked', Franzinelli, *Squadristi*, p. 325.

69 Lucilla Antonelli, *Il santo della palude. Biografia di Giuseppe Massarenti*, dall'Oglio editore, Varese, 1953, p. 66. For Bentivogli see: https://www.stor iaememoriadibologna.it/bentivogli-giuseppe-478603-persona. Bentivogli, who played an active role in the resistance in the Second World War, was shot dead by fascists in Bologna the day the Allies entered the city in April 1945.

70 *Molinella. Alle fonti della fede con lettera di G. Massarenti*, Ufficio stampa del Partito Socialista Unitario, Morara, Rome, 1924, p. 13.

71 Review of Pieroni Bortolotti, *Francesco Misiano* (citing that book, p. 124) in *Il movimento di Liberazione in Italia*, 109, 1972, pp. 119–20. For Misiano, see also: Marzano and Nocera, *Francesco Misiano*. I have also looked at the material in ACS, CPC, b. 3315.

72 The sixteen included Bombacci and Ambrogio Belloni (who was also Misiano's lawyer on occasion).

73 Zama to Celsa Resta, 25 June 1945, cited in Luciano Forlani, *Imola tra le due guerre*, University Press Bologna, Imola, 1998, p. 127; see also: Frank Snowden, *The Fascist Revolution in Tuscany 1919–1922*, CUP, Cambridge, 1989, p. 158.

74 Some claim that that same day Misiano was shaved, threatened, kidnapped and marched through the streets by fascists, with a sign around his neck.

75 *Atti Parlamentari*, Camera dei Deputati, 13 June 1921, p. 3, https://storia. camera.it/regno/lavori/leg26/sed001.pdf.

76 Antonio Gramsci, 'Politica e delinquenza', in *L'Ordine Nuovo*, 14 June 1921, I, n.164, now, in *Socialismo e fascismo. L'Ordine Nuovo 1921–1922*, Einaudi, Turin, 1978, pp. 190–1.

77 Mario Piazzesi, *Diario di uno squadrista toscano, 1919–1922*, Bonacci Editore, Rome, 1980, p. 169.

78 Mussolini, *Opera Omnia*, Vol. XVI, pp. 418–19.

79 'Il nostro bersaglio Claudio Treves', *Il Fascio*, 15 August 1919, cited in Giorgio Fabre, *Mussolini razzista. Dal socialismo al fascismo: la formazione di un antisemita*, Garzanti, Milan, 2005, p. 350.

80 Filippo Turati, Anna Kuliscioff, *Carteggio, V, 1919–1922. Dopoguerra e fascismo*, Einaudi, Turin, 1977, p. 647.

81 Pio Donati, ACS, CPC, 107159.

82 ACS, CPC, 107159.

83 Enzo Levi in Nunzia Manicardi, *Formiggini. L'editore ebreo che si suicidò per restare italiano*, Guaraldi, Modena, 2001, p. 57.

84 Fabre argues that in this case 'the relationship … with anti-Semitism can be proved', *Mussolini razzista*, p. 364.

85 According to the prefect, 'he was seen as morally responsible by the fascists for various murders which have taken place', with reference in particular to 1921, ACS, CPC, 107159.

86 Claudio Silingardi, 'La memoria dei "martiri fascisti" a Modena: il caso di Duilio Sinigaglia', Istituto Storico di Modena, *Annale*, 2010, Modena, 2010, pp. 8–18; 'L'eccidio del 26 settembre 1921 e la memoria dei 'martiri fascisti' a Modena', Istituto mantovano di storia contemporanea (ed.), *Fascismo e antifascismo nella Valle Padana*, Clueb, Bologna, 2007, pp. 129–60.

87 Manicardi, *Formiggini*, p. 51.

88 Silingardi, 'L'eccidio del 26 settembre 1921 e la memoria dei "martiri fascisti" a Modena', p. 143.

89 Ibid., p. 11. Mussolini, it seems, saw the killings in Modena as a political response to the murder of Di Vagno in Mola di Bari.

90 http://www.toscananovecento.it/custom_type/13-aprile-1921-lassassinio-di-carlo-cammeo-segretario-della-federazione-socialista-di-pisa/?print=pdf.

91 Enzo Levi cited in Manicardi, *Formiggini*, p. 56.

92 'I arrived just in time for his last breath', De Felice (ed.), *Dino Grandi: Il mio paese*, p. 145.

93 'Il processo contro Misiano', *Corriere della Sera*, 20 November 1921.

94 'Misiano condannato a 10 anni', *Corriere della Sera*, 30 November 1921.

95 'Come Misiano è uscito dalla Camera. L'elezione contestata dalla Giunta', *Corriere della Sera*, 4 December 1921.

96 'La protesta nell'aula', *Corriere della Sera*, 4 December 1921.

97 Ibid.

98 Cited in Merli, *Autodifese*, p. 161.

99 *Processo agli anarchici*, p. 145.

100 Trento Tagliaferri, *Errico Malatesta, Armando Borghi e compagni davanti ai giurati di Milano*, Milan, 1921; now in Merli, *Autodifese*, pp. 160–4.

101 Mantovani, *Mazurka blu*, pp. 508–12.

102 In July 1921 a mysterious fire broke out in the archive of the *tribunale* (law courts) in Milan. It started in seven different places and damaged a number of files, including some of those relating to the Diana investigation. It appeared to be arson and newspapers claimed that

the intention of the arsonists was to eliminate the trace of specific investigations. It was said that a telegram to the police chief had warned of an attack on the judicial offices with relation to the Malatesta case. Suspicion fell on the anarchists. But most of the Diana material was saved and 'through a long and patient restoration of the burnt papers or those damaged by water, the work of the justice system was allowed to proceed normally', 'Gli incartamenti del processo del Diana', *Corriere della Sera*, 3 September 1921.

103 With two years of *sorveglianza speciale*. See also: 'Complotti terroristici venuti in luce a Milano', *La Stampa*, 20 April 1921. As they were led away in the December 1921 Cova trial, *La Stampa* claimed, the accused cried out 'Long Live Anarchy!' Mariani stated: 'my confession is an explicit and natural act of accusation against the bourgeoise', 'Cinque condanne e undici assolutorie nel processo per l'attentato al Cova', *La Stampa*, 24 December 1921; 'Le ultime battute del processo per l'attentato al Cova', *La Stampa*, 22 December 1921.

104 'Le condanne dei dinamitardi del Diana', *Corriere della Sera*, 2 June 1922.

105 Comitato Anarchico Pro Vittime Politiche (ed.), *Il processo agli anarchici nell'assise di Milano. 9 maggio–1 giugno 1922*, p. 32.

106 One of the defence witnesses was a young fascist called Mario Carità, who testified in favour of the anarchist Cesare Persivale. Carità would go on to become a leading fascist and during the war became notorious for the violence and torture his group inflicted on anti-fascist prisoners, 'Tumultuoso drammatico inizio del processo per la strage del "Diana"', *La Stampa*, 10 May 1922.

107 'La deposizione del Questore di Milano al processo per la strage del "Diana"', *La Stampa*, 19 May 1922.

108 'La tragica sfilata dei sopravvissuti nel processo per la strage del "Diana"', *La Stampa*, 13 May 1922.

109 See Antonio Orlando, 'L'attentato al "Diana" del marzo 1921', pp. 53–73. Répaci's nephew Antonino went on to write the classic account, in 1963, of the March on Rome.

110 See Orlando, 'L'attentato al "Diana"'.

111 Ibid., p. 68, also cited in Mantovani, *Anarchici alla sbarra*, p. 235.

112 'Tumultuoso drammatico inizio del processo per la strage del "Diana"', *La Stampa*, 10 May 1922.

113 Ibid.

114 'Fredda ferocia nelle confessioni dei due anarchici', *La Stampa*, 11 May 1922.

115 Cited in Orlando, 'L'attentato al "Diana"', p. 72.

116 For the trial see the press of the time, and specifically: 'Gli autori della strage del Diana compaiono oggi alle Assise milanesi', *La Stampa*, 9 May 1922.

117 Especially in comparison with the forthcoming D'Accursio and Empoli trials which would take place after Mussolini had taken power.

118 'L'ergastolo a Mariani e Boldrini. 30 anni ad Aguggini', *La Stampa*, 2 June 1922.

119 Maurizio Antonioli et al. (eds), *Dizionario biografico degli anarchici italiani, Volume secondo I–Z*, Biblioteca Franco Serantini, Pisa, 2004, 'Giuseppe Mariani', pp. 92–3. For the Ergastolo, see Antonio Parente, *L'Ergastolo in Santo Stefano di Ventotene: architettura e pena*, Ufficio Studi Dipartimento Amministrazione Penitenziaria, Ministero Della Giustizia, Rome, 2008. See also: Marco Ventura, *Il campione e il bandito. La vera storia di Costante Girardengo e Sante Pollastro*, Il Saggiatore, Milan, 2010.

120 Orlando, 'L'attentato al "Diana", p. 73; *Il Popolo d'Italia*, 10 May 1922.

121 Orlando, 'L'attentato al "Diana", p. 72.

122 In Merli, *Autodifese*, p. 161.

YEAR ZERO: 1922

1 Roberto Farinacci, *Squadrismo: Dal mio diario della vigilia 1919–1922*, Ardita, Rome, 1933.

2 Giuseppe Mayda, *Il pugnale di Mussolini: Storia di Amerigo Dumini, sicario di Mussolini*, Il Mulino, Bologna, 2004, p. 31. See also: 'Come fu ucciso a Cremona il presidente della Deputazione provinciale', *La Stampa*, 13 December 1921; 'a skull too weak to withstand the Fascist cudgels', Fornari, *Mussolini's Gadfly*, p. 50.

3 https://storia.camera.it/regno/lavori/leg26/sed187.pdf.

4 Cited in Rossi, *The Rise of Italian Fascism*, p. 213; Italo Balbo, *Diario 1922*, Lulu.com (Mondadori, Milan) 2017, p. 135.

5 Gramsci often referred to fascist and nationalist violence as a form of pogrom: 'Sugli avvenimenti del 2–3 dicembre 1919', *L'Ordine Nuovo*, 6–13 December 1919: https://www.marxists.org/italiano/gramsci/19/piccolaborghesia.htm; see also: Paul Brass (ed.), *Riots and Pogroms*, Macmillan, London, 1996.

6 Rossi, *The Rise of Italian Fascism*, p. 220.

7 See Balbo, *Diario 1922*, Mondadori, Milan, 1932, p. 11.

8 https://sites.google.com/site/sentileranechecantano/schede/la-cam ere-del-lavoro/movimento-socialista-e-movimento-sindacale-a-fae nza-dal-1900-al-1922.

9 Franzinelli, *Squadristi*, p. 382.

10 'Nuovi conflitti a Ravenna. Un morto e tre feriti', *Corriere della Sera*, 30 July 1922.

11 'A Ravenna i fascisti si accordano coi repubblicani dopo la devastazione delle Cooperative', *La Stampa*, 9 July 1922.

12 Ibid.

13 Balbo, *Diario 1922*, pp. 128, 127, cited in Rossi, *The Rise of Italian Fascism*, p. 213.

14 See for the events before and after that particular fire and an interpretation: Casali, 'Fascisti, Repubblicani e Socialisti in Romagna nel 1922. La "conquista" di Ravenna', pp. 12–36. In the late 1920s and 1930s the fascists built a 'Provincial Palace' in the same spot, completing their elimination of the memory and physical traces of Baldini's cooperative movement. More recently, ninety years on, a plaque remembered the 1922 fire, which 'attempted in vain to destroy the values and the labour of thousands of cooperative members'; see also: Erminio Maria Ferrucci, *Il Palazzo della Provincia di Ravenna: suggestioni di un percorso d'architettura*, Longo, Ravenna, 1993.

15 Balbo, *Diario 1922*, p. 128.

16 http://www.treccani.it/enciclopedia/nullo-baldini_%28Dizionario-Bio grafico%29/ (Gian Paolo Nitti, 1963).

17 *Squadristi*, p. 107; http://www.treccani.it/enciclopedia/nullo-baldi ni_%28Dizionario-Biografico%29/.

18 A different date for the destruction can be found in the biography of Baldini in the *Italian Dictionary of National Biography*, which also repeats Balbo's version that Baldini was not physically harmed by the fascists http://www.treccani.it/enciclopedia/nullo-baldini_%28Dizionario-Bio grafico%29/.

19 Casali, 'Fascisti, Repubblicani e Socialisti in Romagna nel 1922. La "conquista" di Ravenna', p. 12.

20 'A Ravenna i fascisti si accordano coi repubblicani dopo la devastazione delle Cooperative', *La Stampa*, 9 July 1922; see also: 'Concentramenti fascista a Ravenna. La Federazione delle cooperative incendiata', *La Stampa*, 28 July 1922. A further aspect of the semi-mythical idea that fascism acted 'in a loyal way' and 'with honour' towards its enemies is added here by the story that Mussolini himself guaranteed, after a delegation of socialists had visited him, that Baldini would not be touched; see the book by Baldini's daughter, Maria Luigia Nitti Baldini with Stefano Rolando, *Il mio viaggio nel secolo cattivo*, Bompiani, Milan, 2008, p. 21. According to *La Stampa*, 'Baldini stayed at his post but a number of fascists surrounded him, beat him and chased him out.'

21 'Il cooperativismo di Nullo Baldini', *La Stampa*, 29 July 1922.

22 Ibid. Baldini was eventually forced into exile, in 1924, after refusing to join the Fascist Party in return for an offer to be reappointed president of the Cooperative Federation.

23 Balbo, *Diario 1922*, p. 128.

24 Ibid., p. 135.

25 'Nuovi conflitti a Ravenna. Un morto e tre feriti', *Corriere della Sera*, 29 July 1922.

26 Italo Balbo, *Diario, 1922*, cited by Charles F. Delzell in *Mediterranean Fascism, 1919–1945: Selected Documents*, Macmillan, New York, 1970, p. 37.

27 'Una strage proletaria a Ravenna', *Avanti!*, 27 July 1922.

28 Ibid.

29 The motion announcing the resignation of Alfonsine's council can be found in *Comune di Alfonsine, Comitato per le Celebrazioni del XX Anniversario della Liberazione, Breve cronaca della Resistenza in Alfonsine*, Ravenna, Ravegnana, 1965, p. 8, n.3.

30 'L'impresa di Ravenna suscitò nel Paese un'enorme impressione, un'incontenibile ondata di sdegno', Paolo Alatri, *Le origini del fascismo*, Editori Riuniti, Rome, 1962, p. 137.

31 *La Rivolta ideale. Giornale del Fascismo Romagnolo*, I, 1, 6 August 1922.

32 'Nuovi luttuosi conflitti. Sette morti e numerosi feriti in un conflitto con la forza a Ravenna', *Corriere della Sera*, 27 July 1922.

33 Claudio Segrè, *Italo Balbo: Una vita fascista*, Il Mulino, Bologna, 1988, p. 109.

34 Casali, 'Fascisti, Repubblicani e Socialisti', p. 35.

35 'La sede del Comune di Milano occupata dai fascisti. Una giornata di conflitti, attentati e rappresaglie', *Corriere della Sera*, 4 August 1922.

36 'Il discorso di Gabriele d'Annunzio dal balcone del Municipio di Milano', *Corriere della Sera*, 5 August 1922; De Grazia, *The Perfect Fascist*, p. 78.

37 Gabriele D'Annunzio, *Per l'Italia degli Italiani: discorso pronunziato a Milano dalla ringhiera del Palazzo Marino la notte del 3 agosto 1922, con aggiunti il comento [sic!] inedito, il messaggio del convalescente agli uomini di pena, tre preghiere dinanzi agli altari disfatti e sette documenti d'amore*, Bottega di poesia, Milan, 1923.

38 Ercole Sori, *Ancona 1922–1940. Dall'avvento del fascismo all'entrata in guerra*, Le Turbine, Bookstones, Rimini, 2017, Kindle location 90.

39 Sori, *Ancona 1922–1940*, Kindle locations 211–14.

40 In the postwar period Gai was tried, and cleared, for the events of 1922: 'Imputato e assolto dall'accusa di profitti di regime e per i fatti di Ancona dell'agosto 1922', https://patrimonio.archivio.senato.it/inventa rio/fondi-acquisiti-dall-archivio-storico/silvio-gai.

41 Sori, *Ancona 1922–1940*, Kindle location 104.

THE MARCH ON ROME: OCTOBER–NOVEMBER 1922

1 Giulia Albanese, *La marcia su Roma*, Laterza, Bari, 2014, p. 120: 'By 6.30 p.m. on 2 November, according to the police chief, 17 people were dead and 65 had been injured in the city, of whom 20 seriously'; Anthony Majanlahti and Amedeo Osti Guerrazzi, *Roma divisa 1919–1925. Itinerari, storie, immagini*, Il Saggiatore, Milan, 2014, Kindle location 4003.

2 Raffaele Colapietra, *Napoli tra dopoguerra e fascismo*, Feltrinelli, Milan, 1962, p. 203.

3 Colapietra, *Napoli tra dopoguerra e fascismo*, p. 203.

4 'Lo spiegamento fascista di Napoli, *Corriere della Sera*, 25 October 1922.

5 Cited in Patricia Knight, *Mussolini and Fascism*, Routledge, London, 2013, p. 23.

6 Christopher Duggan, *Fascist Voices: An Intimate History of Mussolini's Italy*, Vintage, London, 2013, p. 58.

7 Colapietra, *Napoli tra dopoguerra e fascismo*, p. 208.

8 Cited in Albanese, *La marcia*, p. 202.

9 Fornari, *Mussolini's Gadfly*, p. 63; see also: 'Conflitti a Cremona. Quattro fascisti morti', *Corriere della Sera*, 28 October 1922; Albanese, *La marcia*, p. 87.

10 Emilio Gentile, *La marcia su Roma* (digital edition), Laterza, Rome, 2015, pp. 57–8.

11 Fornari, *Mussolini's Gadfly*, p. 64, see also: Isnenghi, *L'Italia in piazza*, pp. 286–7.

12 Fornari, *Mussolini's Gadfly*, p. 64.

13 Albanese, *La marcia*, p. 88.

14 Répaci, *La marcia su Roma*, p. 31.

15 https://www.sinahotels.com/it/h/sina-brufani-perugia/storia.html.

16 Gentile, *La marcia su Roma*, Kindle locations 206–11.

17 General Diaz cited in Marco Mondini, *La politica delle armi. Il ruolo dell'esercito nell'avvento del fascismo*, Laterza, Bari, 2015, Kindle locations 5543–4. This oft-quoted phrase was first noted in 1946 and related back to a letter from a year earlier which in turn referred to an alleged conversation, which was also reported second-hand, from 1924 or 1925 (twenty years previously) so it may well be apocryphal: see Mondini, *La politica delle armi*, n.110, Kindle location 5862.

18 Adrian Lyttelton, *The Seizure of Power: Fascism in Italy, 1919–1929*, Routledge, London, 2003, p. 74; Duilio Susmel, *Nenni e Mussolini, mezzo secolo di fronte*, Rizzoli, Milan, 1969, p. 152.

19 Répaci, *La marcia su Roma*, p. 18.

20 Denis Mack Smith, *Mussolini*, Paladin, London, 1983, pp. 61–5.

21 Bosworth, *Mussolini's Italy*, p. 180.

22 To cite Seton-Watson, *Italy from Liberalism to Fascism*, pp. 626–7.

23 Répaci, *La marcia su Roma*, p. 31.

24 'Mussolini in Peace and War', *London Review of Books*, 4, 8, 6 May 1982.

25 According to Monelli he told the station master that he wanted to leave on time: Paolo Monelli, *Mussolini piccolo borghese*, Garzanti, Milan, 1950, p. 108.

26 Cited in Alberto Albertini, *Vita di Luigi Albertini*, Mondadori, Milan, 1945, p. 212.

27 For example there are many accounts of the 'wet and hungry black-shirt columns', Christopher Seton-Watson, *Italy from Liberalism to Fascism*, 1870–1925, Methuen, London, 1967, p. 629. 'No provisions were made for lodgings or rations,' Lawrence Rainey, 'Making History', *London Review of Books*, 20, 1, 1 January 1998.

28 According to Monelli, he was wearing a bowler hat, a black shirt, a jacket, and '*le ghette bianche*' (white spats), *Mussolini piccolo borghese*, p. 108.

29 Christopher Hibbert, *Benito Mussolini: A Biography*, Longmans, London, 1962, p. 34; another version is: 'Majesty, I come from the battlefield fortunately bloodless,' Rainey, 'Making History'.

30 Rossi, *The Rise of Italian Fascism*, p. 256. http://www.lorien.it/X_INNI/Pg_Canzoni-D/Disc_BM/Discorso_BM_1922-09-24.html.

31 'Le manifestazioni a Roma. Otto morti in un conflitto coi comunisti', *Corriere della Sera*, 31 October 1922.

32 Antonio Gramsci, *Quaderni del Carcere, Volume secondo, Quaderni 6–11*, Valentino Gerratana (ed.), Einaudi, Turin, 1977, p. 1227.

33 Albanese, *La marcia*, p. 119.

34 http://www.treccani.it/enciclopedia/francesco-saverio-nitti_%28Dizionario-Biografico%29/, see Lucy Hughes-Hallett, *The Pike: Gabriele d'Annunzio, Poet, Seducer and Preacher of War*, Fourth Estate, London, 2013, pp. 465–6, 506–7.

35 'Gli incidenti della mattinata', *Corriere della Sera*, 1 November 1922.

36 'L'esodo degli squadristi da Roma. Nuovi conflitti ed incidenti', *Corriere della Sera*, 2 November 1922. A photo of this incident can be seen in *Modern Italy: Images and History of a National Identity*, Vol. 2, Omar Calabrese, Isabella Pezzini Electa, Milan, 1983.

37 'Un altro morto a Roma. Carte e documenti bruciati all'on. Musatti', *Corriere della Sera*, 1 November 1922.

38 'L'esodo degli squadristi a Roma: Nuovi conflitti e incidenti', *Corriere della Sera*, 2 November 1922.

39 'L'abitazione dell'on. Binotti devastata', *Corriere della Sera*, 1 November 1922.

40 'L'Ordine Nuovo sospende le pubblicazioni', *Corriere della Sera*, 1 November 1922

41 Alessandro Luparini, *Ravenna fascista. 1921–1925, la conquista del potere, con le fotografie di Ulderico David*, Società Editrice 'Il Ponte Vecchio', Cesena, 2017, p. 39.

42 Portelli, *Biography of an Industrial Town*, p. 119.

43 Ibid. p. 120.

44 *Biografia di una città. Storia e racconto: Terni 1830–1985*, Einaudi, Turin, 1985, p. 160. http://www.marx21.it/index.php/rivista/21406-i-comunisti-ternani-dagli-arditi-del-popolo-alla-resistenza.

45 'Devastazione e incendio all'*Avanti!*', *Corriere della Sera*, 1 November 1922.

46 Ibid.

47 'Continuando per la nostra strada', *Avanti!*, 14 November 1922. The last issue before the fire was published on 29 October.

48 Majanlahti and Osti Guerrazzi, *Roma divisa 1919–1925*, Kindle locations 3181–8.

49 *Avanti!*, 13–14 November 1921.

50 See Foot, *Pedalare! Pedalare!*, pp. 24–31, and Fabi, *Enrico Toti*.

51 'Tumulti e conflitti a Roma', *Corriere della Sera*, 25 May 1922.

52 https://www.nuovocinemapalazzo.it/2012/05/24/24-maggio-1922-la-battaglia-di-san-lorenzo/ citing Lidia Piccioni, *San Lorenzo. Un quartiere romano durante il fascismo*, Biblioteca di Storia Sociale, Edizioni di Storia e Letteratura, Rome, 1984, p. 34.

53 Majanlahti and Osti Guerrazzi, *Roma divisa 1919–1925*, Kindle locations 3382–3; Alessandro Portelli, *L'ordine è già stato eseguito. Roma, le Fosse Ardeatine, la memoria*, Donzelli, Rome, 1999, pp. 64–9.

54 Majanlahti and Osti Guerrazzi, *Roma divisa 1919–1925*, Kindle locations 3460–3.

55 Gioacchino Volpe, 'Excerpt from "History of the Fascist Movement' in Jeffrey Schnapp ed., *A Primer of Italian Fascism*, University of Nebraska Press, Lincoln, 2000, p. 25.

56 Majanlahti and Osti Guerrazzi, *Roma divisa 1919–1925*, Kindle locations 3423–6.

57 In Répaci, *La marcia su Roma*, p. 121.

58 Albanese, *La marcia*, p. 71.

59 'La marcia dei fascisti su Roma nella cronistoria di un giornalista', *Corriere della Sera*, 10 November 1922.

60 Ibid.

61 There has been a flowering of research on the Arditi del Popolo in recent years, of varying quality; see for example: Eros Francesangeli, *Arditi del Popolo. Argo Secondari e la prima organizzazione antifascista (1917–1922)*, Odradek, Rome, 2000; Luigi Balsamini, *Gli Arditi del Popolo. Dalla guerra alla difesa proletaria contro il fascismo (1917–1922)*, Galzerano Editore, Atti e Memorie del Popolo, Salerno, 2018; Claudia Piermarini, *I soldati del popolo: Arditi, partigiani e ribelli: dalle occupazioni del biennio 1919–1920 alle gesta della Volante Rossa, storia eretica delle rivoluzioni mancate in Italia*, RedStar Press, Rome, 2016; Valerio Gentili, *La legione romana degli Arditi del Popolo: la storia mai raccontata delle prime formazioni armate che strenuamente si opposero al fascismo*, Purple Press, Rome, 2009; see also: M. Rossi, 'Argo Secondari di tendenza anarchica. Dall'arditismo di guerra agli Arditi del Popolo', *Rivista storica dell'anarchismo*, 1, 1995, pp. 119–30.

62 Albanese, *La Marcia*, p. 119.

63 Majanlahti and Osti Guerrazzi, *Roma divisa 1919–1925*, Kindle locations 3967–9.

64 Mingrino later became a spy for the fascist secret police.

65 https://sto ria.cam era.it/regno/lav ori/leg26/sed 188.pdf.

66 Ibid.

67 Duggan, *Fascist Voices*, p. 65; Salvatore Lupo, *Il fascismo. La politica in un regime totalitario*, Donzelli, Rome, 2005, p. 121.

68 Emilio Lussu, *Marcia su Roma e dintorni*, Einaudi, Turin, 2003, p. 88.

69 http://www.pertini.it/turati/Matteotti90_antologia_Fascismo.pdf.

70 As Giulia Albanese has written: 'in this way Mussolini made clear that the limits to his power were only created by himself', 'Dire violenza, fare violenza. Espressione, minaccia, occultamento e pratica della violenza durante la marcia su Roma', *Memoria e ricerca*, 13, 2003, p. 2.

71 Lussu, *Marcia su Roma e dintorni*, p. 86.

72 Pietro Nenni, 'Una pagina di storia', *Avanti!*, 14 November 1922.

73 Umberto Sereni, 'Carlo Scorza e il fascismo "stile camorra"', in Paolo Giovannini and Marco Palla (eds), *Il fascismo dalle mani sporche. Dittatura, corruzione, affarismo*, Laterza, Rome, 2019, pp. 199–200.

74 Nitti returned to his villa in Acquafredda near Maratea in the south of Italy, but he would not be safe there. There were rumours that he had left for the USA, or had been kidnapped by fascists. In 1923 he was one of the first non-fascists to be forced into exile when his house in Rome was attacked again.

75 'Le riunioni dei gruppi. Cocco-Ortu, contrario al Ministro, si dimette dal gruppo democratico', *La Stampa*, 17 November 1922.

76 Duggan, *Fascist Voices*, p. 64.

77 For a detailed analysis of the debate in both the lower and upper houses see Albanese, *La marcia*, pp. 147–63. See also the judgement of *Avanti!*, which called the parliament 'servile' and 'spineless', 'La servilità della Camera sanziona il colpa di mano fascista', *Avanti!*, 17 November 1922; 'Il censimento degli invertebrati alla Camera', *Avanti!*, 18 November 1922.

78 *La Rivoluzione liberale*, 33, 9 November 1922.

79 See Giorgio Rochat, 'L'esercito e il fascismo', in Guido Quazza (ed.), *Fascismo e società italiana*, Einaudi, Turin, 1973, pp. 98–101; Mondini, *La politica delle armi*; Macgregor Knox, *To the Threshold of Power, 1922/33: Origins and Dynamics of the Fascist and National Socialist Dictatorships*, **Vol. 1**, Cambridge University Press, New York, 2007.

80 My emphasis. Royal Decree 1641: 22 December 1922.

81 *Gazzetta Ufficiale del Regno d'Italia*, No. 300, 23 December 1922.

82 Ibid., p. 3372.

83 Lorenzo Pavanello, *Il processo Burletta. Un omicidio impunito*, ilmiolibro, 2016.

84 *Gazzetta Ufficiale del Regno d'Italia*, No. 300, 23 December 1922, p. 3374.

85 See Marco Nicola Miletti, 'Il processo Di Vagno', *Critica Sociale*, 7, 2011, p. 7, and Vito Antonio Lenzi, 'La revisione tra reazione e democrazia', ibid., pp. 17–19.

86 See the various decrees passed between the end of December 1922 and the middle of January 1923; 28 December; 12 January 1923; 14 January 1923, n.31.

87 Walter Tobagi, *Gli anni del manganello*, Fratelli Fabbri Editori, Milan, 1973, pp. 9–10. Tobagi also pushes the theory of a private 'settling of accounts'; for his full account of the massacre, see pp. 8–20; see also: 'Deposizione di Roveda al processo Brandimarte', *Stampa Sera*, 2–3 August 1950. Roveda also denied that the Prato killings were political, arguing that it was '*a private issue linked to women*'. For Brandimarte's version see 'Brandimarte respinge ogni accusa davanti ai giudici di Firenze', *Corriere della Sera*, 28 July 1950; 'L'interrogatorio di Brandimarte', *La Stampa*, 27–28 July 1950. De Felice also gives space to the 'personal reasons' version, which originated in Renzo De Felice, 'I fatti di Torino del dicembre 1922', *Studi Storici*, 4, 1963, pp. 60–5; Francesco Répaci, *La strage di Torino*, Edizioni Avanti!, Turin, 1924 (reprinted in 1974), p. 14. See also: Franzinelli, *Squadristi*, pp. 193–4, and Antonio Sonnessa, 'The 1922 Turin Massacre (Strage di Torino): Working-class resistance and conflicts within fascism', *Modern Italy*, 10:2, 2005, pp. 92–4 for a well-documented account of the massacre.

88 Historical debates around the massacre have also centred on the distinction between the 'spontaneous' and the 'premeditated' nature of

the violence, and the role of Mussolini; see Sonnessa, 'The 1922 Turin Massacre', pp. 187–205.

89 Giancarlo Carcano, *Strage a Torino. Una storia italiana dal 1922 al 1971*, La Pietra, Milan, 1973.

90 Ibid., p. 38.

91 http://www.gulag-italia.com/w2d3/v3/view/feltrinelli/gulag/db/dettag lio.html?pagina=45&max=1024&ordinale=813.

92 Carcano, *Strage a Torino*, p. 5.

93 Ibid., p. 54.

94 Ibid., p. 55.

95 Ibid., p. 144.

96 Pagella had been hit in the face by a chair thrown by a fascist deputy in parliament in July 1921.

97 'His eyes were pulled out … his body was unrecognisable.' At the 1950 trial Brandimarte's lawyers argued that Ferrero had not been tortured, but 'merely' shot. See also: Ercole Moggi, 'Il martirio di Ferrero segretario della Fiom', *La Nuova Stampa*, 30 July 1950; Ercole Moggi, 'Il processo Brandimarte s'inzia oggi a Firenze', *La Nuova Stampa*, 26 July 1950.

98 'L'assassinio del Berrutti nel racconto dei testimoni', *La Nuova Stampa*, 29 July 1950.

99 Carcano, *Strage a Torino*, p. 70.

100 Francesco Répaci cited in Tobagi, *Gli anni*, p. 14.

101 'Un altro morto a Torino. La Casa del Popolo incendiata', *Corriere della Sera*, 21 December 1922.

102 See Tobagi, *Gli anni*, p. 14.

103 'Mattinata normale a Torino. Le distruzioni nella Camera del Lavoro', *Corriere della Sera*, 19 December 1922; for the development of the massacre see also: 'Sette morti e alcuni feriti a Torino', *Corriere della Sera*, 19 December 1922; 'Cinque morti e sei feriti a Torino', *Corriere della Sera*, 19 December 1922.

104 Vittorio Foa: 'the destruction of an entire social, cultural and educational fabric, a fabric made up of humanity and an individual and collective organisation aimed at helping the weak and the poor', *Questo Novecento. Un secolo di passione civile. La politica come responsabilità*, Einaudi, Turin, 1996, p. 109.

105 'Mattinata normale a Torino. Le distruzioni nella Camera del Lavoro', *Corriere della Sera*, 19 December 1922.

106 'Le salme dei due fascisti trasportate al cimitero', *La Stampa*, 22 December 1922.

107 Ibid.

108 Carcano, *Strage a Torino,* p. 100.

109 Ibid., p. 127.

110 Ibid. Morgagni was a high-level journalist who remained so faithful to Mussolini that he killed himself when Il Duce was deposed in July 1943, penning a suicide note addressed to Mussolini stating: 'I die with your name on my lips'.

111 Ibid., p. 128.

112 Ibid., p. 99. An interview in *Il Secolo,* 19 August 1922 (G. Bongiovanni, 'Come si sono svolti i fatti di Torino. Un colloquio con il console della legione piemontese') was sourced in the National Library in Florence as evidence during Brandimarte's first trial in 1950.

113 Interview in *Il Popolo di Roma,* 24 June 1924, quotes from Carcano, *Strage a Torino,* p. 99.

114 Brunello Mantelli, 'L'antifascismo a Torino' in Tranfaglia (ed.), *Storia di Torino,* VIII, p. 267.

115 Cited in Carcano, *Strage a Torino,* p. 70.

116 For hidden resistance and the power of silence see Luisa Passerini, *Torino operaia e fascismo,* Laterza, Rome, 1984; and for a seminal micro-history and oral history of one neighbourhood before and during fascism see Maurizio Gribaudi, *Mondo operaio e mito operaio. Spazi e percorsi sociali a Torino nel primo Novecento,* Einaudi, Turin, 1987.

117 Franco Rolle interview cited in Gribaudi, *Mondo operaio e mito operaio,* p. 150.

1923

1 'L'on. Modigliani cacciato da Livorno dai fascisti', *Corriere della Sera,* 4 February 1923. Modigliani was acting as a lawyer in a trial in the Livorno law courts. 'The fascists soon found out about Modigliani's arrival.' Some twenty fascists and nationalists broke into the courts and attacked Modigliani. 'The fascists managed to pull off some of his beard.' They also stole his hat and a 'silk scarf'. He was told not to return to Livorno and to leave on the first train out; he left 'among whistles and insults from the crowd'.

2 Santini, 'Quando le barbe erano antifasciste'.

3 ACS, CPC, 3327.

4 Cited in Albanese, 'Il coraggio e la paura', p. 117; Turati, Kuliscioff, *Carteggio,* V, p. 902 (17 November 1922).

5 http://www.orsellistudiolegale.it/2020/04/14/genuzio-bentini-maestro-delloratoria-forense/; Laura Orlandini, *Battista Emaldi: L'assassinio di*

un Sindaco. Fusignano dalla Settimana rossa all'avvento del fascismo, La Mandragora, Imola, 2019.

6 https://massimedalpassato.it/storie-di-avvocati-genuzio-bentini/.

7 'Between 1921 and 1922, Tito Oro Nobili … was assaulted at least fifteen times … He was scalded with cigarette stubs, whipped and left for dead; his house was raided, furniture and books burned': Portelli, *Biography of an Industrial Town*, p. 120; Francesco Bogliari, *Tito Oro Nobili: biografia critica con appendice documentaria*, Preface by Pietro Nenni, Quaderni Regione dell'Umbria, Serie Studi Storici, 1, 1977, p. 25.

8 Bogliari, *Tito Oro Nobili*, p. 26.

9 *Avanti!*, 19 October 1923, cited in Leonardo Varasano, 'La prima regione fascista. L'Umbria e il fascismo (1919–1944)', PhD, Bologna, 2007, p. 212.

10 'The following were sent to trial: Armando Cocchi, Vittorio Martelli, Pio Pizzirani (on the run). Ettore Bidone, Nerino Dardi, Teodorico Frattini, Renato Gaiani, Angelo Galli, Alfredo Gelosi, Corrado Pini, Mauro Raimondi, Abramo Roncaglia, Pietro Venturi … The trial … started on 17 January 1923 … on the 10 March 1923 Venturi was given a sentence of 13 years, 4 months and 10 days for the murders of Giordani and Dardi and nine months and five days for illegal possession of arms. The others were cleared. The three men on the run were tried behind closed doors and with appointed lawyers in a day and were all given life sentences', 'Palazzo d'Accursio, La strage di', in *Gli antifascisti, i partigiani e le vittime del fascismo nel Bolognese (1919–1945)*, Istituto per la Storia della Resistenza e della Società Contemporanea nella Provincia di Bologna 'Luciano Bergonzini' (ISREBO), Comune di Bologna, Bologna, 2005, pp. 197–9.

11 'Not a single fascist was arrested, starting with Leandro Arpinati who led the assault', Onofri, *La strage*, p. 198.

12 Onofri, *La strage*, p. 291. 'The Bolognese fascist movement was more or less able to carry out its violent attacks undisturbed': Jonathan Dunnage, 'The involvement of the Italian State Institutions in the rise to power of Fascism: the Police Forces in the Province of Bologna, 1897–1925', PhD, University of Hull, 1990, https://core.ac.uk/download/pdf/2731661.pdf (p. 269).

13 'L'inchiesta pei fatti di Bologna. Mobilitazione rossa e piani di attentati', *Corriere della Sera*, 26 November 1920.

14 'A proposito dell'oro straniero. Una lettera di Martelli', *Avanti!*, 9 December 1920.

15 See Gianni Isola, *Guerra al regno della guerra! Storia della Lega proletaria mutilati invalidi reduci orfani e vedove di guerra (1918–1924)*, Le Lettere, Florence, 1990; Foot, *Fratture*, pp. 53–95.

16 'Socialisti riparati a San Marino fuggono travestiti', *Corriere della Sera*, 19 April 1921.

17 'La deposizione di E. Gnudi, ex Sindaco di Bologna sull'eccidio di Palazzo d'Accursio', *La Stampa*, 3 February 1923.

18 https://www.storiaememoriadibologna.it/bidone-ettore-507652-persona.

19 'Il tentato suicidio di un imputato', *Corriere della Sera*, 1 January 1923.

20 Floriana Colao, *Il delitto politico tra Ottocento e Novecento. Da 'delitto fittizio' a 'nemico dello Stato'*, Giuffrè Editore, Milan, 1986, p. 230. For legal aspects in general, see: ibid., pp. 229–31.

21 For Grandi's summing up, see: *Il Popolo d'Italia*, 6 March 1923; Chiurco, *Storia*, Vol. II, pp. 186–94.

22 'La deposizione di E. Gnudi, ex Sindaco di Bologna sull'eccidio di Palazzo d'Accursio', *La Stampa*, 3 February 1923.

23 'Figure di imputati nel processo per i fatti di Bologna', *Corriere della Sera*, 3 February 1923; see also: 'La deposizione di E. Gnudi, ex Sindaco di Bologna', *La Stampa*, 3 February 1923.

24 'Il corteo fascista in onore della vedova Giordani', *Corriere della Sera*, 29 January 1923.

25 'Il blocco nazionale vittorioso a Bologna', *Corriere della Sera*, 23 January 1923.

26 Those involved in November 1920 on the fascist and nationalist side – both in the streets and inside the council chamber – found that it did their future career no harm at all. Leandro Arpinati (who led the fascist assault on the streets) became the *podestà* (unelected mayor) of Bologna from 1926–29 and then a minister under Mussolini; Aldo Oviglio (a minority councillor) rose to become Justice Minister in Mussolini's first government; Angelo Manaresi (who was also among the minority councillors that day) was appointed *podestà* of Bologna from 1933–35, and Cesare Colliva, who was shot in the face, would also go on to be *podestà* from 1936–39. Effectively, the losers of the 1920 election ended up governing the city for the next twenty years.

27 'L'insediamento delle amministrazioni bolognesi', *Corriere della Sera*, 5 March 1923.

28 http://www.comune.bologna.it/storiaamministrativa/documenti/sedute/336946: *Atti del Consiglio Comunale di Bologna, Anno 1923*, Volume primo, Cooperativa Azzoguidi, Bologna, 1926, p. 16.

1924

1 The President of the House was Enrico De Nicola, who would become Republican Italy's first president in 1946.

2 Collier, *Duce!*, p. 74.

3 The full speech is in Claudio Modena (ed.), *L'avvocato di Matteotti. Pasquale Galliano Magno*, Apogeo Editore, Adria, 2014, pp. 41–57.

4 Collier, *Duce!*, p. 75.

5 Bosworth, *Mussolini*, p. 171.

6 *La Giustizia*, 13 June 1924.

7 Giuseppe Rossini (ed.), *Il delitto Matteotti tra il Viminale e l'Aventino. Dagli Atti del processo De Bono all'Alta Corte di Giustizia*, Il Mulino, Bologna, 1968, p. 936.

8 Ibid, p. 933. Rossi's 'treachery' meant that he was cut off from the regime, and after he was cleared by the investigating magistrate in the Matteotti case, partly thanks to an amnesty, he went into exile. But he was tempted back to the Italian–Swiss border in 1928 by a clever spy and police plot, illegally snatched by the fascists and brought back to Italy. His capture caused a diplomatic incident. He was then imprisoned and interned until 1943. Tried again in 1947 in line with the second Matteotti investigation, he was again cleared.

9 Spinosa, *Mussolini*, Kindle location 2643.

10 Mack Smith, *Mussolini,* p. 91.

11 Cited in Tobagi, *Gli anni del manganello*, p. 60.

12 *I 535 deputati al Parlamento per la XXVII Legislatura*, Fratelli Treves, Milan, 1924, 'g.b.', (introduction) and pp. 172, 324.

13 Ibid., p. 172.

14 Some were tried in San Marino itself for relatively minor crimes.

15 Ercole Moggi, 'L'inizio a Firenze del più gigantesco processo d'Assise', *La Stampa*, 9 May 1924.

16 Ignazio Silone, *Bread and Wine*, Harper and Brothers, New York and London, 1937, p. 5.

17 'Il processo per l'eccidio di Empoli che si inizierà domani a Firenze', *Corriere della Sera*, 7 May 1924.

18 Moggi, 'L'inizio a Firenze del più gigantesco processo d'Assise'.

19 Ibid.

20 Ibid.

21 'Altri due oratori della difesa al processo per i fatti di Empoli', *Corriere della Sera*, 7 September 1924.

22 Jaurès Busoni, one of those arrested and convicted, published a book on the massacre after the war which made this reference to Innocenti and her

nickname: *L'eccidio di Empoli del 1 marzo 1921. Cronistoria e testimonianze di uno dei protagonisti*, PSI, Rome, 1945, p. 22.

23 Cited in http://divinando.blogspot.com/2008/11/di-silvia-paolo-alena-la-cinquantaccia.html.

24 'La torva figura della "Cinquantaccia" al processo della rossa falange empolese', *Corriere della Sera*, 28 May 1924. See also: 'Le sanguinarie amazzoni rosse alla sbarra', *La Nazione*, 25 May 1924.

25 He appeared to have abandoned 'the impartial attitude which should have been part of his role', Colao, *Il delitto politico*, p. 232. In some studies of the postwar period, various members of the judiciary involved in the case were criticised as pro-fascist. Guerrini wrote of the 'well-known fascist judge' and argued that the president 'supported the fascist version about a ferocious episode perpetrated by subversives', and 'a political climate which conditioned the sentence', cited in Colao, *Il delitto politico*, p. 231.

26 'La torva figura della "Cinquantaccia" al processo della rossa falange empolese'.

27 Busoni, *L'eccidio*, p. 22.

28 There is very little information on Innocenti's life either before or after 1921: see for fragments the notes from a secret report smuggled out and written by fellow prisoner Camilla Ravera in 1932, in Laura Mariani, *Quelle dell'idea. Storie di detenute politiche 1927–1948*, De Donato, Bari, 1982, p. 45, and the comments by Mariani, L. Guerrini, *Il movimento operaio nell'Empolese 1861–1941*, Riuniti, Rome, 1970, p. 319 cited p. 65.

29 'Le pene richieste dal P.M. per i fatti di Empoli', *Corriere della Sera*, 31 October 1924. The final sentence is in Archivio di Stato di Firenze, Corte d'Assise di Firenze, Sentenza Penale, No. 45, del 31, October 1924: 'conosciuto col nome i fatti di Empoli 1921'.

30 As had happened with the individuals who were on the run when the Renzino and Palazzo d'Accursio trials took place.

31 Giuliano Lastraioli and Roberto Nannelli (eds), *Empoli in gabbia. Le sentenze del processone per l'eccidio del 1 marzo 1921*, Le Memoriette, 2, Empoli, May 1995: https://www.dellastoriadempoli.it/empoli-in-gab bia-a-cura-di-giuliano-lastraioli-e-roberto-nannelli/ (Raimondo Cioni, Vasco Ramagli, Dario Parri).

32 The headline in *Il Popolo d'Italia* was: 'Barbaro assassinio dell'on. Armando Casalini a Roma', http://casaliniarmando.blogspot.com ('Barbaric murder of the Deputy Armando Casalini in Rome').

33 Matteo Petracci, *I matti del Duce. Manicomi e repressione politica nell'Italia fascista*, Donzelli, Rome, 2014, p. 195.

34 Cited in Sara Samori, 'La Romagna e l'Emilia', in Severini (ed.), *La Settimana rossa*, p. 199; see also pp. 192, 197.

35 Papini, *Ancona e il mito della Settimana rossa*, p. 66.

36 It is worth noting that this was also used with Augusto Masetti, another high-profile and political case.

37 Petracci, *I matti*, p. xi.

38 Silone, *Bread and Wine*, p. 229.

39 See Amy King, 'Italy's secular martyrs: the construction, role and maintenance of secular martyrdom in Italy from the twentieth century to the present day', PhD thesis, University of Bristol, 2019.

40 Mariani, *Quelle dell'idea*, p. 30.

TRYING TO KILL MUSSOLINI: 1925–26

1 Lyttelton, *Seizure of Power*, p. 103.

2 Simonetta Falasca Zamponi, *Lo spettacolo del fascismo*, Rubbettino, Soveria Mannelli, 2003, p. 123.

3 Walter Boni, 'Introduzione', in Mario Falanga, *Tito Zaniboni. Appunti per una biografia politica e letteraria*, Piovan editore, Abamo Terme, 1991, p. 7.

4 Falanga, *Tito Zaniboni*, p. 23

5 Guido Leto, *OVRA: Fascismo-Antifascismo*, Capelli Editore, Bologna, 1952, p. 20.

6 John Dickie, *The Craft: How Freemasons Made the Modern World*, Hachette, London, 2020, pp. 290–302.

7 'La revoca delle medaglie al valore a Zaniboni, Capello e Nicoloso', *Corriere della Sera*, 9 March 1929.

8 Cesare Rossi, *Il Tribunale Speciale. Storia documentata*, Milan, Casa Editrice Ceschina, 1952, p. 89.

9 Sergio Luzzatto, *Il corpo del duce. Un cadavere tra immaginazione, storia e memoria*, Einaudi, Turin, 1998, p. 25.

10 Capello stayed in custody until 1936 and died in 1941.

11 Vinicio Araldi, *Camicie nere a Montecitorio. Storia parlamentare dell'avvento del fascismo*, Mursia, Milan, 1974, p. 296.

12 Tobagi, *Gli anni del manganello*, p. 60.

13 'Beaten and slightly injured by unidentified people in Naples' (3 July 1926), ACS, CPC.

14 Tobagi, *Gli anni del manganello*, p. 61.

15 Fornari, *Mussolini's Gadfly*, p. 123; Tobagi, *Gli anni del manganello*, p. 61.

16 Fornari, *Mussolini's Gadfly*, p. 120.

17　Mussolini set a strict time limit on the trial, and banned the wearing of black shirts. He also said that the trial should take place 'amidst the indifference of the nation', ibid., p. 120.

18　Roberto Farinacci, *In difesa di Dumini*, Libreria dell'800, Rome, 1944.

19　Modena (ed.), *L'avvocato di Matteotti*.

20　Spinosa, *Mussolini*, Kindle locations 2938–9.

21　Years earlier, in 1912, Mussolini the socialist had poured scorn on his comrades who visited the king after the monarch had survived a failed assassination attempt. He said that such attempts were part and parcel of being a king in the first place: 'in order to avoid dangerous misunderstandings, the only true task of the socialists after the assassination attempt was to say nothing', cited in Paolo Valera, *Mussolini*, Aonia edizioni, Raleigh, USA, 2012, p. 17.

22　Frances Stonor Saunders, *The Woman Who Shot Mussolini*, Faber and Faber, London, 2010; Richard Collin, *La donna che sparò a Mussolini*, Rusconi, Milan, 1988. See also Giovanni Pietro Lombardo ed., *7 Aprile 1926. Attentato al Duce. Violet Gibson, capace di intendere e volere*, Fefè Editore, Rome, 2021.

23　Stonor Saunders, *The Woman Who Shot Mussolini*, p. 113.

24　National Union of Conservative and Constitutional Associations, *Gleanings and Memoranda*, Vol. 63, National Unionist Association, London, 1926, p. 460.

25　Enrico Ferri, 'A character study and life history of Violet Gibson who attempted the life of Benito Mussolini, on the 7th of April, 1926', *Journal of the American Institute of Criminal Law and Criminology*, 19, 2, 1928–9, pp. 211–19; https://scholarlycommons.law.northwestern.edu/cgi/view content.cgi?article=2094&context=jclc.

26　Ferri, 'A character study', pp. 212, 214.

27　Ibid., pp. 211, 215, 215–6.

28　He was listed as a *scalpellino* (quarryman).

29　Sandro Setta, *Renato Ricci dallo squadrismo alla Repubblica Sociale Italiana*, Il Mulino, Bologna, 1986.

30　Riccardo Lucetti, *Gino Lucetti and his attempt to assassinate Benito Mussolini (Il Duce) 11 September 1926*, ChristieBooks, Kindle locations 1502–6.

31　'Against a corner of the car': Luigi Salvatorelli and Giovanni Mira, *Storia d'Italia nel periodo fascista*, Einaudi, Turin, 1966, p. 376.

32　'Even if the bomb had got into the car, I would have had time to throw it out, as an old soldier': Spinosa, *Mussolini*, Kindle locations 2978–9.

33 Salvatorelli and Mira state that 'no accomplices were identified', *Storia d'Italia*, p. 376.

34 Gino Lucetti, ACS, CPC.

35 Ibid.

36 Lucetti, *Gino Lucetti and his attempt to assassinate Benito Mussolini*, Kindle locations 3963–74.

37 Dalla Casa, *L'attentato*, pp. 7–10; also see this book for photos of Mussolini's visit and the gallows.

38 Salvatorelli and Mira, *Storia d'Italia*, p. 380.

39 Dalla Casa, *Attentato al Duce*, p. 19.

40 The fury with which the blackshirts attacked the small boy was reflected in that of the crowd in Milan in 1945 when faced with the body of Mussolini himself.

41 http://www.veneriocattani.it/cronaca.htm.

42 Franzinelli, *Squadristi*, p. 191.

43 Tod, *From Pillar to Post*.

44 Falasca Zamponi, *Lo spettacolo del fascismo*, p. 110.

45 Seton-Watson, *Italy from Liberalism to Fascism*, p. 664.

46 Matteo Millan, ' "Semplicemente Squadristi". Il fascismo post-marcia a Genova', *Contemporanea*, XVI, 2, 2013, pp. 222–4.

47 Bogliari, *Tito Oro Nobili*, p. 67; Varasano, 'La prima regione fascista', p. 212. See also: Portelli, the fascists 'whipped and wounded Tito Oro Nobili' (1 September 1922), *Biography of an Industrial Town*, p. 118.

48 Bogliari, *Tito Oro Nobili*, p. vi; Portelli, *Biography of an Industrial Town*, p. 161.

49 Giuseppe Barbalace, 'Fu segretario del partito negli anni neri', *Avanti!*, 18 August 1977.

50 Stefano Fabbri, *Fascismo d'acciaio. Maceo Carloni e il sindacalismo a Terni (1920–1944)*, Mursia, Milan, 2013, p. 66.

51 Further legal procedings after the war in 1946 re-established the facts of the beating, but amnesties meant that nobody spent any time in prison as a result (a familiar story, which we have also seen in previous cases of violence).

REGIME: 1926–27

1 Giuseppe Massarenti, 5 July 1937, ACS, CPC.

2 ACS, CPC.

3 Ibid.

4 Letter 18 June 1937 to Maglioni in ACS, CPC.

5 Petracci, *I matti*, pp. 61–3. Petracci argues that the repressive tactics used against Massarenti did affect his mental health; see also: Daniela Baratieri, 'Wrapped in passionless impartiality. Italian psychiatry during the fascist regime', in Daniela Baratieri et al. (eds), *Totalitarian Dictatorship. New Histories*, Routledge, London, 2014, pp. 138–56.

6 Enzo Levi in Manicardi, *Formiggini*, p. 57.

7 Silone, *Bread and Wine*, pp. 174–179.

8 Circolo Antonio Gramsci, *Alle origini del PCI. Atti del Convegno su Gastone Sozzi*, Cesena, 1980. For Sozzi's life see the beautifully written 1955 biography by journalist Felice Chilanti and republished as *Gastone Sozzi*, Società Editrice 'Il Ponte Vecchio', Cesena, 2003. This book is notable, especially given when it was originally written, for the attention paid to the private life and relationships within Sozzi's story, although it still adhered to the 'heroic' narrative which was so powerful at the time. See also Patrizia Gabrielli, *Fenicotteri in volo. Donne comuniste nel ventennio fascista*, Carocci, Rome, 1999, p. 166; *Tempo di virilità. L'antifascismo, il genere, la storia*, FrancoAngeli, Milan, 2008, pp. 80–1, 85.

9 Cited in Felice Chilanti, 'Gastone Sozzi: una scelta culturale d'avanguardia', in Circolo Antonio Gramsci, *Alle origini del PCI*.

10 Camilla Ravera 'Un ricordo di Gastone Sozzi', in Circolo Antonio Gramsci, *Alle origini del PCI*, p. 18.

11 Cited in Chilanti, 'Gastone Sozzi', p. 23.

12 Aldo Agosti, 'La formazione di un quadro del PCI alla scuola del Comintern: Gastone Sozzi in URSS (1923–1925)', *Annali della Fondazione Luigi Einaudi*, Vol. XII, 1978, pp. 495–516.

13 Istituto Storico Provinciale della Resistenza-Forlì, V. Flamigni and L. Casali (eds), *Gastone Sozzi, Scritti. Lettere a Norma*, Editrice Cooperativa Libraria di Romagna, Cesena, 1985.

14 'Il martirio di Gastone Sozzi. Le torture orribili erano autorizzati dall'alto', *Avanti!*, 11 March 1928.

15 For women political prisoners during the regime see Mariani, *Quelle dell'idea*.

16 For a denial of this after the war see Guido Leto, 'Ancora sulla questione dell'"OVRA"', *Il Movimento di liberazione in Italia*, 16, 1952, p. 28. The torture/murder version of events was fixed almost immediately, see: 'Gastone Sozzi assassinato in prigione', *Avanti!*, 4 March 1928; 'Il martirio di Gastone Sozzi. Le torture orribili erano autorizzati dall'alto', *Avanti!*, 11 March 1928.

17 For the international campaign see Maurizio Ridolfi, 'La "campagna" Gastone Sozzi. Ruolo e attività del Soccorso Rosso', in Circolo Antonio Gramsci, *Alle origini del PCI*, pp. 189–221.

18 Although after the war there were some who thought that suicide was a possibility, given the ferocity of the torture, as the only way to avoid incriminating other militants, see *L'Unità*, 23 July 1952. Other evidence seems to point to errors in the forms of torture carried out on Sozzi, which proved fatal. Perhaps, the fascists would have preferred to keep him alive. He was a prized asset and had been in Moscow.

1928

1 For Romolo Tranquilli see 'Romolo Tranquilli', in Simonetta Carolini and Fabbio Ecca (eds), ANPPIA, *Antifascisti alla sbarra*, Vol. I, Palombi editore, Rome, 2015, pp. 253–8.

2 Carlo Giacchin, *Attentato alla Fiera. Milano 1928*, Mursia, Milan, 2009, pp. 96, 100–23.

3 Cited in Mimmo Franzinelli, *I tentacoli dell'Ovra, Agenti, collaboratori e vittime della polizia politica fascista*, Bollati Boringhieri, Turin, 1999, p. 330.

4 Further details from Rossi, *Il Tribunale Speciale*, pp. 280–2.

5 Giacchin, *Attentato alla Fiera*, p. 123

6 Ibid., p. 198.

7 Silone, *Bread and Wine*, p. 257.

8 Dario Biocca, *Silone. La doppia vita di un italiano*, Rizzoli, Milan, 2005, p. 153.

9 Biocca, *Silone*, pp. 151–5. Stanislao Pugliese is more sceptical, see for example, *Bitter Spring, A Life of Ignazio Silone,* Farrar, Straus and Giroux, New York, 2009, pp. 300–11. See also for a subtle analysis, Elizabeth Leake, *The Reinvention of Ignazio Silone*, Toronto, Toronto University Press, pp. 18–27.

10 Silone, *Bread and Wine*, pp. 85–6.

11 Ibid., p. 264.

12 ACS, CPC, 3327.

13 Serge also wrote about Modigliani's sense of what was happening in Italy at the time: 'They can hear the timber of the whole edifice in their part of the world giving off loud cracks.' He wrote of Giuseppe and Vera Modigliani that they 'still like to keep in [their] inmost heart the hope that some day [they] can be of service ... Both of them, with their faultless dignity, incarnate the sober, noble Socialism of an age that has passed. What has happened to them now? They are still in France at the

moment when the Nazis took over the unoccupied zone…', *Memoirs of a Revolutionary*, University of Iowa Press, Iowa City, 2002, p. 365.

14 Manlio Brigaglia, 'Introduzione', in Manlio Brigaglia (ed.), *Emilio Lussu. Tutte le opere, 2. L'esilio antifascista 1927–1943. Storia e milizia*, Aisara, Cagliari, 2010, p. xciv.

15 The full story is now in Brunella Dalla Casa, *Leandro Arpinati. Un fascista anomalo*, Il Mulino, Bologna, 2013.

1929

1 Merli, *Autodifese di militanti operai*, pp. 230–1.

2 Carlo De Maria, *Fascismo e società italiana. Temi e parole chiave*, BraDypUS Editore, Bologna, 2016, p. 352.

3 A priest called Don Minzoni was killed by fascists in the Ferrarese countryside in 1923, Giorgio Rochat, *Italo Balbo*, UTET, Turin, 1986, pp. 92–3.

4 Marta Margotti, ' "La soppressione della festa in discorso": Le trattative tra Italia e Santa Sede per l'abolizione della festività del 20 settembre', *Contemporanea*, 2009, 12, 1, pp. 87–104; see also David Kertzer, *The Pope and Mussolini. The Secret History of Pius XI and the Rise of Fascism in Europe*, OUP, Oxford, 2014, pp. 134, 140–3.

5 Cited in Federico Finchelstein, *Transatlantic Fascism. Ideology, violence and the sacred in Argentina and Italy, 1919–1945*, Duke UP, Durham NC and London, 2010, p. 23.

6 For fascism and cycling see Daniele Marchesini, 'Fascismo a due ruote', in Maria Canella and Sergio Giuntini (eds), *Sport e fascismo*, FrancoAngeli, Milan, 2009, pp. 85–98.

7 Erminio Fonzo, 'Giorgio Alberto Chiurco e la Storia della Rivoluzione Fascista', *Ricerche di Storia Sociale e Religiosa*, XLVI, 89, 2017, pp. 289–303. For the rest of Chiurco's life and career, and the legal processes he was subjected to after the war, see Floriana Colao, *Il processo Chiurco. Giustizia e politica nella Siena del secondo dopoguerra*, Edizioni Il Leccio, Monteriggioni, 2013.

8 Colao, *Il processo Chiurco*.

THE 1930S

1 See the essay 'Lauro de Bosis. Icarus', in Iris Origo, *A Need to Testify. Four portraits*, John Murray, London, 1984, pp. 33–78.

2 http://www.bibliotecamarxista.org/de%20bosis%20lauro/storia_della_mi a_morte.htm.

3 Silone, *Bread and Wine*, p. 194.

4 Ibid., p. 229.

5 Ibid., p. 144.

6 *Guida della Mostra della Rivoluzione Fascista*, Stabilimenti Grafici di A. Vallecchi, Florence, 1932.

7 Giorgio Chiurco, *Storia della Rivoluzione Fascista*, Vallecchi, Florence, 1929, five volumes. The regime distributed 10,000 copies of this work alone to various state institutions, at a cost of 1 million lire, a vast sum for the time: Guido Bonsaver, *Censorship and Literature in Fascist Italy*, University of Toronto Press, Toronto, 2017, p. 55.

8 See, for example, Jan Nelis, 'Back to the Future. Italian Fascist Representations of the Fascist Past', *Fascism*, 3, 2014, pp. 1–19.

9 Thanks to the law of 27 December 1930, n. 1726, 28 October became a national holiday. The last national holiday held on this day was in 1942, during wartime.

10 Giuseppe Lauretti quoted in Portelli, *Biography of an Industrial Town*, p. 170.

11 A medal was awarded for taking part in the March on Rome. Renzo De Felice calculated that 227 Italian Jews were officially said to have taken part, as well as three non-Italian Jews, cited in Alexander Stille, *Benevolence and Betrayal: Five Italian Jewish Families Under Fascism*, Penguin, London, 1991, p. 351. See also: Attilio Milano, *Storia degli Ebrei in Italia*, Einaudi, Turin, 1963, p. 392.

12 ACS, CPC, b. 3093.

13 He took part in the Ethiopian war in the mid-1930s. Vittorio Martelli was pronounced officially dead by a court after 1945, on the request of his family.

14 In 1946 it seems Armando Cocchi was on the verge of returning home to Italy. A terminal illness meant that he never made it back: Nazario Sauro Onofri, *Un paradiso infernale: Gli antifascisti bolognesi assassinati e incarcerati nell' URSS di Stalin*, Sapere, Rome, 2000, pp. 78–83, 103 and 108.

15 Adolfo Sandonnini was another of the five. His journey was very similar to that of Morelli, although he survived the gulag and was able to return to Italy from the USSR in 1954. For the trial see also: Lastraioli and Nannelli (eds), *Empoli in gabbia*.

16 For further information on Melacci see: http://www.arivista.org/rivi ste/Arivista/292/47.htm and Cinzia Cardinali and Ezio Raspanti (eds), *Bernardo Melacci. Poeta libertario*, Edizioni Regione Toscana, Consiglio Regionale, 2005. Another of the supposed ringleaders – Galliano Gervasi,

a communist – was given a twenty-two-year sentence. After the war, Gervasi returned home and became Mayor of Foiano and a communist senator; see the account of postwar discussions in Foiano of memory and the legacy of fascism in Victoria Belco, *War, Massacre, and Recovery in Central Italy, 1943–1948*, University of Toronto Press, Toronto, 2010, pp. 208–9.

17 Davide Turcato (ed.), *The Method of Freedom: An Errico Malatesta Reader*, AK Press, Oakland, Edinburgh, Baltimore, 2014, p. 2.

18 Maurizio Antonioli et al. (eds), *Dizionario biografico degli anarchici italiani*, volume secondo I–Z, Biblioteca Franco Serantini, Pisa, 2004, p. 65.

19 Bianciardi, *Argentina Altobelli*, p. 387.

20 http://www.fondazionealtobelli.it/wp-content/uploads/2010/09/Un-prof ilo-di-Argentina-Altobelli-Adolfo-Pepe.pdf.

21 Bianciardi, *Argentina Altobelli*, p. 45.

22 Michelangelo Ingrassia, 'Argentina Altobelli. Politica e sindacato dal Risorgimento al fascismo', *Rassegna storica del Risorgimento: organo della Società nazionale per la storia del Risorgimento italiano*, 94, 2007, 2, p. 275.

23 Letter in ACS, CPC.

24 See Ebner, *Ordinary Violence*, pp. 142–4.

25 Tito Oro Nobili fu Achille, ACS, CPC, 7624.

26 For these letters see Ebner, *Ordinary Violence*, pp. 139–65.

27 Franzinelli, *I tentacoli*, p. 325.

28 ACS, CPC and Archivio di Stato di Bologna, Questura di Bologna, Sovversivi, Ennio Gnudi. Letizia Manaresi, who lived in Bologna, was Gnudi's sister-in-law and the widow of his brother Mario Gnudi, who had died in 1933. Their son was called Oriente Lenin Spartaco – but Gnudi referred to him as Tino. Gnudi also had a sister who lived in Genoa.

1933

1 This section is based on Daniele Marchesini, *Carnera*, Il Mulino, Bologna, 2006.

2 Orio Vergani in ibid., p. 31.

3 Ibid., p. 161.

4 Ibid., p. 173.

5 http://www.casadellarchitettura.eu/fascicolo/data/2010-12-20_375_ 845.pdf.

1934

1 *Corriere Padano*, 20 December 1933, cited in Segrè, *Italo Balbo*, p. 343.

2 Paul Corner, *The Fascist Party and Popular Opinion in Mussolini's Italy*, CUP, Cambridge, 2012, p. 156.

3 Mazzoni, 'Costanzo Ciano' *e famiglia, i grandi ricchi del regime*', in Paolo Giovannini and Marco Palla (eds), *Il fascismo delle mani sporche. Dittatura, corruzione, affarismo*, Laterza, Bari, 2019, pp. 49–70.

4 Mussolini (1923) cited in Colarizi, *Dopoguerra e fascismo*, p. 309.

5 Mazzoni, 'Costanzo Ciano'.

6 Luzzatto, *Padre Pio*, p. 223.

7 Ibid., pp. 295–6.

8 http://vicoinfoeventi.altervista.org/1934-la-visita-di-mussolini-a-foggia-e-lincontro-con-i-cittadini-del-gargano/. See the volume by Silvio Petrucci, *In Puglia con Mussolini: cronache e note di un invitato speciale con il testo integrale dei discorsi editi e inediti pronunciati dal duce nelle giornate pugliesi del settembre XII*, Novissima, Rome, 1935; the film *La visita del Duce in terra di Puglia* (1934); and Stephen Gundle, 'Mussolini's appearance in the regions', in Stephen Gundle, Christopher Duggan and Giuliana Pieri (eds), *The Cult of the Duce: Mussolini and the Italians*, Manchester University Press, Manchester, 2013, pp. 120–2.

9 See Adriano Sofri, *Il martire fascista*, Sellerio, Palermo, 2019.

10 'He began to justify the Libyan war of 1911–1912 which he had once condemned', Mack Smith, *Mussolini*, p. 31.

11 Cited in Giuseppe Finaldi, 'Fascism, Violence, and Italian Colonialism', *Journal of Holocaust Research*, 33:1, 2019, p. 23.

12 Ibid., p. 24.

13 See Michael Ebner, 'Fascist Violence and the "Ethnic Reconstruction" of Cyrenaica (Libya), 1922–1934', in P. Dwyer and A. Nettelbeck (eds), *Violence, Colonialism and Empire in the Modern World*, Palgrave, London, 2018, pp. 197–218.

14 Cited in Kertzer, *The Pope and Mussolini*, p. 219.

15 'Il tricolore su Adua', *La Gazzetta del Popolo*, 7 October 1935.

16 Giuseppe Finaldi, 'Method in their Madness: Understanding the Dynamics of the Italian Massacre of Ethiopian Civilians, February–May 1937', in Phillip Dwyer and Lyndall Ryan (eds), *Theatres of Violence: Massacre, Mass Killing and Atrocity Throughout History*, Berghahn, London, 2012, p. 253. For the military aspects of the war see John Gooch, *Mussolini's War. Fascist Italy from Triumph to Collapse*, Allen Lane, London, 2020, pp. 10–34. For the historical debates, see Giuseppe Finaldi, 'Mussolini's War in Ethiopia', in Gordon Martel (ed.), *A Companion to International History 1900–2001*, Wiley & Sons, Oxford, 2007, p. 220–32.

17 August Simonin, *Il linguaggio di Mussolini*, Bompiani, Milan, 1978, p. 75.

18 Giorgio Rochat, 'The Italian Air Force in the Ethiopian War (1935–1936)', in Ruth Ben-Ghiat and Mia Fuller (eds), *Italian Colonialism*, Palgrave, London, 2005, p. 41; see also Alberto Sbacchi, 'Poison Gas and Atrocities in the Italo–Ethiopian War (1935–6)', in same volume, pp. 47–71.

19 Ras Imru cited in Sbacchi, 'Poison Gas and Atrocities in the Italo–Ethiopian War', p. 52.

20 Cited in Angelo Del Boca, *Italiani, brava gente? Un mito duro a morire*, Neri Pozza editore, Venice, 2006, p. 190.

21 Cited in Del Boca, *Italiani, brava gente?*, p. 191.

22 Paolo Jedlowski, 'Memories of the Italian colonial past', *International Social Science Journal*, 62, 203–4, 2011, p. 40.

23 Ian Campbell, *The Addis Ababa Massacre: Italy's National Shame*, Hurst and Co., London, 2017; Finaldi, 'Method in their Madness', pp. 245–57.

24 Campbell, *The Addis Ababa Massacre*, p. 69.

25 In the years that followed a shameful international cover-up took place (largely orchestrated by the British government, who needed the Italians onside both after they 'switched sides' in the war in 1943 and once the war was over).

26 Finaldi, 'Fascism, Violence, and Italian Colonialism', p. 35.

27 https://ricerca.repubblica.it/repubblica/archivio/repubblica/2011/10/02/la-conquista-delle-baleari.html; http://www.storia900bivc.it/pagine/editoria/ramella207.html; Arrigo Petacco, *Viva la muerte!*, Mondadori, Milan, 2010.

28 Stanislao Pugliese, 'Revisiting an Assassination: the Death of Carlo Rosselli', in Gundle and Rinaldi, *Assassinations and Murder in Modern Italy*, pp. 11–22; Caroline Moorehead, *A Bold and Dangerous Family: The Rossellis and the Fight Against Mussolini*, Chatto & Windus, London, 2017; Mimmo Franzinelli, *Il delitto Rosselli. Anatomia di un omicidio politico*, Feltrinelli, Milan, 2017.

29 Cited in Simon Martin, *Football and Fascism: the National Game under Mussolini*, Bloomsbury, London, 2004, p. 107.

30 Robert Gordon and John London, 'Italy 1934. Football and Fascism', in Alan Tomlinson and Christopher Young, *National Identity and Global Sports Events. Culture, Politics and Spectacle in the Olympics and the Football World Cup*, State University of New York Press, New York, 2006, pp. 41–64.

31 For Carosio, see Alessandro D'Ascanio, *La vittoria del 1934. I campionati mondiali di calcio nella politica del regime*, Solfanelli, Chieti, 2010, pp. 130–3.

32 Paul Dietschy, *Storia del calcio*, Paginauno, Vedano al Lambro, 2014, p. 155.

33 D'Ascanio, *La vittoria del 1934*, p. 70.

34 Gianni Brera, *Storia critica del calcio italiano*, Baldini e Castoldi, Milan, 1998, p. 132.

35 Marco Impiglia, 'The 1934 FIFA World Cup. Did Mussolini Rig the Game?', Stefan Rinke and Kay Schiller (eds), *The FIFA World Cup 1930–2010: Politics, Commerce, Spectacle and Identities*, Wallstein Verlag, Göttingen, 2014, pp. 77–89; on the Spanish protests, see also D'Ascanio, *La Vittoria*, pp. 187–9.

36 Impiglia, 'The 1934 FIFA World Cup', p. 71.

37 David Goldblatt, *The Ball is Round*, Penguin, London, 2006, p. 259.

38 Impiglia, 'The 1934 FIFA World Cup', p. 84.

39 Christian Goeschel, *Mussolini and Hitler. The Forging of the Fascist Alliance*, Yale University Press, London, 2018.

40 PRO minute, 19 January 1934, cited in Peter Beck, 'For World Footballing Honours: England versus Italy, 1933, 1934 and 1939', in J. A. Mangan (ed.), *Europe, Sport, World. Shaping Global Societies*, Routledge, Abingdon, 2001, p. 260.

41 Cited in ibid., p. 247.

42 Eddie Hapgood, *Football Ambassador*, GCR Books Limited, London, 2009, p. 38.

43 Cited in Martin, *Football and Fascism*, p. 205; on the battle of Highbury, see also: Foot, *Calcio*, pp. 479–80, and David Winner, *These Feet: A Sensual History of English Football*, Bloomsbury, London, 2013, pp. 202–6.

44 Hapgood, *Football Ambassador*, p. 38.

45 Ibid., p. 39.

46 'Le mogli dei calciatori Guaita e Scopelli fermate a Ventimiglia con circa tre milioni', *Corriere della Sera*, 29 September 1935. See also: Foot, *Calcio*, pp. 430–1.

47 http://www.succedeoggi.it/2014/05/il-bomber-disertore/; https://gioc opulito.it/enrique-guaita-il-mistero-della-guardia-carceraria-campi one-del-mondo/.

48 Quidam, 'Eroi della domenica', *Critica Fascista*, XIII, 24, 15 October 1935, cited in Marchesini, *Carnera*, pp. 165, 241.

49 'Many people…tried to get the three to leave Italy…there was jealousy, fear and much else besides', La Cronistoria, Rome, 1964, cited in '20 Settembre 1935 - 80 anni fa la fuga dei "Tre Moschettieri"', https://new.laroma24.it/rubriche/ corsi-e-ricordi/2015/09/20-settembre-1935-la-fuga-dei-tre-moschettieri

50 'Le deliberazioni del direttorio', *Corriere della Sera*, 22 October 1935, 'I "risparmi" dei calciatori italo-argentini e la loro mancata emigrazione in Francia', *Corriere della Sera*, 1 October 1935. For this scandal and the issue of the *oriundi* in general, see Martin, *Football and Fascism*, pp. 194–7.

51 There is no biography of Sacerdoti, who became president of Roma again in the 1950s, but see Foot, *Calcio*, p. 430.

52 Joan Tumblety, 'The Soccer World Cup of 1938: Politics, Spectacles, and *la Culture Physique* in Interwar France', *French Historical Studies*, 31, 1, 2008, p. 113. See also: Foot, *Calcio*, pp. 475–8.

53 Paul Dietschy, 'The 1938 World Cup: Sporting Neutrality and Geopolitics, or All-Conquering Fascism?' in Rinke, Schiller (eds), *The FIFA World Cup*, pp. 98–9.

54 Cited in Andrea Sangiovanni, *Le parole e le fi gure. Storia dei media in Italia dall'età liberale alla seconda guerra mondiale* (Donzelli: Rome, 2012), p. 220.

55 Gianni Isola, *L'ha scritto la radio: storia e testi della radio durante il fascismo (1924–1944)*, Bruno Mondadori, Milan, p. xiii.

56 See David Forgacs and Stephen Gundle, *Mass Culture and Italian Society from Fascism to the Cold War*, Indiana University Press, Bloomington, 2007.

57 Ibid., p. 237.

58 Mimmo Franzinelli and Emanuele Marino, *Il duce proibito. Le fotografie di Mussolini che gli italiani non hanno mai visto*, Mondadori, Milan, 2005.

59 In April 1945 the Agenzia Stefani was closed down and the ANSA agency was set up.

60 Philip Cannistraro, *La fabbrica del consenso. Fascismo e mass media*, Laterza, Rome, p. 197.

WAR ON ITALY'S JEWS: 1938

1 Cited in Renzo De Felice, *Storia degli ebrei italiani sotto il fascismo*, Einaudi, Turin, 1993, p. 71.

2 Michele Sarfatti, 'Introduction', in Michele Sarfatti (ed.), *Italy's Fascist Jews: Insights on an Unusual Scenario*, Quest, 11, October 2017: 'I believe that the explanation lies not in a propensity of Italian Jews towards that particular party, but rather in the peculiarly Jewish tendency to engage in political life that arose out of their history as a minority, their higher level of education, and their living predominantly in towns', p. viii.

3 Fornari, *Mussolini's Gadfly*, p. 182.

4 Ibid., p. 185.

5 Ibid.

6 Ibid.

7 Ibid., p. 189.

8 Ibid., p. 187.

9 Preziosi would be given a key role in Mussolini's puppet government in the north of Italy after 1943.

10 It was only in the twenty-first century that roads in honour of some of those who drew up this manifesto were renamed.

11 Simon Levis Sullam, *L'archivio antiebraico. Il linguaggio dell'antisemitismo moderno*, Laterza, Rome, 2008.

12 Valentina Pisanty, *La difesa della razza. Antologia 1938–1943*, Bompiani, Milan, 2006.

13 The *Manifesto degli scienziati razzisti* or *Manifesto della razza* was first published with the title 'Il fascismo e i problemi della razza', in *Il Giornale d'Italia* on 14 July 1938.

14 Paul Baxa, ' "Il nostro Duce": Mussolini's visit to Trieste in 1938 and the workings of the cult of the Duce', *Modern Italy*, 18, 2, 2013, p. 119.

15 Diana De Rosa, 'La visita. Mussolini a Trieste 18–19 settembre 1938', http://www.comunicarte.info/blog/2013/la-visita-di-mussolini-a-trieste/. For the whole trip see also: Baxa, 'Il nostro Duce', pp. 117–28, and the film of the event at https://www.archivioluce.com/2019/09/18/il-discorso-di-trieste/.

16 A small metal plaque put up in 2013 marked the seventy-fifth anniversary of the speech.

17 See Marcella Ravenna and Alessandra Roncarati, 'Delegittimazione degli ebrei nella stampa fascista del 1938', *Psicologia Sociale*, 3, September–December 2008, pp. 473–88.

18 Harry Schneiderman, 'Italy', *The American Jewish Year Book*, 40 (26 September 1938 to 13 September 1939), p. 231.

19 Michele Sarfatti, 'La legislazione antiebraica nell'Italia fascista', *Meridiana*, 29, May 1997, p. 104. The superb book by Ilaria Pavan, *Il podestà ebreo, La storia di Renzo Ravenna tra fascismo e leggi razziali*, Laterza, Bari, 2006, carries a full account of the debate around Balbo, his views on the Jewish community and his 'opposition' to the anti-Semitic legislation.

20 Segrè, *Italo Balbo*, p. 427. But Segrè concludes that 'Balbo stopped well short of the "heroic opposition" which he had asked of Bottai'.

21 Pavan, *Il podestà ebreo*, p. 140.

22 The building no longer exists, as it was blown up by the German army as they retreated north through Italy in 1944. A story later went around that the German occupiers had also cooked and eaten the dromedaries on the estate.

23 https://www.ilfattoquotidiano.it/2018/01/26/giornata-della-memo ria-la-dolce-vita-dei-savoia-a-san-rossore-dove-vittorio-emanu ele-iii-firmo-le-leggi-razziali/4111109/. Years later, the descendants of the

ex-royal family would apologise, in exchange for the right to return to Italy from exile.

24 For the genesis of the laws, see Michele Sarfatti, *Mussolini contro gli ebrei. Cronaca dell'elaborazione delle leggi del 1938*, Silvio Zamorani editore, Turin, 1994.

25 Franco Sabatello, 'Il censimento degli ebrei del 1938', *La Rassegna Mensile di Israel*, January–February 1976, Vol. 42, 1/2, pp. 25–55.

26 Cited in Simona Salustri, 'Angelo Fortunato Formiggini, Parole in libertà', *Storicamente*, 6, 2010, 62; http://www.storicamente.org/bo/formiggini.

27 Manicardi, *Formiggini: L'editore ebreo che si suicidò per restare italiano*, p. 64.

28 For this incident, which led to Formiggini leaving the school in question, see Meris Gaspari, 'La punizione esemplare dello studente Formiggini nel 1896', E-Review 6–2018 Bologna (BraDypUS) #formazione ISSN: 2282–4979 DOI: 10.12977/ere-view278.

29 'Saluti dalla Ghirlandina. A. F. Formiggini', Manicardi, *Formiggini*, p. 160.

30 Ibid., p. 78.

31 Cited in De Felice, *Storia degli ebrei italiani sotto il fascismo*, p. 336.

32 Enrica Asquer, 'Being a Fascist Jew in Autumn 1938: Self-portrayals from the "Discrimination" Requests Addressed to the Regime', in Michele Sarfatti (ed.), 'Italy's Fascist Jews: Insights on an Unusual Scenario', *Quest. Issues in Contemporary Jewish History, Journal of Fondazione CDEC*, 11 October 2017, pp. 2, 4, 18.

33 'Il Tribunale della Razza ha iniziato i lavori', *La Stampa*, 10 October 1939; Law 13 July 1939 XVII 1024.

34 'Il Tribunale della razza…', *La Stampa*, 11 October 1939; 'Il Tribunale della Razza ha iniziato i suoi lavori, *Corriere della Sera*, 11 October 1939.

35 On Il Tribunale della Razza, see L. Garlati and T. Vettor (eds), *Il diritto di fronte all'infamia nel diritto. A 70 anni dalle leggi razziali*, Giuffrè, Milan, 2009, in particular Nicola Rondinone, 'Il "Tribunale della razza" e la magistratura', pp. 195–206.

36 Massimiliano Boni, 'Gaetano Azzariti: dal Tribunale della razza alla Corte costituzionale', *Contemporanea*, 17, 4 (October–December 2014), p. 580. See also the superb book length version of this research, Massimilano Boni, "In questi tempi di fervore e gloria". Vita di Gaetano Azzariti, magistrato senza toga, capo del Tribunale della Razza, Prisdente della Corte Costituzionale, Bollati Boringhieri, Turin, 2022.

37 Boni, 'Gaetano Azzariti', p. 581.

38 René Moehrle, 'Fascist Jews in Trieste', pp. 61–4. This did not save Salem from persecution during the war.

39 Ibid., p. 64.
40 Pavan, *Il podestà ebreo*, p. 109.
41 Ibid., p. 110.
42 Ibid., p. 112.
43 Ibid., p. 113.
44 Ibid., p. 117.
45 Ibid., pp. 120–8.
46 Paolo Frossi (ed.), *Il romanzo di Ferrara. Atti del convegno internazionale di studi su Giorgio Bassani (Parigi 12–13 maggio 2006)*, Quaderni dell'Hotel de Galliffet, XII, Istituto Italiano di Cultura, Paris, 2007. For questions of history and memory see: Stefano Guerriero, 'La fedeltà di Giorgio Bassani alla storia nella rappresentazione della comunità ebraica ferrarese sotto il fascismo', in Fondazione Maria e Goffredo Bellonci, Accademia Nazionale Virgiliana di scienze lettere ed arti, *Narrare la storia. Dal documento al racconto*, Mondadori, Milan, pp. 359–76.
47 Beatrice Pecchiari and Domenico Scarpa (eds), *Giorgio Bassani. Interviste*, Feltrinelli, Milan, 2019, p. 114. 'Giorgio Bassani, the Jewish Italian novelist, claims that he did not know a single Jew who was not a Fascist in his native city of Ferrara,' Arella Lang, *Resistance and Italian Jews in Wartime Italy: Jewish Resistance Against the Nazis*, Patrick Henry, Catholic University of America Press, Washington DC, 2014, p. 141.
48 'L'assalto fascista alla Sinagoga di Ferrara' in P. Pieri (ed.), *Giorgio Bassani: Racconti, diari, cronache (1935–1956)*, Feltrinelli, Milan, 2014, p. 453.
49 Pecchiari and Scarpa (eds), *Giorgio Bassani*, p. 115.
50 Pavan, *Il podestà ebreo*, p. 136.
51 Rossana Rossanda, *La ragazza del secolo scorso*, Einaudi, Turin, 2005, p. 44. It does not seem that this girl was a victim of the Holocaust.
52 After the war not all of those posts were re-assigned to those who had been sacked from them; see for example, for the case of the discipline of psychology, Patrizia Guarnieri, *Italian Psychology and Jewish Emigration under Fascism. From Florence to Jerusalem and New York*, Palgrave, London, 2016.
53 For a letter of expulsion, dated 29 November 1938, see Riccardo Di Donato, 'Materiali per una biografia intellettuale di Arnaldo Momigliano, 1. Libertà e pace nel mondo antico', *Athenaeum*, 83/1, 1995, p. 219, n.25. See also: Simon Levis Sullam, 'Arnaldo Momigliano e la "nazionalizzazione parallela": autobiografia, religione e storia', *Passato e Presente*, 70, 2007, pp. 59–82, http://www.storiaxxisecolo.it/rassegnasta/rassegna_coro50 401.htm.

54 For those few who refused, see Giorgio Boatti, *Preferirei di no. Le storie dei dodici professori che si opposero a Mussolini*, Einaudi, Turin, 2001.

55 Albert Baumgarten, *Elias Bickerman as a Historian of the Jews: A Twentieth Century Tale*, Mohr Siebeck, Tübingen, pp. 195–6.

56 See Giorgio Fabre, 'Arnaldo Momigliano e il Pnf', in *L'integrazione degli ebrei: una tenace illusione. Scritti per Fabio Levi*, Silvio Zamorani Editore, Turin, 2019, pp. 147–66; 'Arnaldo Momigliano: autobiografia scientifica (1936)', *Quaderni di Storia*, 41, January–June 1995, pp. 85–96; 'Arnaldo Momigliano: materiali biografici', *Quaderni di Storia*, 53, 2001, pp. 309–21; 'Ministro mi creda sono un fascista', *La Repubblica*, 16 March 2001. See also: Giorgio Fabre, 'Arnaldo Momigliano: autobiografia scientifica (1936)', *Quaderni di storia*, 1995, 41, pp. 85–96; Riccardo Di Donato, 'Materiali per una biografia intellettuale di Arnaldo Momigliano', in *Athenaeum*, 1995, 1, pp. 213–44, and 1998, 1, pp. 231–44; Alexander Stille, 'Attenti a come si parla di storia', *La Repubblica*, 5 April 2001. And the lengthy debate in the pages of the *TLS*, starting with W. V. Harris, 'The Silences of Arnaldo Momigliano', *TLS*, 4854, 12 April 1996, for example: T. J. Cornell, 'The Politics of Arnaldo Momigliano', *TLS*, 4858, 10 May 1996; Oswyn Murray, 'The politics of Arnaldo Momigliano', *TLS*, 4857, 3 May 1996, p. 17, as well as Carlo Dionisotti, 'Momigliano e il contesto', *Belfagor*, 52, 1987, pp. 633–48.

57 Silingardi, 'L'eccidio', p. 156.

58 Ibid., p. 146.

FATAL ALLIANCE AND THE PACT OF STEEL

1 Cited in Passerini, *Fascism in Popular Memory*, p. 185.

2 Ibid., p. 194.

3 Corner, *The Fascist Party*, pp. 227–64.

4 Ciano's diary, 1947, p. 264, cited in Pollard, *The Fascist Experience in Italy*, p. 104.

5 Corner, *The Fascist Party*, p. 265.

6 Ibid., p. 266.

7 Gooch, *Mussolini's War*, p. 293.

8 See the extraordinary testimonies in Nuto Revelli, *Mussolini's Death March: Eyewitness Accounts of Italian Soldiers on the Eastern Front*, University Press of Kansas, Lawrence, KS, 2013.

TOTAL WAR

1 Claudia Baldoli, 'Spring 1943: the Fiat Strikes and the Collapse of the Italian Home Front', *History Workshop Journal*, 2011, 72, pp. 181–2.

2 Gabriella Gribaudi, *Guerra totale. Tra bombe alleate e violenze nazista. Napoli e il fronte meridionale 1940–44*, Bollati Boringhieri, Turin, 2005, p. 396.

3 Corner, *The Fascist Party*, p. 267.

4 See Foot, *Fratture*, pp. 203–7.

5 My emphasis. Michael Livingstone, *The Fascists and the Jews of Italy: Mussolini's Race Laws*, CUP, Cambridge, 2014, p. 182.

6 Guri Schwarz (ed.), *Diario di un partigiano ebreo: gennaio 1940–febbraio 1944. Emanuele Artom*, Bollati Boringhieri, Turin, 2008 p. 16.

7 'The bombing of Genoa in December 1942 had indeed shown how close the home front was to collapse. After these heavy attacks, popular and spontaneous protests were witnessed in those quarters of the city where there had been no public shelters.' Baldoli, 'Spring 1943: the Fiat Strikes', p. 185.

1943

1 'The Turin Strikes of March 1943', in Jane Caplan (ed.), *Nazism, Fascism and the Working Class*, CUP, Cambridge, 1995 p. 294. More insurrectionary strikes would also break out in 1944.

2 Gooch, *Mussolini's War*, p. 378.

3 Susmel, *Nenni e Mussolini*, p. 346.

4 Gooch, *Mussolini's War*, p. 382.

5 For the memory and history of this event, see the podcast by Alessandro Portelli, *Sulla scena di Roma – Il bombardamento di San Lorenzo: Lezioni di Storia*, Laterza, Rome, 2019.

6 There are numerous accounts of 25 July 1943, many of which contradict each other. For an abundance of detail see: Ruggero Zangrandi, *1943: 25 luglio–8 settembre*, Feltrinelli, Milan, 1964, and for an insider's version, Grandi, *Il mio paese*, pp. 617–60.

7 Kertzer, *The Pope and Mussolini*, p. 191.

8 'Nenni racconta quando vide il Duce prigioniero a Ponza', *Corriere della Sera*, 1 March 1973.

9 Bosworth, *Mussolini*, p. 402.

10 'Piero Brandimarte denunciato per procacciamento di cibarie vincolante', *La Stampa*, 17 August 1943.

11 'Anche Brandimarte ha fatto il gruzzoletto', *La Nuova Stampa*, 30 January 1946.

12 'Il fermo di Piero Brandimarte', *La Stampa*, 28 August 1943.

13 http://www.treccani.it/enciclopedia/giovanni-roveda_(Dizionario-Bio grafico)/.

14 Carcano, *Strage a Torino*, p. 180; 'Dichiarazioni di Roveda sulle accuse contro il quadrunviro', *La Stampa*, 4 September 1943.

15 Story originally recounted in Miriam Mafai, *Pane nero. Donne e vita quotidiana nella seconda guerra mondiale*, Mondadori, Milan, 1987, p. 145, retold and analysed in Arthurs, 'Memory', p. 205.

16 Arthurs, 'Memory', p. 210.

17 Roberto Zani, 'Intervento alla giornata di studi su Augusto Masetti e l'invasione della Libia', Bologna del 30 ottobre 2011: "La sovversione antimilitarista di Augusto Masetti" ', http://circoloberneri.indivia.net/wp-content/uploads/intervento_zani_masetti.pdf. p. 11.

FORTY FIVE DAYS

1 Other members of the *tribunale* also moved seamlessly into key roles in postwar Italy. One of them, Antonio Manca, also ended up in the Constitutional Court itself.

2 https://www.didaweb.net/fuoriregistro/leggi.php?a=7206 for the text, and see also: https://www.patriaindipendente.it/persone-e-luoghi/anni versari/25-luglio-43-45-giorni-badoglio/.

3 https://www.istoreco.re.it/28-luglio-eccidio-reggiane/.

4 See Bruno Marani, Michele Sartori, Moreno Simonazzi, 'Le Officine Reggiane centro della Resistenza antifascista (1919–1945)', *Ricerche Storiche*, 17–18, 1972, https://www.istoreco.re.it/wp-content/uploads/2017/07/28-luglio-reggiane.pdf.

5 On 25 September Badoglio himself signed a longer peace agreement in Malta.

8 SEPTEMBER 1943

1 For details, see Gooch, *Mussolini's War*.

2 Luca Baldissara and Paolo Pezzino, *Il massacro. Guerra ai civili a Monte Sole*, Il Mulino, Bologna, 2009.

3 Foot, *Fratture*; Paolo Pezzino, *Guerra ai civili. Occupazione tedesca e politica del massacro (Toscana, 1944)*, Marsilio, Venice, 1997.

4 Zangrandi, *1943*, p. 700.

5 See Claudio Pavone, *A Civil War. A History of the Italian Resistance*, Verso, London, 2014, and Phil Cooke, *The Legacy of the Italian Resistance*, Palgrave, London, 2011.

6 Gribaudi, *Guerra totale*, pp. 510–71.

ITALY'S HOLOCAUST: DEPORTATION AND SLAUGHTER, 1943–45

1 Giuseppe Mayda, *Storia della deportazione dall'Italia 1943–1945. Militari, ebrei e politici nei lager del terzo Reich*, Bollati Boringhieri, Turin, p. 96; Marco Nozza, *Hotel Meina. La prima strage di ebrei in Italia*, Editoriale Diario, Milan, 2007. In a strange twist of fate the Petacci family also stayed in Meina in 1943 as they tried to escape capture.

2 Eugenio's sister Lina managed to avoid deportation in Venice.

3 Elsa Morante, *Opere*, Mondadori, Milan, 1988, p. 541.

4 Anna Foa, '16 ottobre. Deportazione degli ebrei di Roma', in Alessandro Portelli (ed.), *Calendario civile*, Donzelli, Rome, 2017, pp. 267–72. These figures sometimes differ. See Robert Gordon, *The Holocaust in Italian Culture, 1944–2010*, Stanford University Press, Palo Alto, 2012, pp. 86–108. The last survivor from that deportation died in October 2018.

5 Enzo Gradassi, *Sesto Senso. Una famiglia ebrea in Casentino. Biforco, 1943*, Zona, Arezzo, 2009; Mayda, *Storia della deportazione dall'Italia*, p. 79.

6 Paolo Ravenna, 'Il sequestro dei beni delle sinagoghe e altre notizie sulla comunità ebraica di Ferrara dal 1943 al 1945', *La Rassegna Mensile di Israel*, terza serie, 69, 2, *Saggi sull'ebraismo italiano del Novecento in onore di Luisella Mortara Ottolenghi*, Tomo II (May–August 2003), p. 534.

7 Ravenna, 'Il sequestro dei beni', p. 538.

8 Ibid., p. 530.

9 Ibid., p. 538.

10 Rolando Balugani: *La scia di sangue lasciata dai Tupin (1943–1945). Seguirono Vezzalini da Ferrara a Novara e dalla Bassa modenese a Dongo (Como)*, Sigem, Modena, 1999. However, Vezzalani's activities against Jews were not mentioned at the trial, apart from a reference to the theft or sequestration of Jewish property.

11 For 'having saved at least 800 Jews' according to the official justification for the medal.

12 Michele Sarfatti, 'Gino Bartali e la fabbricazione di carte di identità per gli ebrei nascosti a Firenze', *Documenti e commenti*, 2, http://www.michelesarfatti.it/documenti-e-commenti/gino-bartalie-la-fabbricazione-di-carte-di-identita-gli-ebrei-nascosti-firenze. For the heroic version, see: Ali and Andres McConnon, *Road to Valor. A True Story of World War II Italy, The Nazis and the Cyclist who Inspired a Nation*, Crown, New York, 2002. For the value of the Bartali myth for the Church and in postwar Italy, see: Emiliano Perra, 'Good Catholics, Good Italians: Religion and Rescue in recent Italian Holocaust Dramas', *The Italianist*, 34, 2, June 2014, pp. 156–69. The classic and pioneering work on the Bartali myth

is Stefano Pivato, *Sia lodato Bartali. Ideologia, cultura e miti dello sport cattolico (1936–1948)*, Edizioni Lavoro, Rome, 1996.

13 I also accepted this version in my history of Italian cycling published in 2011, Foot, *Pedalare! Pedalare!*, pp. 126–7.

14 Marco and Stefano Pivato, *L'ossessione della memoria. Bartali e il salvataggio degli ebrei: una storia inventata*, Castelvecchi, Rome, 2021. See also: David Bidussa, et al., *Il caso Bartali e le responsabilità degli storici*, Lit Edizioni, Rome, 2021.

15 https://it.gariwo.net/dl/ComunicatoPalatucciFarkas.pdf.

16 David Bidussa, *Il mito del buon italiano*, Il Saggiatore, Milan, 1995; Filippo Focardi, *Il cattivo tedesco e il bravo italiano. La rimozione delle colpe della seconda guerra mondiale*, Laterza, Rome-Bari, 2013.

17 'Deficit etico-politico e continuità nella storia italiana. Interviste di Giuliano Ferrara a Renzo De Felice', *Corriere della Sera*, 27 December 1987 and 8 January 1988.

18 Schwarz (ed.), *Diario di un partigiano ebreo*.

19 Primo Levi, 'Un parco dedicato a Emanuele Artom', *La Stampa*, 11 April 1984.

20 Nazario Sauro Onofri, *Ebrei e fascismo a Bologna*, Grafica Lavino, Bologna, 1989, p. 33; http://www.bibliotecatrisi.it/Archivio-notizie/Le-leggi-razzi ali-e-gli-ebrei-a-Lugo-1938-1945; http://curba.racine.ra.it/_static/materi aleStud/olocausto/comunita_ebraica_lugo.htm.

21 http://www.smbr.it/lugo-lapide-famiglie-ebree-deportate/.

22 Liliana Picciotto, *Il libro della memoria. Gli ebrei deportati dall'Italia (1843–1945)*, Mursia, Milan, 1991, pp. 27–35; https://www.mosaico-cem. it/cultura-e-societa/personaggi-e-storie/ebrei-di-rodi-un-film-e-un-sito.

23 Varian Fry, *Surrender on Demand*, Johnson Books, Boulder, 1997, pp. 22–3. See also: Arfé in *Giuseppe Emanuele l'altro Modigliani*. p. 15.

24 Joyce Lussu, *Fronti e frontiere*, Laterza, Rome-Bari, 1967, p. 77.

25 Ibid., p. 80.

26 Ibid., p. 83.

27 Ibid., p. 82.

28 On his return to Italy, 'Mené bent down, touched the land with his finger and then brought it to his lips', *Giuseppe Emanuele l'altro Modigliani*, p. 183.

29 Pugliese, *Bitter Spring*, pp. 184–5. See also: Viviana Simonelli, 'Testimonianza', in Angelo Pedani (ed.), *Giuseppe Emanuele Modigliani: il fratello 'maggiore'. Socialismo, pace e libertà*, Atti del Convegno, Livorno, 28 October 2012, Firenze: Consiglio regionale della Toscana, 2015, p. 31. Modigliani briefly took part in the work of the Constituent Assembly

after 1945, by which time he was old and unwell, before dying in 1947. He is buried, alongside Vera, in the vast Verano cemetery in Rome.

30 He went on to be part of the Constituent Assembly after 1946, which drew up and debated the Italian constitution, and continued to support the workers of Terni after the war.

LIBERATION: 1944

1 Portelli, *Biography of an Industrial Town*, pp. 210–11.

2 Guido Crainz, 'Il conflitto e la memoria. Guerra civile e triangolo della morte', *Meridiana*, 1992, 13, pp. 17–55; Francesco Catastini, *Una lunga Resistenza. Microstorie a confronto. Roccastrada e Calenzano (1922–1946)*, Pacini Editore, Pisa, 2015; Foot, *Fratture*, pp. 349–71.

3 Crainz, 'Il conflitto e la memoria', pp. 17–55; Pavone, *A Civil War*; Foot, *Fratture*.

MUSSOLINI BETWEEN LIFE AND DEATH: A STORY IN FRAGMENTS

1 The eighteen bodies comprised: the fifteen fascists shot in Dongo; Mussolini, Claretta and Claretta's brother, Marcello. Starace would be captured and shot in Milan itself.

2 Franco Loi, cited by Romeo Cerri in *Brianza Popolare*, 10 August 2022. brianzapopolare.it/sezioni/storia/milano_loreto_1944_loi_2002ago10.htm

3 Carlo Gentile gives the correct figure as nine: 'Piazzale Loreto 10 agosto 1944. Dai fondi fotografici degli archivi tedeschi', *Italia contemporanea*, 205, 1996, p. 751.

4 See https://www.doppiozero.com/materiali/piazzale-loreto-immagini-di-una-strage, and the painting by Aligi Sassu, *Guerra civile* (*I martiri di piazzale Loreto*) which he created in 1944 but which was only seen in 1952, at the Venice Biennale, and can now be viewed in the Galleria Nazionale d'Arte Moderna e Contemporanea di Roma. See also: Gentile, 'Piazzale Loreto 10 agosto 1944', pp. 749–53. Gentile discovered a series of photos of the 1944 reprisal in archives in Germany. He notes how in the photos Italian fascists stand guard over the bodies, and there is no sign of any Germans.

5 'Mussolini, mistress executed by firing squad', James E. Roper, United Press Staff Writer, 29 April 1945, https://www.upi.com/Archives/1945/04/29/Mussolini-mistress-executed-by-firing-squad/7511360114334/.

6 'Italy's former Dictator Shot After Trial – Other Fascists Executed', *New York Times*, 30 April 1945.

7 Cited in Mirco Dondi, 'Piazzale Loreto 29 aprile: aspetti di una pubblica esposizione', *Rivista di Storia Contemporanea*, 2, 1990, p. 220. See also: Mirco Dondi, 'Piazzale Loreto', in Isnenghi (ed.), *I luoghi della memoria*, pp. 487–99; Ilaria Favretto, 'Rough Music and Factory Protest in Post-1945 Italy', *Past and Present*, 228, 1, 2015, pp. 232–3; Isnenghi, *L'Italia in piazza*, pp. 364–70.

8 Milton Bracker, 'Italy's former Dictator Shot After Trial – Other Fascists Executed', *New York Times*, 30 April 1945, also in R. F. Collins, P. S. Washburn, *The Greenwood Library of American War Reporting: World War I & World War II, the European Theater*, Greenwood Press, Westport, 2005, p. 374.

9 See 'Milton Bracker, Chief of Bureau for the Times in Rome, Dead', *New York Times*, 29 January 1964.

10 Milton Bracker in 'Duce's Demise', *New York Times*, 29 June 1952, writes that he was one of eight journalists in the *piazzale* that day. On the 30th he claims that they 'retraced' Mussolini's attempt to escape up to Lake Como. He also states that the bodies were buried that night at 6 p.m. in Musocco.

11 'Last Days of Mussolini', *New York Times*, 24 April 1955.

12 Collier, *Duce!*, p. 363.

13 https://www.hfsbooks.com/books/combat-correspondents-sterne/.

14 *Baltimore Sun*, 30 April 1945. For the choice of Piazzale Loreto, see also: Giovanni Scirocco, 'Caduta e morte del tiranno a piazzale Loreto', in M. Isnenghi (ed.), *Gli Italiani in guerra. Conflitti, identità, memorie dal Risorgimento ai nostri giorni*, Vol. IV, Tomo II, *La seconda guerra mondiale*, UTET, Turin, 2009, pp. 617, 622, n.8.

15 It is said that the photos of Mussolini reached Hitler's bunker 'by telex' and that this pushed Hitler towards suicide: see Mimmo Franzinelli and Marcello Flores, *Storia della Resistenza*, Laterza, Rome, 2019, p. 500.

16 https://www.youtube.com/watch?v=wOCecmSa-Mo.

17 Cited in Dondi, 'Piazzale Loreto 29 aprile', p. 220.

18 As a kind of added form of mockery, someone had placed a fascist staff in his hand. His face was grotesquely swollen.

19 Monelli, *Mussolini piccolo borghese*, p. 198.

20 Dondi, 'Piazzale Loreto 29 aprile', p. 221.

21 Ibid., p. 240; there were also accounts of people shooting at the body in the morgue itself, see Franco Vernice, 'Cercavamo in lui la prova della follia', *La Repubblica*, 13 December 1994.

22 Dondi, 'Piazzale Loreto 29 aprile', p. 248.

23 Monelli, *Mussolini*, p. 298.

24 Cited in Dondi, 'Piazzale Loreto 29 aprile', p. 236; the Official proclamation, supposedly written by Luigi Longo, was issued by the CLNAI on 29 April 1945, https://it.wikisource.org/wiki/Comunicato _29_aprile_1945.

25 Isnenghi, *L'Italia in piazza*, p. 264.

26 Alberto Scerbanenko, *Le cinque vite di Giorgio Scerbanenco*, Feltrinelli, Milan, 2019, p. 202. His father was Giorgio Scerbanenco, who would go on to write a series of extraordinary crime novels set in Milan in the 1950s and 1960s.

27 Cited in Isnenghi, *L'Italia in piazza*, p. 269.

28 Giorgio Pisanò, *Gli ultimi cinque secondi di Mussolini. Un'inchiesta giornalistica durata quarant'anni*, Il Saggiatore, Milan, 2009. For a concise run-through of all the various theories concerning Mussolini's death see Didier Musiedlak, 'The Metamorphoses of Mussolini's Body', *Journal of Genocide Research*, 20, 2, 2018, pp. 236–46.

29 Roberto Rossellini, *Paisà*, 1946; in general see: Giovanni De Luna, *Il corpo del nemico ucciso. Violenza e morte nella guerra contemporanea*, Einaudi, Turin, 2006, and Mario Isnenghi, 'L'esposizione della morte', in Gabriele Ranzato (ed.), *Guerre fratricide. Le guerre civili in età contemporanea*, Bollati Boringhieri, Turin, 1994, pp. 330–52.

30 Isnenghi, *L'Italia in piazza*, pp. 369, 370, and see also, in general, the analysis on pp. 364–70.

31 Luisa Passerini, *Fascism in Popular Memory: the Cultural Experience of the Turin Working Class*, CUP, Cambridge, p. 101.

32 'Revenge is Sour', *Tribune*, 9 November 1945, Sonia Orwell and Ian Angus (eds), *The Collected Essays, Journalism and Letters of George Orwell*, Vol. IV, *In Front of Your Nose, 1945–1960*, Secker and Warburg, London, 1968, p. 5.

33 http://www.piccolimartiri.it/01-PAGINE-IN-ITALIANO/L-entrata. htm. In this list there are three victims with a Beccari surname and three victims called Carretta, but in interviews collected on the site one of the victims in each case appears to be a cousin of the others.

34 Collier, *Duce!*, p. 363.

35 Collier, *Duce!*, p. 363.

36 Passerini, *Torino operaia e fascismo*, p. 120.

37 Ibid., p. 273, n.90.

38 Sergio Temolo, son of one of the 1944 victims, Libero Temolo, cited in Giovanni Scirocco, 'Christian Schiefer, un fotografo a piazzale Loreto',

in Maurizio Guerri, *Le immagini delle guerre contemporanee*, Meltemi editore, Milan, 2017, p. 51.

39 Monelli, *Mussolini*, p. 298. For Claretta, see: Richard Bosworth, *Claretta: Mussolini's Last Lover*, Yale University Press, London, 2017, and Bee Wilson, 'Il Duce and the Red Alfa', *London Review of Books*, 39, 6, 16 March 2017. Not all the bodies were hung up, only the 'most important' ones. Claretta's was the second to be lifted into place.

40 Monelli, *Mussolini*, p. 298.

41 Temolo and others, cited in Dondi, 'Piazzale Loreto 29 aprile', p. 237.

42 Monelli, *Mussolini*, p. 298.

43 Cited in Scirocco, 'Caduta e morte del tiranno a piazzale Loreto', p. 617.

44 Claudio Fogu, *The Historic Imaginary. Politics of History in Fascist Italy*, University of Toronto Press, Toronto, 2003, p. 197.

45 Milton Bracker, 'Last days of Mussolini', *New York Times*, 24 April 1955; James Roper, 'Mussolini, mistress executed by firing squad', *United Press*, 29 April 1945, https://www.upi.com/Archives/1945/04/29/Mussolini-mistress-executed-by-firing-squad/7511360114334/; Milton Bracker, 'The End of Mussolini', *New York Times*, 30 April 1945.

46 https://www.huffingtonpost.it/2019/04/27/alessandra-mussolini-il-25-apr ile-ero-in-mezzo-ai-migranti-con-la-croce-rossa-la-boldrini-dovera_a_2 3718160/.

47 *Avanti!*, 30 April 1945, cited in Scirocco, 'Caduta e morte del tiranno a piazzale Loreto', p. 618.

48 C. Levi, 'Morte dei morti', *La Nazione del Popolo*, 30 April 1945, now also in P. L. Ballini (ed.), *La Nazione del Popolo. Organo del Comitato Toscano di Liberazione Nazionale (11 Agosto 1944–3 Luglio 1946)*, Regione Toscana, Florence, 1998, pp. 295–7, cited in Filippo Benfante, 'Carlo Levi a Firenze e la Firenze di Carlo Levi (1941–1945). Vita quotidiana e militanza politica dalla guerra alla Liberazione', EUI, Unpublished thesis, 2003, p. 210.

49 See Foot, *Modern Italy*, pp. 182–3.

50 Cited in Dondi, 'Piazzale Loreto 29 Aprile', p. 227.

51 Collier, *Duce!*, p. 365.

52 Giovanni De Luna, *La passione e la ragione. Il mestiere dello storico contemporaneo*, Bruno Mondadori, Milan, 2014, p. 173.

53 Cited in Dondi, 'Piazzale Loreto 29 aprile', p. 221.

54 Ibid., p. 245.

55 Unpublished manuscript notes, cited in Benfante, *Carlo Levi a Firenze*, p. 209.

56 *New Left Review* 49, January–February 2008: https://newleftreview.org/issues/II49/articles/rossana-rossanda-the-comrade-from-milan.

57 Scirocco, 'Caduta e morte del tiranno a piazzale Loreto', p. 620.

58 Cited in Scirocco, 'Caduta e morte del tiranno a piazzale Loreto', p. 619; For the presence, or not, of Montanelli in Piazzale Loreto, see: Renata Broggini, *Passaggio in Svizzera, L'anno nascosto di Indro Montanelli*, Feltrinelli, Milan, 2021, pp. 150–3. For Montanelli and fascism see, for example, Isnenghi, 'La marcia su Roma', pp. 328–9, and Cristina Baldassini, *L'ombra di Mussolini: l'Italia moderata e la memoria del fascismo, 1945-1960*, Rubbettino, Soveria Mannelli, 2008.

59 See Scirocco, 'Christian Schiefer, un fotografo a piazzale Loreto', in Maurizio Guerri, *Le immagini delle guerre contemporanee*, Meltemi Editore, Milan, 2017, pp. 35–56, and: https://www.milanolibera.it/storie/christ ian-schiefer-un-fotografo-a-piazzale-loreto/. For other photographs see http://www.lombardiabeniculturali.it/percorsi/29-aprile-1945/1/; Mario Chiodetti, 'Schiefer e la sua Leica a Piazzale Loreto', *L'Unità*, 23 August 1996; Giovanni Scirocco, 'Il fotografo di matrimoni che portò Piazzale Loreto sul New York Times' (24 April 1915): https://www.glistatigenerali. com/storia-cultura/christian-schiefer-piazzale-loreto/.

60 Chiodetti, 'Schiefer e la sua Leica a Piazzale Loreto'.

61 Antonio Spinosa, *Starace*, Rizzoli, Milan, 1981, p. 289.

62 Scirocco, 'Christian Schiefer', p. 41.

63 Spinosa, *Starace*, p. 289.

64 Ibid., p. 290.

65 Dondi, 'Piazzale Loreto 29 aprile', p. 230.

66 Bottai, *Diario, 1935–44*, Milan, 1982, p. 102, cited in Ebner, *Ordinary Violence*, p. 10.

67 https://www.marxists.org/archive/serge/1945/05/bombacci.htm.

68 S. Orwell and I. Angus (eds), *Collected Essays, Journalism and Letters of George Orwell, Vol. II, My Country Right or Left 1940–1943*, Secker and Warburg, London, 1968, p. 324. 'And, above all, no solemn hypocritical "trial of war criminals", with all the slow cruel pageantry of the law, which after a lapse of time has so strange a way of focusing a romantic light on the accused and turning a scoundrel into a hero'; George Orwell, 'Who are the War Criminals?', *Tribune*, 22 October 1943.

69 Orwell and Angus (ed.), *The Collected Essays*, pp. 324–5.

70 Guglielmo Scotti, *Nicola Bombacci: un comunista a Salò*, Mursia, Milan, 2008; see also: Annamaria Bombacci, *Nicola Bombacci rivoluzionario 1910–1921*, Santerno edizioni, Imola, 1983; Serge Noiret, *Massimalismo e crisi dello Stato liberale. Nicola Bombacci (1879–1924)*, FrancoAngeli, Milan, 1992;

Steven Forti, 'Partito, Rivoluzione e Guerra. Un'analisi del linguaggio politico di un transfuga: Nicola Bombacci (1879–1945)', Albanese, 'Dire violenza, fare violenza'. Espressione, minaccia, occultamento e pratica della violenza durante la marcia su Roma', *Memoria e Ricerca*, 17, 31, 2009, pp. 155–75.

71 Scotti, *Nicola Bombacci*, p. 11.

72 Contini, 'Il comizio', p. 187; 'Noiret, *Massimalismo e crisi dello Stato liberale*, p. 380.

73 Isnenghi, *L'Italia in piazza*, p. 355, see also pp. 355–7.

74 R. W. Johnson, 'Le Grand Jacques', *London Review of Books*, 8, 17, 9 October 1986.

75 *Nel tempo del fascismo*, Riuniti, Rome, 1975, pp. 226–7.

76 https://www.marxists.org/archive/serge/1945/05/bombacci.htm.

POST-FASCIST ITALY: GHOSTS AND MEMORIES

1 http://www.comune.bologna.it/storiaamministrativa/media/files/comme morazione_di_enio_gnudi.pdf.

2 Luzzato, *Il corpo del duce*, pp. 47–8, see also pp. 6–9.

3 Mayda, *Il pugnale di Mussolini*, p. 318.

4 Ibid., p. 323.

5 Simona Colarizi, 'Giuseppe Di Vagno. Il Matteotti del Sud', *Critica Sociale*, CXX, 7, 2011, p. 1. http://www.criticasociale.net/files/60_000 0008_file_1.pdf.

6 In Rome, the crowd had occasionally taken justice into their own hands, as in the case of Donato Caretta, who was, it seems, wrongly identified as being in part responsible for the 1944 Fosse Ardeatine massacre in September 1944 (although there is a debate about his responsibility as director of the Regina Coeli prison in Rome), he was forced out of a courtroom, beaten, thrown into the Tiber and pushed underwater until he drowned; his body was then hung up outside Rome's prison, Gabriele Ranzato, *Il linciaggio di Carretta, Roma 1944*, Il Saggiatore, Milan, 1994. See also: the film footage of this event in the documentary directed by Luchino Visconti and others, *Giorni di gloria*, 1945.

7 'Aperto il processo al "ras di Torino"', *Avanti!*, 27 July 1950. By this time Brandimarte had been amnestied for the crime of collaborationism.

8 'Brandimarte non è fuggito dal carcere di Firenze', *Stampa Sera*, 1–2 October 1947.

9 Carcano, *Strage a Torino*, p. 202.

10 Ibid., p. 203.

11 Walter Tobagi described him as 'the small fat leader of the Turinese squadristi', *Gli anni*, p. 10, but Enrico Deaglio calls him 'a big and large man', *Besame Mucho: diario di un anno abbastanza crudele*, Feltrinelli, Milan, 1995, p. 16.

12 Carcano, *Strage a Torino*, p. 205.

13 '26 anni e 3 mesi al Brandimarte ma col condono di due terzi della pena', *La Nuova Stampa*, 5 September 1950.

14 This was less than had been asked for by the Public Prosecutor, see 'Trent'anni di reclusione chiesti per Brandimarte', *Avanti!*, 4 August 1950; 'Trent'anni di reclusione per il Brandimarte e il Napoli', *Stampa Sera*, 3–4 August 1950; '26 anni e 3 mesi al Brandimarte ma col condono di due terzi della pena', *La Nuova Stampa*, 5 September 1950.

15 'Chiesti 26 anni per Brandimarte', *Avanti!*, 1 May 1952. See also: 'Ordinò le stragi del 1922 a Torino', *Stampa Sera*, 1 May 1952; 'L'ex-gerarca Piero Brandimarte assolto per insufficienza di prove', *La Nuova Stampa*, 1 May 1952; 'Il processo contro Brandimarte si concluderà forse questa sera', *La Nuova Stampa*, 30 April 1952; 'Si è iniziato ieri in appello il processo contro Brandimarte', *La Nuova Stampa*, 29 April 1952.

16 Carcano, *Strage a Torino*, p. 230; see also: 'Torino antifascista protesta contro l'assoluzione di Brandimarte', *Avanti!*, 7 May 1952.

17 'Il ricorso del Procuratore Generale contro l'assoluzione di Brandimarte', *La Nuova Stampa*, 4 May 1952.

18 'A Memorial Tablet in Via Mazzini', in Giorgio Bassani, *Within the Walls*, Penguin, London, 2016, pp. 61–91.

19 'Sul raduno squadrista a Torino interrogazioni da ogni settore', *Avanti!*, 26 January 1955.

20 Massarenti, ACS, CPC, 3137, 3878.

21 Ibid.

22 Petracci, *I matti*, pp. 13–15.

23 Ibid., p. 15.

24 'Commosso omaggio di Einaudi alla salma di Giuseppe Massarenti', *Corriere della Sera*, 3–4 April 1950.

25 Minguzzi later won a more prestigious competition to design the huge fifth bronze door of the Duomo di Milano.

26 For Bucco in Dachau, see Edmond Paravel, *De Béleyme à Dachau ou, La vie d'un handicapé physique dans les prisons de Vichy et les camps de concentration de l'Allemagne hitlérienne*, E. Paravel, Bergerac, 1983, p. 160 and his listing at https://stevemorse.org/dachau/dachau.php?...70454=&offset=1951.

27 Giovanna d'Amico et al. (eds), *Il libro dei deportati, Vol. 1, I deportati politici 1943–1945*, Tomo 1, A–F, Mursia, Milan, 2009, p. 412.

28 Guido A. Grimaldi, *Zaniboni racconta: perché non partì la pallottola fatale e liberatrice*, Periodici Epoca, Rome, 1945.

29 Luzzatto, *Il corpo del Duce*, p. 168.

30 'Chiuso l'albergo dove Zaniboni preparò l'attentato contro Mussolini', *Corriere della Sera*, 7 March 1963.

31 'Piazzale Loreto, 1948, si demoliscono le strutture metalliche della tettoia dello "storico" benzinaio Esso', Foto Giancolombo.

32 http://anpi-lissone.over-blog.com/article-11669404.html (although the date here is wrong), 'Milano antifascista celebra i Martiri di Piazzale Loreto', *Avanti!*, 10 August 1961.

33 The trial sentence can be seen here. http://www.difesa.it/Giustizia_Milit are/rassegna/Processi/Pagine/SaeveckeTheodorEmil.aspx. See also: Carlo Gentile, 'Piazzale Loreto 10 Agosto 1944. Dai fondi fotografici degli archivi tedeschi', *Italia contemporanea*, 205, 1996, pp. 749–53; Luigi Borgomaneri, *Hitler a Milano. I crimini di Theodor Saevecke capo della Gestapo,* https://web.archive.org/web/20120112090218/http://www. fondazioneisec.it/include/spaw/uploads/files/saevecke.pdf; Guido Acquaviva, 'Sävecke', *Oxford Companion to International Criminal Justice*, OUP, Oxford, p. 902.

34 Luzzatto, *Il corpo del duce*; see also: Mario Isnenghi, 'Il corpo del duce', in Sergio Bertelli and Cristiano Grottanelli (eds), *Gli occhi di Alessandro. Potere sovrano e sacralità del corpo da Alessandro Magno a Ceausescu*, Ponte alle Grazie, Florence, 1990, pp. 170–83.

35 Belletti and Carnoli, *L'Ardito*, p. 91.

36 Ibid., p. 104.

37 John Foot, 'The Tale of San Vittore. Prisons, politics, crime and fascism in Milan, 1943–1946', *Modern Italy*, 3, 1, May 1998, pp. 25–48.

38 'In 1968 Caradonna's squads were active against workers and students', Martin Clark, 'Italian Squadrismo and Contemporary Vigilantism', *European History Quarterly*, 18, 1988, p. 45.

39 Rhiannon Evangelista, 'The particular kindness of friends: ex-Fascists, clientage and the transition to democracy in Italy, 1945–1960', *Modern Italy*, 20, 4, 2015, pp. 411–25.

40 For Graziani see Victoria Witkowski, 'Remembering Fascism and Empire: The Public Representation and Myth of Rodolfo Graziani in 20th Century Italy', PhD Thesis, EUI, 2021.

41 In Ferrara 432 people were classified officially as 'being part of the Jewish race' in November 1943. In January 1944, over a hundred Jews were

rounded up. The most accurate recent calculations state that over seventy Jews from Ferrara died in the Holocaust: Livingston, *The Fascists and the Jews of Italy*, pp. 160–97, https://resistenzamappe.it/ferrara/fe_persecuzi oni. But these figures vary, http://www.museoferrara.it/view/s/e4ceccda8 55c49158083f20f98babco5.

42 Pavan, *Il podestà ebreo*, p. 194. See also: for the survivors https://stori amestre.it/2017/03/la-vera-storia-geo-josz/, and https://storiamestre. it/2016/04/il-25-aprile-un-fiore-per-geo-josz/.

43 Pavan, *Il podestà ebreo*, p. 194.

44 'Una lapide in via Mazzini' in Giorgio Bassani, *Cinque storie ferraresi*, Einaudi, Turin, 1956, pp. 103–48.

45 Bassani, 'Una lapide in Via Mazzini' cited in Pavan, *Il podestà ebreo*, p. 193, see also: p. 192.

46 For Predappio, see Sofia Serenelli, 'A town for the cult of the Duce: Predappio as a site of pilgrimage', in Gundle, Duggan and Pieri (eds), *The Cult of the Duce,* pp. 93–109; 'It was like something that you have at home which becomes so familiar that you don't even pay attention to it': 'Memories of Mussolini and Fascism in Predappio, 1922–2010', *Modern Italy*, 18, 2, 2013, pp. 157–75; Simona Storchi, 'The ex-Casa del Fascio in Predappio and the question of the difficult heritage of Fascism in contemporary Italy', *Modern Italy*, 24, 2, 2019, pp. 139–57; Paolo Heywood, 'Fascism, uncensored', *Terrain* (online), 72, November 2019, http://journ als.open edit ion.org/terr ain/18955,1.

47 https://www.bbc.co.uk/news/world-europe-50164806.

48 *L'Unità*, 4 December 1955.

49 'Il discorso del Presidente Azzariti davanti alla Corte costituzionale', *L'Unità*, 7 April 1957.

50 Ibid.

51 See Claudio Pavone, *Alle origini della Repubblica. Scritti su fascismo, antifascismo e continuità dello Stato*, Bollati Boringhieri, Turin, 1995.

52 'Gaetano Azzariti gravissimo per un attacco di broncopolmonite', *La Stampa*, 5 January 1961; 'La morte di Gaetano Azzariti presidente della Corte costituzionale', *La Stampa*, 6 January 1961.

53 'Un solo impegno lavorare con devozione', *La Stampa*, 6 January 1961.

54 'Saragat alla commemorazione del giudice costituzionale Azzariti', *La Stampa*, 7 March 1965. Azzariti was described as a 'brilliant legal mind'.

55 Ilaria Pavan, 'Prime note su razzismo e diritto in Italia. L'esperienza della rivista "Il Diritto razzista" (1939–1942)', in D. Menozzi, R. Pertici, M. Moretti, *Culture e libertà. Studi di storia in onore di Roberto Vivarelli*, 2006, pp. 404, 415–6; Giovanni Focardi, 'I magistrati tra la RSI e

l'epurazione', in Sergio Bugiardini (ed.), *Violenza, tragedia e memoria della Repubblica sociale italiana*, Carocci, Rome, 2006, pp. 320–1.

56 Massimiliano Boni, 'Gaetano Azzariti: dal Tribunale della razza alla Corte costituzionale', *Contemporanea*, 17, 4 (October–December 2014), pp. 577–607. See also: Barbara Raggi, *Baroni di razza. Come l'università del dopoguerra ha riabilitato gli esecutori delle leggi razziali*, Riuniti, Rome, 2012.

57 https://roma.corriere.it/notizie/cronaca/15_marzo_31/via-busto-dell-antisemita-azzariti-palazzo-consulta-d08a5444-d767-11e4-82ff-02a5d 56630ca.shtml; https://roma.corriere.it/notizie/cronaca/15_marzo_29/ corte-costituzionale-il-busto-presidente-antisemita-resta-qui-9ce77 7d8-d5d8-11e4-b0f7-93d578ddf348.shtml.

58 https://www.osservatorioantisemitismo.it/articoli/il-nipote-di-gaetano-azzariti-difende-il-nonno-presidente-del-tribunale-della-razza-fascista/.

59 https://ricerca.repubblica.it/repubblica/archivio/repubblica/2015/10/15/ una-pianta-al-posto-del-busto-di-azzariti30.html.

60 https://www.beni-culturali.eu/opere_d_arte/scheda/-busto-ritratto-di-gaetano-azzariti-scorzelli-lello-1921-12-01030297/167114.

61 Roberto Zani, 'Intervento alla giornata di studi su Augusto Masetti e l'invasione della Libia Bologna del 30 ottobre 2011: "La sovversione antimilitarista di Augusto Masetti"'; http://circoloberneri.indivia.net/ wp-content/uploads/intervento_zani_masetti.pdf, p. 13. In 1955 a debate had broken out between communists and anarchists concerning the nature of Red Week. A meeting had been held in Ancona in support of the positive memory of Red Week, and Masetti had sent a message of support, see also: 'Gli anarchici respingono in un pubblico comizio le responsabilità dell'eccidio della "settimana rossa"', *Voce Adriatica*, 19 December 1955; Massimo Papini, 'L'ombra sul mito. Le polemiche tra gli eredi negli anni Cinquanta', in Severini (ed.), *La Settimana rossa*, p. 387; Massimo Papini, *Ancona e il mito della Settimana rossa*, Le affinità elettive, Ancona, 2013, p. 99, and for the commemorations in 1964, pp. 109–14.

EPILOGUE

1 Silone, *Bread and Wine*, p. 32.

2 Francesco Filippi, *Mussolini ha fatto anche cose buone. Le idiozie che continuano a circolare sul fascismo*, Bollati Boringhieri, Turin, 2019.

3 See Ben-Ghiat, *Strongmen*.

4 Federico Finchelstein, *A Brief History of Fascist Lies*, University of California Press, Berkeley, 2020.

5 Finchelstein, *Transatlantic Fascism*, p. 15.

6 Heywood, 'Fascism, uncensored'.

7 Simona Storchi, 'Mussolini as monument. The equestrian statue of the Duce at the Littoriale Stadium in Bologna', in Gundle et al. (eds), *The Cult of the Duce*, p. 206.

8 'La dittatura fascista', in *Scritti sul Fascismo*, Vol. 1, Feltrinelli, Milan, 1961, p. 204.

9 Silone, *Bread and Wine*, p. 256.

10 Ibid.

11 Finchelstein, *Transatlantic Fascism*, p. 33.

Acknowledgements

The research for this book was carried out in libraries and archives in Bologna, Ferrara, Fiesole, Florence, Milan, Parma and Rome in Italy, and in Bristol, Edinburgh, London and Oxford in the UK. I would like to thank the staff at the Archivio di Stato in Florence, the Archivio Centrale dello Stato in Rome and the Sala Riservata of the Biblioteca Nazionale in Florence – my favourite place to study in the whole world – for their patience and advice.

Given that this book was written in Bristol amidst the unusual and difficult circumstances of a pandemic, many other libraries and archives sent me material which I could not view in person. Over the years, a number of individuals helped me in various ways with the research upon which this book is based, or with simple questions, or by just listening to often incoherent ideas. I would like to thank above all: Giulia Albanese, Josh Arthurs, Maurizio Avanzolini, Emma Barron, Ruth Ben-Ghiat, Roberto Bianchi, Phil Cooke, John Dickie, Michael Ebner, Kate Ferris, Steven Forti, Paul Ginsborg, Christian Goeschel, Robert Gordon, Hilary Horrocks, Maurizio Isabella, Mike Jones, Pieter Judson, Amy King, Giovanni Pietro Lombardo, Alessandro Luparini, Sergio Luzzato, Hannah Malone, Simon Martin, Sergio Noiret, Silvana Patriarca, Stefania Placenti, Enrico Pontieri, Lucy Riall, Marla Stone, Simon Levis Sullam. At Bloomsbury I received excellent support as ever from Michael Fishwick, Kate Johnson and Sarah Ruddick. Georgina Capel backed the project from the beginning and was always ready to hear about progress, or lack of it, at various key moments. Thanks also to Irene Baldoni at Georgina Capel Associates.

The research was funded by a Leverhulme Trust Major Research Fellowship. I would also like to thank the European University Institute for a Fernand Braudel Fellowship. My colleagues in the Italian Department in Bristol have always been extremely supportive and friendly – Rhiannon Daniels, Ruth Glynn, Tristan Kay and Catherine O'Rawe. I was lucky to have very useful discussions about my work through seminars in the EUI, the History Department in Bristol and during events online organised with the British School at Rome and the Italian Cultural Institute in London. Writing a book during a pandemic, with the schools closed, was an interesting process, which was only possible due to mutual support and understanding between me and my partner, Sarah, as well as the constant good humour of my daughter, Corinna, and the eccentric behaviour of our cats, Connie and Mimmi.

Select Bibliography

Albanese, Giulia, *La marcia su Roma*, Laterza, Bari, 2006

Araldi, Vinicio, *Camicie nere a Montecitorio. Storia parlamentare dell'avvento del fascismo*, Mursia, Milan, 1974

Arthurs, Joshua et al. (eds), *The Politics of Everyday Life in Fascist Italy*, Palgrave, New York, 2017

Asquer, Enrica, 'Being a Fascist Jew in Autumn 1938: Self-portrayals from the "Discrimination" Requests Addressed to the Regime', in Michele Sarfatti (ed.), 'Italy's Fascist Jews: Insights on an Unusual Scenario', in *Quest: Issues in Contemporary Jewish History, Journal of Fondazione CDEC*, 11, October 2017, pp. 1–28

Balabanoff, Angelica, *My Life as a Rebel*, Hamish Hamilton, London, 1938

Balbo, Italo, *Diario 1922*, Lulu.com (Mondadori, Milan) 2017

Baldissara, Luca and Paolo Pezzino, *Il massacro. Guerra ai civili a Monte Sole*, Il Mulino, Bologna, 2009

Baldoli, Claudia, 'Spring 1943: the Fiat Strikes and the Collapse of the Italian Home Front', *History Workshop Journal*, 2011, 72, pp. 181–9

Baratieri, Daniela, et al. (eds), *Totalitarian Dictatorship, New Histories*, Routledge, London, 2014

Belco, Victoria, *War, Massacre, and Recovery in Central Italy, 1943–1948*, University of Toronto Press, Toronto, 2010

Belletti, Giulia, and Saturno Carnoli, *L'Ardito: Vita provocatoria di Ferruccio Vecchi, Ravennate, Fondatore del Fascismo*, Edizioni Moderna, Ravenna, 2013

Ben-Ghiat, Ruth, *Strongmen: How they Rise. Why They Succeed. How They Fail*, Profile Books, London, 2020

Ben-Ghiat, Ruth, and Mia Fuller (eds), *Italian Colonialism*, Palgrave, London, 2005

Bianciardi, Silvia, *Argentina Altobelli e 'la buona battaglia'*, FrancoAngeli, Milan, 2013

Bidussa, David, et al., *Il caso Bartali e la responsabilità degli storici*, Lit Edizioni, Rome, 2021

Bidussa, David, *Il mito del buon italiano*, Il Saggiatore, Milan, 1995

Biocca, Dario, *Silone, La doppia vita di un italiano*, Rizzoli, Milan, 2005

Boatti, Giorgio, *Preferirei di no. Le storie dei dodici professori che si opposero a Mussolini*, Einaudi, Turin, 2001

Bonsaver, Guido, *Vita e omicidio di Gaetano Pilati. 1881–1925. Contadino, poeta, socialista, soldato, inventore e costruttore*, Franco Cesati editore, Florence, 2010

———, *Censorship and Literature in Fascist Italy*, University of Toronto Press, Toronto, 2017

Bosworth, Richard, *Mussolini*, Arnold, London, 2002

———, *Mussolini's Italy: Life under the Dictatorship, 1915–1945*, Penguin, London, 2007

Busoni, Jaurès, *L'"eccidio" di Empoli del 1 Marzo 1921. Cronistoria e testimonianze di uno dei protagonisti*, PSI, Rome, 1945

Campbell, Ian, *The Addis Ababa Massacre: Italy's National Shame*, Hurst and Co., London, 2017

Canali, Mauro, *Le spie del regime*, Il Mulino, Bologna, 2004

Cannistraro, Philip, *La fabbrica del consenso: Fascismo e mass media*, Laterza, Rome, 1975

Carcano, Giancarlo, *Cronaca di una rivolta. I moti torinesi del '17*, Stampatori nuovasocietà, Turin, 1977

Casali, Luciano, *Bologna 1920: le origini del fascismo,* nuova universale cappelli, Bologna, 1982

Chiurco, Giorgio, *Storia della Rivoluzione Fascista*, Vallecchi, Florence, 1929, five volumes

Ciani, Nadia, *Fuori da un secolare servaggio: Vita di Argentina Altobelli*, Ediesse, 2011

Circolo Antonio Gramsci, *Alle origini del PCI. Atti del Convegno su Gastone Sozzi*, Circolo Antonio Gramsci, Cesena, 1980

Colao, Floriana, *Il delitto politico tra Ottocento e Novecento. Da 'delitto fittizio' a 'nemico dello Stato'*, Giuffrè Editore, Milan, 1986

———, *Il processo Chiurco. Giustizia e politica nella Siena del secondo dopoguerra*, Edizioni Il Leccio, Monteriggioni, 2013

Colapietra, Raffaele, *Napoli tra dopoguerra e fascismo*, Feltrinelli, Milan, 1962

Colarizi, Simona, *Dopoguerra e fascismo in Puglia (1919–1926)*, Laterza, Bari, 1971

Collier, Richard, *Duce! The Rise and Fall of Benito Mussolini*, Collins, London, 1971

Collin, Richard, *La donna che sparò a Mussolini*, Rusconi, Milan, 1988

Cooke, Phillip, *The Legacy of the Italian Resistance*, Palgrave, London, 2011

Corner, Paul, *The Fascist Party and Popular Opinion in Mussolini's Italy*, CUP, Cambridge, 2012

D'Ascanio, Alessandro, *La vittoria del 1934. I campionati mondiali di calcio nella politica del regime*, Solfanelli, Chieti, 2010

Dalla Casa, Brunella, *Leandro Arpinati. Un fascista anomalo*, Il Mulino, Bologna, 2013

De Felice, Renzo (ed.), *Dino Grandi. Il mio paese. Ricordi autobiografici*, Il Mulino, Bologna, 1985

De Felice, Renzo, *Storia degli ebrei italiani sotto il fascismo*, Einaudi, Turin, 1993

De Grazia, Victoria, *The Perfect Fascist: A Story of Love, Power and Morality in Mussolini's Italy*, Harvard University Press, Cambridge, MA, 2020

Del Boca, Angelo, *Italiani, brava gente? Un mito duro a morire*, Neri Pozza editore, 2006

Dickie, John, *The Craft. How Freemasons made the Modern World*, Hachette, London, 2020

Dietschy, Paul, 'The 1938 World Cup. Sporting Neutrality and Geopolitics, or All-Conquering Fascism?' in Stefan Rinke and Kay Schiller (eds), *The FIFA World Cup 1930–2010: Politics, Commerce, Spectacle and Identities*, Wallstein Verlag, 2014, pp. 85–101

———, *Storia del calcio*, Paginauno, Vedano al Lambro, 2014

Dondi, Mirco, 'Piazzale Loreto 29 aprile: aspetti di una pubblica esposizione', *Rivista di Storia Contemporanea*, 2, 1990, pp. 219–48

———, 'Piazzale Loreto', in Mario Isnenghi (ed.), *I luoghi della memoria*, Vol. 1, *Simboli e miti dell'Italia unita*, Laterza, Roma-Bari, 1996, pp. 487–99

Duggan, Christopher, *Fascist Voices. An Intimate History of Mussolini's Italy*, Vintage, London, 2013

Dunnage, Jonathan, *The Italian Police and the Rise of Fascism: a case study of the province of Bologna, 1897–1925*, Praeger, Westport/London, 1997

———, *Mussolini's Policemen: Behaviour, Ideology and Institutional Culture in Representation and Practice*, Manchester University Press, Manchester, 2012

Ebner, Michael, 'Fascist Violence and the "Ethnic Reconstruction" of Cyrenaica (Libya), 1922–1934, in P. Dwyer and A. Nettelbeck (eds), *Violence, Colonialism and Empire in the Modern World*, Palgrave, London, 2018, pp. 197–218

——, *Ordinary Violence in Mussolini's Italy*, CUP, Cambridge, 2011

Evangelista, Rhiannon, 'The particular kindness of friends: ex-Fascists, clientage and the transition to democracy in Italy, 1945–1960', *Modern Italy*, 20, 4, 2015, pp. 411–25

Fabbri, Fabio, *Le origini della guerra civile. L'Italia della Grande Guerra al fascismo*, UTET, Turin, 2009

Fabi, Lucio, *Enrico Toti. Una storia tra mito e realtà*, Persico, Cremona, 2005

Fabre, Giorgio, *Mussolini razzista. Dal socialismo al fascismo: la formazione di un antisemita*, Garzanti, Milan, 2005

Falanga, Mario, *Tito Zaniboni. Appunti per una biografia politica e letteraria*, Piovan editore, Abamo Terme, 1991

Falasca Zamponi, Simonetta, *Lo spettacolo del fascismo*, Rubbettino, Soveria Mannelli, 2003

Farinacci, Roberto, *Squadrismo: Dal mio diario della vigilia 1919–1922*, Ardita, Rome, 1933

Favretto, Ilaria, 'Rough Music and Factory Protest in Post-1945 Italy', *Past and Present*, 228, 1, 2015, pp. 207–47

Ferris, Kate, *Everyday Life in Fascist Venice, 1929–1940*, Palgrave, London, 2012

Finaldi, Giuseppe, 'Fascism, Violence, and Italian Colonialism', *Journal of Holocaust Research*, 33, 1, 2019, pp. 22–42

——, 'Method in their Madness: Understanding the Dynamics of the Italian Massacre of Ethiopian Civilians, February–May 1937', in Phillip Dwyer and Lyndall Ryan, *Theatres of Violence: Massacre, Mass Killing and Atrocity Throughout History*, Berghahn, London, 2012, pp. 245–57

——, 'Mussolini's War in Ethiopia', in Gordon Martel (ed.), *A Companion to International History 1900–2001*, Wiley & Sons, Oxford, 2007, pp. 220–32

Fincardi, Marco, 'Contro il "nemico interno": la gioventù squadrista', in Mario Isnenghi and Giulia Albanese (eds), *Gli Italiani in guerra. Conflitti, identità, memorie dal Risorgimento ai nostri giorni*, Vol. IV, Tomo 1, *Il Ventennio fascista. Dall'impresa di Fiume alla Seconda guerra mondiale (1919–1940)*, UTET, Turin, 2008, pp. 94–101

——, 'I riti della conquista', in *Regime e società civile a Reggio Emilia 1920–1946*, Mucchi, Modena, 1988, pp. 7–137

Finzi, Paolo, *La nota persona. Errico Malatesta in Italia dicembre 1919–luglio 1920*, La Fiaccola, Ragusa, 1990

Focardi, Filippo, *Il cattivo tedesco e il bravo italiano. La rimozione delle colpe della seconda guerra mondiale*, Laterza, Rome-Bari, 2013

Fogu, Claudio, *The Historic Imaginary: Politics of History in Fascist Italy*, University of Toronto Press, Toronto, 2003

Fonzo, Erminio, 'Giorgio Alberto Chiurco e la Storia della Rivoluzione Fascista', *Ricerche di Storia Sociale e Religiosa*, XLVI, 89, 2017, pp. 289–303

Foot, John, *Calcio. A History of Italian Football*, Harper Perennial, London, 2007

———, 'Guerre delle memorie nelle esperienze europee. Italia, Gran Bretagna e Irlanda a confronto', in Adolfo Mignemi (ed.), '*Nessuno potrà tenersi in disparte*', *La Grande Guerra: Memoria, territorio, documentazione*, interlinea edizioni, Novara, 2009, pp. 85–114

———, *Fratture d'Italia*, Rizzoli, Milan, 2009

———, *Italy's Divided Memory*, Palgrave Macmillan, New York, 2011

———, *Pedalare! Pedalare! A History of Italian Cycling*, Bloomsbury, London, 2011

Forgacs, David and Stephen Gundle, *Mass Culture and Italian Society from Fascism to the Cold War*, Indiana University Press, Bloomington, 2007

Fornari, Harry, *Mussolini's Gadfly. Roberto Farinacci*, Vanderbilt UP, Nashville, 1971

Forti, Steven, ' "Tutto il potere ai Soviet!" Il dibattito sulla costituzione dei Soviet nel socialismo italiano del biennio rosso: una lettura critica dei testi', *Storicamente*, 4 (2008)

Francesangeli, Eros, *Arditi del Popolo. Argo Secondari e la prima organizzazione antifascista (1917–1922)*, Odradek, Rome, 2000

Franzinelli, Mimmo and Emanuele Marino *I tentacoli dell'Ovra. Agenti, collaboratori e vittime della polizia politica fascista*, Bollati Boringhieri, Turin, 1999

———, *Squadristi. Protagonisti e tecniche della violenza fascista*, Mondadori, Milan, 2003

———, *Il duce proibito. Le fotografie di Mussolini che gli italiani non hanno mai visto*, Mondadori, Milan, 2005

———, *Il delitto Rosselli. Anatomia di un omicidio politico*, Feltrinelli, Milan, 2017

Gabrielli, Patrizia, *Fenicotteri in volo. Donne comuniste nel ventennio fascista*, Carocci, Rome , 1999

———, *Tempo di virilità. L'antifascismo, il genere, la storia*, FrancoAngeli, Milan, 2008

Gentile, Emilio, *La marcia su Roma*, Laterza, Bari, 2015

Giacchin, Carlo, *Attentato alla Fiera. Milano 1928*, Mursia, Milan, 2009

Giovannini, Paolo, and Marco Palla (eds), *Il fascismo dalle mani sporche. Dittatura, corruzione, affarismo*, Laterza, Bari, 2019

Giulietti, Fabrizio, *Gli anarchici italiani dalla grande guerra al fascismo*, FrancoAngeli, Milan, 2015

Gooch, John, *Mussolini's War. Fascist Italy from Triumph to Collapse*, Allen Lane, London, 2020

Gordon, Robert and John London, 'Italy 1934. Football and Fascism', in Alan Tomlinson and Christopher Young, *National Identity and Global Sports Events. Culture, Politics and Spectacle in the Olympics and the Football World Cup*, State University of New York Press, New York, 2006, pp. 41–64

Gordon, Robert, *The Holocaust in Italian Culture, 1944–2010*, Stanford University Press, Palo Alto, 2012

Gradassi, Enzo, *Sesto Senso: Una famiglia ebrea in Casentino. Biforco, 1943*, Zona, Arezzo, 2009

Gribaudi, Gabriella, *Guerra totale. Tra bombe alleate e violenze nazista. Napoli e il fronte meridionale 1940–44*, Bollati Boringhieri, Turin, 2005

Gribaudi, Maurizio, *Mondo operaio e mito operaio. Spazi e percorsi sociali a Torino nel primo Novecento*, Einaudi, Turin, 1987

Guerrini, Libertario, *Il movimento operaio nell'Empolese 1861–1941*, Riuniti, Rome, 1970

Gundle, Stephen, Christopher Duggan and Giuliana Pieri (eds), *The Cult of the Duce: Mussolini and the Italians*, Manchester University Press, Manchester, 2013

Impiglia, Marco, 'The 1934 FIFA World Cup. Did Mussolini Rig the Game?', Stefan Rinke and Kay Schiller (eds), *The FIFA World Cup 1930–2010: Politics, Commerce, Spectacle and Identities*, Wallstein Verlag, Göttingen, 2014

Isnenghi, Mario, *L'Italia in piazza. I luoghi della vita pubblica dal 1848 ai giorni nostri*, Mondadori, Milan, 1994

Isola, Gianni, *Guerra al regno della guerra! Storia della Lega proletaria mutilati invalidi reduci orfani e vedove di guerra (1918–1924)*, Le Lettere, Florence 1990

———, *L'ha scritto la radio: storia e testi della radio durante il fascismo (1924–1944)*, Bruno Mondadori, Milan, 1998

Kertzer, David, *The Pope and Mussolini: the Secret History of Pius XI and the Rise of Fascism in Europe*, OUP, Oxford, 2014

Knox, Macgregor, *To the Threshold of Power, 1922/33: Origins and Dynamics of the Fascist and National Socialist Dictatorships, Vol. 1*, Cambridge University Press, New York, 2007

Lastraioli, Giuliano and Roberto Nannelli (eds), *Empoli in gabbia. Le sentenze del processone per l'eccidio del 1 marzo 1921*, Le Memoriette, 2, Empoli, May, 1995

Levis Sullam, Simon, *L'archivio antiebraico. Il linguaggio dell'antisemitismo moderno*, Laterza, Rome, 2008

Livingstone, Michael, *The Fascists and the Jews of Italy. Mussolini's Race Laws*, CUP, Cambridge, 2014

Longhini, Carlo, *Le giornate rosse: 1919 a Mantova. Storia di una sollevazione popolare e storie di rivoluzionari senza rivoluzione*, Editoriale Sometti, Cremona, 2009

Lotti, Luigi, *La Settimana rossa con documenti inediti*, Felice Le Monnier, Florence, 1965

Lucetti, Riccardo, *Gino Lucetti and his attempt to assassinate Benito Mussolini (Il Duce) 11 September 1926*, ChristieBooks, Hastings, 2012

Luparini, Alessandro, *Ravenna fascista: 1921–1925, la conquista del potere, con le fotografie di Ulderico David*, Società Editrice 'Il Ponte Vecchio', Cesena, 2017

Lussu, Emilio, *Enter Mussolini: Observations and Adventures of an Antifascist*, Methuen London, 1936

———, *Marcia su Roma e dintorni*, Einaudi, Turin, 2002

Lussu, Joyce, *Fronti e frontiere*, Laterza, Rome-Bari, 1967

Luzzatto, Sergio, *Il corpo del duce. Un cadavere tra immaginazione, storia e memoria*, Einaudi, Turin, 1998

———, *Padre Pio: Miracles and Politics in a Secular Age*, Henry Holt and Company, New York, 2010

Lyttelton, Adrian, *The Seizure of Power: Fascism in Italy, 1919–1929*, Routledge, London, 2003

Mack Smith, Denis, *Mussolini*, Paladin, London, 1983

Majanlahti, Anthony and Amedeo Osti Guerrazzi, *Roma divisa 1919–1925. Itinerari, storie, immagini*, Il Saggiatore, Milan, 2014

Manicardi, Nunzia, *Formiggini. L'editore ebreo che si suicidò per restare italiano*, Guaraldi, Modena, 2001

Mannino, Salvatore, *Una domenica di sangue. 17 aprile 1921: i fatti di Renzino fra storia e mito*, Il Mulino, Bologna, 2011

Mantovani, Vincenzo, *Mazurka blu. La strage di Diana*, Rusconi, Milan, 1979

Marchesini, Daniele, *Carnera*, Il Mulino, Bologna, 2006

Mariani, Giuseppe, *Memorie di un ex-terrorista. Dall'attentato al 'Diana' all'ergastolo di Santo Stefano*, ultima spiaggia, Genoa, 2009

Mariani, Laura, *Quelle dell'idea. Storie di detenute politiche 1927–1948*, De Donato, Bari, 1982

Martin, Simon, *Football and Fascism: the National Game under Mussolini*, Bloomsbury, London, 2004

Mason, Tim, 'The Turin Strikes of March 1943', in Jane Caplan (ed.), *Nazism, Fascism and the Working Class*, CUP, Cambridge, 1995, pp. 274–94

Mayda, Giuseppe, *Il pugnale di Mussolini: Storia di Amerigo Dumini, sicario di Mussolini*, Il Mulino, Bologna, 2004

————, *Storia della deportazione dall'Italia 1943–1945. Militari, ebrei e politici nei lager del terzo Reich*, Bollati Boringhieri, Turin, 2002

Mazzoni, Gianna, *Un uomo, una città. Giuseppe Massarenti a Molinella*, Coop Il Nove, Bologna, 1990

Merli, Stefano, *Autodifese di militanti operai e democratici italiani davanti ai tribunali*, Comune di Venezia, Avanti!, Milan-Rome, 1958

Millan, Matteo, ' "Semplicemente Squadristi". Il fascismo post-marcia a Genova', *Contemporanea*, XVI, 2, 2013, pp. 209–38

————, *Squadrismo e squadristi nella dittatura fascista*, Viella, 2014

Missiroli, Mario, *La Repubblica degli accattoni*, Zanichelli, Bologna, 1916

Modena, Claudio (ed.), *L'avvocato di Matteotti. Pasquale Galliano Magno*, Apogeo Editore, Adria, 2014

Mondini, Marco, *La politica delle armi. Il ruolo dell'esercito nell'avvento del fascismo*, Laterza, Rome, 2015

Monelli, Paolo, *Mussolini piccolo borghese*, Garzanti, Milan, 1950

Moorhead, Caroline, *A Bold and Dangerous Family: The Rossellis and the Fight Against Mussolini*, Chatto & Windus, London, 2017

Morris, Penelope, Francesco Ricatti and Mark Seymour (eds), *Politica ed emozioni nella storia d'Italia dal 1848 ad oggi*, Viella, Rome, 2012

Nozza, Marco, *Hotel Meina: La prima strage di ebrei in Italia*, Editoriale Diario, Milan, 2007

O'Brien, Paul, *Mussolini in the First World War. The Journalist, the Soldier, the Fascist*, Berg, Oxford, 2005

Onofri, Nazario Sauro, *Il triangolo rosso. La guerra di liberazione e la sconfitta del fascismo (1943–1947)*, sapere 2000, Rome, 2007

————, *La strage di palazzo d'Accursio. Origine e nascita del socialismo bolognese*, Feltrinelli, Milan, 1980

Papini, Massimo, *Ancona e il mito della Settimana rossa*, Le affinità elettive, Ancona, 2013

Passerini, Luisa, *Fascism in Popular Memory: the Cultural Experience of the Turin Working Class*, CUP, Cambridge, 1987

Pavan, Ilaria, *Il podestà ebreo, La storia di Renzo Ravenna tra fascismo e leggi razziali*, Laterza, Bari, 2006

Pavone, Claudio, *A Civil War: A History of the Italian Resistance*, Verso, London, 2014

Pedani, Angelo (ed.), *Giuseppe Emanuele Modigliani: il fratello 'maggiore'. Socialismo, pace e libertà*, Atti del Convegno. Livorno, 28 October 2012, Regione Toscana, Florence, 2015

Petracci, Matteo, *I matti del Duce. Manicomi e repressione politica nell'Italia fascista*, Donzelli, Rome, 2014

Pezzino, Paolo (ed.), *Empoli antifascista. I fatti del 1 marzo 1921. La clandestinità e la Resistenza*, Comune di Empoli, Pacini, Pisa, 2007

Piazzesi, Mario *Diario di uno squadrista toscano, 1919–1922*, Bonacci Editore, Rome, 1980

Picciotto, Liliana, *Il libro della memoria. Gli ebrei deportati dall'Italia (1843–1945)*, Mursia, Milan, 1991

Pieroni Bortolotti, Franca, *Francesco Misiano. Vita di un internazionalista*, Riuniti, Rome, 1972

Pisanty, Valentina, *La difesa della razza. Antologia 1938–1943*, Bompiani, Milan, 2006

Pivato, Marco and Stefano, *L'ossessione della memoria. Bartali e il salvataggio degli ebrei: una storia inventata*, Castelvecchi, Rome, 2021

Poli, Matteo, *Giuseppe Massarenti. Una vita per i più deboli*, Marsilio, Venice, 2008

Portelli, Alessandro, *Biography of an Industrial Town: Terni, Italy, 1831–2014*, Palgrave, London, 2017

Procacci, Giovanna (ed.), *Stato e classe operaia in Italia durante la Prima guerra mondiale*, FrancoAngeli, Milan, 1983

Pugliese, Stanislao, 'Revisiting an Assassination: the Death of Carlo Rosselli', in Stephen Gundle and Lucia Rinaldi, *Assassinations and Murder in Modern Italy: Transformations in Society and Culture*, Palgrave, London, 2007, pp. 11–22

Quazza, Guido (ed.), *Fascismo e società italiana*, Einaudi, Turin, 1973

Répaci, Antonino, *La marcia su Roma*, Canesi, Rome, 1963

Revelli, Nuto, *Mussolini's Death March: Eyewitness Accounts of Italian Soldiers on the Eastern Front*, University Press of Kansas, Lawrence, KS, 2013

Rossanda, Rossana, *La ragazza del secolo scorso*, Einaudi, Turin, 2005

Rossi (Tasca), Angelo, *The Rise of Italian Fascism 1918–1922*, Methuen and Co. Ltd, London, 1938

Rossi, Cesare, *Il Tribunale Speciale. Storia documentata*, Casa Editrice Ceschina, Milan, 1952

Rossini, Giuseppe (ed.), *Il delitto Matteotti tra il Viminale e l'Aventino. Dagli Atti del processo De Bono all'Alta Corta di Giustizia*, Il Mulino, Bologna, 1968

Sacchetti, Giorgio, *L'imboscata Foiano della Chiana 1921: un episodio di guerriglia sociale*, Arti tipografiche toscane, Cortona, 2000

———, *Sovversivi e squadristi. 1921: alle origini della guerra civile in provincia di Arezzo*, Aracne, Rome, 2010

Sarfatti, Michele (ed.), 'Italy's Fascist Jews: Insights on an Unusual Scenario', *Quest*, 11, October 2017, pp. i–xvii

———, *Mussolini contro gli ebrei. Cronaca dell'elaborazione delle leggi del 1938*, Silvio Zamorani editore, Turin, 1994

Sauro Onofri, Nazario, *Un paradiso infernale: Gli antifascisti bolognesi assassinati e incarcerati nell' URSS di Stalin*, Sapere, 2000

Schnapp, Jeffrey, *Anno X: La Mostra della Rivoluzione Fascista del 1932*, Istituti Editoriali e Poligrafici Internazionali, Pisa-Rome, 2003

Scirocco, Giovanni, 'Caduta e morte del tiranno a piazzale Loreto', in Mario Isnenghi, *Gli Italiani in guerra. Conflitti, identità, memorie dal Risorgimento ai nostri giorni*, Vol. IV, Tomo II, *La Seconda guerra mondiale*, UTET, Turin, 2009, pp. 617–23

Segrè, Claudio, *Italo Balbo. Una vita fascista*, Il Mulino, Bologna, 1988

Setta, Sandro, *Renato Ricci dallo squadrismo alla Repubblica Sociale Italiano*, Il Mulino, Bologna, 1986

Silingardi, Claudio, 'L'eccidio del 26 settembre 1921 e la memoria dei "martiri fascisti" a Modena', Istituto mantovano di storia contemporanea (ed.), *Fascismo e antifascismo nella Valle Padana*, Clueb, Bologna, 2007, pp. 129–60

———, 'La memoria dei "martiri fascisti" a Modena: il caso di Duilio Sinigaglia', Istituto Storico di Modena, *Annale*, 2010, Modena, 2010, pp. 8–18

Silone, Ignazio, *Bread and Wine*, Harper and Brothers, New York and London, 1937

Simonini, August, *Il linguaggio di Mussolini*, Bompiani, Milan, 1978

Snowden, Frank, *Violence and Great Estates in the South of Italy. Apulia, 1900–1922*, CUP, Cambridge, 1986

Sofri, Adriano, *Il martire fascista*, Sellerio, Palermo, 2019

Spinosa, Antonio, *Mussolini. Il fascino di un dittatore*, Mondadori, Milan, 2017

Spriano, Paolo, *The Occupation of the Factories, Italy 1920*, Pluto Press, London, 1975

Stille, Alexander, *Benevolence and Betrayal: Five Italian Jewish Families Under Fascism*, Penguin, London, 1991

Stonor Saunders, Frances, *The Woman Who Shot Mussolini*, Faber and Faber, London, 2010

Susmel, Duilio, *Nenni e Mussolini, mezzo secolo di fronte*, Rizzoli, Milan, 1969

Thompson, Mark, *The White War: Life and Death on the Italian Front 1915–1919*, Faber and Faber, London, 2008

Tobagi, Walter, *Gli anni del manganello*, Fratelli Fabbri Editori, Milan, 1973

Tumblety, Joan, 'The Soccer World Cup of 1938: Politics, Spectacles, and *la Culture Physique* in Interwar France', *French Historical Studies*, 31, 1, 2008, pp. 77–116

Turcato, Davide (ed.), *The Method of Freedom: An Errico Malatesta Reader*, AK Press, Oakland, Edinburgh, Baltimore, 2014

Zangrandi, Ruggero, *1943: 25 luglio–8 settembre*, Feltrinelli, Milan, 1964

Index

A Note on the Author

John Foot is the author of seven books, including *The Archipelago: Italy since 1945; Calcio: A History of Italian Football; Pedalare! Pedalare!: A History of Italian Cycling; Italy's Divided Memory* and *The Man Who Closed the Asylums*. Five of his books have been translated into Italian. He has written for the *Guardian, Independent on Sunday, London Review of Books* and the *TLS*. He is Professor of Modern Italian History at the University of Bristol and lives in the city with his partner and daughter. He is a regular contributor to the Italian magazine *Internazionale*.

A Note on the Type

The text of this book is set Adobe Garamond. It is one of several versions of Garamond based on the designs of Claude Garamond. It is thought that Garamond based his font on Bembo, cut in 1495 by Francesco Griffo in collaboration with the Italian printer Aldus Manutius. Garamond types were first used in books printed in Paris around 1532. Many of the present-day versions of this type are based on the Typi Academiae of Jean Jannon cut in Sedan in 1615.

Claude Garamond was born in Paris in 1480. He learned how to cut type from his father and by the age of fifteen he was able to fashion steel punches the size of a pica with great precision. At the age of sixty he was commissioned by King Francis I to design a Greek alphabet, and for this he was given the honourable title of royal type founder. He died in 1561.